# Fritz Müller
# A Naturalist in Brazil

Based on *Fritz Müllers Werke, Briefe, und Leben*
by Alfred Möller

David A. West

Pocahontas Press, Inc.
Blacksburg, Virginia
2003

David A. West: *Fritz Müller, A Naturalist in Brazil*
Based on *Fritz Müllers Werke, Briefe, und Leben* by Alfred Möller

Cover: *Placidula eurynassa*, a Müllerian mimic
Cover photo and design by the author

Pocahontas Press, Inc., P.O. Box F, Blacksburg, VA 24063-1020

First printing 2003
ISBN 0-936015-92-6

for

Lindsay

# Contents

# List of Illustrations

## Figures

## Maps

*An epiphytic bromeliad (*Vrisea*), Santa Catarina, Brazil
(photo by author).*

# Introduction

Charles Darwin called him "prince of observers" and counted him among those whose opinions he valued most. Ernst Haeckel acknowledged a debt to him for his own biogenetic law, "ontogeny recapitulates phylogeny." And at his death in 1897 the obituary writer in *Nature* questioned "whether any other naturalist, save Darwin himself, has given the world so large and original a mass of observations of the kind by which natural selection has been most strongly supported." Yet today Fritz Müller is largely ignored in books about the great nineteenth-century naturalists, most of whom, at least to English-language readers, would seem to have been Englishmen. Müllerian mimicry, usually applied to butterflies, is in every biology text but, perhaps because Müller's interests covered such a breadth of organisms and topics, his vast output has been difficult to pigeonhole, and no attempt has been made to place it in the context of his life since his German biography was published in 1920.

It was Fritz Müller's cousin, Alfred Möller (1860–1922), mycologist and Director of the Forestry Academy in Eberswalde, who ensured that his legacy would not be lost. Immediately after Fritz Müller's death in 1897 Möller, who had recently spent three postdoctoral years with him in Brazil, started an almost single-handed effort to gather every document connected with him: publications scattered in scores of journals, manuscripts and drawings left unpublished, letters, and reminiscences of surviving friends. He intended to publish as much of this great archive as he could, and for more than twenty years he doggedly organized it, despairing at times that he could do the job on top of his own research and administrative duties. The First World War intervened, but in 1915 Möller succeeded in bringing out a republication of all of Müller's published work including 85 redrawn plates, the first volume of *Fritz Müller. Werke, Briefe und Leben*, published by Gustav Fischer in Jena. The biography

1

(*Leben*) followed in 1920. Möller feared that the subsidies for the publication from government ministries and the Prussian Academy of Sciences would be consumed by the inflation then rampant in Germany, but fortunately he completed the project with some of the scientific correspondence and unpublished manuscripts (*Briefe*) in 1921 before he himself died suddenly in 1922 from complications following a minor operation (Falck 1927). Alfred Möller had by then preserved in published form almost all that we have about Müller's personal life, as well as the majority of his scientific correspondence, now lost. Without that documentation, it would now be impossible to write a life of Fritz Müller.

After Alfred Möller's labor of love, Fritz Müller rarely regained center stage. His Brazilian town of Blumenau erected a statue of its favorite son in 1929, and a small museum was later established in his house by the Itajaí River on the outskirts of town. Several brief biographies of Fritz Müller have been published in Brazil, including Roquette-Pinto (1979) and Castro (1992), based on the *Leben*.

In 1982, fresh from field work on mimetic swallowtail butterflies in Fritz Müller's part of southeastern Brazil, I read the biography, hoping to find a description of the landscape when European settlers first arrived. Although the city of Asunción, on the large navigable river system 800 kilometers to the west, had been founded in 1537, the heavily forested interior of southern Brazil only a short distance from the Atlantic coast was scarcely touched by Europeans until the German settlements of the mid-nineteenth century. As I read about Müller's education in Germany, his decisive break with religion at the age of 24, and the liberal views that led to his emigration in 1852 as a pioneer farmer and naturalist in the Brazilian forest, however, I became fascinated with the man himself. After he read Darwin's *Origin of Species* in 1861, he became a staunch defender of Darwin's theories, not only descent with modification but also natural selection as the agent of evolution, and until his death in 1897 he continued to believe in the preeminence of natural selection in times when its adherents were dwindling. He applied those theories to everything at hand: marine and freshwater crustaceans, climbing plants, orchids, butterflies, caddis fly cases, stingless honey bees, fig wasps, bromeliads, and floral variation; and his research touched on development, behavior, ecology, and inheritance, nearly always in an evolutionary framework. He corresponded significantly with biologists abroad, including Darwin, Haeckel, August Weismann, Alexander Agassiz, and his brother Hermann Müller, reporting observations, criticizing ideas, and sometimes pressing Darwinism on the unconverted. His discoveries are still being cited more than a century after they appeared.

For these reasons a new biography of Fritz Müller seems desirable, using for its narrative framework a translation of Alfred Möller's *Leben* of 1920. Möller wrote in the style of his time, and for a modern reader he says too little about Müller's published work, perhaps because he felt that his readers could always consult the original papers that he had just republished. But the many letters and other documents that intersperse his narrative are almost our only source of information about Müller's personal life. My contribution has therefore been to edit Alfred Möller's story and give it my own voice; to edit the documents that he included in the *Leben* for greatest effect; to add material from Müller's scientific correspondence in the *Briefe* and from unpublished letters and reminiscences, some of them unknown to Alfred Möller; to develop some of Müller's scientific themes of interest to the modern reader; and to describe through Müller's writings the rich natural history of his Brazil.

Fritz Müller was urged to write a book about his life as a naturalist in Brazil, in the tradition of Henry Walter Bates on the Amazon (1863), Alfred Russel Wallace in the Malay Archipelago (1869), and Thomas Belt in Nicaragua (1874), but he never did so, and my distillation is intended to serve that purpose for a new audience a century after his death.

Blacksburg, Virginia
November 2002


**Editorial Note**

In each chapter the first note gives the sources of material. All translations from German and Portuguese are by the author unless otherwise stated.

Aufnahme 1891 von Alfred Möller

*Fritz Müller, 1891. A. Möller, 1920, from* Fritz Müllers Leben.

# 1
# Childhood and Early Education in Thuringia, 1822–1841

Johann Friedrich Theodor Müller, known throughout his life as Fritz, was born 31 March 1822 in the parsonage of the Thuringian village of Windischholzhausen, an hour's walk east of Erfurt (Map 1), the eldest son of pastor Johann Friedrich Müller and Caroline Trommsdorff Müller.[2]

Fritz Müller's paternal grandfather Müller was a theologian[3] and the director of the Erfurt Gymnasium. His maternal grandfather, Privy Councilor Johann Bartholomäus Trommsdorff (1770–1837), a manufacturing chemist and owner of an apothecary shop, was a scion of an established Erfurt family mentioned repeatedly beginning in the fourteenth century among the councilors and magistrates of the town of Erfurt. Trommsdorff[4] was widely known as a scholar in pharmacy, which then comprised chemistry and botany. He founded the Pharmaceutical Institute of Erfurt in 1795, brought it to fame and managed it until 1828. In 1794, when only 24 years old, he started the first German pharmacological journal, of which 50 volumes had appeared by 1824. Justus Liebig then continued it as the *Annals of Pharmacy* (*Annalen der Pharmacie*). When Napoleon passed through Erfurt in 1807 he asked Trommsdorff whom he considered the greatest chemist, and Trommsdorff is said to have answered: "Chemistry no longer has a head since Lavoisier lost his." Napoleon was not amused.[5]

Fritz's father had started his career in 1818 as pastor of Windischholzhausen, which was one of the lowest paid ecclesiastical

5

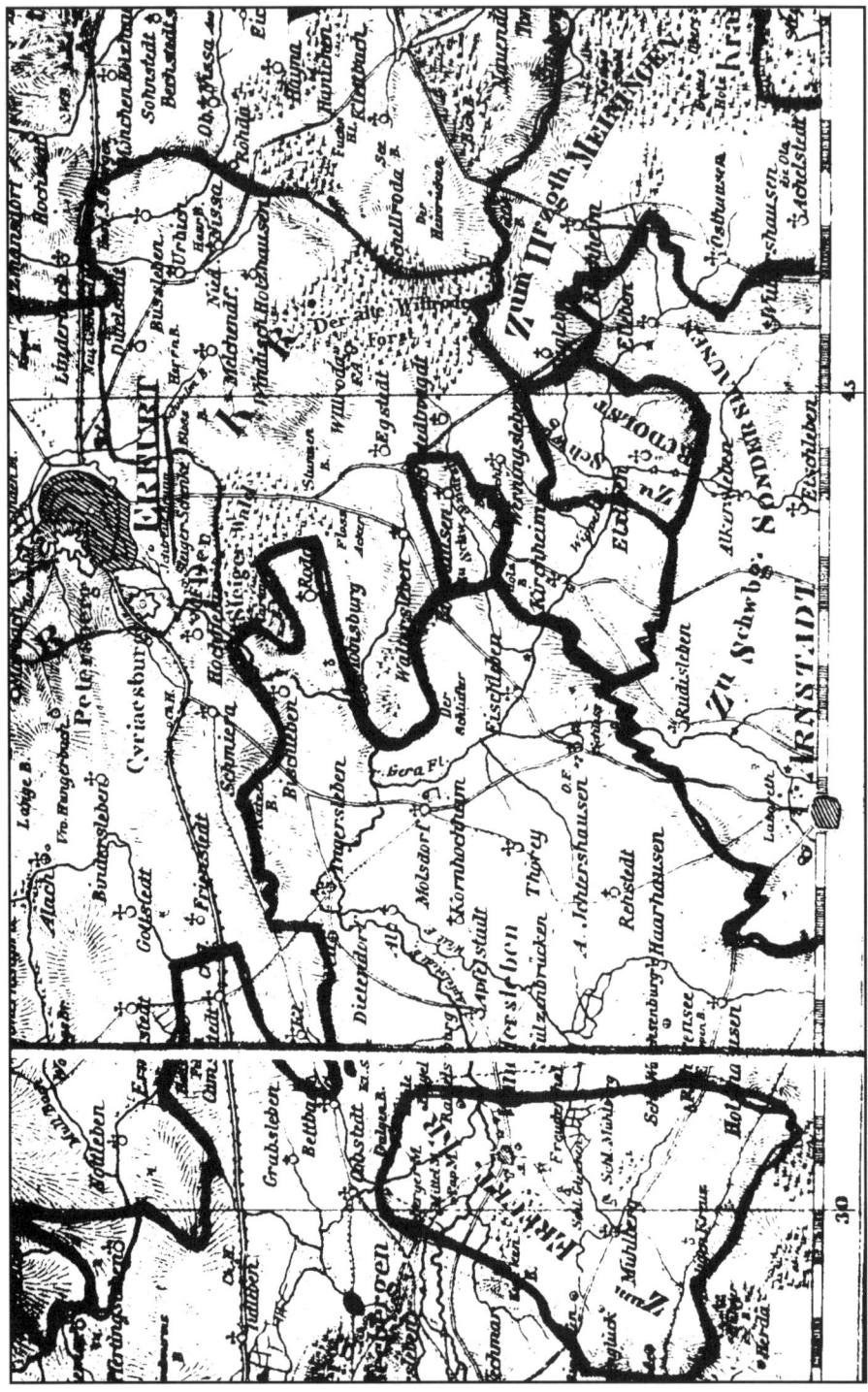

livings in Germany. Even in 1856 the income there for a pastor with a large family was 336 talers[6] (less than $240, when a book cost about $2). But although Fritz's parents may have had limited means, their children[7] never mentioned any privation in their childhood, which was evidently a happy time for all of them in the little parsonage in Windischholzhausen as well as in the more spacious one to which they later moved in Mühlberg. "I wish all children as happy a childhood as we had," his sister Rosine later wrote. "Father rejoiced with Mother when we were happy and amused, but he took our upbringing very much to heart, and we were encouraged from an early age to keep ourselves occupied."[8] The cheerful atmosphere of the house emanated chiefly from their father, who was described by Fritz's cousin Lina Walther as "serene, good-natured, and full of humor and nearly constant banter," while their delicate and often ailing mother was the "quiet star of the house. One had to be very sensitive to recognize her deep religious feelings, so much did she keep them to herself; when we were all still romping about in the yard at dusk or in the moonlight, she stood quietly with folded hands at the window, as I sometimes found her, looking heavenward; for, as she said to my mother, 'I pray for my children.'"[9]

Fritz's father, on the other hand, cared little for formalities and was in fact quite untidy, the gentle weapons of his wife being powerless against his disorderliness. He fulfilled his duties conscientiously in the parish and the school, but he had independent religious views, inclining toward rationalism, and he was fond of natural history and encouraged his children's interest in it from early childhood.[10] "Rationalism" at that time in Germany implied a theology that declined "to accept the authority of the Bible as the infallible record of divine revelation and [was] practically synonymous with free-thinking."[11] It is certain that Fritz's father did not carry it that far, but Fritz's later rejection of religion, although driven primarily by his training in science, probably owed something to his father's liberal views. His brothers August and Hermann followed much the same path.

---

*Map One. Vicinity of Erfurt, c. 1844. Detail from* Der Regierungs-Bezirk Erfurt. *Magdeburg: Albrecht Platt. Courtesy of the Syndics of Cambridge University Library.*

"On Sundays, even while practicing his sermon on the way to one of his parishes, nothing eluded him, whether it was an interesting plant growing by the path, or a beetle, bee or other animal roving about."[12] "We brothers inherited our delight in living things from our father," wrote Fritz to Ernst Krause,[13] and of his first lessons in natural history at his father's side he said,

> [In Windischholzhausen] my enjoyment of nature was awak-
> ened in my earliest youth by my father, who was a keen student
> of the rich local flora. Among my earliest memories are walks
> with Father and Mother through the woods and fields. Bee
> orchids, lady's slippers in the open woods, grass iris (*Iris sibirica*),
> globe flowers (*Trollius*) in the wet meadows, dwarf iris (*Iris
> pumila*) on the low wall of our little garden, houseleeks (*Semper-
> vivum*) on the roof, still appear vividly before my eyes, although
> I had already left my birthplace by the time I was six and none
> of those plants grew in Mühlberg, a large town in the
> Thuringian Forest to which my father was transferred in 1828.
> Of course I met with some of them again at
> Windischholzhausen in later years.[14]

In 1828 Fritz's family moved to Mühlberg, twenty kilometers southwest of Erfurt (Map 1), at the foot of the Mühlberger Gleiche,[15] where there was once again a rich flora. He established his own herbarium of the Mühlberg region, and the children, especially Fritz and later Hermann, were his enthusiastic helpers. In January 1828 Fritz's parents wrote a joint letter to Caroline's brother Hermann Trommsdorff, then studying in Berlin, about the new appointment and the impending move to Mühlberg. Fritz's father stressed the benefits, including the local flora:

> The region to which I am going cannot be entirely unfamiliar to
> you, for you have certainly more than once visited the Gleichen
> and will remember that the area really deserves the term "charm-
> ing." From the upper story of my future home the Mühlberger
> and Wanderslebener Gleichen present the most beautiful view.
> The parsonage is more spacious and nicer than my present one
> and is right beside the church. There is a vegetable garden and
> orchard as well, which is especially welcome to my children.
> Mühlberg itself is rather large for a village and numbers 250
> hearths and 1000 inhabitants. . . . Of course there is also much

work for my wife and myself. This move will probably be put off until Easter, and I am already looking forward to guiding you around my future residence one day and being able to acquaint you with the surroundings of Mühlberg and its curiosities. Among these there is also a spring, a very strong source which never freezes in winter and which drives the mills, of which Mühlberg has six. It was a surprise to me that Mühlberg has good watercress, which I hitherto took to be a characteristic product of Erfurt. . . . You will therefore probably not botanize with me again in Windischholz-hausen, but rather on the Gleichen and only a few hours away in the Thuringian Forest, which will give us no small yield.

Caroline, on the other hand, stressed the expected increase in her work load in the new parish:

Though I liked it here very much, I am also pleased with [the move] because the income was too small for us to have stayed here forever and because it is better to go to a place with more beautiful surroundings and a nicer house than we have here. Of course I will have more work; since we are willing to assume responsibility for the agricultural activities themselves, I am taking on a large household. We will probably have five or six cows, two horses and 60 sheep, surely more to do than with our present single cow.

Caroline Müller had had rheumatic fever after the birth of her daughter Rosine late in 1827, and "again recently," she added, "I was so ill that I had accustomed myself to thoughts of death. But the good Lord has helped once again, for which I am deeply grateful, for though we should always be ready for death yet I freely admit that I fear it. I would like to go on living for the sake of my husband and our children."[16] Despite recurrent illness over the next 15 years, she gave birth to three more children and supervised an increasingly complicated household.

Lina Walther described life in Mühlberg a few years after the move:

Once when I was spending harvest time there, the faithful farm hand Scheibe knocked on the door of our room at 3 o'clock, and we had to get up right away; that is, no one would have forced me to, but I would have deemed it a disgrace to stay in

bed while my cousin (Fritz's sister Charlotte) got up. The servant
girl attended to feeding and milking the cows, and the farm
hand was occupied with the horses, while we put up lunch for
the men. We were soon done and then helped with the milking.
Thereupon the men were off, and our first errand took us across
the dewy lawn to the Victoria plum tree, whose tempting golden
fruits one could always find in the grass; that was our first
breakfast. Then one of us went to the cellar for the skimming,
the other swept and cleaned the house as quietly as possible.
That done, we sat in the front doorway with a piece of black
bread in hand and shared a bowl of skimmed milk between us.
Our third breakfast came around 6:30, when we drank coffee
with Aunt and Uncle [Fritz's parents]. Later in the day, when the
fully-laden harvest wagons followed one another, we had to help
with the unloading.[17]

In 1993 the Mühlberg spring was still flowing freely, and the
parsonage, with roofed gate, half-timbered farm buildings and walled
garden and orchard, appeared close to its original state (Fig. 2);  the
Windischholzhausen parsonage had been a private dwelling for many
years.

The unpleasant side of the agricultural operation in Mühlberg
was the annual winter slaughtering "festivities," which Caroline
described in a letter to her brother in January 1838 as "a couple of
nasty days."[18] But, Lina Walther's idyllic description notwithstanding,
there was also hard work in the fields during harvest, foot rot in the
livestock, and times in the winter when they were effectively snowed
in. Caroline's post-Christmas letters to the Trommsdorffs in Erfurt in
the 1830s are full of thanks for Christmas presents received, and
apologies for not being able to reciprocate. She sent milk, butter and
fruit in season to the Trommsdorffs in the city, but there was no spare
cash in the Mühlberg household.

Although Fritz's father had his hands full as pastor and district
school inspector, as well as from his own farming operation, he found
time for the thorough education of his sons.

Fritz's mother reported to her brother in Berlin in 1827, when
Fritz was not yet five, that he "has an hour every day with his father
and is so eager to learn that he would be happy to spend the whole
day spelling. He was just now quite delighted at having spelled out

*Figure 2. Mühlberg parsonage, gate, and church in 1993. Photo by the author.*

*Berlin,* because that was the name of the city where you were."[19] But the daily load of the children was still hers; their quarreling would keep her from letter-writing or force her to break off, and when she was trying to finish the letter of 30 January 1828, two-year old August got hold of her pencil while Fritz and Charlotte were scrapping and scribbled across the paper.

Lina Walther recalled many years later being aghast as a young girl when she first attended a lesson that Fritz's father was giving his sons Fritz and August. "Tall as he was, he lay on the sofa pipe in mouth; one leg hung to the floor, the other over the sofa arm. The little ribbons of his underwear dangled between his trousers and his slippers, his shirt front was fastened only at the top and otherwise dangled freely; but both youngsters, Fritz especially, hung attentively on his words, for what he had to say was always profound."[20] "One got something worth listening to from the lesson, especially when it dealt with world history, for then his words rang out so nobly and arrestingly that one couldn't help staying and listening."[21] He prepared his sons so well that Fritz was admitted to the 4th form of the Erfurt Gymnasium when he was 13 and finished his studies within a year.[22] Along with his sons, Fritz's father prepared a few other Mühlberger boys for gymnasium or seminary with the help of the very capable tutor,[23] and the stimulating headmaster of the Mühlberg village elementary school, Tänzer, who suggested Fritz's vivacity by his remark that things were pretty calm in Mühlberg after Fritz left for Erfurt.

Although busy with their own children, Fritz's parents always had an open hand for others. The son of his father's widowed sister lived in the parsonage for a year as brother to the siblings until he entered school, and the Mühlberg parsonage saw many young people come and go, for even Fritz's frail mother liked to have youngsters around her. And there were always festive times at the parsonage in later years when the brothers brought guests home for vacations.[24]

"In the middle of the yard," wrote Lina Walther, "stood an old linden in the top of which Uncle had put up a spacious tree-house, reached by a set of steps. There we liked to sit with my Aunt when there was a quiet day during the harvest. Right by the tree stood the beehive, above us cooed the doves, below us the cock and hens carried on a lively exchange, and from the stables came the bleating of sheep and the bawling of cows."[25] That linden was apparently also one of Fritz's favorite places, for he later remembered it nostalgically while a student in Greifswald: "Whenever I stroll now under the flowering lindens in front of the university, I wish myself there in our old linden tree."[26] By then he had left forever Mühlberg and a young woman with whom he was in love, but like the similar protagonist of Wilhelm Müller's poem *The Linden Tree*, which Schubert set in his song cycle *Winter Journey*, Fritz may have felt the tree's call, "Here you would find peace."

At Easter 1835 Fritz left his parents' home to enter the Gymnasium in Erfurt, where he lived happily in the family of his grandfather Trommsdorff. His grandfather's "beloved old Swan Apothecary Shop" (Fig 3), which is commemorated by a plaque on the post office building that replaced it in 1860,

> was at the corner of Schlösserstraße and the Anger. It was an old house to which his grandfather had added the one next door, and was planted round with acacias, the leaves and flowers of which decked out the windows of the first floor. Through the joining of the two houses there were created around the court-yard all sorts of mysterious nooks and passageways of which we children were inordinately fond. There was also an upper floor, a loft for instruments and for drying herbs, which we respected all the more because, to keep us from disturbing anything, we were not allowed to set foot in it without an adult.[27] When the grandchilds assembled from various households, grandfather led us up to the instrument loft. There was an electrostatic machine connected to a little house which gave off a bang when struck by lightning; grandfather also had us form a living chain through which he passed a weak current.[28]
>
> Every year our grandparents rented a summer cottage on the Steiger, a wooded hill overlooking Erfurt from the south, which was an ideal playground for high-spirited children. It lay at the edge of the forest in the midst of a little garden, behind a thick hedge which also enclosed a few modest flower beds, a bit of sandy ground, a big linden tree and two sandstone busts whose weathered noses could only hint at their original beauty. The cottage had only a single large room the whole front of which was taken up by glass doors. When the doors were thrown open we were quite in the open air and enjoyed a lovely view across the green valley to Erfurt beyond. Grandmother enjoyed

*Figure 3. The Swan Pharmacy, Erfurt, on the site of the present post office, as it appeared in Fritz Müller's time, with laboratories on the ground floor of the main building and student lodgings on the ground floor of the adjoining house. Rosenhainer & Trommsdorff 1913,* Johann Bartolomäus Trommsdorff (1770–1837). *By permission of the British Library, shelfmark 010705.f.35.*

entertaining her children and grandchildren on fine summer days, and we were always delighted when our grandparents invited the extended family to their Steiger cottage and treated us to cold strawberry soup and sliced meats. When it got dark, grandfather let off fireworks: squibs, catherine wheels, crackers.[29]

Fritz's Trommsdorff grandparents died in quick succession, grandmother in 1836 and grandfather on 8 March 1837. The estate passed into the hands of their son Hermann Trommsdorff, the founder of the Trommsdorff chemical works in Erfurt, and Fritz stayed on with his uncle Hermann in the Swan Apothecary Shop while he was a student in the Erfurt Gymnasium. His friend and contemporary Ernst Biltz (1822–1903) recalled that Fritz was at the top of his class in mathematics,[30] and indeed his fondness and talent for mathematics stayed with him all his life. He amused himself with mathematical problems in his few spare hours, even in his maturity, and his continuing interest in phyllotaxy, the arrangement of leaves on stems, was based largely on his fascination with the mathematical approach that it required. He easily satisfied the school requirements in the subject, and in other respects too the gymnasium was not especially difficult. But it also gave him no real challenge or feeling of satisfaction, and he moved quickly through the grades, leaving no trace of his achievements there except that he passed the final examinations at Easter 1840. In later years he remained as grateful for his Mühlberg education as he was bitter about the Erfurt Gymnasium. In the Latin *vita* appended to his dissertation at the University of Berlin he praised the Mühlberg school "which still flourishes under its rector Tänzer, an outstanding teacher who forever deserves my adulation with a faithful and grateful mind," but of the Erfurt Gymnasium reported only that he had attended it for five years. At the death of Tänzer he wrote his brother Hermann: "I have often asked myself how completely different my life would have been if there had been a single teacher in that dull Erfurt Gymnasium who knew as well as Headmaster Tänzer did how to lay hold of and stimulate a young mind."[31] Thirty years after leaving the gymnasium Fritz was still galled by the experience:

> I began so many things in my life the wrong way round and have had to suffer bitterly for many of them, yet I look back happily: "Sweet is the memory of adversity endured." It is only those lovely years lost in the gymnasium that I can never recall without bitterness.[32]

Fortunately for Fritz, the Swan Apothecary Shop provided what the gymnasium lacked:

> There was at that time a great deal of scientific activity among the apprentices and assistants at the Swan and other Erfurt pharmacies, thanks chiefly to the influence of my grandfather. In that circle I found fresh stimulation and sustenance for my predilection toward the natural sciences, which lay claim to my thoughts and inclinations far more than did the school.[33]

Those interests grew during his daily association with his uncle Hermann Trommsdorff. "My mother was much devoted to your father, who was her only brother," Fritz wrote to his cousin Hugo Trommsdorff, Hermann's son, years later,

> and she passed those feelings on to her children. The first and last points of contact between your father and me were botany. On one of your father's rare visits to Mühlberg before I came to the gymnasium in 1835, I was proud to be able to accompany him to the Wanderslebener Gleiche, to collect *Nepeta nuda* [a catnip] with him, and to dry it for him in my plant press. In 1845, during the few months that I lived in your house, we spent nearly every evening together examining and arranging his herbarium. Even of the Compositae, he had at that time most of the specimens from the Berlin Botanic Garden.[34]

Fritz's love of botany, the encouragement of his grandfather, his uncle and of a very capable shop assistant in the Swan, inspired him with a taste for pharmacy as a profession.[35] His interest was strengthened by his close friendship with Ernst Biltz, son of an Erfurt pharmacist's widow, who had already decided on the profession when he took over his mother's business. Fritz apparently saw pharmacy not only as a useful professional course in itself but also as a step toward the study of pure science.[36] And his decision may also have been influenced by thoughts of emigration, for "well-known German pharmacists' assistants were being beckoned to lucrative appointments in Capetown."[37] Although it was not until he was an apprentice pharmacist in Naumburg in 1840 that he took the first steps toward emigrating with his school friend to Capetown,[38] he seems already to have thought of it while in Erfurt.[39] His father agreed to his choice of profession but insisted that he first get his school-leaving certificate from the gymnasium. Fritz, however, had already learned the rudiments of the trade in the Swan during his last year at school,

Ernst Biltz and Fritz got to know one another through their association with the apprentices and assistants in their respective family pharmacies, who organized joint botanical excursions in which the two of them eagerly joined. The friendship also brought Biltz, among other things, a gracious invitation from Fritz's parents to spend Easter 1837 with them in their delightful Mühlberg parsonage.

> I passed unforgettable holidays with Fritz and his brothers in the pleasures of warm hospitality and daily rambles through the

lovely Mühlberg countryside, and I could also observe how carefully his father managed the activities and interests of his sons and seized every opportunity to guide them in the observation and understanding of nature and its creations. I cannot forget how on an especially bright and starry night Papa Müller lit a hand lantern, took a rolled-up sheet of paper under his arm and scrambled with us up the Mühlberger Gleiche to an open patch of grass where we could see the sky. Guided by the star chart which he spread on the ground and lit with his lantern, he showed us the easily visible constellations. Only years later, when Fritz became increasingly known as a prominent observer in the natural sciences, did it become clear to me from that recollection, as well as from other experiences, how the teaching methods that Pastor Müller practiced on his children from the tenderest age had influenced their later development, and how those methods made the brothers Fritz and Hermann into such master observers of nature.[40]

By Michaelmas (29 September) 1838 Ernst Biltz had already apprenticed himself to a apothecary in Naumburg-on-the Saale, where Fritz would eventually follow after taking his final examinations in Erfurt. In the meantime, however, Fritz was enjoying part-time work in his uncle's apothecary shop, as he reported in a free-wheeling letter to Biltz:

You ask how I like being a pharmacist, how it suits me to stay home, doing time, crushing capsules, selling ointments, etc. So far, my good Ernst, I can't complain of being bored with pharmacy. And what a pleasure it will be, Ernst, to be a pharmacist at your side. Oh, how I long to see you! The farther off you are, the more I realize what you have been to me. Cousin E. [unidentified] still reproaches me for being such a proper bore, not to say Melancholicus, after your departure. I would rather trap arctic foxes in Siberia with you, Biltz, than pick oranges in Italy or elsewhere by myself. You will find little coherence in this letter, Ernst, with many sentences ending with etc. Those are sentences which John Q. Public has interrupted with a groat for jalap.[41] As you know, mischievous impudent fun is in my temperament and now and then interrupts polite slush, but I am especially jolly today because my Old Man filled my nearly empty purse with lettuce (What kind of lettuce is not yet determined, perhaps *Lactuca aurea*!?)[42] But for now farewell and again farewell! Give [Hermann] Koch [a fellow apprentice] my greetings and think occasionally of your faithful friend Fritz Müller, pedant as well as tyro in Erfurt-on-the-Gera. It goes without saying that you will write soon![43]

In his last year in the Erfurt school Fritz took an independent step that his mother found especially painful. Without asking his parents, he applied for an apprenticeship (probably in Erlangen) with an apothecary Martius, who was a friend of his grandfather but who turned him down. It was probably boredom with his detested school that impelled him, but at 17 he was already expressing in his typical way the tug of self-determination.

His mother's diary for 1839, which reports Fritz's independent step, also shows her love for her son, whom she takes care to call "my Fritz" or "good Fritz" in various places:

20 January. Fritz's letter pained me deeply, because he applied for an apprenticeship without saying or writing anything about it before hand. I shall sit down immediately and write him just how I feel about his rashness.

21 January. Yet one should not write or respond in the first flush of emotion. All day I feared that I had written too strongly and had hurt him. Of course it was thoughtless of Fritz to take such an important step without saying anything to his parents.

25 January. I wrote Fritz again more calmly so that he would realize that I am not too cross.

26 January. Fritz wrote very sadly because he had pained us so, and promised to guard against such indiscretions. Martius refused him; I am sorry, because he very much wanted to go there.[44]

Fritz already showed a predilection for foreign languages in the 6th form. "If I had met with any sort of help in my endeavors to learn Italian, Russian, Syriac, and Arabic, I would probably have become a linguist instead of a naturalist," he wrote in 1881 to his brother Hermann. In fact he had an uncommon gift for languages. Although he had never spoken with an Englishman and knew nothing of English pronunciation, he wrote such fluent English to Darwin years later that his letters could be published almost without alteration. Fritz later read English, French, German, Swedish and Italian literature with no trouble and attempted Hungarian and Russian with good results. But he commanded Portuguese, his vernacular in later years, with the subtlest mastery of idiom and wrote perfectly in that language on specialized topics in zoology for which Portuguese had hardly ever been used. His skill in languages, however, was most clearly evinced in the way he treated German, his native tongue. Clarity and plain-speaking were second nature to him.

After finishing his final school examinations in mid-April 1840, Fritz moved out of the Trommsdorff household in Erfurt to be with his family in Mühlberg,[45] and then on 8 May 1840 entered a term of apprenticeship in Mr. Beneken's Baytree Apothecary Shop in Naumburg-on-the Saale, where his friend Biltz was already ensconced. "Everything that Fritz and I hoped for ourselves was realized during that time of living and studying together," Biltz wrote after Fritz's death.

> We pursued botany most keenly under the mutual stimulus of the two of us and Hermann Koch, another apprentice and a boyhood friend from Erfurt, who also encouraged us to correspond with scholarly botanists on matters of particular interest. Koch had written to Professor Koch in Erlangen[46] about finding *Epipactis microphylla* [a rare orchid, now extinct in Germany] near Naumburg, and Fritz and I had turned to the famous Wallroth[47] for information about parasitic cryptogams that we had observed on *Vaccinium oxycoccos* (cranberries) and *Allium ursinum* (ramsons). We received the nicest replies: Wallroth addressed us as "my dear friends in flora", and in reference to the rarity with which apprentice pharmacists became interested in botany, delighted us by calling us "rare birds." Fritz, however, unfortunately found himself increasingly alienated from his apprenticeship in pharmacy, which was still a relatively inflexible subject. After giving up his position without authorization in December 1840 because of some incident based on that inflexibility, he was induced by his father to return in atonement, so to speak. But after a short trial period, which he endured with great self-denial, he walked out in February 1841 with the consent of the director of the apprenticeship program and said

farewell to pharmacy for ever. Thus did our fine dreams of years of life together in the profession meet with a sudden end.[48]

Fritz was especially fond of his uncle, Wilhelm Möller, who was pastor of a village near Naumburg and, according to Alfred Möller, his mother's youngest brother-in-law. During his apprenticeship Fritz often visited the parsonage, and later remembered his uncle affectionately from Brazil: "He was my favorite by far among all of the older relatives, and nowhere else did I feel so much at home. How often have I thought of him at the sight of our thorn-apple trees thickly hung with foot-long flowers; he tended such a *Datura* with great care and was delighted when it once produced a couple of isolated blooms."[49]

Lina Walther, Fritz's sister Rosine, and his friend Biltz described Fritz's character and appearance during that first phase of his youth in letters to Alfred Möller.[50] They liked him for his intelligence and quick wit, and for his modesty and amiability. From Lina Walther: "I can still see him in his dark blue, gold-buttoned confirmation robe, a handsome youth with a long narrow pale face and highly intellectual features." From Rosine Müller: "During his school days and as an apprentice, Fritz's manner was thoroughly engaging, his figure slender, and because he wore his blond hair long and falling over his shoulders one might speak of him as a fair-haired youth. His manner was shy and almost girlish, much resembling that of his uncle Hermann Trommsdorff." Biltz recognized in Fritz's letters, as we have seen above, a "natural sensitivity as well as a streak of roguish fun."

The young apprentice's plans to emigrate began to take shape while he was in Naumburg. Yearning for the tropics and its rich natural history, he started negotiating with an agent in Hamburg about employment as a pharmacist in Capetown and tried to persuade his friend to go with him.[51] But Biltz was kept back by his mother's shop, and Fritz was gradually moving away from the profession. He then decided to take a university degree in mathematics and natural sciences and to become a teacher.

# 2

# University Days in Berlin and Greifswald, 1841–1845

After abandoning a career in pharmacy, Fritz entered the University of Berlin in the spring of 1841. The university had been founded in 1809 by a group of "neo-humanists," including Wilhelm von Humboldt (1767–1835, brother of the great naturalist Alexander von Humboldt), the philosopher Johann Gottlieb Fichte (1762–1814), and the theologian and philosopher Friedrich Schleiermacher (1768–1834). The founders were intent on restoring the preeminence of the philosophical faculty (what we would call Arts and Sciences), with the aim of educating the whole man, "influencing the higher mental training," as Schleiermacher wrote,[2] as distinct from the three professional tracks of theology, law, and medicine then dominant in older German universities. It was thought that the members of the Prussian Academy of Science in Berlin and the city's collections and research laboratories could provide inexpensive resources for the new university. In addition, as the first German university in a large city, it might avoid the sort of student terrorism that prevailed in small-town universities, as in fact it did.[3] By 1841 the faculty of philosophy had achieved its aim of imparting its own research results rather than handing down "accepted truths," and was demanding of the students that they "learn to work and to think in a scientific way."[4] A starry collection of scholars was lecturing, giving seminars and providing research opportunities for the students by the time Fritz arrived. These men would give him the intellectual breadth that characterized his life.

In Fritz's first term, on the science side he attended Lichtenstein's General Zoology, Elements of Botany with Kunth, Encke's Celestial Astronomy, and Erman's Geographic, Magnetic, and Meteorological Orientation. On the arts side it was Werder's Logic and Metaphysics and Benary on Sallust's *Cataline Conspiracy*,

It must have been a stimulating term. Fritz remembered Jules Lichtenstein (1816–1866), a French-German entomologist and naturalist, for having given him an excellent introductory zoology course. Karl Sigismund Kunth (1788–1850) had spent 16 years in Paris working up the vast South American plant collection brought back by Alexander von Humboldt;[5] in addition to attending his botany lectures Fritz went plant hunting with Eduard Regel (1815–1892), a fellow Thuringian and horticulturist then employed at the Berlin Botanic Garden. Johann Franz Encke (1791–1865) was an eminent astronomer who computed the orbit of the comet named for him, directed the Berlin observatory, and constructed star charts that would lead to the discovery of Neptune in 1846.[6] Georg Adolph Erman (1806–1877) was an earth scientist with broad interests, who had traveled round the world in 1828–30 on a geographic and geodesic survey,[7] Karl Friedrich Werder (1806–1893) was a prominent philosopher, and Karl Albert Agathon Benary (1807–1861) a comparative philologist at a gymnasium in Berlin.[8] Fritz was being exposed to experienced scholars who all ranked him at the term's end as "extremely diligent."

In winter term 1841–42 he took Johannes Müller's Theoretical and Practical Anatomy and met the great zoologist in the classroom for the first time. Johannes Peter Müller (1801–1858), Professor of Anatomy and Physiology, whose *Handbuch der Physiologie* of 1833–40 was a milestone in experimental medicine, had broad research interests including embryology, nervous systems and comparative anatomy, as well as experience in marine zoology that would provide the foundation of Fritz's own research on marine invertebrates in Brazil. Other courses that term included Solid and Analytical Geometry with Martin Ohm (1792–1872, brother of the better-known physicist), and Meteorology and Climatology with Heinrich Wilhelm Dove (1803–1879), who first recognized a system in weather changes.[9] Fritz evidently never missed a lecture, and a characteristic comment appended to Fritz's certificate at the time that he had "not hitherto been charged with participating in forbidden organizations among students at the local university," suggests that his indignation over religious and political repression in Prussia had not yet been aroused.

German university students in Fritz's day commonly changed universities once or twice during their academic careers,[10] and it was therefore no surprise when he moved at Easter 1842 to Greifswald University, 210 kilometers miles north of Berlin near the Baltic coast (Map 2), where he spent the next year. We have only one contemporary impression from that year, in a letter to his favorite sister Rosine, whom he usually called "my dearest little sister," or "Rosie," and with whom he was close. He had been on an excursion to the Rügen, a scenic and historic island on the Baltic north of Greifswald, and on 5 December 1842 for her birthday he sent her a little picture, evidently of a boat and some coastal scenery:

> Imagine if you will that the boat has a little mast with a brown-tarred sail, and that in it, besides two old fishermen, are seven Greifswalder students, who smoke their pipes in comfort and lift their voices through wind and darkness, and you will have our journey from Stubbenkammer to Arcona. When I come home at Easter, I will tell you more about particular places in the picture, show you where we bathed, where we climbed the chalk cliffs, where we spent the night, where we tasted pickled eels, etc.[11]

Fritz's warmest reception in Greifswald was in the home of the bryologist Christian Friedrich Hornschuch, Professor of Botany. Hornschuch evidently recognized talented undergraduates and treated them as colleagues, for "the subject of mosses is a sort of youthful memory for me," Fritz wrote to Ernst Krause in 1882. "It is now some 40 years since I helped the well-known bryologist, my teacher and fatherly friend Hornschuch, to organize his moss collection in Greifswald."[12]

Fritz's mother was once again seriously ill in December 1842. She wrote to Auguste, her brother Hermann's wife, that a fever which appeared after she went to church on Christmas day had developed into a severe sore throat, which after much gargling led to facial neuralgia that kept her from sleeping. The application of horseradish

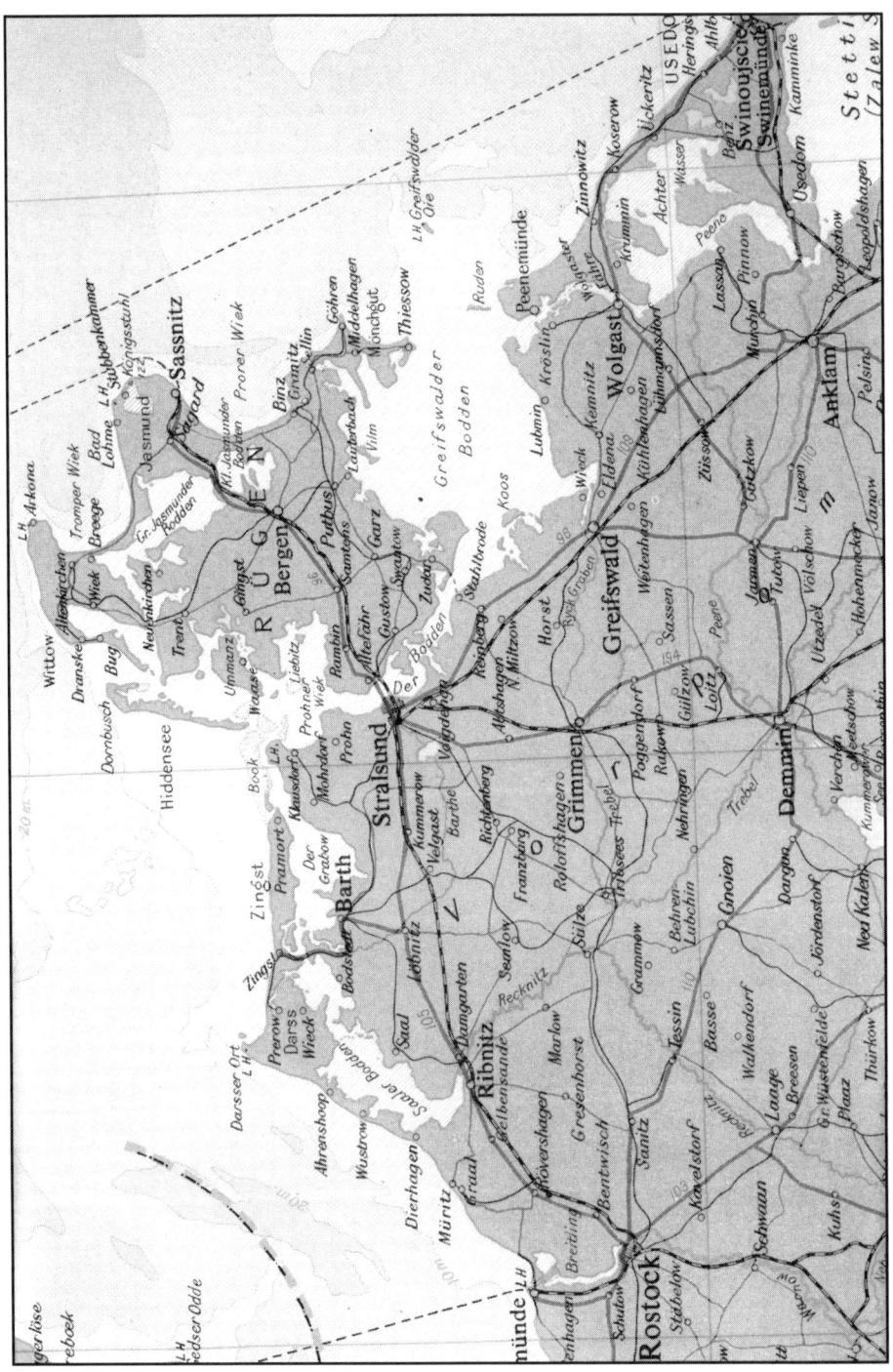

to her neck cured that problem, but she was left too weak to do any work and she abandoned any idea of going into Erfurt to see her Trommsdorff relatives.[13] She died six weeks later, on 6 February 1843. In a letter to Fritz that day she entreated him not to stop off in Halle and Bernburg during his holiday travels, but to come home as soon as possible. She did not see her eldest son again. "I have thought about home a good deal these past days!" he wrote to his sister Charlotte in February 1844.

> It is now a whole year since our dear mother passed away, but I still can hardly believe that I will never see her again. It still seems to me that she will give me a kindly greeting when I come home. O, truly, dear sister, time will never efface her from our memory. In the past few weeks I have read over all of the letters of hers that I still have and have felt once again what a deep and irreparable loss we have suffered. How tenderly she always cared for us, how urgently she exhorted us always to be diligent and virtuous and to have true brotherly and sisterly love. In living by her precepts and following her example we would also honor her memory.[14]

Fritz returned from Greifswald in summer term 1843, after his mother's death, to finish his university education in Berlin. That term he attended lectures on Number Theory given by Gustav Peter Lejeune Dirichlet (1805–1859), who was known not only as a brilliant mathematician — he was appointed to Berlin University in 1828 at age 23, and "exerted a strong influence on the development of Berlin mathematics"[15] — but an excellent teacher. Perhaps it was that experience that stimulated Fritz's interest in phyllotaxy, to which number theory has direct application. The rest of his lectures must have kept him busy: Conic Sections with Jakob Steiner (1796–1863), who encouraged independent thought and ran his courses as colloquia;[16] Experimental Physics with Dove; Comparative Physiology of the Infusoria [17] with Christian Gottfried Ehrenberg (1795–1876), whose specialities included single-celled marine and fossil organ-

*Map Two. The Greifswald region of northeastern Germany.*
*Detail from* The Times Atlas of the World, *volume 3, 1955, Plate 63.*
*© Bartholomew Ltd. 2002. Reproduced by kind permission of HarperCollins Publishers.*

isms;[18] Entomology with Wilhelm Eduard Erichson (1809–1848); and Philology with the classical scholar and antiquarian August Böckh (1785–1867). Winter 1843/44 brought History of Philosophy with the Aristotelian philosopher Friedrich Adolf Trendelenburg (1802–1872); Mineralogy with Gustav Rose (1798–1873), an innovative crystallographer;[19] Geognosy (the materials and structure of the earth) with the paleontologist Heinrich Ernest von Beyrich (1815–1896); and a Colloquium in Zoology with Ehrenberg. In summer term 1844 he finished his undergraduate course work with Comparative Anatomy and General Physiology (both taught by Johannes Müller), Logic (Trendelenburg), Philosophical Exercises, and the Natural History of Mollusks with Franz Hermann Troschel (1810–1882). After eight terms of university, Fritz was now ready to prepare for the secondary teaching examination.

Fritz recalled Johannes Müller's major influence on him in a letter to Max Schultze 15 years later:

> I am grateful to Johannes Müller and to Lichtenstein for having set the course of my scientific endeavors. The latter led me first through his eloquent lectures on zoology; Johannes Müller became for me a nearly perfect model, first through his writings and then even more through his course of lectures. I was fortunate to be close enough to him personally to learn that the prejudice against his stern inaccessibility that prevailed in my time at the University of Berlin was unfounded, and I was thankful to discover for myself how willingly he encouraged and supported any serious scientific endeavor. The first microscope that I had at my disposal was a Schiek belonging to Joh. Müller. I showed him something in *Clepsine* [a genus of leeches and subject of Fritz's Ph.D. dissertation]. "Have you a microscope?" — "No." — "Take this one and examine the newly-laid eggs." (He wanted to know whether the movements discovered at that time in planarian eggs were also found in *Clepsine*.) And he made that offer to me, a very shy young man, in our very first conversation. A few weeks later he mentioned my study of the genitalia of leeches, without naming me ("one of you"), in his lectures on comparative anatomy. After that I showed him everything remarkable that I came across in the Berlin fauna, and although much was surely of very little interest to him, I

was always kindly received and almost never left without instruction and encouragement.[20]

As Fritz's letter shows, Johannes Müller encouraged students to do independent research, and Fritz devoted himself to it wholeheartedly. His simple digs at 22 Dorotheenstraße, a few blocks from the university, were apparently a regular zoo, according to a fellow student, and he himself told his younger brother Hermann, who was still in the Erfurt Gymnasium, of his "cherished menagerie." Glass jars and pots holding lizards, frogs, snails and especially leeches, occupied lots of space, and his lodgings were often in a wild state of confusion, especially when, to the dismay of his landlady Madam Hintze, the animals left their containers. Leeches were his particular interest and the subject of his first scientific paper, at age 22, "On *Hirudo tessulata* and *marginata*" in the *Archiv für Naturgeschichte*[21]. He described a new species, *Clepsine costata*, which he found among some Armenian leeches that Johannes Müller passed on to him from a collection made by the botany professor Karl Heinrich Koch (1809–1879) during an adventurous expedition to the Caucasus in 1843-44.[22] In 1844, on an excursion with his friend Hoffmeister to the Tegler See, a lake just north of Berlin, he discovered a rare sort of aquatic earthworm new to science. It was distinguished by its quadrangular spindle-shaped egg-cocoon attached to water plants and roots and was described by Hoffmeister the following year as *Criodrilus lacuum*. Fritz was clearly in his element. "I hope that there will soon be more time for such investigations," he wrote to Hermann at the time.

> They are quite the most interesting in zoology. As long as you stay only with external morphology, what do you get but a dim view of the endless diversity of nature? The careful study of a single animal gives more pleasure than a whole zoological museum, as you observe its way of life, study its internal structure and can sense the infinite wisdom which fits the smallest part to the common purpose of the whole animal; as you see the harmony in which each member stands in relation to all the rest, in which all work with and for one another![23]

Although Fritz continued to emphasize the integration of ecology, structure and physiology, he was soon to reject the role of "infinite wisdom" and would ultimately side with Darwin in favor of natural selection as the cause of such interrelationships.

On 14 December 1844, when Fritz was not yet 23, the philosophical faculty conferred on him the degree of Doctor of Philosophy based on a dissertation "On the leeches of the Berlin region," approved by Johannes Müller.[24] The doctorate in philosophy was useful for a prospective gymnasium teacher, and it was also a "sign of independent scientific and scholarly achievement."[25] Fritz then passed the secondary school teacher's examination at the beginning of 1845, and with that his first university course came to an end.

The Latin motto which Fritz placed at the head of his dissertation was typical of his approach. It was a quote from the Danish biologist Otto Frederik Müller (1730–1884) "I am echoing no one else's ideas and have not depended in any way on the findings of others; I am setting forth here only what I have studied myself and observed repeatedly and at different times."[26] When the Berlin faculty renewed his diploma 50 years later, they could well have used that motto in their citation, so true had Fritz remained to it throughout his scientific career.

The theses appended to his dissertation are also remarkable, and reflect the unusually independent opinions of a 22-year old:[27]

1. The peristome[28] alone is not sufficient for determining the natural genera of mosses.

2. The genus *Andreaea* [mosses related to *Sphagnum*] should be included with the mosses, not with the true liverworts.

3. Neither Treviran's nor Henle's theory about the genitalia of leeches is defensible.

4. The study of languages is less suited than the study of mathematics and natural history for developing the power of judgement in children.

5. Lungs and gills are not clearly distinguishable.

6. There is no reason to consider some animals more perfect, others more imperfect.

7. The so-called animalcules of animal semen do not exist.

Fritz's social contacts during his studies in Berlin were limited to a small circle of fellow-students; he had a low opinion of most of the students. In 1885, when Max Sagemehl, a young zoologist in

Amsterdam, complained to him that few university students there were interested in pure science, Fritz replied:

> You complain about the lack of interest in science among present day students, but I believe it has never been otherwise. Even forty years ago most students divided their time between the bars and taking curricula for making money, and despite the matchless men whom Berlin possessed as teachers (Johannes Müller, Lichtenstein, and others) and the large number of students, the circle of those who became fascinated by science because of those teachers and were stimulated to take it up as an occupation was vanishingly small.[29]

At the beginning of the twenty-first century, Fritz's comments about bars and money-making curricula are as true as ever.

Of his friends in Berlin only Franz Wenzlaff (1810–1866), who died as Director of the Berlin Royal Municipal Gymnasium, carried on a long-term correspondence with him. Fritz found in Wenzlaff a partisan for his own increasingly free and independent religious and political beliefs, and one who stuck by his convictions. "Even though we differ in age, outlook and entire personality," he wrote to his sister later in 1845, "I still esteem him as a very good friend. There are so wretchedly few men these days who have any real depth and are really capable of sacrificing everything for their convictions."[30]

With those words Fritz first suggests the stress and turmoil which filled the next few years and was to be of such immense difficulty for him and so fraught with consequences. The coincidence of his own upheaval with that of the whole nation in the period before the Revolution of 1848 could scarcely have eased his inner strife, but at that time, given his innocence, his love of truth and craving for freedom, it affected him with particular force. He was to fight for the freedom of his personal beliefs, and from the bitterness of such a fight to emerge victorious, not yielding a hair's breadth on any point. "Ask not, what will I be? Always ask yourself, What must I be!"[31] He followed those words, and they set the course of his life far from convention.

At Easter 1845 the young Doctor of Philosophy started his probationary year as a teacher in Erfurt, where his uncle Hermann Trommsdorff's Swan Apothecary Shop once again offered him a home. "After knocking about in foreign parts for five years, it's really comforting to be home once again with one's relations," he wrote to one of his sisters.[32]

Fritz had to teach seven lessons a week at the Erfurt Gymnasium: one section of Botany, three of Algebra, one of Mineralogy, and two of Natural History. A young cousin who was then a pupil at the school later described Fritz's innovations in the curriculum: "Fritz introduced the first proper course in natural science at the gymnasium. Before him, each teacher taught the subject if he was not fully occupied with his own speciality, whether that be religion, history or languages, and used a textbook that gave only a classification of the animal, plant and mineral kingdoms."[33] Fritz also privately tutored three boys, including Werner and Heinrich Kühne, the sons of a privy councilor in whose household he eventually lived.[34] He was especially fond of children, judging from his bittersweet remark to his sister shortly before he left Erfurt: "When I wake Heinrich in the morning and he gives me a happy look and puts his arm around my neck, or when Fritzie [youngest son of his uncle Hermann Trommsdorff] babbles sweet childish gibberish to me in the pharmacy, tears sometimes come to my eyes (and weeping is not really my thing) when I think that I might have to give up the great happiness of such a cozy family life for ever."[35]

Fritz willingly allowed his brother Hermann, who was seven years younger and was attending the Erfurt Gymnasium, to join his school boys or private students on excursions around Erfurt and Mühlberg, or deeper into the Thuringian Forest. They made long trips with modest provision for food and lodging, and bad weather scarcely dampened the gaiety and simple pleasures of their hikes. Once they walked twenty-two kilometers from Mühlberg to the Inselberg (a high peak in the Thuringian Forest, over 900 meters), as he wrote to his brother August:

> The path led up a steep slope, the clouds were so thick around
> us as to cut off the view, and only the tips of a few firs were
> suspended before us in dim outline like shades of Tartarus. We
> then saw a strange and wonderful spectacle, as a brisk wind
> suddenly gathered this uniform gray chaos into definite form,
> drove it into another valley and revealed a lovely green vale over
> which the thick mass had only just been hanging. I am too

inept, however, to describe to you the magical fascination of those clouds swirling and drifting all around us, above and below. Even the unpoetic dampness, and a most unpleasant chill, could not disturb our poetic pleasure.[36]

Something of the "unpoetic dampness" of those swirling clouds was soon to return to Fritz's life, however, for he was on the threshold of renouncing religion and with it all hopes of becoming a school-teacher in Prussia or of marrying within his social class. That step, coupled with the impending revolution of 1848, had a momentous effect on his life, setting it firmly toward emigration and a new start in Brazil. But for the moment the future appeared unclouded.

Fritz, now 23, had fallen in love with the daughter of one of the principal nurserymen of Erfurt, and his shy affection was evidently reciprocated. Her mother and Fritz's mother had been friends, and the Müller children had often visited the family. Their relationship is only hinted at in Alfred Möller's narrative, even the identity of the woman being suppressed, or having been lost with lost letters, but witnesses of those years suggested to Möller that Fritz was then remarkably happy and untroubled. He was heading toward a profession for which he was trained and talented, and also toward a union with a young beloved whom his family would have received with open arms. After his mother's death his father married the eldest daughter of a land-owner named Schmidt from Kirchheim near Erfurt[37], and Fritz remained on cordial terms with his expanded family. Hermann Müller's diary of 1845[38] tells of a warm reception during frequent visits by himself and Fritz to their new grandparents in Kirchheim.

Despite all the promise, however, Fritz remained only half a year as a probationer in the Erfurt Gymnasium and at the end of summer semester 1845 gave up his post and the teaching profession to study medicine. He probably decided on medicine because of his zoological training, and because he was less fearful of stirring up a scandal with his religious views as a doctor than as a teacher. But he had also thought of becoming a ship's doctor and satisfying his heart's desire to travel abroad and especially to study the natural history of the tropics. His father could not finance his medical course but placed at Fritz's disposal the small inheritance from his mother, and Fritz chose Greifswald because of its familiarity and because he knew that he could keep himself there with modest means. Not surprisingly, even his close associates thought him "reckless" or "fickle," and people misunderstood him and turned away with a shake of the head. The evidence of his surviving letters and of the rest of his life, however, suggests that it was the pressure of his conscience that compelled him to give up what had once been his cherished plans, and to begin still another university course with the scantiest of means. The naturalist in him had evidently lost faith in the creed of the church in which he was raised. What had been taught in his parents' house as eternal truths, what his uncle Friedrich Möller had firmly fixed in him in confirmation class and he had acknowledged wholeheartedly at his own confirmation, had now been shaken. The Bible, as he later wrote, was now for him just a human document, belief in miracles impossible, and Christ only a man. His own goal was now a useful, industrious, and virtuous life, and life after death was unthinkable. Although he would never think of forcing these convictions on anyone else, he could also never deny them, and he realized increasingly that it was impossible for him to teach in the public schools of the Prussian state. For him there was no compromise or easy middle course; as painful as it was, his decision was unavoidable.

To his cousin Wilhelm Mensing he wrote:

> Truth and virtue are unthinkable without freedom. Yet despite all guarantees of freedom of conscience, etc., our Prussian government maintains such an intolerant propagandist line, and secular power has already intervened so often in religious battles that were being fought only with intellectual weapons[39], that soon no one who speaks his views openly and freely and does not hypocritically follow the line popular with the authorities, will be able to depend on any forbearance from the State.[40]

Of his decision to switch careers he wrote to his sister Rosine:

> I regret that my letter [now lost], brief though it was, has alarmed you so. It can't be helped. You can well believe that I thought it over carefully and did not make the decision lightly. It has been difficult enough for me, and — Oh, I may in fact tell you — as irresistibly as my desire to travel draws me abroad, I would far rather lay the whole world of my ideals at her (my beloved's) feet and offer her my most passionate youthful dreams. But it must be! I neither will be nor can be a slave.[41]

# 3
# Medical School, Freedom of Conscience, and the Revolution, 1845–1849

At the beginning of October 1845 Fritz left Erfurt with the feeling that this farewell was unlike the previous ones and that he was leaving forever his youth and the society that had formed him. In November he wrote his sister Rosine,

> I couldn't tell you the slightest thing about my journey to Berlin, I was so preoccupied. . . . I lodged in Berlin with Ernst Biltz and visited Madam Hintze [his undergraduate landlady], who was quite beside herself with joy. . . . I stayed several days in Berlin. The last evening I had a jolly time with Wenzlaff and some other acquaintances. . . . From Berlin I went by rail to Passow, and thence overnight to Greifswald. I could not sleep, and I didn't have Wenzlaff any more to whisper an intimate little word now and then.
>
> I was now for the first time completely alone and only then had the sad feeling that no departure had ever been as difficult as that last one from Erfurt. Of course, it's perfectly easy to say: Farewell! But, oh so hard to bear: Farewell! Even in Greifswald I was at first quite melancholy and could not master the thought that I had probably said goodbye for ever to her [his beloved in Erfurt] whom I would so much rather have called my own for ever and whom I can neither now nor ever forget. Even Hornschuch said to me, "You no longer seem to have your old *joie de vivre*."[2]

By December, however, Fritz was looking ahead, as he wrote his cousin Wilhelm Mensing:

> I cannot dream of the lovely days in Erfurt, the heavenly time in Mühlberg, the whole sweet past, lest I make myself needlessly melancholy. My destiny is now irrevocably set; I have had to give up my sweetest hopes. Hence, I do not look back longingly to that favorable star which for me has set for ever, but rather ahead to the stars which now guide my course. That is at least my laudable resolution, to which I fear I will too often be unfaithful.[3]

His sister Rosine evidently expected Fritz to outgrow his rebelliousness and to settle down, because at the beginning of 1846 he wrote to her again, evidently referring once more to the woman with whom he was in love but who had become unattainable because of his radical views:

> It is perfectly natural for most people to suppose that after looking around the world for a time I would come home and build my cottage there, because they no doubt still regard ambition and adventurous curiosity as my motivation. But it astonishes me that you, too, expect that of me. You know very well the tie that would have bound me to my homeland (if only it would pull me to some distant place). I've told you, of course, that I must sever that tie because, given my religious and political views in the present climate, I could have pursued my former career only as a hypocrite and slave. But I know only too well: that tie is forever broken! I don't have to tell you with what painful melancholy that certainty fills me. And yet, Rosie, there is an inexpressible bliss in the knowledge of having sacrificed everything for one's own convictions![4]

Fritz applied himself diligently to his courses. From the list of lectures for which he registered over the next three years until summer term 1848, Alfred Möller concluded that he grudged himself no spare time but took advantage of all the courses and clinical work that the University offered. In 1848/49 he assisted in the obstetrical clinic. There was little time for scientific research or field work, but he made use of whatever free afternoons he had. He published a series of zoological articles at that time, but never a word in the medical literature, showing that his outlook had not changed from naturalist to medical man. In fact he never thought of himself as a physician at all, even in later years in Brazil where his medical skills would be in demand.

Languages captivated him once more: he took up Swedish for relaxation and was enthusiastic about its richness and melodious sound.[5] After work he sought diversion in merry evenings in the company of friends or fellow students; "because I enjoy myself thoroughly and no one takes the least notice when I sometimes have to dry a tear over thoughts of home."[6]

The closest of Fritz's Greifswalder friends were the zoologists Max Schultze, Oscar Schmidt, and Anton Karsch,[7] and in 1846 Hornschuch, whose own speciality was mosses, enlisted their help in a zoological endeavor. The Danish zoologist Johannes Steenstrup[8] had asked Hornschuch to translate his "Studies of the occurrence of hermaphroditism in nature" into German.[9] Steenstrup tried to show that hermaphrodites do not occur in nature, believing that qualities as different as male and female could not exist together in the same individual. Hermaphroditic reproduction, he wrote, "disagrees completely with the whole way in which nature works, as well as with the surest principles of physiology, comparative anatomy and development; because of the improbability of hermaphroditism, as presented here, consideration will be given to the way in which its reality must be investigated and to the arguments which alone could persuade science of its occurrence."[10] Hornschuch, who was responsive to anything new, was completely charmed by the work and told his young friends a great deal about it. But they gave Steenstrup's views a poor reception and before the translation was finished had convinced Hornschuch that there really were hermaphroditic animals, whatever Steenstrup said. Hornschuch then asked Müller, Schultze, and Karsch to write up their observations on hermaphroditism in animals: Fritz on leeches,[11] Max Schultze on hydra, and Karsch on snails, and he published them as an appendix to his translation, much to Steenstrup's annoyance.[12]

Characteristically, Fritz still worried years later about his criticism of Steenstrup, justified though it was, thinking that he and his fellow students might have been rude or inconsiderate toward a scientist whose work he valued highly in other respects. In 1885, writing an essay on hermaphroditism but lacking a copy of the translation, he asked Ernst Krause, editor of *Kosmos*, to look it up and see whether there was any impropriety which he might now withdraw. In his essay[13] Fritz criticized the idea that hermaphroditism was the primitive state in the evolution of sexuality and sided with Steenstrup on this point. Curiously, although Müller did not have Hornschuch's translation at hand in 1885, he apparently did have the Danish original, because he translated several passages anew and included the Danish words to clarify some of his German equivalents.

Fritz joined Hornschuch's botanical excursions whenever possible and was again offered the hospitality of his home: "You must stay to lunch so that I can represent you to the family as the returned prodigal son."[14] With these words came the first invitation to the lunches that constituted the Lucullan high point of Fritz's life as a medical student in Greifswald. Otherwise, because of his limited resources, it was usually short rations. Through Hornschuch, who was then in charge of the student hostel, he got a laid-on lunch. Supper in the neighboring New Church, "where the hostess, Sister Stining, knew how to fry a most delicious and inexpensive omelet," was already among his pleasures.[15]

A friend from his Greifswald days, a physician named Oehlschläger, later wrote of Fritz's frugal life style: "I have seldom known a man so modest and unassuming and yet so highly intelligent. When he called on me in the evening, often worn out by hours of botanical-zoological ramblings in the countryside, I had to read between the lines rather than from his own words that he had carried a piece of dry bread in his pocket during his long walk only to delude himself over the lunch hour. Naturally I summoned up everything needed to remedy the deficiency as soon as possible."[16] Fritz's pleasures as a student in Greifswald were also frugal and innocent. He took part with almost childlike delight in the Greifswald Festival, the Schützenfest,[17] and in student larks, as he reported to his sister in July 1846:

> Four years ago [while an undergraduate] I lived close to the
> town ramparts by the garden where the more refined members
> of the public gather during the Schützenfest, and yet I was

scarcely even fleetingly on the ramparts and never at all in the garden. This time I have more than made up for it; the whole of Monday afternoon was spent on the ramparts throwing dice for gingerbread, listening to hair-raising tales on the barrel organ, and inspecting dwarfs and other curiosities; and in the evening we sat till midnight in a beautifully lit arbor of the Lauterschen Garden where there was of course plenty of music. Thus can one change with the times.[18]

There was at that time student unrest in every German university. For several years the faculty had demanded freedom of teaching and research, earning the admiration of their students and the reprimands of the government. Valentin quotes an "exceedingly well-informed contemporary" that "the freedom of the lectern was at no time so much at the mercy of ministerial despotism as it was then."[19] Robert Prutz, for example, whose poetry Fritz quoted for its liberal sentiments, was forbidden by the Minister of the Interior to give his lectures on literary history at the University of Halle in 1846, and in what Valentin calls "beautiful teamwork" the Minister of Education and Culture simultaneously stopped Prutz's popular science lectures, leaving him without a platform.[20] Press censorship contributed to the atmosphere of suppression to which students not surprisingly reacted, and Greifswald was no exception, as Oehlschläger recalled many years later:

> An "anti-duelling" society was formed, and an "exchange tax" society on the Communist model in support of a progressive tax on domestic bills of exchange to even out excessive inequalities. A reading room was established that displayed, in addition to the liberal press, the latest and most liberal writings of the time, such as those of Bruno Bauer, of Feuerbach and Strauss, Max Stirner's *The Individual and his Individuality* and the writings of the Communist [Karl] Marx. It says something that among scarcely 180 students in the whole university, 60 belonged to that student reading association. About sixteen closer friends banded together in a tighter society under the innocent name of "The Circlet." Fritz Müller was a member of that society and through his determination was soon one of its leaders.[21]

Oehlschläger's book list includes David Strauss[22] and Ludwig Feuerbach,[23] perhaps the two most influential and radical writers on theology in the pre-revolutionary period. David Strauss's *Life of Jesus* was almost certainly in that reading room in one of its editions, and Strauss had raised a storm at its publication in 1835. He accepted Jesus as an historical figure but had stripped away all of the supernatural events in the Gospels as myths, carefully showing how they were Old Testament prophecies applied after the fact to justify Jesus as the Messiah.[24] In another book that may have been there as well, *Christian Doctrine* (1840/41), Strauss, among much else, rejects the Creation stories in Genesis on the basis of advances in astronomy and geology,[25] subjects with which Fritz was already familiar. Strauss also articulated an attitude that may have promoted Fritz's tolerance towards other points of view (provided they were held with conviction). "So then, let the believer leave the intellectual to go his own way in peace, as the intellectual does the believer; we leave their faith to them; let them leave our philosophy to us."[26]

Ludwig Feuerbach's *Essence of Christianity* (1841) went further and declared that God was only "the reflection of human thoughts and aspirations," and was "a name for man's own idealized essence projected into a transcendental sphere."[27] Feuerbach provided what Gregory calls "the conceptual point of departure for . . . the German scientific materialism of the 1850s."[28] Although Fritz makes no mention of Feuerbach's influence on his acceptance of Darwinism, he was already affected by Feuerbach's arguments in the religious sphere, as we shall see when he renounces the church at the end of 1846, and he carried Feuerbach's name to Brazil and named a genus of orchids after him 20 years later.

No other author on the book list appears to have had much influence on Fritz. Bruno Bauer and Max Stirner were extremists, the former attacking the Gospel sources in the early 1840s far more severely than Strauss had done,[29] the latter asserting that "the individual must not allow himself to be checked by any higher power, such as God or the state, or by abstractions, such as humanity and natural law."[30] As for Karl Marx, whose *Communist Manifesto* appeared in 1848, Fritz never really took the political opposition very seriously.

"How I actually came to be regarded as a great Darwinian, I do not really know," wrote Fritz to Oehlschläger in 1893:

It is neither surprising, nor much to my credit, that during my years here [in Brazil] I observed many new things in living plants and animals that had not been seen over there in stuffed and impaled corpses or in dry hay.[31] But if now and then I have sought to probe the meaning of those observations more deeply, I believe that I have in large part to thank our Greifswalder "Circlet" for giving me the necessary training; less, I admit, the radical religious, political and social books and newspapers that we read than our lively verbal sparring over those topics at nearly every meeting. You will remember, as I do, hours of heated dispute with Basset, or how Fabrys once sprang onto the table with a shout during a drinking party in order to defend his religious viewpoint against us heathens. Even though I have had little use for what I learned as a medical student in Greifswald, I consider the years spent there as the most important for my intellectual development.[32]

As a member of the reading society, Fritz was keenly interested in all of the topics of the day. According to Alfred Möller, he read Prutz's political satire,[33] the liberal writings of Glaßbrenner,[34] Gervinus on establishing a national church by uniting all Christian confessions in Catholicism,[35] and Vischer on Gervinus and the German Catholics.[36] But it was the aspirations of the Friends of Light and their successors that he followed with the greatest interest. The Friends of Light (Lichtfreunde) was founded in 1841 by the liberal theologian Leberecht Uhlich (1799 –1872) in protest against the government-backed Protestant harassment of rationalist clergy[37] who had "rejected obscurantist orthodoxy and called for a return to simple Christianity,"[38] and in 1844 was taken over by the more radical Gustav Wislicenus, an Evangelical pastor in Halle.[39] The group, which became an organ of political opposition, was outlawed by the Prussian government in 1845, but Wislicenus remained a critic of government church policy and was dismissed from the national church in 1846. Writing that "the standard of Protestant consciousness should be, not Holy Scripture but rather our own inherent intellect,"[40] he assembled a Free Congregation in Halle and started a monthly journal on church reform for "free Protestants of all persuasions," which remained a step ahead of the authorities for the next seven years. Before long there were eighty Free Congregations with

35,000 members, and once again they comprised a party opposed to the government as well as to the national church[41]. In 1853 Wislicenus published *The Bible in the light of contemporary learning*, which was suppressed, and he avoided imprisonment only by escaping to the United States.[42]

Fritz's letters of the 1840s, available to Alfred Möller and partly published in *Leben* but now lost, express his inner conflicts, his resolute and uncompromising feelings, and his burning hatred of hypocrisy, superficiality, and indifference, as well as his tolerance toward dissent of every sort, provided that it was based on the deepest conviction. The letters also tell of his withdrawal from the established church, which he effected toward the end of 1846 by allying himself with Wislicenus's Free Congregation in Halle. Alfred Möller believed that it was religious rather than political convictions that really stirred Fritz. "He stood securely on his own two feet in the religious sphere but was not at home in politics and hence was influenced by the political slogans of friends who agreed with him on religious matters."[43]

Fritz, now in his early 20s, was clearly heading towards a major crisis in his life, and in January 1846 he informed his brother August of an impending step:

> Three of the five medical men with whom I mainly associate, and I, are radical rationalists,[44] both in college life and in matters of religion, and draw our conclusions with inexorable consequences, painful though it may be to give up ideas to which we have clung fervently from childhood.
>
> These are all questions that one has to fight one's way through in order to reach one's own firm conviction out of the faith once accepted with ingenuous childlike confidence from others. Perhaps at least in their practical consequences nearly all religious beliefs lead to the same result, that is that all honorable people who have not been ruined by selfish ambition for pleasure, glory and power will at least act alike, even though one person may do for Christ's sake what another does for mankind's sake, even though the goal of one may be future salvation and of the other the greatest perfection possible on earth.

To me each is honorable, whatever his belief, but only if that belief is really a matter of solemn inner conviction, penetrating his whole being and being proclaimed fearlessly in word and deed. But I hate (there is nothing Christian, but something human, about hating), I hate all of that respectful half-heartedness that carries one creed on the lips but another in the mind, and the hypocritical servility that professes an inwardly foreign belief, for fear of the opinion of the masses or of the powerful arm of authority.

I firmly believe that everything would quickly change for the better the moment everyone expressed his innermost conviction freely and frankly, regardless of external considerations, and what is most painfully difficult, regardless of the selfish interests of his own mind! I consider such frank truthfulness to be one's most solemn responsibility, and I also believe that the individual may not excuse himself because of the indifference of others.

Consequently, you will find neither unnatural nor incomprehensible a step which I must take before long, that is when I come legally of age on my next [24th] birthday and have to answer for my own beliefs, a step which in present circumstances will probably shatter my future hopes and may sever all of my ties with the family, but which I must take in order to curtail for myself a wretched existence as a cowardly hypocrite scorned by all good fortune — namely that I openly renounce Christianity, openly declare that I will not be a Christian, but rather a human being.

It goes without saying that I will not trumpet it to everybody. I have hitherto professed no creed to the world and therefore owe it no recantation. I will explain everything to our parents and to Uncle Möller, to whom I swore a belief in the Christian Creed at confirmation. Moreover, although not forcing my views on anyone unbidden, I will never hold them back, and on the day when I have to express them I will say frankly what I really believe.

Lucky would be the man who could remain coolly indifferent to all the inevitable consequences that I anticipate, when many a beloved heart that hitherto has beaten warmly for me will turn away in disgust! Including the One [his beloved in Erfurt]. You yourself know why I must abandon my sweetest hopes, and you know that it is not vainglory that drives me away. Why conceal it from you? It has cost me many, many a tear, and even as a child it was my boast not to weep!

But will you still stand by me, August? It breaks my heart to think that even Rosie, who has stuck with me so wholeheartedly, might now begin to have doubts about me! And yet, on the other hand, you would not believe how splendidly I feel and what immense joy fills my whole being, now that I have firmly resolved to sacrifice everything for the sake of truth!

Farewell, and write soon, and may I still truly continue to call myself your faithful brother,

Fritz.[45]

In February 1846 Fritz wrote further to his cousin Wilhelm Mensing,

Where it is really a matter of inner conviction, an orthodox adherence to old beliefs is to me more honest than the semi-rationalism that is now customary. Here, too, reason should have its claim, and yet everywhere the courage to assert it is lacking, with serious consequences. To renounce reason completely must be a heroic decision; in present circumstances, to shake off all religious authority and to recognize human reason as the only standard, as of course it is, also requires the greatest sacrifice (that is if one abjures saying one thing and thinking another). It is prudent and easy to squirm into the twilight between light and darkness, into indecision between faith and reason.

Do you know Lessing's remark about so-called rational Christianity? "It is still, of course, far more than simple faith, but what a pity that no one really knows the seat of either his reason or his Christianity."[46]

You will ask, "What then do you really believe?" Stated briefly, my whole creed is that we need look for our salvation neither above nor beneath mankind. That is, I believe that to be human is our highest destiny; but that will be unappreciated as long as supernatural phenomena, dogmas and myths are given equal value with reason, and it is unattainable so long as fixed creeds endure.

You know perfectly well that no one with such views can be a civil servant in a Christian country, and you understand the moral necessity for me to give up the prospect of a secure position, with all the fine hopes that I had attached to it, in order to be a human being - though I may starve for it.

In my mind, I could certainly have been a heathen, as indeed thousands are who still call themselves Christians. But I am unable to appear other than I am.

> What we, alone with grief o'ershadowed,
> Have only thought with beating heart,
> What we have whispered only in secret
> And uttered only before God:
> Let it now be told the world!
> Let it now from every mouth,
> From the depth of the heart
> Undisguised be proclaimed! (Prutz)[47]

There is certainly a difference between not speaking the truth (that is keeping silent) and lying; but not, to my mind, between speaking falsehood and lying. There are certainly countless situations in which I am asked: to what denomination do you belong? Do I answer: "Protestant," as now? Do I keep back the truth or speak falsely? Do I want to cause a sensation out of vanity? - I know that I am exempt from that rebuke; but if I must speak, I will speak only the truth. Since that can easily lead to ugly conflict, I deem it my duty to make an open confession of my creed to my family, and that I am ready to do.[48]

"I declare freely and openly to anyone who wants to hear," Fritz wrote to his brother August later that year,

that I can respect and regard as friend and brother only he who chooses truth, goodness and honor, as dearly fought for as they may be, over stultifying happiness! Freedom and health are all the happiness that body and soul need! Just as the body breathes freely, so must the mind think freely! Faith and religion spring from free thought and the noble pursuit of truth and virtue. Away with dogmatism and religious intolerance. Illumine the spirit, ennoble the mind, then there will be true faith and true religion! What good does a drop of reason do in our brain cases if we stifle it and cling to mindless rubbish![49]

In January 1846 Wislicenus launched his radical journal *Kirchliche Reform* (Church Reform) in Halle. He expressed its aim with two principles, the first,

> . . . that there cannot and will not be church reform from above in our time. . . . [It] must be achieved by the people and the whole community. And the second is that it will not . . . be achieved by a return to broken traditional beliefs, but only by reason. The *universal application of reason*, the great craving of our time, is the only path to real church reform . . . and only it will reawaken genuine love and action.

Wislicenus closed with an expression of tolerance: "We trust that our convictions will eventually prevail, even without any freedom, and if the power were given us to take away the free expression of opposing opinions we could not use it, because by that practice our own belief must immediately crumble."[50] Fritz demonstrated his genuine agreement with Wislicenus's call for tolerance in a letter to his uncle Hermann Trommsdorff, February 1846. The small community of Catholics in Greifswald, having been refused its request to use local churches for occasional services, petitioned the University for the use of its assembly hall, and Fritz joined with other students in asking the faculty to grant the petition, "in the interest of the Catholic students and of the free practice of religion."[51]

Fritz saw Wislicenus's new journal, and on 15 November 1846 he wrote the following letter to Wislicenus:

> I hope you will not think me presumptuous, Honored Sir, if I feel impelled to lay in your hands my declaration of complete agreement with the principles of the Halle Free Congregation enunciated in your journal *Church Reform,*[52] and if I entreat you to consider me as a member of your community of free men. In times of conflict I believe that it befits a man to enter into the ranks of those whose goal is the truth, rather than to wait in the safe seclusion of the party circle. Well do I know how little an individual's connections matter in advancing a good cause, but I hope that you will not reject a young man who can no longer tolerate the oppressive feeling of appearing, even if only by his silence, to belong to a church, to acknowledge a creed, from which his mind is alienated.

In directing to you this petition to admit me among your number, however, I deem it my duty to tell you briefly about the path that led me out of the confines of dogma to that free-thinking point of view of which you are such a bold champion, and thus to assure you, as far as I can, that I am guided not by rash blasphemy but rather by a serious striving for truth.

Through early education at home as a pastor's son (up to my fourteenth year), I was already more than usually familiar with the Christian viewpoint, and took it more than usually to heart. But it was chiefly the moral influence of my uncle the present Bishop Möller of Magdeburg [in Prussian Saxony], that fine man who prepared me for confirmation, that aroused my purest and most ardent enthusiasm for the creed in which he instructed me. He was too saintly for me to find fault with him for not understanding my mind, or to let myself be confused by mocking freethinkers.

At Easter 1841 I went to the university for an education in the natural sciences. Through that curriculum I became increasingly convinced of the eternal constancy of the laws of nature, a conviction that could not coexist with the Christian belief in miracles, but one that had already become an irresistible force within me as I became aware of the conflict. The belief that with God nothing is impossible had been replaced by the certainty, founded on the firm basis of science, that "with God, no absurdity is possible." With that, however, I had already set my mind in judgement of faith, doubt was awakened, and I was compelled to apply to the entire content of my faith the criterion of common sense. As a result, the Bible has been replaced by the intellect, the supernatural God by the eternal laws of nature, life hereafter as the end of all striving by life on earth as an end in itself, and enervating sentimental gushing by a conscious passion for truth, freedom and justice. A Christian has become a human being! [An echo of Ludwig Feuerbach in 1841: "Unbelief has taken the place of belief, reason the place of the Bible, politics the place of religion and the church, earth the place of heaven, work the place of prayer, material want the place of hell, man the place of the Christian."[53]]

That transformation has not been without influence in my life. I had chosen the teaching profession as a career and had already passed the examination and begun the legally prescribed year of probation when, last summer, the steps that the Prussian regime took against the rights of religious freedom, the prohibition of meetings of the Friends of Light, the proceedings instituted against you, etc., convinced me that the free expression of my opinions was incompatible with any position that depended on the State. It was that conviction in particular that strengthened my resolve to exchange an objective of imminent certainty for an uncertain future, and to take up a medical course, to which I have now applied myself over the past year.

With what joy I greeted the news of the formation of your Free Congregation, how my heart beat when I thought, according to its declared principles, that I might even be considered one of its members - how can I describe it? It is uplifting and invigorating to know that one is linked to others of like mind.

I, too, place my trust in the "spirit of truthfulness and love, of righteousness and strength," a spirit that I strive always to keep alive in myself and to practice in my life, and I therefore express once more the hope that you will not reject me.[54]

Wislicenus asked Fritz's permission to publish the letter in his journal, and it appeared in December 1846. Thus, although it had not been his intention, Fritz now went public with his atheism, a stand that he reiterated from time to time for the rest of his life.

Fritz's uncle, Johann Friedrich Möller, the Lutheran bishop of Prussian Saxony, had since his appointment in 1843 led the fight of the Lutheran church against the Friends of Light.[55] He must have seen the letter in *Kirchliche Reform* and was appalled to have his nephew join the foe. The Bishop reacted immediately and with passion on 3 January 1847:

In your letter of 15 November last year to the director and spokesman of the Free Congregation in Halle, my forever beloved nephew, you mentioned my name and reflected on that holy hour in which I thought to unite your soul in faith with Jesus Christ, your savior from sin and death, but from which, to my deep sorrow, your tree has now yielded useless fruit. There may even be in this a well-deserved punishment for me because I did not pray enough or struggle enough for you, because my effort was too weak. But that punishment, with all its pain, will not silence me as long as I can still speak. While you publicly shred before all the world the baptismal covenant repeated then under solemn oath (I would say before God, but you no longer believe in Him), I am reminded that you can still ask of me what you are throwing away, the everlasting salvation of your soul.

For that reason I write to fulfill the last duty of a minister, I come to you now in the name of Him whom you no longer wish to know, but who some day in a grievous hour will receive your quaking "Yes" to his question, "Do you know me?" That is why I extend my hand in love, and God forbid that I should be speaking for the last time, and why I admonish you to think once more about your rash and superficial account before you build in your mind altars to false Gods and at the stroke of a pen dispose of treasures on which depend your dignity, your strength, your peace of mind and your last triumph at the eternal gates."

After recalling how Fritz's mother had reacted with religious fervor at his baptism, Möller continued in horror:

On 15 November 1846, (God comfort his mother for it) that son announced: "A Christian has become a human being!" and joyfully welcomed a community which rejects the sacrament of baptism as contrary to its fundamental ideas. "A Christian has become a human being:" that phrase, brief to be sure but horrible, signifies the shift which you have taken since you turned away from the countenance of Jesus Christ and from the true witnesses who saw His majesty as the only-begotten son of the Father, full of mercy and truth. And in so doing you descend from the heights of Him who has said: "I would draw all of you to me." At the same time you persistently renounce every blessing which transfigures Man in the dust, brightens his prospects, ennobles his mind, arouses him to the most solemn devotion. You renounce not just the blessing of the Christian communion, the true creed, the mercy and the intercession, which can join us blessedly even with the simple and illiterate, and place yourself and your children after you, and your loving wife from whom you shall receive them, in the desert of a godforsaken life. No, you also expressly renounce a belief in the holy witnesses of the scriptures, before whom the wise men of all

47

Christian centuries, before whom Copernicus and Newton, bowed humbly down. The great naturalist Blumenbach, our compatriot, set as a motto at the head of his Natural History a passage from the Psalms, "Great are thy wonders and thy purposes which thou makes manifest to us," and Linnaeus set Psalm 111:2 at the top of his *Systema*: "The works of the Lord are great, sought out of all them that have pleasure therein."[56]

Later that year Fritz appealed to his sister Rosine,

My dear sweet Rosie! The last lines that I received from your hand are of 30 March; a full half-year has flown by without a word from you, but I know that it is my fault - my last letter to you - rather than your fault, that our regular correspondence was so abruptly interrupted. So it is up to me to resume it if we are not to become increasingly estranged from one another, and that would be an even more irreparable loss to me than to you. You have other brothers and can easily dispense with "godless" Fritz. Yours was the only womanly nature, the only sympathetic mind, to which I could reveal all my feelings without fear of misunderstanding; may I still do so, Rosie? Serious matters must be discussed seriously with men, and one must take manly action for a perceived goal; lamentations and fanciful dreams are rightly derided. But the mind will either atrophy or lapse into melancholy if one is forced mutely to conceal all of one's emotions. One needs a loyal and sympathetic woman friend to listen to one's laments, to share one's joys, to protect one's rights against people with prosaic minds. You were that friend to me for a long time, my dear Rosie; will you continue to be so?

You see, dear Rosie, what selfish motives have put the pen in my hand, yet I still come with conditions which must accompany our correspondence, conditions for which I have already given up forever a correspondence that was very dear to me (you are well aware of it). [Fritz refers again to his former beloved in Erfurt.] You know how our religious views differ and how the open confession of mine has permanently affected my public position. You also understand that all my inner feelings, my fears and desires, my hopes and longings, are fused with an ideology inspired by religious views that are very different from yours. You will then realize how impossible it is for me to avoid expressing my opinions directly or indirectly in my letters. As a condition of our further correspondence (primarily for your sake) you must therefore consider whether you might fear falling into doubt through an exchange of ideas on those opinions, or being led to an inner conflict to which you would not feel equal. I need hardly assure you that I will not attack your beliefs with philosophical subtlety. If I am to share my thoughts with you, as I must, then I desire only to be able to reflect on and to represent things from my perspective. If you are afraid of being made miserable because of confusion about the rightness of your viewpoint, then there is of course no alternative to silence.[57]

There is no record of what Fritz's father thought of his oldest son's withdrawal from the church, no word of a formal break or of his son's offence, but there was evidently a deep estrangement. In a short letter to his sister Rosie on 6 December 1847 Fritz rejoices that he is going to have a chance to talk with her again at Christmas. They probably did meet, but he never saw his parents' house in Mühlberg thereafter, and he stopped corresponding for several years with his sister, who felt far more sorrow than anger but who would not write him secretly in the presence of her parents. The family was saddened in 1846 when August gave up theology for horticulture and not unfairly blamed his older brother's influence for the change in career. Fritz thus became isolated from them for a time, as he had of course feared. Only the unswerving loyalty of his two brothers consoled him, and he kept up a regular correspondence with them, and with his cousin Wilhelm Mensing.

In September 1847, at the end of his second year, Fritz was looking ahead to the end of his medical training, which should have concluded with the state examination, but he knew that he could take the examination only after graduation, and as he reported to August, he had a problem:

According to many precedents, I can easily imagine the answer that I must expect to the enquiry which I sent to the Ministry of Culture about three weeks ago. As you know, at the graduation of medical doctors, one takes an oath with the concluding phrase: "so help me God and his sacred gospel." I have asked whether I might replace it with a simple promise, as is customary in Berlin at the graduation in Philosophy. I am of course prepared for a negative answer, yet curious to see if they will qualify that "no" in order to avoid declaring publicly that one cannot even become a physician in Prussia without believing in a certain system of dogma, or at least pretending to do so. You are in a position to get information, as chance arises, about opportunities in Hamburg for employment as a ship's doctor or surgeon. For in the very likely event that I cannot take my degree in Prussia and therefore cannot sit the state examination, I intend to stay here only until I feel qualified for an independent practice, and then either seek employment as a ship's doctor, or emigrate.[58]

Fritz's "enquiry" went through the medical faculty on 28 October 1847 to the Greifswald government, and on to the Minister of Ecclesiastical, Educational and Medical Affairs, who replied in the negative in February 1848, for the reason that Fritz had "not joined a religious society whose members were excused from the rules regarding the wording of the oath."[59]

The Revolutionary upheavals in Europe reached Berlin in March 1848. They had many ultimate causes, including the crop failures and famines of 1845-46, rural overpopulation and economic downturn, from which the working class sought relief, but to these stresses on the authorities were added the demands of intellectuals for freedom of the press, civil rights and freedom of conscience. The King of Prussia, Frederick William IV came to the throne in 1840 with promises to lift press censorship and restore civil liberties, but he soon retreated to an autocratic position. In 1842 he made a gesture of liberalization by establishing provincial assemblies (diets) elected on the basis of class, but even they opposed the King, who then summoned them to Berlin as a United Diet in 1847. When that body in turn refused in June 1847 to approve a loan which the government sought, it was dissolved, but although most liberals in the Diet were not revolutionaries, it became a forerunner of the revolutionary spirit that would rise in 1848. In the autumn of 1847 there were further calls for a militia to replace the regular army, for a progressive income tax, and for freedom of conscience and of the press.

Similar currents were stirring in all of the major capitals of Europe, culminating in early 1848 in a series of crises, the first in Paris, where the King abdicated in February, and Vienna and Berlin followed in March. A workers' demonstration in Berlin was brutally suppressed on 13 March, but news of the success of student revolutionaries against the Austrian government in Vienna a few days later "put the situation in Berlin out of control completely," and on the 18th the King agreed to free the press, revive the United Diet, and grant a constitution. The presence of troops at the palace when the King made these concessions destabilized the situation, however, and there was violence and barricade-building. On the 19th the King gave in to popular pressure for a Civic Guard to replace the troops at the palace and was then "entirely under the protection of his subjects."[60]

Not surprisingly, the revolutionary year of 1848 found Fritz on the side of the Democratic Party. Oehlschläger later recalled, "One may gauge the mood of the times among educated people in the university town by how Barthold, Professor of History, burst into my room when the news of the Berlin Revolution of 18 March reached us, and with an embrace told me all the joyful details. Of course our 'Circlet' also took part appropriately in the general joy, and Fritz swam in a sea of happiness."[61]

Fritz became secretary of the Peoples' Union, mostly workers and students, which together with the middle class Union of Townspeople formed the Democratic Party. Even the Constitutional Club, founded by professors and civil servants, was changed into a "Democratic-Constitutional" club after the withdrawal of the extreme conservatives. Fritz was almost completely occupied in the obstetrical clinic until 1 July of the revolutionary year, and a severe attack of dysentery confined him to bed for several weeks in the late summer. Only in the autumn, when he was completely free, could he devote his activities entirely to the party machinery. He reckoned 24 September 1848, the day of the Congress in Greifswald "to bring about the unification of all the democrats of Lower Pomerania," the finest day of his life because he "became acquainted with such a number of splendid people,"[62] but although he was at times enthusiastic about spreading enlightenment across the flat countryside and reforming the "rotten and still completely medieval state institutions," his heart was not really in it. What had motivated him were questions of religion and the practical conclusions that he drew for the individual from his answers to those questions. "Only religious freedom, though at the moment repressed by politics, can form the firm and unshakable foundation for the free shaping of political and social conditions,"[63] and the likelihood of such freedom was fast diminishing.

On 21 October 1848, he wrote to his brothers,

> The old nuisance with the examination is coming back again. I hardly expect that the revolution has advanced us in this respect and that I will be able to graduate without that Christian oath to which I will of course never submit. Today I have therefore appealed to the faculty. My immediate future is thus completely in the dark.[64]

Fritz's second petition to the medical dean, dated that same day, is a ringing defense of his principles and points out that the denial of his request to omit the religious formula from the oath would be a "slap in the face" of the civil rights proclaimed in Prussia after the March (1848) Revolution. The faculty, however, declared that it lacked the authority to alter the existing rules, and the new Minister in Berlin concurred.[65] Probably early in 1849 the Minister rejected Fritz's renewed request that he be allowed, "like Jews, to take the oath without its concluding phrase."[66] Irene Lauterbach, in her publication of the documents, justifies the stand of the medical dean and the ministry by the fact that the proclamation of "civil rights" had changed nothing in the university statutes. She points out that it was really Fritz's own fault for being so stubborn, and that he could have graduated and taken the medical exam if he had just compromised.[67] Although his inflexibility on this point is undeniable, there is something in her argument of "blaming the victim." People have often taken principled stands on civil rights and thereby had trouble with the authorities, but would we ask them to compromise their principles to avoid that trouble? Nevertheless, there is no evidence that Fritz's participation in the revolutionary events of March 1848 was a factor in the rejection of his petitions, as McKinney suggests. [68]

"For me to emigrate is to some extent an act of desperation," he wrote to Wilhelm Mensing in March 1849.

> Because of my stubborn personality, which, to be true to my principles, is in reckless rebellion against the current situation and would rather be shattered than submit, I have reached the point where nothing remains for me here but to seek my livelihood as a private tutor, a writer or a day laborer. I largely

foresaw from the outset that I would get into this situation but would even now without hesitation take all the "idiotic, ill-advised" steps that brought me to it. For I know that I would be miserable forever were I to forswear a jot of my convictions for the sake of any superficial gain.[69]

By October 1848 the forces of reaction in Prussia were strengthening, as the workers' movement failed from lack of effective leadership and the middle class recognized the danger of social instability and backed off from confrontation with the King. Changes in the electoral law in Prussia led to a largely conservative assembly in June 1849, as Fritz was finishing his medical course, and it would have been clear to him that any religious reforms that he favored were now dead. Early in 1850 the King's authority was effectively restored and the revolution was over.[70]

After finishing his studies in science and medicine, Fritz stood nearly destitute before the question: What now?

# 4

# Respite in the Country, 1849–1852

On the recommendation of a friend, Fritz (Fig. 4) took a position as a private tutor with the Lamprecht family in Rolofshagen near Grimmen in western Pomerania (Map 2), in the futile hope that the reactionary wave in Prussia would not last much longer. After the turmoil, bitterness, and disappointment of the revolutionary year and his depressing inactivity and uncertainty about the future, he found the place a peaceful sanctuary among congenial people. "I have now been here six weeks," he wrote to his brother Hermann in late November, 1849:

> and have long since settled in completely. After the revolutionary year, which was also a turbulent time for me personally, I feel very much at home in this comfortable quiet existence. My job is almost exclusively limited to the education of my charges, a boy of 13 and three girls of 11, 10 and 5 years. In addition I am now studying some (popular) astronomy on my own and plan to review physics and some higher mathematics in the course of the winter. I have absolutely no acquaintances outside the family and so far have not missed them. We read the Berlin Democratic Paper. Herr Lamprecht is a man of the extreme left, well educated, especially in history, and a keen thinker. My interaction with him is therefore a real pleasure.[2]

To his sister Charlotte, who had married in 1848 and was now living on an estate in Bavaria, he wrote early in 1850, "I too now live in the quiet seclusion of the countryside, almost completely confined

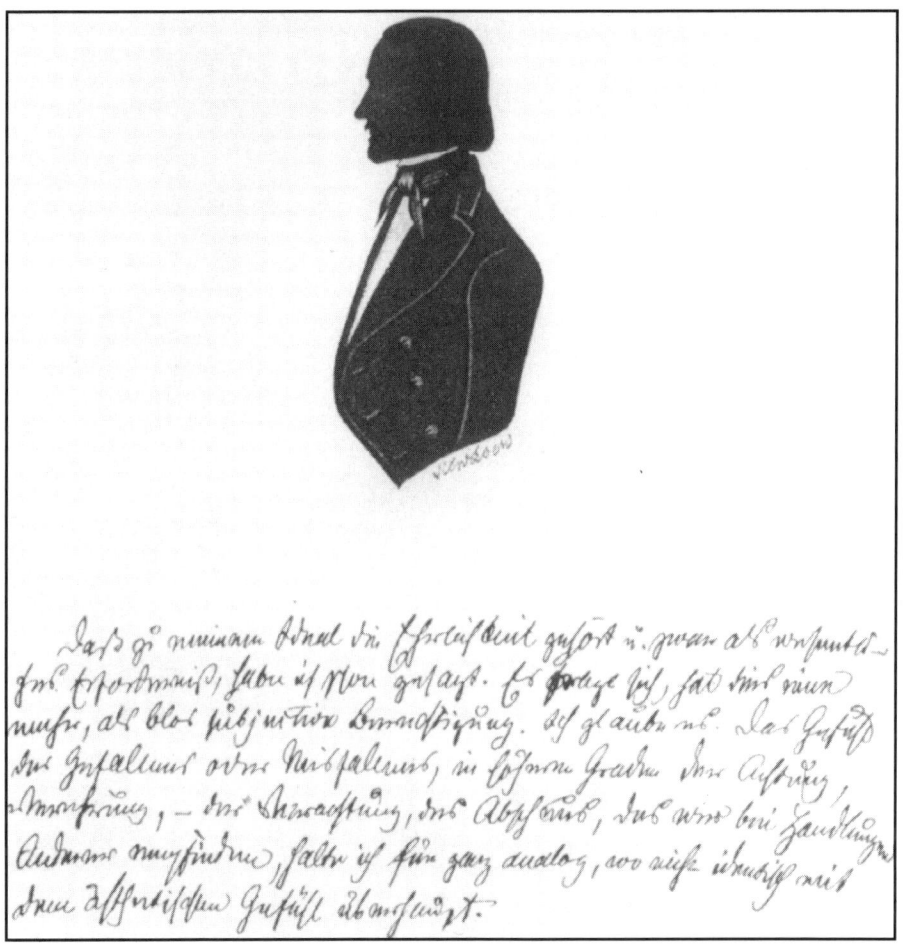

*Fig. 4. Silhouette of Fritz Müller while in Rolofshagen (1849–1852)
and sample of his handwriting, 1851. A. Möller, 1920,* Fritz Müllers
Leben.

to the one family of which I have become as it were a member, and
have discovered how strongly, in that isolation, ties of loyalty bind
together even those who are not bound by ties of kinship."[3]

Fritz later recalled in his letters to Lamprecht from Brazil how
much he had enjoyed that family circle:

> in which I found such a snug refuge during the political turmoil
> that forced me from my career.[4] I don't want the few threads
> that link me to my homeland to be completely broken, and it is

that period when I lived in your home, in the midst of your family, which I recall most fondly. . . . I was especially pleased by the letters from your children and Minnas . . . and must grate-fully acknowledge that among the many children whom I have taught I have never encountered any whose enthusiasm and willingness to oblige made a teacher's work so agreeable."[5]

Whatever reputation he may have had as an atheist and anarchist overturning altar and throne, Fritz's letters from his time in Rolofshagen reveal a personality full of kindness and innocent amuse-ment rather than of strife.

In the summer of 1850 he wrote to Hermann that he had been:

vegetating, careless and without plans, idly enjoying whatever the moment offers: genial family life, frittering away time innocently with the children, loitering about the countryside, enjoying the plants and animals and observing their habits, but without any coherent purpose; all sorts of reading matter, almost as chance offers it, including Macaulay's *History of England* in translation,[6] Sue's *Mystères du peuple*,[7] Proudhon's *Confessions d'un révolutionnaire*,[8] Kolatschek's *German Monthly Magazine for Politics, Science, Art and Lifestyle*.[9]

As for "loitering about the countryside," despite what he told Hermann in 1849 about his complete lack of social life outside the Lamprecht family, he had had what Alfred Möller called a "free love" association since 1848 with Caroline Tollner, daughter of a day-laborer in Loitz, a village near Greifswald, with whom he had a daughter Louisa on 14 May 1849, even before he joined the Lamprecht family.[10] He and Caroline were later married, and she emigrated with him to Brazil, bore him ten children and was a faith-ful and hard-working companion until her death in 1894. According to Alfred Möller, who knew Fritz's family in Brazil while on research there in the 1890s, however, she never took any part in his intellectual life and never really appreciated his stature in the community, much less his international reputation as a naturalist. Unfortunately scarcely anything is known about her from any other source.

Fritz did not hide his joy of fatherhood from his brothers August and Hermann, and told them openly of the frequent visits to "my family" in Loitz, where Caroline lived with her parents, although he seems not to have let them know until after his letter to Hermann late in 1849. His parents in Mühlberg and his sister Rosine must have known about the affair, which violated all their hallowed traditions, but there is no record of what they thought.

Fritz had expressed his thoughts on love and marriage in a letter to his brothers in the autumn of 1848, when Caroline must have been pregnant:

> Sometime when you are going to Mühlberg, take along Fröbel's *Politics*[11] and have Mother [actually his stepmother] read the passages about marriage and the relationship of the sexes. A long time ago she asked for my views on the subject, but I had neither time, nor even any real inclination, to explain that difficult subject in writing. She will find my views expressed pretty well in Fröbel's book, though certainly more by implication than by a developed argument. Christians are always so proud of their morality; it may have its good points, but its weakest point surely concerns the relationship of the sexes. One shudders at the inevitable consequences of that affected Christian morality and begins to doubt human intelligence in the face of the prejudice that prevails on the subject. The most monstrous relationship is turned around and made respectable by a priest's blessing. I had ample opportunity in my former situation, and still do to some extent, to become acquainted with the social, moral and material evils that arise from those prejudices and that monkish priestly-morality.[12]

Perhaps Fritz was referring to the subordination of women in marriage, but it is not clear what passage in Fröbel's book he had in mind. Fröbel thought that women were dominated by what we might call "instinct," that is that they responded to stimuli, while men were reflective about their thoughts and feelings,[13] but also that the development of our sexual natures could be satisfied only by freedom and abundant contact between the sexes.[14]

Oehlschläger, his fellow student in Greifswald, rationalized Fritz's attraction to Caroline Tollner, recalling many years later that Fritz was "shy and absolutely chaste and found sensuality deeply repugnant. For him, flitting from girl to girl was completely out of the question, and as long as I was in Greifswald he had no relationship with any woman at all. What must have attracted him to

[Caroline] was that she was unpretentious like him and had a certain simplicity which fascinated him as a child of nature."[15] Goethe's taking of a "simple" wife has often been explained the same way.[16] Whether by intention or not, Caroline's pregnancies confirmed that she and Fritz were a fertile couple, an important consideration for future emigration.

McKinney, in the *Dictionary of scientific biography*, took a cue from Alfred Möller's phrase "freie Liebe" and wrote that Fritz "believed in free love."[17] He certainly had at that time a sexual relationship outside of marriage, but to say that he "believed" in free love implies something further, perhaps licentious, which would be utterly wrong, as Oelschläger's reminiscences and Fritz's own future behavior show.[18]

Although Fritz was not then in direct correspondence with his sister Rosine, as a consequence of his earlier break with the church, he heard about her reaction to the affair through his brothers, who evidently stood by him. She was apparently unhappy about it, but Fritz thought that he saw through to her real problem. "I am in complete agreement with the point which you told me about in your letter to Rosie," he wrote to Hermann at the end of 1849:

> Perhaps I would have added two points: Firstly, that Rosie was not sorry for me, but rather envied me, when she began to be aware of the true circumstances of her development under the influence of Christian ethics, with all that physical and spiritual infirmity and misery, and when she understood how difficult it is in those circumstances for her to live according to the demands of nature without giving up some of her human dignity or offending the dignity of others. Secondly, that anyone must be a fool who remains true to his principles when they demand sacrifice and renunciation in the face of universal condemnation, and who renounces them when they offer him pleasure.[19]

In his continued soul-searching, Fritz told Hermann in 1851 why he was so open about his beliefs:

> To begin with, why do I wish to be candid? The real driving force of all human behavior is the pursuit of pleasure, satisfaction, or happiness; that is egoism, or whatever you want to call it. Each of us, even the most passionate preacher against egoism,

does what seems most effective to promote his own happiness. Just as I myself reject any authority that would tell me what happiness I should strive for, and by what path I am supposed to attain it, so do I acknowledge everyone else's right to seek happiness in his own way. For myself at present, the essential condition for my own satisfaction and happiness is complete accord between an understanding of science and one's creed, between knowledge and action. Unfortunately, in recent years I have often had to decide between prudent silence (or open denial of my views) and the renunciation of many of life's pleasures. So far I have always chosen the latter, not often without a hard struggle. Although this stunting of my own development has been painful and at times impossible to surmount, I would purchase for the price of that inner conflict neither the realization of my long sweet dream of love, nor the path to a successful scientific career, nor the opportunity to widen the practical influence of my views. I have never yet regretted my choice. Hence I am "candid," or at least have the intention of being so, because I consider candor the most expedient approach to my ultimate goal, which is my own happiness. So little virtue do I see in it that I would not lay it down as a rule for others, though it has served me well and has stood the test of my own experience.

I have already said that candor is part of my ideal and is indeed its prerequisite. The question is, has it more than a merely subjective justification? I believe so. I consider the feeling of pleasure or displeasure, or more largely of esteem and respect — or of disdain and disgust, that we have about the deeds of others to be perfectly analogous to, if not identical with, our aesthetic sense. But it is that which is simple and in harmony with itself that pleases us the most.[20]

Fritz produced no important scientific work while at Rolofshagen, only a note on copulation in a leech which he had collected near Loitz before he left Greifswald. Beginning in 1851, however, he sent a few contributions to Wislicenus's journal, now called *Neue Reform*. As Fritz reported to his brother Hermann in March 1851:

Dr. Douai had written an essay "On the holiness of God," from (approximately) Hegel's point of view, naturally with the usual arrogant disdain of speculation on ordinary "consciousness," and with all the pretensions of our new "philosophy" to impose its subjective and arbitrary fantasies as new dogmas. I was so annoyed that I wrote a critical rejoinder,[21] as I also did against Herr Rossmässler,[22] a very honorable man and an excellent naturalist but still rather biased in religious matters, who in a "nature sermon" wanted among other things to make nature out as a moral standard for Man.

Meanwhile the matter of Fritz's future became increasingly urgent: "There is still the question of what I should take up next year," he wrote to Hermann:

> when I shall probably leave Rolofshagen. Emigrate? I would probably lose the pleasures of civilization which even my present position more or less offers me. And that is a high price. In the event, the closer I come to breaking away, the more I realize how strongly I am rooted in all of my local relationships.[23]

Fritz had been thinking for some time about emigration and was vacillating between southern Brazil and southern Chile as a destination, in reaction to a brochure on southern Brazil by Hermann Blumenau[24] and highly favorable reports about southern Chile from deputies in the provincial diet and members of the Frankfurt National Assembly and the Halle Free Congregation. "The chief advantages of both these southern countries," he wrote to Hermann, "are a nice mild climate, rich natural history, proximity to the sea and, although Catholicism is the state religion in both, a greater tolerance than in North America, where bigotry prevails and at the very least Sunday is strictly observed nearly everywhere by law and by custom. In addition, 'make money' [English in the original] seems nowhere to be such a universal principle of life as in the Union."[25]

While Fritz was a student in Erfurt, he had known Hermann Blumenau as an apprentice in the Lion Apothecary Shop and as an enthusiastic botanist who later worked in the chemical factory of Fritz's uncle Hermann Trommsdorff and visited in his home. In 1848 Blumenau bought 100,000 acres (over 40,000 hectares) of virgin forest in the southern Brazilian province of Santa Catarina, which was actively recruiting German immigrants. In 1850 he established a colony on the land with a partner and returned to Germany, where he published a brochure to attract emigrants. After a fulsome description of the beauties and riches of Brazil, Blumenau admitted that the only parts of the country that were suitable for German settlers were the southern states of Rio Grande do Sul and Santa Catarina, and the highlands of São Paulo. Blumenau undoubtedly recognized that there would be a flood of emigrants from central Europe after the failed revolutions of 1848, but his colony had no ideological basis. It was a business venture, and he wanted to attract serious settlers. Blumenau wrote at the time, "My colony could and ought to become a refuge for German-speaking immigrants of German origin who seek by the sweat of their brows a means of livelihood and a future for themselves and their children secure and without worry."[26] Blumenau attracted seventeen settlers to his new colony in September 1850, but after the colony failed in 1852 he bought out his partner's share and tried again, and Fritz was among the first settlers that year.[27]

Fritz had intended to take a good look at possible destinations by making a preliminary trip as a naturalist-collector and covering the cost by the sale of his collections. He had sought information about the possibilities when, as he wrote to Hermann in November 1851:

> simultaneously with the letter that brought me that information came a second one, from brother August, informing me of his resolve to emigrate as well. I decided immediately to give up my preliminary travel plans, in the event that he was agreeable to a joint colonization, and to proceed at once with emigration. He has just agreed, and we will therefore leave Europe together early next year and fell the trees for our cabin in the virgin forest of Brazil or Chile. In this country, even those with considerable vigor lose most of it fighting against old deeply-entrenched circumstances. Most of the time they can scarcely find the conditions for a successful, let alone creative profession, and all the pleasure in their lives is lost in bitter struggle. Over there, an individual is free to shape according to his best beliefs a society just emerging and probably facing a great future; that is, once he has endured the first tough fight against the wilderness and has struggled for an existence freer of care, though always full of toil. Thus satisfied with himself, any sensible man will also be able to exert in that embryonic society a disproportionately greater influence on its formation and further development than in our

ossified states. His activities could benefit his children, and his children's children far into the future. There is the prospect of satisfying not merely one's material needs, but also one's ideals. It is principally for that reason that I prefer the nascent German colonies in South America to the Union, where everything has already taken on a more stable but to me somewhat less pleasing form, and where the Anglo-American race has a marvelous capacity to assimilate all sorts of heterogeneity.[28]

Fritz expanded these thoughts in 1852 in his last communication to Wislicenus's journal, where he presented his views on a suitable destination for members of the Free Congregations who had decided to emigrate. Southern Brazil, southern Chile (Valdivia), Australia, Central America, and the United States were named as possibilities. Fritz evidently acquired all of his information about Brazil from Blumenau's brochure. Central America was rejected because of its tropical climate and because the German Society of Emigration and Colonization had been unsuccessful in establishing a colony there. Australia was too far away and the land too expensive; southern Chile was also far, and the Pacific offered no convenient markets for goods. The United States had slavery in the south and was too cold in the north, which was in any event best suited to cereal crops that members of the Free Congregations, as city-folk, would have difficulty learning how to grow. The Germans in Texas had managed to keep slavery out of their settlements, but otherwise the institution was fiercely defended in the southern states. Brazil also had slavery, but Fritz believed that there was much opposition to it and that its end was in sight. In fact, complete emancipation came only in 1888, but many slaves had bought their freedom long before. In his own colony Blumenau forbade slavery, and although he reserved land for churches and schools, publicly-funded schools had to be secular.[29]

On religious freedom, Fritz added to what he had written to Hermann that Brazil was officially Roman Catholic and that other sects could build meeting houses only if they did not look like churches, especially in not having steeples. Although Fritz considered such a limitation "ridiculous and degrading," he recognized the irony that for free-thinkers it would be "for all practical purposes a matter of complete indifference." His greatest concern was that the German culture of the emigrants not be swallowed up, as had already happened in North America, and he quoted the Göttingen professor Johann Eduard Wappäus[30] on the dangers of Anglo-American society in this respect and the greater likelihood of being able to form a uniquely German-American culture in southern South America. In the end Fritz decided that the "nine square miles of Blumenau's colony on the Great Itajaí in Santa Catarina"[31] was best suited to that goal, and he concluded his article, "I have myself chosen it for my new home and hope soon to be able to report further details about it from personal experience."[32]

On 6 March 1852 a second daughter, Anna, was born and on 14 March was recorded in the baptismal register of Loitz Parish as Johanna Frederike Caroline. The baptism was probably Caroline Tollner's doing, as Fritz never agreed to it for any of the children born after their marriage. The parents' joy was clouded, however, by the death soon after of her older sister Louisa, then nearly three years old. In early April Fritz left Rolofshagen and moved for a short time to Loitz to prepare for emigration. Here, on 27 April 1852, according to the marriage register of the Loitz church, he and Caroline Tollner were married by the Lutheran pastor, with Fritz's father's consent. One can imagine what it must have taken to move Fritz the Unbeliever to that first and only denial of his principles. He was then 30 years old, but his stubbornness was evidently overcome by the wishes of his elderly parents and his sister Rosine, and the persuasion of his brother August, who was married by his father in Mühlberg shortly before emigrating. Alfred Möller suggests that August wanted to save his future sister-in-law from later trouble, and that Caroline, looking forward to an uncertain future in Brazil, might not have wanted to appear inferior to her new sister-in-law by not having a wedding ceremony.

Fritz never saw his relatives or the scenes of his youth again. On 6 May 1852 he wrote a farewell to his parents from Loitz:

> This is my last letter to you from Europe, and even that with only a fleeting pen in the midst of preparations for our departure. But I would not leave without expressing once more my thanks for the love and concern which you show yet again for us emigrants. Not infrequently have you grieved and worried about

me in recent years. Our divergent views were often the cause of it, and in those instances I could not even with the calmest reflection have acted otherwise. Often, however, when I was upset or irritated, I have let myself be swept away to say things against you which I should not have said. I hope that I will never again grieve you thus and that the differences in our opinions will never again affect our sincere good feelings toward one another.

On Monday the 10th we shall go from here by omnibus to Stralsund, the next day by the same to Rostock, and on the 12th by rail to Hamburg. What a cheerful birthday Louisa would have celebrated there on the 15th, among so many novelties. Our little one [Anna] is a robust and lively child. Affectionate greetings to my brother and sisters, and to the Old World for the last time farewell! Your Fritz.[33]

# 5
# Emigrant and Pioneer in Brazil, 1852–1856

Fritz and his brother August, their wives, and Fritz's two-month old daughter sailed from Hamburg in May 1852 and arrived in Brazil in July after a two-month voyage. The following "Notes on the journey for friends and acquaintances" were written by the brothers from their first settlement, on Velha Brook in the Blumenau Colony, 25 August 1852, four days after arriving at their destination.[2]

The departure of the *Florentin*, Captain Lofgrén,[3] which was to take us to São Francisco [Santa Catarina] in south Brazil, was set for 14 May [1852]; but the ship was only ready for us to board on the 17th. More than 200 Swiss had arrived shortly before us, mostly poor people from the canton of Schaffhausen whose passage money to Dona Francisca [colony inland from the port of São Francisco, now Joinville] had been advanced by their community. They were quite busy loading their luggage, and everything was still in the most unspeakable confusion. We obtained two nice little staterooms, each with a lower and an upper berth, washstand etc., lit by a porthole, and adjacent to a most elegant main cabin which was lit from above and had a mirror, sofa and gilt trim on the walls.[4] Most of the cabin passengers, on the other hand, were quartered in a packed space below decks without air or light, separated from steerage by a wooden partition. We owed our material advantage to having sent earlier notice. Next day many visitors came on board, most of whom, having seen other emigrant ships, thought ours overloaded and made us fear for our health. Indeed, the air rising from the overcrowded luggage-crammed lower deck was truly stifling.

On the afternoon of the 19th we weighed anchor and were towed by a steamer to the vicinity of Stade, where we lay at anchor for the night. The next morning we went downstream with a good wind. About midday we sailed past Cuxhaven into the [North] sea, and about 4 o'clock, scarcely two hours after we lost sight of the mainland, heavy weather came up and most of the passengers were seasick. Toward evening Helgoland was visible on our right. For the next few days the wind was light, the weather foggy and rainy. On the evening of the 22nd the wind increased and the fog grew still thicker. All night we heard the Dutch fishing boats tooting around us, and our ship's bell was rung from time to time to avoid a collision. On the evening of 24 May, in a high sea in which their dinghies tossed like nutshells and often vanished behind the crests of the waves, a couple of English ships came alongside to exchange some fresh fish, a lobster and a crab, for meat. That night we entered the English Channel with a good wind. On the morning of the 25th we saw the first stretch of the English coast, and about midday we were opposite Beachy Head. At approximately 4 o'clock in the afternoon we sailed past the chalk bluffs of the Isle of Wight and by the following morning we had left the Channel. The wind blew a full gale in our favor, so that only three sails were unfurled, although in calmer weather we sailed with more than twenty.

On the 29th, at the latitude of Cape Finisterre, the wind was very weak and the weather mild and pleasant. Most passengers were now over their seasickness; many of the men had not been affected at all, and most of them, including both of us, had been only slightly affected with some vomiting and dizziness for part or all of a day. It was worse for most of the women, some of whom were plagued by seasickness for the whole journey.

On the afternoon of Whitsunday [28 May], and by moonlight on Whitmonday evening, there was a dance on board; the space in front of the main cabin served as a dance hall, music was supplied by the barrel organ of the captain, who generally made every effort possible to keep the passengers amused during the trip, and who, like the whole crew, was worthy of highest

praise. On 1 June, 15° W of Greenwich, we passed the latitude
of Lisbon; on the 4th and 5th those with sharp eyes could see
Madeira on our left. We then reached the region of the NE
Trades, and could count on a regular favorable wind until close
to the Equator. On the 6th Palma was seen to our left. On the
evening of the 9th we crossed the Tropic of Cancer and at
midday of that and the following day the sun was nearly straight
overhead, about 1° from the zenith. On the former day still to
the south of it, on the latter day for the first time, but probably
forever, to the north. It amused us to see tiny shadows nearly
lacking under that vertical sun.

The heat was not especially great and was easily bearable
because of the fresh trade winds; the highest temperature during
those days was 21.5° R (27°C),[5] that is lower than in Hamburg
harbor at our departure. For some time now flying fishes had
appeared, sometimes singly, sometimes in great schools; splendid
jellyfish, called by the sailors "Man of War" or "Portuguese",
often floated by us on spread violet sails, and every evening the
play of marine phosphorescence delighted us.

On 12 June we caught sight of São Antonio in the Cape
Verde Islands; from there we steered southward, parallel to the
African coast; on the 13th the islands of Fogo and Brava appeared on the left, and in the evening the steersman called our
attention to the Southern Cross. On the 14th we reached 13.5°
N latitude, steering south-southeast, and on the following day
the northeast trade wind ceased; in oppressive heat, and nearly
calm and often cloudy, rainy weather, we moved only slowly
forward; on the 18th we were at 9°15' N latitude, 21° W of
Greenwich, on the 21st at 6°30' N latitude. We had midday
temperatures of 29°C, and on the longest day it was the same
until 6 pm.

Fritz had the pleasure for about a week during those sultry
days of having to stay in his berth, ill with measles. Measles had
already turned up in one child in Hamburg, and a second family
was put ashore in Cuxhaven for that reason. At Whitsuntide it
appeared again and remained with us for the whole trip, affecting most of the children and some adults. Despite its generally
very mild course, twelve children died of it in the stuffy atmosphere of the overcrowded steerage. Nearly all of the children

under two years died for lack of a suitable diet, and only two of the fourteen nursing infants arrived in South America alive and well. Diarrhea and other illness prevailed among the adults, mainly because of bad air and water. On the afternoon of 22 June a putrid blackish liquid was dispensed as drinking water, and on the morning of the 23rd we lowered the remains of five children together into the sea. On the 24th of June, 4° 30' N latitude, a stronger wind finally sprang up from the south, and on the 27th we crossed the Line around noon without further ceremonies. It was 26.2°C at midday, and that whole day the temperature scarcely changed a degree. It was thus not as dangerous on the equator as we feared, for at midday in Germany at that time it would probably have been just as hot. The southeast trade winds pushed us quickly ahead, sometimes in bright and sometimes in cloudy weather, and always at a even temperature of around 25-27.5°C. We were at 4°S 27°W on 30 June, on 3 July at 14°S 33°W and on the 6th at 21°S 33°W. The southeast trades ceased, we caught a strong north-northwest wind, and we then sailed west-southwest, the waves consequently beating perpendicularly against the starboard and breaking over the side for many a merry baptism.

The following day the American mainland came in sight for the first time: Cabo Tomé and later Cabo Frio, which project eastward from Rio de Janeiro. Simultaneously there appeared many dainty little petrels, so-called cape-pigeons, which accompanied the ship from then on and which were hooked with bacon, harpooned, or shot.

The American mainland had been greeted with joy; we hoped to be at our destination in two or three days, but here our luck deserted us. Sometimes with a contrary wind, sometimes in complete calm, we moved along at a snail's pace, often scarcely four leagues a day (about 4 English miles). On the evening of the 17th in a most beautiful sunset, we saw our long-awaited São Francisco. On the morning of the 18th the island lay unmistakably before us. We were near the southern end of the island, and finally with a favorable wind we sailed past many little rocky islets to its northern end, entering here the Rio São Francisco. Soon we could distinguish vegetation, rocks, sand dunes, and breakers on the beach, and finally individual trees, including slender towering palms, and white houses at the edge of the forest. As we entered the river a pilot came aboard from a small canoe, and with his guidance we cast anchor opposite the town of São Francisco about 5 o'clock.

Our first sight was most cheerful; white houses in a picturesque situation at the foot of beautiful hills wooded to the water's edge. The captain, however, laughed at our delight in the lovely town, and when we were set ashore the next day, after a cursory customs inspection of our goods and chattels, it turned out that he was right. The streets and all the closely-built houses were dirty and neglected; of many houses there stood only a few bare walls or stone columns overgrown with bushes, giving the streets a forbidding and ruinous air. What the town lost at close inspection was made up for by nature; orange trees loaded with golden fruit, palms, bananas, papayas and giant castor beans made a show around the houses. For the time being we stayed with our things on the shore, stared at by people of every color, and negotiated with the ship's captain, who for 100 milréis [$54] was willing to go on to Santa Catarina in about a week and would take us close to the mouth of the Itajaí River, though he later asked 80 [$43].[6] That was too expensive for us; moreover, we were told so many good things about the island of São Francisco, and so many bad things about the Itajaí, that we decided to take a closer look at both localities before making our final choice of a new residence. Meanwhile, for 2 milréis [$1.08] per week, we rented very spacious lodgings, quite elegant by Brazilian standards. There were no fewer than seven rooms with wooden floors, connected by large folding doors, in all two windows with glass panes, and at the back a kitchen, that is to say a miserable shed with a few bricks laid together ad lib for the hearth. Ten paces from the door was the shore, close behind the house a neglected coffee and orange plantation and beyond that, forest. On the next day, 20 July, we looked over the island in nearly continuous rain.

On 21 July August Müller set out with two companions to reconnoiter. They traveled mostly on foot, though by canoe up and down the Itajaí River, and spent only a day in Blumenau, but the lovely river meandering through rolling hills and plains was appealing, and the spot that Dr. Blumenau had chosen for his Colony, where Garcia Brook entered the Itajaí, seemed to fulfill all their require-

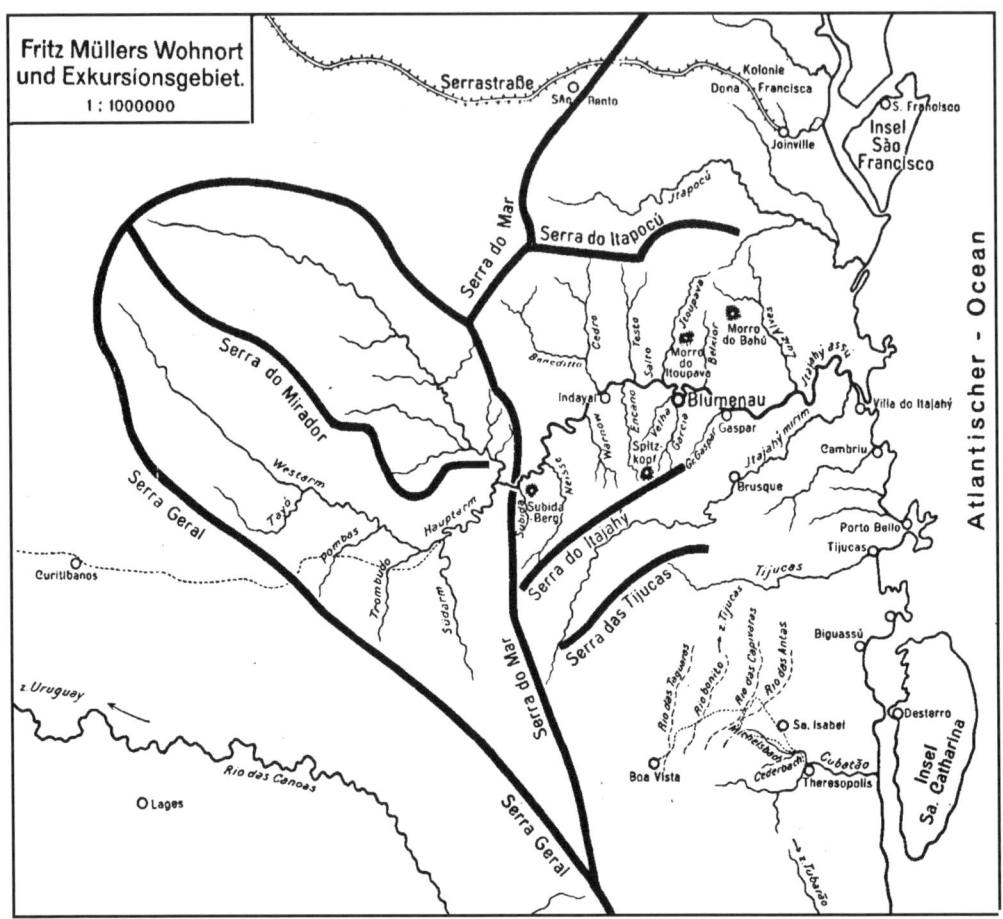

*Map Three. The region of Santa Catarina traveled by Fritz Müller, 1852–1897. A. Möller, 1920,* Fritz Müllers Leben.

ments for a healthy spot with good soil right on a navigable stream. After a ten-day absence, August had no trouble persuading his brother to stick to their original plan, especially now that Fritz had inspected the colony of Dona Francisca on the mainland opposite the island and been unfavorably impressed with its situation in a mangrove swamp. To reach their destination with their wives, the baby, and all the luggage, however, was not going to be easy. August made another trip to the Itajaí, where he finally secured a little coastal sailboat to carry them to the Itajaí. They finally embarked from São Francisco on 14 August, and after an uncomfortable voyage with bad weather and seasickness reached the mouth of the Itajaí on 18 August.

Here they assembled a raft of two canoes bound together by cross-planks, making a platform large enough for several people and their luggage. The upstream journey took three days, and finally on 21 August, three months after leaving Hamburg, the travelers reached their destination (Maps 3 and 4). They lodged temporarily in Blumenau's own cabin on the Velha, a tributary of the main river. The brothers' narrative continues:

> The next day the two of us went with Schneider[7] to the settle-ment on the Garcia to inspect two properties which were situated in front of the lands that were to be distributed free, and which Blumenau offered to us at a cheap price. [The lots, No. 1 for Fritz and No. 2 for August Müller, were of 49.5 hectares each and cost 100 milreis ($54).[8]] They met with our approval, and on the following day, the 24th of August, we took possession, picked out a place for a temporary cabin and began to build. It was finished yesterday the 27th, and on Monday, day after tomorrow, we shall move in with bag and baggage. With that our journey ends, and appropriately also the first account of our adventures. For we still have too little experience to give our own opinion about the climate and healthfulness of the country and of our settlement, and about the advisability of emigrating, and we do not wish to tempt anyone to follow us here by a hasty judgement. However, in the interest of those who wish to make a new home in Brazil it is perhaps not superfluous to mention something that should be self-evident but is seldom considered over there in Europe, as we know from many instances. Anyone wishing to settle in the virgin forest must be aware that for years he will forego all European comfort, all European pleasures. Here for a long time he will have no dwelling but a hut with walls of lath from split palm trunks, a roof of palm leaves and a floor of bare earth; likewise, year in and year out his midday meal will be dried meat, manioc meal[9] and black beans today, manioc meal, dried meat and black beans tomorrow, and black beans, dried meat and manioc meal the day after. No beer, fresh meat, bread, eggs, milk, or potatoes, no chair, table, or soft bed. Dreadful, isn't it? And yet, in spite of it all, we are all of us

extremely happy and in good spirits and would not for all the world return from our virgin forest to civilized Europe.[10]

The next day Fritz wrote to his parents,

You have already seen from our description of the trip and from August's letters that we are fully satisfied so far. I have been in good health except for boils which continue to plague me. I had six of these nasty visitations in close succession under my left arm, then one under my right arm, and at the moment I have one on my chest by the right shoulder. I hope that they will soon be gone. My family has remained well except for my wife's seasickness, during which, however, she always had a good appetite and abundant milk. Our Anna is the only child of such a tender age to have survived the sea voyage on the *Florentin*; she left the ship as chubby-faced as when she boarded it. She was by day a restless spirit who shrieked and laughed as much as others wept, and she slept like a top at night and never disturbed her fellow-travelers. Hence she was my daily and hourly joy and cheered me up when I was bored or irritated by shipboard life. You can imagine how little pleasure it was being a doctor in that gloomy space overflowing with humanity, unable to provide good air and a proper diet. Moreover, I usually got little reward for my pains.[11]

Later that year August described his cabin in more detail:

Our properties lie on Garcia Brook, an hour from its junction with the Itajaí. These are the first building sites in the Blumenau colony, which so far comprises twelve families.[12] Our house is about 100 paces from the Garcia on a rise which flattens out beyond us. Farther back in the forest we also have some hilly land which is admirably suited for growing coffee and manioc. On the other side of the river stretches a rather high steep range of mountains, covered like all the land here with virgin forest. All the homesteads are like little oases in a great desert. Our house, which is also Fritz's at the moment, is built of palms in the Brazilian manner. Uprights and rafters are palm trunks; the roof is covered with palm leaves and is perfectly watertight; the walls are of palm laths which are sunk in the ground and bound in the middle to slats with "cipós." Cipós are the roots of various epiphytic plants [chiefly philodendrons, family Araceae] which

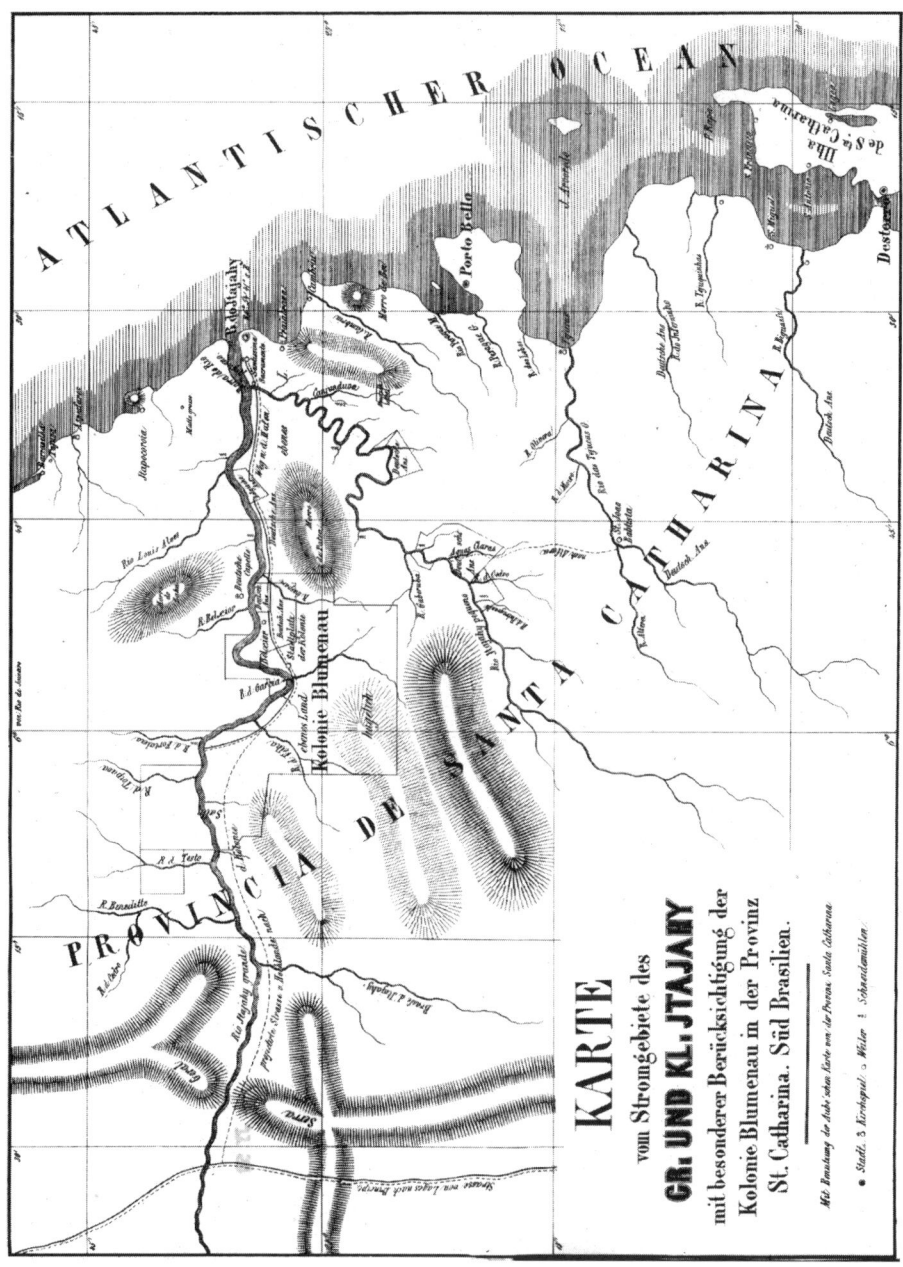

*Map Four. The Great and Little Itajaí Rivers, Santa Catarina, Brazil, showing the Blumenau Colony around the time of Fritz Müller's arrival, 1852. Blumenau, 1856,* Deutsche Kolonie Blumenau. *By permission British Library, shelfmark 10480.a.34.(4).*

grow on the tallest trees and send their roots through the air to the ground. They are often 100 feet long, and are very tough and of uniform thickness. They serve here in place of nails, cord and wicker. Houses and palings are built without nails and are merely bound with cipós. The rigging of Brazilian coasting ships is made of cipós, and during long spells of rainy weather we weave them into all sorts of baskets. Along the back gable wall of the house, a few feet from the ground, we have built a frame for our mattresses and bedding and above it a little loft. In the middle of the room in front of it stands the zinc chest on four posts as a table and around it the other chests as benches. We have also made a couple of chairs and a makeshift settee on our homemade carpenter's bench. At the front of the room is a workshop with a chopping block, our makeshift carpenter's bench, tool cupboard, etc. To the right is the kitchen, with hearth, baking oven, sideboard and kitchen cupboard (formerly an ice box). The fire burns on the hearth day and night, and some smoke drifts through the room and keeps the mosquitoes away.[13]

A few months later, during the summer, Fritz wrote to his sister Rosine about the trials of those first months in Brazil.

Blumenau Colony, Santa Catarina Province, Brazil

6 January 1853

My dear Rosie! An unusually hot sun has driven me from work into the house sooner than usual (it is not even 10 o'clock), but at least I will use this long midday rest to start a letter to you.

You will be glad to hear that I am wholly satisfied with the country in which we chose to seek a new home, and that I feel very happy and at ease in my present way of life. We started as settlers with every possible difficulty and have learned all the evils of this country from our own experience, and there have been moments when we cursed Brazil. From our entry into the virgin forest around the end of August until mid-November the weather was cloudy and rainy. Often we could scarcely leave the hut for a week; mildew and rust damaged our clothing and our tools; seedlings rotted in the garden; forest that had been felled didn't dry out; the time for putting in crops passed before we could get the land ready, and we had to put off our first big planting till February. Germans who have been 20 years in the country could not recall such incessantly bad weather. At the end of October on top of the rainy weather came a flood such as there had not been for many years. The Garcia stood a good 20 feet above its usual level. No damage was done to my property, where the land rises steeply from the river. At August's, most of the cleared land ("roça," as they call it here) was under water, the muddy twigs and branches would no longer burn, the whole thing cleared at great pain and expense and all that hard work in vain. It was worse for many of the settlers living below us, who built their cabins too low down; several were completely under water, much was ruined, and famine followed the flood, because the swollen stream blocked the road and canoes could not navigate the swiftly-flowing Garcia.

After that wet period came intense heat; around the end of November we repeatedly observed 36°C in the shade. We had to clear forest during those hot days and we sweated as never before. Once, when Schneider and I were at work on a very thick magnolia, the sweat ran down our shirts in streams. The heat discouraged us even more than the dampness; we feared that we would not be able to work at all in the approaching hottest months of January and February. Happily this fear proved groundless; the heat has been bearable for a long time now, and we are assured that such a heat wave is quite unusual before Christmas and that midsummer itself is never any hotter. During those hot days we also had some weather of strange and frightful intensity to us Europeans: constant lightning and thunder, a veritable Deluge of rain, the palms in front of the house swaying like reeds, and falling trees crashing in the forest.

We had to endure yet another plague, noxious insects, and according to all the long-time settlers it was, like the rainy weather and the early heat wave, of unusual severity. As hot weather followed the long wet spell there were immense swarms of sand-flies, quite similar to the German ones. Walking in the forest one immediately had a black cloud of them at one's back, and if one stood still for a moment one's face, hands and legs were covered with bites. Several times the flies chased us home from work. Our poor Anna was as spotted as if she had measles. These long-legs have now nearly disappeared; they could really make life miserable, while we can put up with the various other vermin.

In addition, all provisions became scarce, both manioc meal (which here replaces bread) and dried meat. The latter was for a long time nearly impossible to obtain, and then we had to pay 0.12 milréis [$.06] a pound for the worst stinking stuff, more skin and sinew than meat. Potatoes cost 2 milréis [$1.08] a sack, and are moreover scarcely to be had. A bag of manioc meal now costs 3.5 milréis [$1.90], a sack of beans 8 to 10 milréis [$4 or $5]. [The average daily cost of food per person in Blumenau about this time was something over 0.2 milréis ($.10).[14]]

Other hazards that threaten us have been called vividly to mind by recent events. One of the settlers, a universally-liked and amiable young man of about 20 years, drowned on December 21st in the Itajaí. He had gone with his father-in-law and two other Germans by canoe to a settlement lying above us on the Itajaí, and then farther by himself to deliver a letter from Germany. After a long and futile wait for his return his companions saw the empty canoe go by; he had fallen out. He was moreover one of the best oarsmen among the Germans. A craft as unstable as our canoes, which are often scarcely two spans [not quite half a meter] wide, capsizes quite easily, and one can even more easily lose one's balance standing up to paddle. Swimming is therefore an indispensable skill which my wife must also learn.

Soon after that, we were greatly excited by another incident; [on 28 December] Indians (bugres, as the natives are called here[15]) made a surprise attack on Blumenau's settlement on the Velha, scarcely half an hour from here. They had presumably twice seen a canoe with men in it leaving in the morning (downstream in the middle of the river so to take advantage of the current) but had not noticed the canoes returning close to shore. At midday they had probably not seen anyone either, because both tenants in the settlement happened to be busy repairing their guns, and so thought the house empty. As one of the tenants, Schramm, stepped out of his house about 3 o'clock, he saw five naked brown figures armed with bows and arrows approaching from a manioc plantation on a nearby hill; a sixth remained on the hill. He approached them, showed them his gun, laid it at his feet and signaled with a green branch that they might approach peacefully and without weapons. They seemed to be considering it, but at a call from the leader they gave a dreadful war cry, beat their hands against their thighs and attacked him. The other tenant, Töpsel, hearing the noise and Schramm's summons, shot over their heads to scare them off; they paused a moment but then advanced again. Schramm and Töpsel turned toward the house and sent Schramm's wife with a companion to the Garcia for safety and to fetch help, and then hid themselves in an adjoining house. The Indians approached with a great din (apparently to scare away any remaining whites), shot arrows into several rooms (for the same purpose), and then got on with their plundering. They seized sacks lying in the yard, some of them forced their way into Blumenau's room (he had gone to Desterro), and Schramm could hear them already breaking into the cupboard. One Indian, who was about to enter the room, looked nervously around, saw Schramm at the attic window of the neighboring house and was at that moment shot by him in the side. With a loud cry he flung his weapons aside and fled; the others likewise abandoned their weapons and fled after him. As they went they capered about to right and left, fearful of being shot, but in spite of it another was struck, probably fatally, in the back, and their wild howling could still be heard far into the forest. The next day the first one to be shot was found dying in the forest. I have seen his head, and although the mouth and nose are rather thick the features are not at all ugly: better looking than many Brazilians, far better than Negroes. His smooth black hair had been shaved off on top of the head and neatly cut all round, and he had almost no eyebrows or beard. In the lower lip he wore a potok, a peg of araucaria wood, which is just as decorative as ear rings, in other words no more disfiguring. The arrows were rather crudely made of bamboo, usually with a wooden point bearing six to ten barbs and with jacú feathers [a pheasant-like bird of the genus *Penelope*] at the other end. There was one among the eight arrows found with an iron point.[16]

After the Indians' surprise attack our guns were put in order and are now always handy and ready to be fired, and for the first few days scarcely a palm leaf fell in the forest without our looking round, though no Indian emerged from the under-growth. (A ten-foot palm leaf naturally makes more racket in falling than the leaf of a German linden.) The Indians do not

attack at night, and in the daytime with a firearm one has
nothing to fear even from superior numbers.

Ferreira da Silva reports that despite such an attack on his own
property, Hermann Blumenau was "opposed to the use of brute force
against the Indians; in his letters and reports he condemned the
blood-thirsty 'reprimands' which nearly always resulted in the massa-
cre of the unfortunate Indians, especially women and children who
were less able to escape pursuit through the entangling forest. Unfortunately, that was the method in vogue" among the German settlers.
Troops of "forest scouts" were created to drive Indians away from the
settlements, but their aims were both to kill Indians and to scout out
new territory for the expansion of the settlements, and they often left
the Indian men dead or dispersed and brought the women and
children back to "civilization." These Indian-hunters were still active
in southern Brazil in the first decade of the twentieth century.[17]

Although there were at first so many difficulties that could have
spoiled this beautiful land for us, yet a visit to the German
settlers by the river suffices to revive our spirits. If you could see
a family that started four years ago with nothing but plenty of
labor now making 1000 talers [1250 milréis, or $675] a year in
sugar and having a surplus of livestock and vegetables, or look at
the rapid growth of coffee plantations and orchards, and the
splendid banana and orange groves, then you would surely be
convinced that any enterprising person with sound limbs could
make a comfortable life for himself and could create a little
Paradise out of the chaos of half-burnt trees which now sur-
round his cabin.

You will ask how anyone could be so happy in such a
miserable dwelling, with such monotonous and strenuous work.
But if you could compare the present condition of this bit of
land, which can now be surveyed at a glance, with what it was
only a few months ago when I chose the site for our house in
thick virgin forest and opened up a barely passable route to the
water through thick undergrowth; if you could recall the gradual
transformation of the surroundings and of the view and could
then say to yourself: it was nearly all due to my own labor; I
cleared the house-site of trees with my own hands, I hewed the
posts, the joists and lath, gathered roofing leaves and made

matting of them, built steps to the water, poured my sweat on this tree and that; if each evening, from a high-lying tree over-looking the roça [the cleared land], you could watch it increase little by little at the expense of the chaos of twigs and branches, you would surely be as fond of your cabin and land as I am and would find as much pleasure in your work as I do.

I am so much at home here in the forest that I usually do not leave it without special reason, even on Sundays; such reasons include running short of provisions, which we have to lug half an hour on our backs because the Garcia unfortunately cannot be navigated by canoe at its usual water level. I once made a longer journey with Schneider by water down the Itajaí to buy a pig. We got a rather fat little one of about 60 pounds for 6 milréis [$3.25], but of course we then had to carry it half an hour through the woods on our shoulders. Several times ailing people have had me fetched down river, for there is no doctor on the whole Itajaí. On New Year's we went with August and his wife to Blumenau's place on the Velha for a cup of chocolate.

Yet I must also tell you that on one occasion I nearly lost my young life while felling trees. It was on 26 November; we had cleared a piece of forest on August's property and still had to cut up the branches of the downed trees so that they would dry for better burning. I was standing with my axe among the branches of an orange tree, when suddenly I heard a shout, "Fritz, Fritz." I looked up, and saw a palmito [the edible juçara palm, *Euterpe oleracea*] which August had cut on the edge of the forest falling straight toward me. It had brushed a liana as it fell and was deflected from the direction in which August had aimed it. I could not escape from my unsteady perch, and before I could think about it the palm trunk struck me right across the head and l lay bleeding on the ground. Many a man has been killed instantly by a falling palmito while clearing forest, for the tall limbless trunks acquire tremendous momentum as they drop. I was all right and quickly regained consciousness, and after cold compresses were applied in the afternoon and evening the pain had nearly gone. I had a heavy head for several days and was very sensitive to the sun for some time. One cannot be careful enough when clearing forest because trees are so often deflected as they fall.[18]

A month later Fritz thanked his parents for having prepared him for a life of hardship by not pampering him as a child. Otherwise,

> I would probably strike up just as miserable a lament as do many of our fellow colonists, who surely lived more humbly than I in Germany and yet now never tire of complaining about food, housing, heat, vermin, everything. Thanks to my upbringing, I have the good fortune to be receptive to all the beauties and pleasures of the world, yet a slave to no necessities and at ease in any situation.
>
> Anna already walks very nicely, barefoot of course like a true Brazilian. She just feasted with great gusto on a piece of pineapple; it is of a bigger and more fragrant sort than I ever saw in Europe, and we already have a dozen plants of it in our garden.
>
> We have now added as an outbuilding to our homestead a poultry house with an enclosed yard. Therein live three hens and a rooster which I purchased mainly for Anna's sake, so that she at least has a proper diet, since milk is practically impossible to obtain and butter and eggs only with difficulty.[19]

Fritz first expressed his yearning for scientific colleagues in a letter to his brother Hermann a year after arriving in Brazil. Hermann was seven years younger than Fritz and spent 1853–1855 in probationary teaching posts before he took a position at the secondary school in Lippstadt, which he held until his death in 1883. At first interested in mosses, he later pioneered the study of insect pollination and was one of FM's most active correspondents. This is apparently the first of Fritz's many letters from Brazil to Hermann.

> You will be able to deduce what I miss the most, and it is really the only thing: I should like the spare time and the literature necessary to be able to make the most of our beautiful natural surroundings for science, and of course even more I should like someone with whom to share such a scientific enjoyment of nature.
>
> We are not going to learn to speak Portuguese here in Blumenau because we seldom have contact with Brazilians; if necessary I can make myself understood to them. Besides, the language is easy, like Latin with broken bones. If you omit the consonants from a Latin word and squash it out, you have the Portuguese. For example, personales becomes pessoas; potest

becomes pode; population becomes povoação (pronounced povoassaung); bonas noctes, boas noites; germanus (brother), irmão (pronounced irmaung). It is amusing what long names our cities usually have, for example Cidade de São Sebastião do Rio de Janeiro, City of Saint Sebastian on the January River, usually called Rio, River; or Cidade de São Salvador de Bahia de Todos os Santos, City of the Holy Savior of All-Saints Bay, commonly: Bahia, Bay; Villa de São Salvador dos Campos dos Goyatacases, City of the Holy Savior of the Goyatacasen Plains, commonly Campos, Plains; Cidade de Nossa Senhora de Desterro, the City of Our Lady in Exile, commonly Desterro, Exile.[20]

Early in 1854 Fritz wrote to Lamprecht about the latest depredations on the settlement:

What's new is seldom any good, they say, and I also believe that as a rule what's old is worth even less, yet the saying suits the one extraordinary event that has recently interrupted the monotony of our smoothly flowing life in the virgin forest and has aroused the whole settlement. That was the repeated visits of some ounces or jaguars. One morning shortly before New Year's, my neighbor reported that a "tiger", as they call the jaguar, had carried off his dog during the night; I listened in some disbelief. But indeed two nights later two piglets belonging to my next neighbor were killed, and in the morning we also found distinct footprints on the path that runs close by our open house. The animal must have been rather large, judging from paws the size of a hand, and was accompanied by a young one that by its tracks must have been as big as a very large cat. Naturally the dogs and pigs were made as secure as possible, spring guns were set, weapons were checked over, and so forth. After the brutes had eaten still another dog, my brother was awakened one night by a sudden shriek. He hastened outside with Schneider, but all was quiet. They took a light to the pigsty and found two of the palmito trunks that form the roof of the sty forced apart, and on the ground the pig, dead with a crushed skull. As the bloody trail showed, the jaguar had already lifted its booty to the roof of the sty. They tied the pig to a tree stump right in front of a window and then spread dry roofing leaves under it, the better to see it in the darkness. Scarcely had they settled themselves in

81

ambush with their loaded weapons behind the window when the jaguar came trotting back again and was immediately welcomed with two shots. For a moment the animal appeared stunned, then escaped with tremendous bounds into the forest. They could not follow the bloody trail far into the forest the next morning, but the beast had apparently had enough and has not reappeared since.

Of course our homesteads are gradually becoming more comfortable, and we are becoming increasingly self-sufficient. I am having a little cottage built of a more European design. It is nearly finished and including some simple furniture will cost about 50 milréis [$27]. The roof is from my own workshop, and I have several times lent a hand myself.[21]

But there were always accidents, as in May 1854 when Fritz injured his foot so badly with an axe that he was immobilized for two weeks and had difficulty getting around for a long time thereafter, leaving his wife to shoulder all responsibility for the family, the stock and the plantation.

In 1892 Fritz wrote an autobiographical sketch for the German popular journal *Ausland* in which he recalled his early years in Blumenau, when the Itajaí River was the only road, and access to the settlers' cabins that were scattered in the forest was by narrow trails. Although the Müller brothers were the first to clear homesteads on the Garcia, beginning in August 1852, they were followed a few weeks later by ten more German families, and the settlement increased steadily over the next year. Trapped game provided occasional fresh meat and three times a year, at Easter, Whitsun and Christmas, Hermann Blumenau had an old cow slaughtered. For lamp oil Fritz mentions both castor oil, which they extracted themselves from the beans, and train-oil. Once, however, when their oil had run out, he found an old arariba[22] trunk in the forest "by the light of whose brightly-burning splinters my wife knitted and sewed in the evenings, while I read aloud to her."[23]

During the early years all the settlers came over at their own risk and expected and received no subsidy at all. Blumenau took care only of bringing in necessary provisions, which he sold at cost, and he paid a German who had settled on the Gaspar River several years before to teach us how to hunt game, build cabins, plant crops, make traps, and so forth. All of those who became accustomed to a simple life in the virgin forest from the outset have gotten on well and remain in good spirits, despite all the pains and privations of those early days. But of course they had no one to blame for their discomforts. What a contrast to many of the later colonists who were enticed here by unscrupulous agents and who, despite a generally far easier start with support from the government, had a hard time acclimating and complained constantly!

Right after the first maize harvest we purchased chickens, and as soon as the taro grew up, pigs as well, and these, together with our diverse and tasty tubers (cassava, yams, sweet potatoes, etc.) and our flourishing European vegetables, brought variety to our diet.

For four years I dwelt thus in the virgin forest with axe and hoe and was very happy. There was a certain fascination in being so completely self-sufficient: having to build one's own house, henhouse and pigsty from materials in the forest, to clear the woods for one's plantations, to weave one's own baskets, to slaughter one's own pigs, and so forth.[24]

In 1853, less than a year after his arrival, Fritz gave more credit to Blumenau's efforts on behalf of the settlers than he seems to have recalled 40 years later. In a letter to Wislicenus, who was now in the United States, Fritz reported on his year in Brazil and on the prospects for members of the Free Congregations who might wish to emigrate there, and Wislicenus published the letter the following year in *Aus Amerika*, a little book about his own American experiences. Blumenau's "every thought is the Colony," wrote Fritz. One colonist had written that Blumenau was a "little tyrant," but Fritz couldn't understand the point of view, unless "going quickly in a business-like way from cabin to cabin giving well-meant advice on this or that was tyranny." When Blumenau told someone "you must fence in your chickens or get rid of them," or "you must plant your bananas farther apart in August," Fritz wrote, "neither he nor anyone who knows him considers his 'must' to be anything but good advice." Blumenau, however, touched one sensitive spot: "You have read [his] first annual report [on the colony] in the *General Emigration News*." wrote Fritz.

"I find him completely truthful, except that he makes me Protestant, to which I must protest."[25]

Fritz was often on call for his medical services, but as he reported to his father in 1853 it was not always a welcome change from his daily work as a settler:

Now and then I have to make a medical trip down the Itajaí; my patients are usually old people for whom there is no hope. As a rule they have already tried all sorts of quackery and will continue to do so. It all makes medical practice here unpleasant, and I wish that another doctor would come so that I could refuse it completely. What is nice about those trips is that one can stock up on bananas and oranges and can usually also bring back some new kind of seed or plant for the garden. The income is also useful, although it scarcely makes up for the time lost.[26]

Fritz described some of that medical quackery to his father two years later:

A few years ago a chimney sweep came over on a German immigrant ship, enticed by the rumor of how profitable a business it would be over here. Disembarking in Santos [the port of São Paulo], he offered his services, but no one knew anything about his craft and he heard that people had their humble chimneys swept by their own slaves. In despair he went back on board; the captain tried to console him, gave him an old folio volume of some sort, and advised him to use it as a signboard and to set himself up as a doctor. The chimney sweep, who knew nothing else to take up, followed the advice and must now be enjoying an extensive practice in Curitiba [capital of Paraná, the province to the north.]

A young merchant in Dona Francisca (with whom I travelled three years ago from São Francisco to Dona Francisca) had among other goods a large quantity of boot-polish: a worthless commodity in a country where everyone goes barefoot. So, what to do with it? It occurred to him to sell it as a remedy, and it found a ready market for every possible illness. He subsequently heard it praised everywhere as an especially good and powerful "remédio," such a fine purge, emetic, and so forth.[27]

Fritz followed the growth of his daughter Anna with fatherly pride, and in December 1853, with his wife expecting another child in a few months, he wrote his sister Rosine to tell her how Anna was developing and to solicit Rosine's help in the future education of his children:

> Just as we have prospered this year and everything has grown well, so, too, has our vigorous little plant, Anna. She often delights us with her good memory and her alertness to everything around her; as fast as she trots on her way, no flower, spider or beetle that she encounters escapes her eye, and after the new moon she is usually the first to observe the slender crescent in the evening sky. Our situation here is in most respects extremely favorable for a child's development, with a beautiful natural environment in which she can romp about freely and which furnishes her ample amusement. Her favorite objects, after flowers and birds, are in particular the moon and stars, which she never tires of watching, and the beautiful big fireflies. Our tasks are mostly so simple and intelligible even to a child that they offer ample material for her imitative instincts. That being so, we can usually have her around us and can keep track of her without much interruption in our work. What she chiefly lacks at the moment is playmates, and in the future, once she starts proper lessons, there will not be enough time to give her the range of instruction that I would like, although the essence of education is not in a mass of facts.
>
> It would be invaluable to us for you to come and help us raise the children. Because of the children, it would be desirable for our otherwise so good and capable wives to a have a little more education, and above all to have more free time. Cooking, washing, sewing, and taking care of the livestock and the garden leave them little spare time for the children. You could of course easily find a larger field of activity in Germany, but scarcely a one in which you would be so irreplaceable, I might almost say, and in which you would be repaid by other parents for your efforts with their children with any more affectionate thanks than by your brothers. Our children are after all the most precious of all we have; on their prosperity our own happiness depends.

But Fritz's religious views imposed some conditions:

> What I consider especially important, as you will probably
> agree, is that absolutely nothing should be pressed upon children
> that they do not understand; consequently, even for the smallest
> child no words for which they have no clear image or concep-
> tion, and later on no poems or stories that they do not com-
> pletely understand. But above all, they should not be indoctri-
> nated with a strict interpretation of life's most important
> questions before they are capable of forming their own opinions.
> In other words, not only are creeds to be avoided, but also
> religious instruction of any sort nearly to the end of childhood,
> as well as a strict avoidance of all so-called "articles of faith" in
> any of their other lessons or in the course of life. All of those
> questions are too far beyond a child's mental grasp for it to reach
> an independent opinion from a premature treatment of them.
> Any profound mind craves an independent answer to those
> questions in harmony with all the rest of his education, and it
> would be indescribably difficult if, on beginning that task, his
> heart and mind had already been possessed by a viewpoint
> implanted by an outside authority and made habitual from
> infancy. To let children grow up without "God and Faith" may
> appear to you irresponsible; I think that we really would agree
> on the matter, and that you too would find that only by strict
> avoidance of everything dogmatic, all religious doctrine, every-
> thing drummed superficially into their heads, will children be
> able to escape the present apathy and become truly devout.
> Surely you will admit even now that an inclination towards
> truth, goodness and beauty, and an abhorrence of meanness and
> vulgarity, may be awakened without any religious instruction.[28]

Although Fritz and August quickly established suitable homes
for themselves where they first settled, by 1854 they were already
beginning to look for a better location. The soil on the Garcia was not
nearly as fertile as that by the Itajaí, a decent road to town was still far
in the future, and they had to fetch many things from town and were
increasingly taking some of their own produce there. It was hard slow
work carrying goods up hill and down dale, through quagmires, along
a narrow forest path that was always growing over again, while the
settlers on the Itajaí had their lightweight canoes for handy transport.
A location on the Itajaí would also be more convenient for Fritz's

medical practice, which, "though it matters little to me, I cannot forgo."[29]

The sale of their well-established homesteads came at a propitious moment. In 1854 several hundred new settlers arrived in Blumenau, and in more than twenty localities the forest was cleared and cabins built. Some of the newcomers were glad to find the hard work already done; August sold his homestead at the beginning of 1854 and Fritz his at the end of the year, and the brothers settled again close together on the north bank of the Itajaí. From May 1854, when August moved to his new homesite, until December, Fritz lived alone with his family on the Garcia. Despite the daily work and his isolation from anyone who shared his interests, he remained alert to the natural world around him.

On 31 August 1854, in the first of Fritz's letters to his brother Hermann that Alfred Möller published in *Briefe*, he contrasted the flora of the Itajaí valley with that of central Europe, especially in the relative abundance of monocots. Although there are fewer species of monocots in tropical than in temperate regions, he wrote, they dominate the landscape far more in the tropics, both in the forest and on cultivated land:

> In the virgin forest there are majestically towering palms, aerial roots of philodendrons, bamboos, and brightly-colored bromeliads emerging from impressive leafy rosettes on the trunks of trees whose branches are hung with old-man's beard (*Tillandsia*, also a bromeliad); in the understory there are tucums (spiny palms, *Bactris setosa*) and uricanas (shadow palms, *Geonoma pumila*), and on the ground heliconias, young palms, and here and there masses of rotten fallen branches crowded with bromeliads, aroids and orchids. On the river banks there is canna brava (plume grass) and bird-of-paradise flower (*Strelitzia*), and in our plantations, bananas, sugar cane and yams. These plants have the greatest influence on the general character of our vegetation.
>
> The number of palms is not great; I have seen seven species so far. Most common is the juçara, usually called palmito [*Euterpe oleracea*], which is reckoned the most beautiful species in this proud family, even by travellers who have seen the rich palm flora of equatorial America. Its slender smooth white trunk

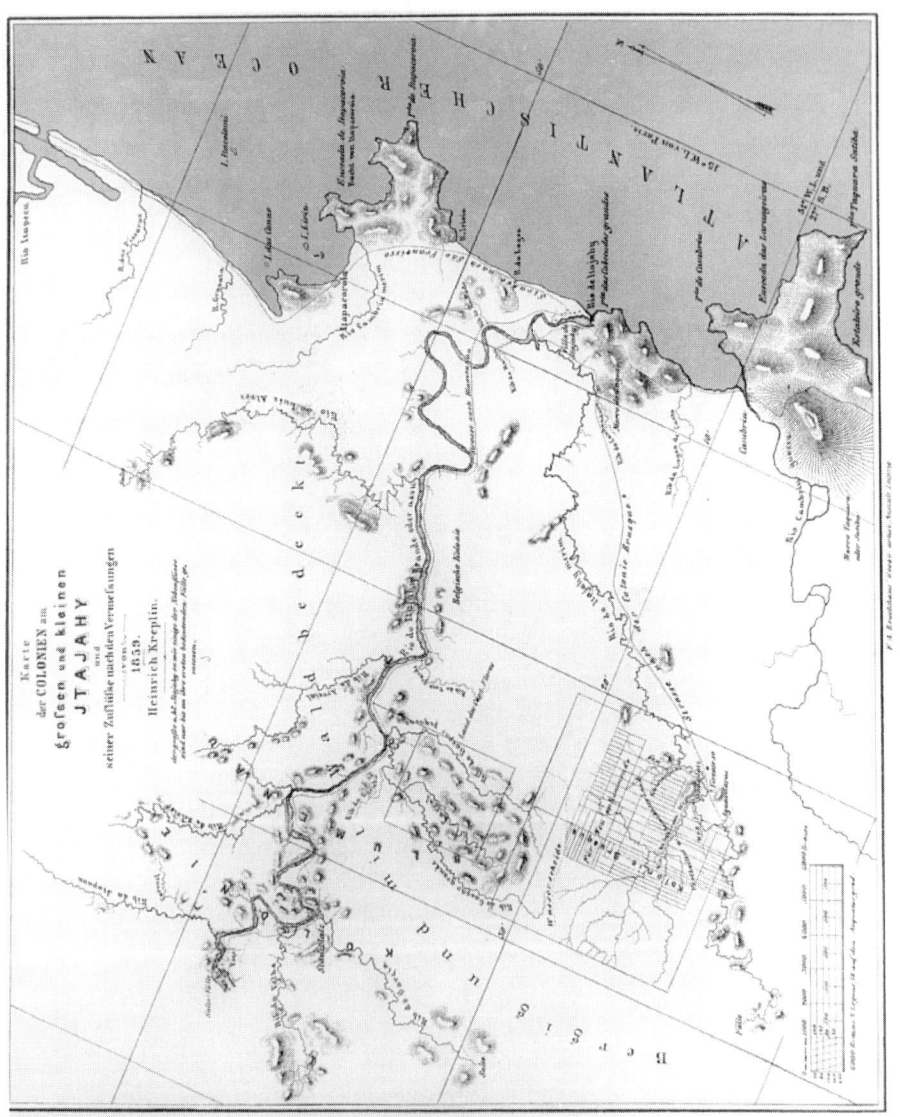

*Map Five. The Colonies on the Great and Little Itajaí Rivers, Santa Catarina, Brazil, 1859. Tschudi, 1868-69,* Reisen durch Südamerika III. *Courtesy of the Syndics of Cambridge University Library.*

reaches 70 feet (the tallest I have measured), and on a thick green cylindrical extension of sheath-like clinging petioles it carries an open crown of perhaps a dozen glistening feathery fronds with narrow leaflets that swing to and fro in the lightest breeze. The yellowish inflorescence appears in spring below the cylinder of petioles, and later there are round black fruits the size of hazel nuts, a favorite repast of parrots which often perch in screeching flocks in the palmito crowns.[30]

By then he already had a box full of natural history specimens to send to his brother and was asking for information about the names of many of the most striking kinds of plants and animals that he was encountering. He also asked his brother to find for him Carl Vogt's *Zoological Letters*[31], Spinoza's works, "in the original Latin, of course, I am opposed to translations,"[32] Julius Fröbel's *Social Politics*[33], and the Yearbook of the Longitudes Office. He had determined the phyllotaxy, the disposition of leaves on a stem, of bananas and of imbaúba (*Cecropia*) and begged for literature on the subject, enquiring after the extracts from the monograph on the subject by the Bravais brothers,[34] which he had studied in Rolofshagen but had not brought with him to the forest.

Fritz could have made a business of his medical practice; there were plenty of opportunities, and his wife urged it on him, but he answered medical calls only when they were unavoidable and was paid for his lost time at the rate of a day laborer on the Itajaí. His relatives often reproached him for his complete indifference to making money, and with a growing family we can see why. On 7 May 1854, while Fritz and Caroline were still on the Garcia, their daughter Rosa was born. Her vigorous intellectual and physical development and early expression of a talent for natural history were Fritz's greatest joy, just as her premature death in Berlin 25 years later was to cause him the deepest grief.

The 500 milréis ($270) from the sale of the property on the Garcia amply covered the cost of Fritz's new homestead on the Itajaí River. Shortly before Christmas 1854 his family, now four in number, moved down to live temporarily with August until their own cabin, "built entirely of monocotyledons," was ready in February 1855.

"Our new property," he wrote to Hermann, "is very nicely situated. The beautiful big river is in front of the house, with several German homesteads across it, and at some distance a wooded range of mountains. Between my dwelling, now under construction, and August's house there is still forest, but it will go in the course of the year."[35]

Fritz described his doings to Lamprecht. Once again he had to face the tasks of a pioneer farmer. What his family did not grow itself was largely unobtainable, and that meant clearing forest again, planting and weeding, although everything was far easier now that they lived on the river:

> The river, which small coastal vessels often ascend this far, is the chief advantage of our new residence, and the soil moreover is looser and more fertile than that of the Garcia Valley. For the present all our work goes to growing the immediate necessities of life: maize, beans and potatoes, as well as feed for chickens and pigs; to planting coffee and all sorts of fruits and vegetables; and to putting in pasture.[36]

> Until I had my own black beans again, it cost me far more time than money to procure what I needed. One practically has to do without eggs until one has one's own chickens, and to forgo chickens until one harvests one's own maize. Because lamp oil is often unobtainable, even at an exorbitant price, we are spending our evenings by a bright fire until we can once again extract our own castor oil.

> Bread made from cornmeal alone is too dry and crumbly, manioc flour by itself makes bread that is doughy and tasteless; but to my taste, bread made from the two together leaves nothing to be desired.[37]

In May 1856 Fritz wrote to Lamprecht the following vivid account of an Indian raid during the previous summer and of the flood that followed. There were still hazards in that raw land.

> On 9 November my friend Kellner[38], aided by Swiss and Belgian friends, was building a dam for a sawmill on his land a few hours above the highest existing settlement on the Little Itajaí, the principal tributary of the Itajaí [Map 5]. He had shifted the first barrow load after lunch and was loading the second, when

the Belgian suddenly cried out "Indians!" He looked up and saw on a little rise a few paces away about eight naked copper-brown fellows who were quite calmly drawing their bows. Kellner, a powerful and courageous man, sprang at them with his shovel; one of the Indians jumped back, the shovel struck the bow of the second just as he fired, and the arrow, aimed at Kellner's chest, pierced his arm a hand's breadth below the shoulder. Simultaneously his two companions fell, shot through with arrows. As Kellner hurried to the house about 80 paces away, he received a second arrow in the back. He called to the wife of the Swiss to bring him a weapon; she, terrified out of her senses, met him with a firebrand. With two five-foot arrows in his body, Kellner fetched himself a weapon and shot five or six times at the Indians, who slipped behind tree trunks and gradually withdrew into the nearby forest. The Swiss had a wooden arrow through his heart and died on the spot. The Belgian, the biggest and strongest of the three, was hit by two iron arrows which had penetrated his back to the front of his chest. Kellner and the Swiss wife helped him into a canoe, and Kellner then began paddling down that difficult river. Seriously wounded as he was, he would scarcely have reached the next place of habitation, the sawmill at Aguas Claras, without the good luck of meeting up in a quarter-hour with his younger brother and another man, who had been away a few days getting supplies from the mouth of the river. Thus they came to Aguas Claras, where the Belgian died that evening. Kellner had his own arrows pulled out; it took three men with all their might to pull the arrow out of his back, where it had penetrated obliquely upward eight inches into his chest cavity. Its barbed point lodged against a rib, where I later removed a broken piece of it. The next day Kellner was taken to a friend's house at the confluence of the Little Itajaí and the big river.

People from Aguas Claras went up to Kellner's land and found his chests and cupboards broken open, weapons, tools, clothing and linens completely gone. Flour was dumped out, the sacks taken away. A large demijohn of schnapps stood undisturbed on the table. The wall-clock lay intact by the door and showed 5:30, apparently the time when it was taken down. His violin was also still there, a chess game taken. The dog was gone, no doubt eaten by the Indians. The Swiss had been stripped and

91

his clothes taken away. Kellner has recovered surprisingly quickly from his wound and has been building his mill since the New Year. The President of the province, João José Coutinho,[39] has granted him 500 milreis in compensation.

On 17 November I was still at the mouth of the Little Itajaí, half an hour from where the big Itajaí empties into the ocean, as Kellner's medical attendant. Blumenau and some other friends had also come down to take care of him. We had set our return journey for that midday, but a violent storm coming in from the ocean delayed us, and that afternoon there began a really frightful downpour, driven by a strong sea wind, which persisted with unabated force the whole of the 18th and continued more gently for several days. The river swelled visibly with a speed and to an extent that people whose memories reach back 50 years had never experienced. Early on the 19th I noticed a conspicuous dark line between the distinctly-colored waters of the big and little Itajaí rivers; it was an unbroken line of tree trunks. Where the big river was blocked by the Little Itajaí flowing in nearly at right angles, a regular island of trees and all sorts of debris collected, and out of that chaos tree trunks would slip forward to the meeting point of the two rivers and then drift down stream strung out in a straight line. Now and then a head of cattle came by, or a canoe shot past like an arrow, with a family escaping the surging water that had forced them from their home. I most pitied an old German who had been near death for several days and now had to escape the raging water in the tempest. The river bank near our lodging crumbled away bit by bit, the river advancing from 50 paces away to half that distance. We had our hands full saving lumber that we had stored here, a good deal of which was still washed away. On the morning of the 20th we heard that the walls, floors and roof of a house had washed ashore at the mouth of the big river, and from papers and other things found in it, it soon appeared that it was Blumenau's house, which had stood opposite the mouth of the Garcia. We thought his house had been on rather high ground, and we had to fear the worst for the whole upper course of the river. You can imagine our situation, so far from our own people. Finally, at midday of the 23rd the strength of the current allowed us to return home, but it still often took all the strength of five oarsmen to move the canoe forward. Everywhere on the way there was the most dreadful devastation. We sailed along over manioc and sugar fields, over cotton plants and coffee bushes, among orange trees and behind houses. For the most part the houses stood empty; here and there people were going round their homes in canoes to save their things; others were cleaning out the deep mud deposited in their rooms. Some had spent days hanging onto tree trunks, many were still living wretchedly in the forest in temporary shelters. Only a few houses remained habitable. I got back home on the 24th. My house, like my brother's, had been spared; our neighbors opposite had had to flee. The river had risen about 43 spans [nearly ten meters] above its present level, but still about five spans [a meter] short of my house. In our former house on the Garcia the water ran through the windows.[40]

Very serious damage was done to the Itajaí valley by that powerful flood. As for me, the high water ruined a nice patch of maize, most of my beans and my fine yam plantation. It did not reach most of my arable land, but I still feel the loss of those yams; they themselves have grown back, of course, but the piglets that were slaughtered off for lack of fodder can not be brought back to life, and nowhere can I find others to eat up the now superabundant food. However, I am expecting a litter from my own stock shortly. Because I am not yet producing many commodities myself, especially coffee, manioc flour and meat, I have also experienced the ridiculous prices that spiralled up after the flood.[41]

Indians played an important role in the life of the Blumenau Colony during the 1850s, not so much for the damage as for the uneasiness they caused by their occasional raids, and they continued to be a problem for colonists in Santa Catarina into the twentieth century. Between 1851 and 1914 there were 61 Indian attacks causing 41 deaths in the colony.[42] In 1856 Fritz added further impressions of the natives to those written to his family in Germany during the first year in Brazil:

Perhaps you would be interested in the little that we know about those malicious neighbors of ours. As to their appearance, Schramm and Kellner describe them as well-built, slender but strong, with shiny copper-colored skin and smooth black hair.

They wear absolutely nothing that could be called an article of clothing, merely a binding of cord around the hips and a similar pair around the ankles. Their weapons are bow and arrow; a white man can scarcely draw one of their bows, probably more for lack of practice than for insufficient strength. The arrows are as tall as a man, some with wooden, some with iron points. [Fritz drew a sketch of an iron point 5 cm long with maximum width of 3.5 cm.] The wooden points are about a foot long and of very tough wood and carry about 10 barbs of which the forward ones are thinner and more widely spaced. The shaft consists of several pieces of bamboo inserted into one another, wound with the peel of cipó d'imbe [a philodendron] and smeared on the inner surfaces with wild bees' wax. At the other end of the shaft two jacú feathers are fastened, also with cipó-peeling or with tough fibers from the leaves of the tucum palm.[43] Behind the feathers is a knob, sometimes very gracefully woven of tucum fiber, which they grasp with their hand when pulling the bow.

The chief occupation of the Indians seems to be hunting, at which they appear to be exceedingly skilled. The whites, despite their firearms, do not know how to catch tapirs without specially-trained dogs, whereas the fresh remains of a tapir eaten by the Indians were found in the course of an excursion after their last raid; the remains of monkeys, jacú, and other game are usually found at their resting places. Their favorite game, however, must be peccaries, which usually roam through the forest in very large herds; when peccaries are around, they say, Indians are also not far away. They use flints to chop the nests of bees out of trees; in order to stay on the trunk while hacking with their hands, they place around it a bamboo hoop which supports their backs while they press their feet against the tree.

With hunting as their sole food source, they can of course neither live together in large groups nor have permanent dwellings. Accounts of them vary, and it may well be that even in this province there are several tribes with different ways of life. Their raiding parties are invariably small troops of around four to ten. It is said that they always spy on a locality and on the activities of the whites for days before a raid and wait for the most favorable moment. Signs of their long presence, campsites with remains of game, etc., have always been found nearby after the

raids of recent years. Summer seems to be the favorite time for
their sorties, yet they had already appeared at our neighbors' in
September, and last year were still around in March and April.[44]
They have sometimes approached with loud shouts, and sometimes crept in softly, the former, so it seems, when they supposed
that there were only women and children in the house and
hoped to scare them off by their uproar. More often they have
also killed women and children, but sometimes they carry them
off, as happened last year to a 12-year old boy in Uruçanga in
the southern part of the province. They used to appear particularly around Piçarras, on the coast between São Francisco and
the Itajaí, and the worst raid was certainly the one suffered by
the Italian colony on the big Tijucas River in 1839, in which
some dozen people lost their lives. In the last six years the Itajaí
seems to have become their favorite locality, and they have
probably never had such good plunder as here in recent years.
Up to now, however, only the remote colonies and the furthest
outposts have been attacked; houses that can be seen by a larger
number of neighbors are quite safe. It is more risky working in
the forest and its immediate vicinity. Ever since our recent sad
experiences, of course, we never fail to take along a gun. The
savages still seem to have great respect for firearms and usually
flee at the first report. A Brazilian who was attacked five or six
years ago, and who had killed several natives, had only flint and
percussion caps left, no powder or shot. Yet he held off a whole
troop long enough for his son to come to his aid. In the highlands of Lajes the savages are said sometimes to be on a friendly
footing and in communication with the whites, as is the case in
many other parts of Brazil. Other Indians are in fact quite
civilized, and even here we sometimes see them serving as
soldiers or sailors.[45]

In his letter to Lamprecht in May 1856 Fritz stressed still other
dangers that faced the pioneer in the forest:

Though we are somewhat safer here where the homesteads are
close together, the Indians remain everpresent and inhospitable
neighbors. Nevertheless, don't suppose that it is just those
neighbors that cause us anxiety; there is as much in such perils
as snakes and falling trees. One becomes increasingly careful the
more one is aware of the dangers, but at the same time less

anxious. At first one saw danger where there was none and did not know what to do in real danger whereas now there is peace of mind when no danger threatens and quick circumspection when it does. How many careless blows I struck that first year felling trees, when I then realized how close I had been to mortal danger, and then how many more besides, and every one the same. Now I have a sharp eye not just for threatening branches and the like, but especially for any vine or stump on the ground which could keep me from jumping sideways. It is a miracle that more accidents don't befall newcomers. Among the new settlers only one has lost his life to a falling limb, and he himself had called it to the attention of his fellow workers: he was snared by a liana while trying to get out of the way.[46]

Hermann Blumenau praised Fritz and August's work habits to their uncle Hermann Trommsdorff in March 1855, although he was less happy in other respects:

I can by no means reconcile myself to their religious views, especially those of the Doctor (Fritz), and I am not at all pleased with his influence on the rest of the people, although it has somewhat diminished since the two of them left the colony proper and settled a little downstream. I did not like to see them move away, because their energy and example fired up others as well, but it may eventually be for the better because of the effect of their religious views. Nothing can be said against those who can think and manage for themselves as your nephews do, for there should be freedom of thought and civil liberty; but it is disastrous, almost criminal at the same time, to deprive people of that faith to which their weak morality clings as to a single supporting staff. It really is a shame that Fritz, who is effective and energetic and has such a splendid intelligence, buries himself in the virgin forest. I have already told him so, but he seems completely to have retired from the world and to be as happy as a hermit.[47]

The following year, however, Hermann Blumenau would be instrumental in getting Fritz out of the forest by recommending him for a teaching job in the provincial capital. Fritz's third daughter, Agnes, was born on 21 April 1856, and his life as a pioneer in the virgin forest soon came to a close.

# 6
# Teacher in Desterro, 1856–1867

In 1856, after nearly four years as a pioneer farmer, Fritz was offered a post teaching mathematics in a new secondary school being established on the coast in the provincial capital Desterro, now Florianópolis (Map 3). It was to be a momentous move, for he would now have the opportunity to study marine invertebrates once again and, stimulated by Darwin's *Origin of Species* a few years later, would produce his first major work, a defense of Darwinism. He recalled the sequence of events in his autobiographical sketch written 36 years later:

> In the early 1850s there was a Jesuit college in Desterro of which I had heard nothing but good things. When yellow fever overran the province of Santa Catarina for the first time, in 1852, the epidemic carried off seven of the fathers and the institution consequently ceased to exist. In 1856 the provincial assembly decided to establish a new secondary school, a provincial lycée. At Dr. Blumenau's suggestion, the president of the province, João José Coutinho, had the position of mathematics teacher offered to me. When Blumenau told me this at Whitsuntide 1856, I little desired to accept the offer, but he persuaded me to look the matter over more closely, and so in July I went to Desterro. The route took me for long stretches along the seashore, and the rich zoological treasures that I found strewn there and around Desterro itself reawakened my former pleasure in the study of marine fauna, which I had enthusiastically pursued on the Baltic near Greifswald with my friend Max Schultze. The chance to explore at leisure the superabundant life of a nearly tropical ocean, instead of the depauperate Baltic, was

an exceedingly tempting prospect. I liked what the President of the province told me about the school and my position in it. But above all I liked the man himself, whose plain straightforward manner was a pleasant contrast to Prussian bureaucracy as well as to empty Brazilian courtesy. I took the post offered me, returned once more to Blumenau to put my affairs in order, and travelled back to Desterro in the company of Becker, a German lawyer who had recently settled in Blumenau and was assigned to teach Latin in the new school.[2]

When the summons came, however, it was hard for Fritz to leave the virgin forest. "I almost fear that the transition from man of the wilderness to townsman, from farmer to teacher, will be more difficult than the reverse has been," he wrote to Lamprecht on 12 May 1856. And the following year he reflected from Desterro on having changed his dwelling place yet again, and on the fact that he had hardly been able to enjoy the fruits of his sweat.

> Scarcely had I transformed a few acres from nearly impenetrable wilderness to a cozy homestead, cut my first bunch of bananas and dug up the first ginger to season the first of our chickens, seen the first snowy flowers among the glossy foliage of our coffee bushes and the first young fruits among the spiny leaves of the pineapples which edge the road; scarcely had the passion flower foliage been bedecked with its magnificent scented flowers and set its first big savory fruits, then I was offered a post as Professor of Mathematics. After considerable vacillation over whether I should exchange the axe for the pen, and the unbound freedom of life in the virgin forest, even with its hardships and dangers, for a far easier and more lucrative but nevertheless dependent position, I finally decided that here close to the seashore I could indulge at leisure my former favorite occupation, the study of marine animals, and would generally have ample time and opportunity for intellectual pursuits.[3]

After meeting the President of the province and arranging the terms of his appointment, Fritz returned directly to get his household in order on the Itajaí. He leased the land to a young settler, who immediately took over the care of Fritz's wife and children, while they remained there alone for the time being. In lieu of rent the settler took on the responsibility of planting 100 coffee trees annually. Fritz went back to Desterro in August, primarily to improve his Portuguese, something he could not do on the Itajaí. His trips between Blumenau and Desterro were not easy, as he had to travel along the coast for the most part on foot. Each trip took several days, with scanty food in Brazilian cottages along the way and hard sleeping quarters on the ground, but bodily discomfort never dampened Fritz's good spirits or his susceptibility to the beauties of nature. Of one such trip from Desterro back to Blumenau he wrote:

> My walking tour was made doubly difficult by a most uncomfortably heavy travelling-bag strapped to my back. Nevertheless, being inured to physical hardship, I had no trouble keeping pace with my unladen companions G. and H. [not identified], and their cheerful company sweetened the hardships of the march, the first of which was the ascent of a steep hill at noon. From there we descended to the insignificant village of Porto Bello, pleasantly situated by the sea. The afternoon was rather cloudy and our route generally level, running for the most part right along the shore. A rain shower drove us into a big shed where manioc meal was made [from the tubers of the poisonous form of cassava, *Manihot esculenta*, from which the hydrocyanic acid is removed by roasting[4]]. We encountered a nearly naked, grey-haired Negro busily chopping the stems of aipim into cuttings [the non-poisonous form of cassava, the tubers of which are boiled and eaten like potatoes[5]], and we persuaded him with difficulty to brew us coffee and to sell us an egg apiece. That was our generous midday meal; and we refreshed ourselves with a midday nap on a reed mat spread on the ground. In the evening we were graciously received along the way in a house that was imposing by local standards. We had already had many lovely views during the walk, but the setting of this house was remarkable for its scenic beauty. To left and right were bushy hillocks, before us, with isolated palms, a grassy expanse serving as a pasture, and at the bottom of it a stream with sheds for making sugar and manioc meal. Manioc, sugarcane, banana and other plantings covered the low hills as far as the nearby sea, which was edged by a smooth sandy strand. Close to shore was a fantastic rocky island crowned with glorious palms, white breakers frothing high up on its rocks. The horizon was

bounded in part by the endless expanse of open ocean, in part by the hills of Porto Bello, hazy with bluish vapor.

The many young people of the house went to a dance (fandango) nearby, while their aged mother prepared supper for us. A reed mat was spread with a little tablecloth, and on it was a gourd cut in half and filled with manioc meal, a plate of dried fish roasted on coals, and a saucer of vinegar and crushed red pepper. Each of us now got a dish of hot water in which we stirred manioc meal to our liking, forming a stiff mush. The fish was picked up by hand and dipped in the peppery vinegar. A cup of excellent coffee, as Brazilians always make it, ended the meal. The same mat then served as a sleeping place; G. and I slept soundly, while H., less accustomed to such arrangements, could not complain enough about the hard bed.

The next day, shortly before noon and rather tired, we reached the mouth of the Itajaí, where we could once again enjoy good German cooking.[6]

It was also possible to sail between Desterro and the mouth of the Itajaí on a little coasting vessel, though seldom without unforeseen delays because of a contrary wind or because the Brazilian skipper found an excuse in some place for a stop that none of his passengers wanted. Paddling up the Itajaí in a canoe took more than a day, at some cost in sweat, and sometimes also with an involuntary bath, as in December 1857 when a fellow passenger's careless movement capsized the unsteady craft with three people in it. Fritz never complained about the discomforts of these journeys, but he did complain of sore feet from having to wear shoes again "in the city," after going barefoot so long in the forest.

Fritz was welcomed into the home of a German merchant in Desterro, but he was unhappy being separated from his family, and his only recreation was walking along the shore, which promised a rich harvest of observations. He was therefore glad when his family joined him in December 1856 and they could have a home of their own in a modest cottage on the Praia de Fora (outer beach). It was small even for a family of five and, as one of Fritz's colleagues wrote at the time, was of spartan simplicity in accordance with its occupant's wishes. Its location outside the town freed Fritz from having to deal with municipal affairs, and its proximity to his research area, the ocean, was invaluable. It also proved to be a healthy spot; the various epidemics that swept the town never reached the outer beach and the Müller girls were spared. "A few paces from my window the ocean waves rush foaming up the sandy shore; the white sails of cruising ships stand out against the dark mountains on the mainland and are proudly passed by steamers, those postmen of the sea. We often go with them in our thoughts to our homeland so far away!"[7]

Although there were plenty of Germans around Desterro, Fritz had limited social contact with them; they were mostly well-off but uneducated farmers who were adopting Brazilian ways, and he did not find them attractive. Leisure time after teaching and research was spent with his family. "He who finds happiness at home longs for little outside, he who lacks it in his own home will seek it elsewhere in vain," he wrote in 1857.[8]

"The provincial lycée opened early in 1857," Fritz wrote in his autobiographical sketch,

> at first with four professorships: Latin, French, English and Mathematics (including arithmetic, algebra to quadratic equations, and geometry). Becker[9] became Director, because I declined the post in order to live by the shore and to be able to spend more of my spare time on marine animals. Geography, History and Philosophy were later added to the course offerings, and also for a short time Natural History, which I had already expressed my willingness to take on.
>
> The President of the province, João José Coutinho, was the last to hold that post longer than ten years[10]; after him, scarcely anyone lasted more than two. He had a real feeling for the province, regarded himself as its father and as such was as exemplary and conscientious as if he were the head of a large well brought-up family. He had found the provincial till in the sorriest condition, but he soon put it in good order. For example, not only was money set aside by the provincial assembly for public works, roads, bridges, and the rest, but it was also spent properly, as seldom before or since. He kept track of expenditures and of the activities of his officials inconspicuously but effectively, and nowhere is such supervision more necessary than here. He was particularly interested in his favorite creation,

101

the lycée, and attended lectures regularly, especially at the beginning, and particularly those of the German teachers. At first he seemed disinclined to our usual rather variable teaching methods, but he was soon won over and readily granted our wishes. At my request, I was allowed to use a piece of the large yard surrounding the schoolhouse for a small botanic garden, and without my asking he obtained for me seeds for the garden and plants of the only fan-palm in our province, the lovely burití [*Mauritia vinifera*], which is not native in the coastal region. After attending the zoological lecture in which I discussed cephalopods, he sent me next day for the school a beautiful argonaut (paper nautilus) that he had himself collected years before near Rio de Janeiro. And when I told him that I would like to teach the more mature students a few elementary ideas in Physics and Chemistry, he immediately allotted me more than twice the sum for procuring apparatus and chemicals that I had wanted.

The school was rather different from the concept of a German Gymnasium. There were no fixed classes that every student had to finish in succession, and hence also no standardized curriculum. Anyone could enroll in any class that he or his parents wished, just as in our German universities. One person started with Latin, another with French, a third with Mathematics; one with a single subject, another with two, a third with all four subjects that were represented in the school at the beginning. Many attended the third-year class in one subject, the second year in another, and the first-year class in a third subject. It was therefore an enormous job drawing up schedules at the start of every year to provide each an opportunity to attend his desired lessons.[11]

The school finally opened in February 1857. Fritz's activities were limited in the first year to only three hours of instruction a day with two students; all the better for being able to familiarize himself with Portuguese. In the second year the number of pupils climbed to four, in the third year to twenty-two with four hours of lessons. For someone who always enjoyed languages, the acquisition of Portuguese delighted him, and he was soon fluent. "Portuguese literature," he wrote to Hermann, "is in every respect among the poorest, especially in the exact sciences. How rich by comparison are Danish and Swedish; although those are still smaller nations, they have, for example, produced good original works in all the natural sciences and many fine scientists."[12] On the other hand, he thought Portuguese made for the teaching of mathematics: "Through its endless participial and infinitive constructions it allows the expression of formulas and theories with a precise brevity of which neither German nor any other modern languages that I know is capable."[13]

Fritz used his first summer vacation (Christmas, 1857/58) to visit his brother and his own rented property on the Itajaí. He embarked on a coasting vessel on the evening of 4 December but reached his destination only after many difficulties and quite exhausted on the afternoon of the 9th.

> I spent several very pleasant weeks here in the relaxing life of the virgin forest and in visiting old acquaintances on the Itajaí and in the Blumenau Colony. You will laugh when I tell you what a particular pleasure it was to walk about barefoot for a few weeks and to be able to do all my visiting in shirt and pants, or that I felled trees for pleasure one whole hot December day, and if you can imagine it, how nice it was to be able to swing an axe once again.[14]

Fritz never ceased yearning for the Itajaí and usually spent his vacations there during the following years. "If the sea did not keep me here, I would go back to the Itajaí at the end of the year," he wrote Hermann in 1857. "Because of the sea I will be happy to have my position confirmed and will endure perhaps a dozen years here; then, however, I will have to change my tastes completely and return to the virgin forest as a farmer by August's side, and also for the sake of my children, whom I do not wish to become too Brazilian."[15] Fritz's teaching activities were not completely satisfying, but it pleased him when in 1858 an acquaintance from his youth, Dr. Burkhart, who had been a sixth-former in the Cathedral school during Fritz's apprenticeship in Naumburg, was appointed Professor of History and Geography in the Desterro lycée. Burkhart, who had already been a few years in Brazil (in Dona Francisca and on the Itajaí), was a broadly educated man, although strictly orthodox in religion. Fritz got on well with him and with the director Becker, and these two colleagues were almost his only close acquaintances during his years in

Desterro. His appointment as Professor of Mathematics was made final in 1858, following an examination that gave him scarcely any difficulty. The examiners posed him a tough problem, and after Fritz solved it with ease, one of them blurted out "You should be examining us, rather than the other way round."[16]

Fritz was highly regarded by his students, as he well knew, and according to one of his colleagues, "combined friendliness with rigor, and even stimulated the indolent to action. He was no sullen scholar but loved to crack a good joke and kept up a lively conversation with his colleagues."[17]

There was at least one descendant of former slaves in the school, and Fritz revealed his unorthodox racial views in a letter to his brother Hermann in 1860:

> Among my current pupils the best by far is a black man of pure African lineage. He has an easy grasp of things and a zeal for learning such as I had not previously encountered here and as is rather rare even in your more invigorating climate. That black man is fresh evidence for my opinion, contrary to the prevailing view that the Negroes are an altogether inferior race and are incapable of rational development on their own. It is alleged that they have failed to reach a high level of civilization in their native land and are therefore incapable of it, but the Greeks and Romans could have said the same of our ancestors 2000 years ago. If Burmeister[18] found nothing very lofty in his conversations with Negroes, he would surely have had no better luck with German day-laborers in Pomerania or Mecklenburg. I know plenty of blacks with noble and expressive faces such as are scarcely more common among Caucasians of the same oppressed social status, and if that status on average causes great moral depravity, yet I have often observed unmistakable signs of profound and refined feelings. I also attribute to that status the general reticence of those born in Africa to talk with whites about their homeland; I have always been answered evasively about it. But it does not seem to me generally true, as Burmeister asserts, that they soon forget their homeland and are happier here. A few years ago a whole community of them who had bought freedom with their own savings returned from Bahia to Africa, and I myself witnessed the joy of a sullen old Negress at the sight of an African palm fruit brought to her by a friend.

It is known that most children of mulattos and whites excel in their intellectual talents, while their common moral failings are largely to be accounted for by their social position. It is plainly foolish of Burmeister, in discussing this question, to talk about the characteristic smell of the perspiration of many Negroes, unpleasantly strong though it may be to European noses.[19]

In Desterro Fritz's bevy of daughters increased to six with the births of Emma, 2 January 1859[20]; Thusnelda, 26 October 1860; and Selma, 8 September 1863. Another daughter, Martha, was born 18 July 1865 but died of a respiratory infection four months later. Fritz's wish for a son, however, remained unfulfilled. "How I envy you, you lucky one, being the father of two sons!" he wrote to Max Schultze in 1858. "Fate seems to bestow on me only daughters and denies me one of my most fervent desires."[21] A son, Fritz, was born 7 October 1862 but died within a few hours. "A fresh and beautiful springtime of my life would have blossomed with him," he wrote to Schultze the following week:

> You will understand, dearest Max, just how I, whose own development was frequently curtailed by fate, whose lofty youthful dreams so often found bitter disappointment in harsh reality, how I, whose lonely situation has concentrated all my happiness in my family circle, could cherish more fervently than many others the wish to live my youth again in my son, to see my own ideals awake in him, and to lead him with a careful hand over the obstacles by which I myself was frustrated. You will understand how deeply the sudden loss of my long wished-for happiness has affected me and what thick clouds of sorrow have hung over me. Forgive my long lament, but there is not a person here who would understand that in that little one I carried more to the grave than has any other father.[22]

Earlier that same year Fritz wrote to Schultze about a case of snake bite in the family.

> A fortnight ago we had a terrible fright; my youngest daughter, Thusnelda, 17 months old, was bitten by a small jararaca [a pit viper of the genus *Bothrops*], the snake we fear most, and in her cradle! She has come through it with no bad after-effects, although we only found the snake and recognized the wound as a snake bite two days later. I thus had the rare opportunity, may

fortune protect me from it ever happening again, of observing the effects of a snake bite of minimal dose without their having been obscured by anxiety for the patient or by medical intervention. Our child had been bitten at midday; toward evening she would no longer step on her somewhat swollen foot. In the evening she was very excitable and instead of going to bed at 7 she was awake till 10. She was unusually jolly, looking at pictures, babbling, laughing and full of tricks; we had never seen her so. Only when she bumped her foot did she think of the "ant" which we all thought had bitten her. The next day she was tolerably cheerful except that she could not walk. That night she had a rather high fever, slept little, but when awake was not out of sorts. The following morning, when we found the snake, her leg was swollen to the knee. There were several small spots of subcutaneous bleeding on her ankle and instep (where upon closer examination we now found the two closely adjacent punctures that only a snake could have made). From then on she improved, and in a couple of days the little one was cheerfully running around again. The bite of an adult jararaca often leads to a long illness and is frequently fatal, and surely the exaggerations which Oesterlen (in his *Materia Medica*) imputes to travellers could be no farther from the truth than the contempt with which he himself treats snake bite almost like that of a mosquito.[23]

Fritz devoted himself to the education and rearing of his daughters while living in Desterro. He would not entrust them to the miserable Desterro elementary school, and above all he wanted to keep them from becoming Brazilian in language and outlook: German must remain their first language.[24] He educated his two eldest daughters, Anna and Rosa, together with the son of the German merchant who had befriended him. He had observed that most German children in Desterro hardly understood their parents' language, or spoke it poorly, and that experience taught him to pay strict attention to his own children, because they tended to prefer the far easier Portuguese. His brother Hermann had to send textbooks and readers from Germany because the Portuguese ones, to the extent that they were not translations from French, proved to be utterly useless. The two eldest children enjoyed reading and soon ran out of suitable books, which they now knew by heart. Soon after arriving in Brazil

Fritz wrote to his sister Rosine, "I wish some day we could have here someone like Hey[25], who would write poems for our children, to whom the lovely European tales of the raven, the snowman, and the rest are mostly incomprehensible; our hummingbirds, parrots, monkeys, toucans, gambás (marsupial rats), jaguars, etc. would provide abundant material. Someone here is going to have to write a reading book for his own children."[26]

In fact, beginning in 1859 Fritz himself wrote and illustrated poems for his children in the style of Hey, based on their Brazilian experience. The subjects include leaf-cutting ants, turtles, fire-flies, the comparable complexities of the virgin forest and the subtidal zone, poisonous snakes, and a comparison of the growth rate and longevity of papayas and date-palms. From Fritz's experience on the sea coast comes the following.[27]

### Minnows and Jellyfish
In the swells that rise and fall
The flashing minnows play.
How they glimmer with silvery shimmer,
And dart with delight
Through gold beams of light.

A clear glass bell,
A quivering crystalline mass,
Moves slowly into their path.
"Minnow, minnow, let it be,
Minnow, minnow, quickly flee."

Long tentacles trailing by
Catch the minnow's eye.
"Are they really worms?"
"Minnow, minnow, now beware,
Minnow, now avoid that snare."

Too closely swims the minnow past.
"O woe, O woe, It holds me fast.
How tightly its tentacles cling me,
How deadly its nettles do sting me."
Minnow struggling, minnow slithering,
Jellyfish tugging, jellyfish shivering,
Soon poor minnow's ceased its quivering.

For arithmetic, he created "number symbols to illustrate the teaching of elementary sums." In a document left among his papers he described a system using small pieces of cardboard arranged in unique patterns for the numbers 1 through 10 and combined for arithmetic operations, in contrast to the conventional system of the time in which numbers were represented by rows of dots or strokes. "I doubt whether any child, by merely looking, can recognize at first glance a set of more than 5 or at the most 6 strokes. . . . I do not know whether this illustrative method would be feasible in larger schools. In any case it is recommended for a small number of students, whom one can gather around a table. For such a number it seems to me best to use this method for easy calculations under 100, and only then turn to calculations with numerals."[28]

Politics soon began affecting the lycée in Desterro, as Fritz later wrote:

> Coutinho was unfortunately ousted about four years after the opening of the lycée [actually 1859], when the Liberal party once more came to the State trough.[29] Other presidents followed in quick succession, each trying with more or less incompetence to reform the lycée, and with that the school, which till then had developed promisingly, began its decline. Coutinho's successor was Brusque[30], founder of the German colony of the same name. He began by dismissing for no reason two of the foreigners, the North American teacher of English [Willington], and a very capable German who had only recently been called from Dona Francisca to the professorship of Geography and History [Burkhart]. The directorship was taken from Becker, who was also a foreigner, and given to the new English teacher, Amphiloquio Nunes Pires, a Brazilian educated in North America, who proved by the way to be a good teacher as well as director. I could not stand Brusque from the start and took my release from teaching Natural Sciences. (I had taught zoology only a year in that capacity but had keen students.) The modest physical and chemical apparatus that had arrived from Germany shortly before was sold unused for a trifle, and the beginnings of my botanic garden soon vanished again under rampant weeds.[31]

Brusque actually initiated some reforms that were to Fritz's benefit. The summer vacation was lengthened to three months, the number of hours of instruction per day decreased and teachers' wages raised 20 percent. He then had more time for his children's education and his research, but it was more than hours and wages that bothered Fritz, and on 4 August 1861 he wrote to a friend that he would gladly give up school mastering and take up an axe once more. He chronicled the further decline of the school in his autobiographical sketch:

> The following year the school lost several teachers to other posts, Becker died, and only the English and French teachers and I remained. But the empty positions were not filled because, as we soon noticed, our "liberals" had it in mind to replace the lyceé with a Jesuit College. That transpired, the lycée was dissolved, and the pious Fathers took possession of our rooms in September 1864. Since we had permanent appointments, we could neither be dismissed nor be retired unwillingly as long as we were competent, and our positions became "cátedras avulsas" (separate chairs without common administration); but at least we were assigned schoolrooms together in the same building. In the first year nearly all of the studious youngsters flocked to the Jesuits, with only a few remaining faithful to us, but the following year many of our old students returned to us, and new ones applied.[32]

Because Fritz was never comfortable among either the Brazilians or the German-Brazilians of Desterro, it is no surprise that be began thinking of returning to Blumenau. "I am still as unaccustomed to the local way of life as on my first day here," he wrote his brother Hermann in 1862, "and would probably still be just as complete a stranger in twenty years as I am now, because the Brazilian character is completely alien to me. On the Itajaí I live among Germans."[33] When his brother and Ernst Haeckel[34] urged him four years later to return to a German university to carry on the vigorous and successful research that he had begun, he rejected the possibility. To Hermann he wrote:

> My yearning is in exactly the opposite direction, back to the virgin forest on the Itajaí. From the beginning I regarded my sojourn here as "desterro" (exile) and never stopped longing for the day when I could return to the Itajaí without having to

support my family exclusively by my own hands and therefore needing to spend all of my time working the land. Unfortunately those hopes have been frustrated this year, but I reckon it pretty certain that I will be rid of my present appointment under reasonable conditions next year. In addition, I hope to have at least as much spare time when I return to the Itajaí as I have here, and of course the virgin forest offers just as much as the sea to keep a naturalist occupied.[35]

By this time he had become a Darwinian and to Haeckel he pointed out that attractive as it would be to influence a new generation with Darwin's ideas, no German university would want a member of a Free Congregation on its faculty. Even though the political climate of Brazil was no better than that of Germany, as a foreigner he could treat much of it with impunity.[36] Although Fritz never returned to Europe, he told Haeckel in 1869 what was wrong with scientific education and what he would do about as a professor. Pointing out the contributions made by non-specialists like Darwin and Sprengel[37], and the evils of specializing, he wrote:

> Were I a Professor, I would urge my students above all not only to maintain an active interest in the progress of natural science as a whole (and that is easily done in Europe through journals and annuals), but also to familiarize themselves with several disparate areas through their own specific research.[38]

Given Fritz's feelings about Desterro, it is ironic that Haeckel in his obituary of Müller (1897) suggested calling him "Fritz Müller-Desterro" to memorialize the place in which he did so much significant research, and to distinguish him from the many other Müllers. As Alfred Möller wrote, "It would certainly not have pleased him to have his name enduringly linked with Desterro."[39] Haeckel was no doubt biased by his own interest in marine invertebrates and undervalued the rest of Fritz's output on terrestrial and freshwater organisms.

The year 1866 still did not release him from exile (Fig. 5). An agricultural and industrial exhibition in Rio de Janeiro, in which the German colonies took a particularly active part, put heavy demands on him, although Fritz himself never left Santa Catarina. The following year, with the school offering nothing more in the way of satisfy-

*Fig. 5. Fritz Müller in Desterro in uncharacteristic city
clothes, around 1866. A. Möller, 1920,* Fritz Müllers
Leben.

ing activity and the government making no decision about the continued engagement of the teachers who had been displaced by the
Jesuits, Fritz initiated his own proposal to the provincial government
for future employment with the following terms, as he reported to
Hermann in 1867:

> "The Professor of Mathematics offers, for the guarantee of a
> permanent position at his present salary, to undertake the
> following:

111

"1. to investigate the natural riches of the province, especially those of the plant kingdom, by collecting and studying all objects that might be useful in medicine or industry or that would yield a commercial product, and by planting on his land on the bank of the Itajaí those native plants the study of which would be of scientific or practical interest;

"2. to introduce and cultivate those foreign plants which are worth trying to acclimate in the province, while he studies their potential benefits and the best methods of culture and use;

"3. to cultivate for seeds or cuttings those plants which the government may send for distribution in the province, nearly all of which have hitherto been lost before anyone found out if their cultivation was profitable;

"4. to place the seeds and the cuttings that he grows at the disposal of the provincial government for distribution in the province;

"5. to write a detailed annual or semi-annual report on the results of his labors;

"6. to undertake any surveys and observations of the natural history of the province with which the provincial government charges him."

The proposal, which naturally has a very elaborate introduction following local taste, has been favorably received, and the appropriate commission has already drawn up a bill of assent whose adoption I consider probable.[40]

The offer was accepted by the provincial legislature in June 1867. "Because we were troublesome competitors of the pious Fathers, the assembly gladly agreed to my proposal. Our professorships were abolished (literally *extinctos*, wiped out), and in July 1867 I returned to the Itajaí, to take up once again my old free and easy life in the virgin forest."[41]

# 7

# Marine Zoology and the Defense of Darwin, 1856–1869

In November 1856, soon after moving to Desterro (Maps 3 and 4), Fritz recorded his impressions of the coast near his house, on the sheltered west side of Santa Catarina Island:

in part a flat sandy shore dipping very gradually beneath the sea, partly rugged rocky regions often broken up into a wild confusion of isolated blocks. The summits of these rocks are adorned with giant cacti, splendid orchids and bromeliads, and over them in the sunshine run thousands of *Ligium* [isopods] about the size of our slaters and up to two inches long. They hide themselves from danger in the rocky crevices with the agility of the German *Ligium agile*. Just at the upper level of spring tides there is a thick covering of small barnacles with masses of little periwinkles packed together in the cracks and crevices. Below the barnacles comes a layer of small oysters with limpets crawling among them. Below that, also uncovered by nearly every tide, the irregular blackish entwining tubes of *Serpula* form a literal mass of stone which extends over the rocks in a belt nine inches wide and a few inches thick. In the interstices of those serpulas are nereids [annelid worms], small crabs and sea anemones, while numerous *Lithodomus* (boring clams) dwell enclosed in the living stone. Only low tides uncover the rocky regions where various snails, sea stars, tunicates, anemones, etc. are found, as well as a variety of sea weeds, among which clamber numerous caprellids (skeleton-shrimp) and other small amphipods. Under the cast-up seaweed on sandy shores above

the level of ordinary tides there are innumerable *Orchestia*
[amphipods] and crabs. A large gray crab with chalk-white claws
sometimes runs about on the sand in the sunshine with incredible agility.

Other crabs, especially *Lupea*, come in close to shore but flee
into deep water at one's approach. There is also a variety of
jellyfish in quiet waters close to shore. The commonest is a large
rhizostomid (probably a new genus), often a foot in diameter
with 32 deep indigo-blue marginal lobes. I have already observed about ten different acalephs[2], among them a ctenophore,
*Mnemia*.

Fritz went on to describe bottom-dwelling sea cucumbers, and
sea urchins bedecked with pieces of mussel shell, and concluded, "You
can see that I will not soon lack for material for anatomical studies. In
particular I intend to follow the development of various animals that
have not yet been studied in that respect. My first task, as soon as I
acquire a microscope, however, will be the natural history (anatomy
and development) of the local jellyfish."[3]

Fritz began sending his notes and manuscripts on marine invertebrates to Max Schultze, who was his most important correspondent
during the early years in Desterro and who also supplied him with the
latest literature and with equipment. Until Schultze sent him a
microscope via Burmeister in 1856,[4] Fritz worked in a little window
seat with no instruments or apparatus save a loup. It was a festive day
when the clerk at the Desterro post office handed him something
from Schultze. In June 1856, just before he left the Itajaí valley, Fritz
had sent notes on land planaria to Schultze, who submitted them as
Fritz's first publication from the New World, pointing out that since
Darwin had called attention to the rich variety of these unusual
animals in the forests of South America in his *Journal of Researches*,[5]
very little had been learned of their natural history, and that even
without optical devices Fritz had made important observations of this
group of free-living flatworms. "An obvious question," Fritz wrote, "is
whether [these animals] carry cilia on the body surface like their
aquatic relatives. Lacking a microscope, and remembering an experiment in Johannes Müller's physiology lectures, I sprinkled a little
arrowroot flour on a rather large specimen of *Geoplana rufiventris* and

watched the flour move steadily forward and sometimes outward on the dorsal side, and backward on the ventral side. From those observations the existence of cilia seems established beyond doubt."[6]

Fritz's papers, principally in the *Archiv für Naturgeschichte* (Archives of natural history), on the rich annelid fauna of Santa Catarina Island, and on the anatomy and development of brachiopods, jellyfish, and ctenophores, followed between 1858 and 1861 and brought him to the attention of naturalists in Europe and North America; his papers on jellyfish would soon bring a response from Alexander Agassiz.

But even as he continued to study acalephs, he began in 1861 to look in earnest for juvenile stages of Crustacea, and he characteristically discovered other things in the process, as he wrote to Schultze:

> For some weeks the sea has not been calm a single day and has driven off the ctenophores. Consequently I have for the time being taken up once again a subject frequently begun, the juvenile stages of crabs, primarily the zoëa. I don't expect anything suitable for publication for some time, but while searching for egg-bearing *Porcellana* [a porcelain crab], I chanced upon two most wonderful parasites of those crabs. I am sending you an article about them, perhaps by the next ship. Seldom have new animals misled me as did these two parasites. I think that I have already sent you a sketch of one of them; at that time I took it for a worm; but it is a *Lernaea* [a parasitic copepod] in which I have not yet found a trace of mouth parts or vestiges of feet, and on which even the two characteristic egg clusters are lacking; it is a live-bearer, and its juveniles remind one almost more of young barnacles than of the larvae of *Lernaea* by the horns into which the wide front margin of the body is extended, and even by the legs.[7]

By the time Fritz had written up this discovery he realized that his new species was not a copepod but a member of a previously unrecognized group of parasitic Crustacea. "I have lived through a regular novel of misunderstandings, confusions and surprises with my crustaceans," he wrote to Schultze on 1 August 1861, enclosing his paper on "The Rhizocephala, a new group of parasitic Crustacea."[8] Though at first believing the Rhizocephala to be copepods, Fritz soon recognized them as barnacles that had degenerated through their parasitic mode of life, as he wrote Schultze the following April,[9] and in May 1862 he dispatched his evidence in a description of the second stage in their development:

> About three days after the young rhizocephalans have left their mother's brood pouch as nauplii, they are transformed, as I recently observed in three different species, into a new form very different from the first and most closely agreeing with the second developmental stage of barnacles.[10]

Fritz was the first to witness the transformation directly, as Max Schultze wrote in his footnote to Fritz's paper, although Anderson and Lilljeborg had already recognized the Rhizocephala as parasitic barnacles in 1861.[11]

Late in 1861 Fritz wrote to Schultze that he was

> still occupied with the Crustacea, in fact for several weeks now with a subject which seems to me of the greatest importance for a natural phylogenetic arrangement of that class and for its morphology. Even among crabs there is metamorphosis, and the youngest stages are Cyclops-like. Then follows a Zoëa-like stage which I know already in three species. Finally a *Mysis*-like form, this last seeming by its three pairs of claws to point the way toward the genus *Penaeus*. . . . The Crustacea overwhelm me with so many questions, and shrimp larvae hold such promise for my hope of finding in their development the key to a definitive natural classification, that I will probably not be free of the group for years![12]

Fritz's increasing attention to natural classification may have been due to his discovery of Darwin's evolutionary theories, for he probably received the German edition of *The Origin of Species*[13] in 1861 from Schultze. On 30 October 1861 he wrote to his parents, "Darwin's book on the origin of species in the animal and plant kingdoms has given me, and still gives me, much to think about."[14] This is the first comment from Fritz on the work that had an increasingly decisive influence on his ideas and activities, and on the man whom he came to admire the most. Early the following year, to Schultze, he first explicitly related his studies of crustacean development to a test of Darwinism:

I had in mind publishing some general observations in favor of Darwin's theory of natural selection, but I gave up the idea. The best proof of the theory will be if it can be applied without constraint to quite specific circumstances and brings clarity and order to an apparent chaos. I hope that I can thus apply it to crustacean development and thereby benefit the theory more than by the usual deductions, with which after all only those who already adhere to the same general viewpoint can be expected to agree. This hope has induced me to devote myself exclusively to that class of animals.[15]

To his brother Hermann he wrote:

I have been almost exclusively occupied with Crustacea this past summer, particularly with the development of shrimp, which throws an entirely new light on the relationships of crustaceans and on the whole morphology of the arthropods, and I hope will provide important evidence in favor of Darwin's theory of the origin of animal and plant species. It is a most time-consuming and difficult task, using larvae fished from the sea to compare the development of animals that pass through a long series of different forms, but it is also most interesting and absorbing, often full of truly fantastic complexities, disillusions and surprises. I know only one pursuit that I might set equal to fishing for larvae, or might even prefer to it: carving a cozy homestead out of uninhabited virgin forest.[16]

In December 1862 Fritz wrote to Hermann, delighted that his brother had been won over to Darwin's views, and told him that *The Origin* has suggested a plan:

namely to attempt to draw up a phylogeny of the Crustacea, that is to show in what sequence the various living forms diverged from the ancestral form and what different stages they passed through; for example, what the actual structure was of the common ancestor of all shrimps, then of all Macrura [lobsters, crayfish, shrimps], then all Decapoda [Macrura plus crabs], all Podophthalmata [decapods plus other stalk-eyed crustaceans], all higher Crustacea. If Darwin's theory is correct, it can hardly be doubted, for example, that all Crustacea descended from a nauplius, because it is in that form that Rhizocephala, Cirripedia, Lernaea, Copepoda, all Phyllopoda and even — you have probably read my paper on the subject[17] — some of the highest Crustacea (*Penaeus*) now leave the egg. All higher Crustacea will probably be traceable back to a zoëa, all Macrura, perhaps all Decapoda, to a *Mysis* [Schizopod]-like ancestor. Some day when I have a chance, I will explain to you how I believe many such questions can be answered with the help of development. But whatever the upshot may be, these reflections afford me great pleasure, and they have yielded more new data for my colleagues in one year than the whole of the last decade has furnished.[18]

Fritz developed these thoughts in a manuscript entitled *Für Darwin*, which he finished in September 1863, and by February 1864 he had sent the last revisions and additions to Schultze.[19] The book was published by Engelmann in Leipzig around the middle of the year[20], advertisements for it appearing in a new journal, the *Jenaische Zeitschrift für Medizin und Naturwissenschaften*, from December 1864 through the middle of 1865, and was reviewed favorably in 1865 by the zoologist Karl Gerstaecker (1828–1895) in his "Report on scientific accomplishments . . . 1863–64."[21] An unsigned review of most of its main points appeared in Geneva early in 1865, and a translation of that review in the *Annals and Magazine of Natural History* later that year brought Fritz's book to the attention of English readers.[22]

The author of the Geneva review described Fritz's attempt to construct a "natural classification or genealogical tree for the class of Crustacea" and to deduce from it certain necessary consequences:

> These deductions he has endeavoured to verify. If they could not be verified, this would be a fatal blow to the Darwinian theory; but if proved true, they would furnish, if not a proof, at least a strong presumption in favour of the theory. Hitherto his deductions have been verified; and thus his work presents us with a remarkable example of important results in natural history obtained by a purely deductive method, in opposition to most of the discoveries in that science, which are made by means of a sort of inductive groping.[23]

*Für Darwin* was also given a long review by Charles Spence Bate in the *Zoological Record* of 1864[24], but unfortunately most of Fritz's points, including a "joke" genealogy of the Crustacea, were misunderstood, perhaps from Bate's ignorance of German.

Darwin may have become aware of Fritz's book through a letter from Ernst Haeckel in October 1864,[25] or he may have already received his copy. He told Haeckel in November that he had found the German difficult and had employed a translator.[26] In May 1865 Edward Cresy, an acquaintance, wrote to Darwin in favor of Fritz's argument for natural selection in the evolution of the air-breathing apparatus of crustaceans, as reported in the review in *Annals and Magazine of Natural History*.[27] Although Darwin sent reprints on climbing plants to Fritz around this time, it was only in August that Darwin wrote him the first of a series of letters that was to continue until Darwin's death in 1882:

> I have been for a long time so ill that I have only just finished having read aloud your work on species. And now you must permit me to thank you cordially for the great interest with which I have read it. You have done admirable service in the cause in which we both believe. Many of your arguments seem to me excellent, & many of your facts wonderful. . . . Your observations on Classification and Embryology seem to me very good and original. They shew what a wonderful field there is for enquiry on the development of Crustacea, and nothing has convinced me so plainly what admirable results we shall arrive at in Natural History in the course of a few years. What a marvellous range of structure the Crustacea present, & how well adapted they are for your enquiry![28]

Already Darwin had struck on the "facts" and "arguments" that would form the title of the English translation four years later.

Fritz received Darwin's letter on 8 October[29] and responded the next day with observations on the evolution of sponge spicules, on climbing plants, the circumnutation of plants and the probable link between barnacles and Rhizocephalans. It was a typical Müller letter, even to its expression of a preference for the original English edition of *Fertilisation of Orchids* over the German translation which Darwin had offered. He had already written Darwin twice that year, in response to a paper on climbing plants that Darwin had sent, "as an experiment to see whether it w^d reach you."[30] Darwin submitted the appropriate parts of all three of Fritz's letters on climbing plants to the Linnean Society, and they were eventually published as his first paper in English.[31] Fritz wrote to Darwin in English, a language which he knew only academically and had never spoken. Darwin told him, however, "I have slightly modified the arrangement of some parts and altered only a few words, as you write as good English as an Englishman."[32]

In response to one of those earlier letters, Darwin wrote, "Does it not often strike you that Natural History is rendered extremely interesting by such views as we both hold."[33] And Fritz answered:

> To be sure! Ever since I read your book *On the Origin of Species* and was converted to your point of view, many facts which I used to view with indifference have become quite remarkable; others which formerly seemed meaningless oddities have acquired great significance, and thus has the countenance of all Nature been transformed.[34]

Although Darwin told Haeckel in 1865 that he was going to have *Für Darwin* translated, he did not pursue the idea for several years. In 1866 he told J.D. Hooker, one of his allies,[35] that the book was perhaps the most important contribution in support of his ideas,[36] but it was only early in 1868 that W. S. Dallas suggested that a translation would sell well and offered to do it.[37] Darwin wrote Hermann Müller the next day that he would undertake the publication of an English translation of *Für Darwin*,[38] and after hearing from Hermann[39] he wrote to Fritz:

> Your brother, as you will have heard from him, felt so convinced that you would not object to a translation of "Für Darwin," that I have ventured to arrange for a translation. Engelmann has very liberally offered me "cliches" of the woodcuts for 22 Thalers; Mr. Murray has agreed to bring out a translation (and he is our best publisher) on commission, for he would not undertake the work on his own risk; and I have agreed with Mr. W. S. Dallas (who has translated Von Siebold on Parthenogenesis, & many German works and who writes very good English) for the sum of from 12 to 15 sovereigns to translate the book. He thinks (and he is a good judge) that it is important to have some few corrections or additions, in order to account for a translation

appearing so long after the original; so that I hope you will be able to send some.[40]

Having heard from Hermann of Darwin's intentions, Fritz had already sent Darwin six English additions for the translation, including a long section on the evolution of the Rhizocephala from typical barnacles,[41] and he now added a memo in which he argued that the "so-called 'complete metamorphosis' of Insects, in which these animals quit the egg as grubs or caterpillars, and afterwards become quiescent pupae incapable of feeding, was not inherited from the primitive ancestor of all Insects, but acquired at a later period."[42]

Darwin also raised the question of an appropriate title for the translation. He had proposed "Für Darwin" or "For Darwin," but Charles Lyell[43] and Dallas were strongly opposed, and Lyell suggested "Facts and arguments in favour of Darwin." Fritz agreed but thought that "Darwinism tested by Carcinology" or "Carcinology as bearing on the origin of species" would be more precise.[44] Darwin was blunt: "I feel sure however that Murray w$^d$ object to so unusual a word as Carcinology."[45]

Dallas started translating in mid-March 1868[46] and finished in late November, calling it a "difficult job,"[47] and in mid-March 1869 John Murray brought out, at Darwin's suggestion, an edition of 1000 copies, though Darwin feared the number "might be foolish."[48] Darwin's caution was not misplaced; only four hundred copies had been sold by 28 April 1869, and ten years later total sales were less than 700.[49]

Darwin was familiar with barnacles from his taxonomic work some years before on living and fossil Cirripedia, and he wrote to Fritz shortly after the book's publication, "I have re-read many parts, especially that on cirripedes, with the liveliest interest. I had almost forgotten your discussion on the retrograde development of the Rhizocephala. What an admirable illustration it affords of my whole doctrine! A man must indeed be a bigot in favour of separate acts of creation if he is not staggered after reading your essay; but I fear that it is too deep for English readers, except a select few."[50] *Facts and Arguments* (Fig. 6) was never easy reading. Darwin introduced several of Fritz's ideas into the next edition of *The Origin*.[51]

# FACTS AND ARGUMENTS

FOR

# DARWIN.

## BY FRITZ MÜLLER.

WITH ADDITIONS BY THE AUTHOR.

TRANSLATED FROM THE GERMAN

By W. S. DALLAS, F.L.S.,

ASSISTANT SECRETARY TO THE GEOLOGICAL SOCIETY OF LONDON.

WITH ILLUSTRATIONS.

LONDON:

JOHN MURRAY, ALBEMARLE STREET.

1869.

*Fig. 6. Title page of Müller, 1869,* Facts and Arguments for Darwin.

Favorable reviews appeared in *The Academy*[52] and *Scientific Opinion*[53], and a critical one in *The Athenaeum*.[54] This last reviewer believed that "the real value of the facts here brought forward, for their ostensible purpose, can only be estimated by a specialist in the Crustacea . . ." [which he was not], but that although few naturalists were familiar with crustacean embryology, "this little treatise contains many somewhat important facts in the developmental history of several of the Crustacea, and will be acceptable to those who interest themselves in this branch of research." As to "observations on the progressive evolution of Crustacea," the reviewer reported that:

> Dr. Müller concludes by expressing the hope that in one thing he has succeeded, viz, "in convincing *unprejudiced* readers that Darwin's theory furnishes the key of intelligibility for the developmental history [by which Fritz meant "evolution"] of the Crustacea, as well as for so many other facts inexplicable without it." It must be admitted that this is a large conclusion to be drawn from comparatively few facts. But . . . only specialists in Crustacean development can test Dr. Müller; and he himself confesses that "the most profound students of the animal kingdom are amongst Darwin's opponents."

The reviewer shows that his premises are different from Fritz's when he continues:

> It will probably occur to some readers that at least a few of the noted facts may be cited for other purposes than that of this book. Take, for example, the remarkable provisions with which that "charming, lively crab, *Aratus Pisonii*," is furnished [for air-breathing]. . . . Let any *unprejudiced* reader of these facts say whether they do not impress him with a conviction of special provision, and of the high improbability of such a result from developmental evolution.

Fritz's mocking of Louis Agassiz,[55] however, receives the sharpest comments:

> The author twice or thrice indulges in sneers which certainly are not "arguments for Darwin." No scientific writer should allow himself to say, as Dr. Müller does, "Just as in Christian countries there is a catechismal morality, which every one has upon his lips, but no one considers himself bound to follow, or expects to

see followed by anybody else, so also has Zoology its dogmas, which are as universally acknowledged, as they are disregarded in practice."[56] It is to be feared that Dr. Müller's moral code is rather Crustacean than Christian. Nor does it enforce his argument to say that "to read this remarkable writing we need the spectacles of Faith, which seldom suit eyes accustomed to the microscope."[57] It is obvious enough that the spectacles of Faith do not suit Dr. Müller's eyes; but he should not forget that they have suited and do still suit the eyes of some of the most eminent microscopists. To point this sneer against [Louis] Agassiz is not the best way of aiding Darwin.

Fritz received the reviews from Darwin on 11 June 1869 and wrote to his brother the next day that the *Athenaeum*'s reviewer "took great offense at my unchristian expressions as unworthy of a 'scientific writer.' The witticism [about Fritz's moral code] is not so bad and amused me greatly."[58]

The "Facts" in Fritz's book include adaptations for aerial respiration, asymmetrical limbs, sexual dimorphism, polymorphism, and the morphology and development of larval forms; his "Arguments" touch on convergent evolution, the value of shared derived characters in classification, the significance of variation in life histories, and the evolutionary history of the Crustacea.

Fritz opened *Facts and Arguments* with an acknowledgment of Darwin's *Origin* as its inspiration, and with thanks for its "instructions and suggestions." We have seen that within a few months of reading *The Origin*, he had devised a plan to test Darwin by establishing a genealogy of some group of organisms and seeing whether the application of Darwin's theory of descent was supported, or whether it led to such contradictions as would falsify Darwin. He chose Crustacea as his testing ground, for three reasons: most of the diversity in living Crustacea was represented around Desterro; the mutability of crustacean species, especially parasitic ones, was already widely acknowledged; and the classification of the group was in a stable state compared with that of annelid worms and acalephs, with which he was also familiar.

"A false supposition, when the consequences proceeding from it are followed further and further," wrote Fritz, "will . . . lead to absurdities and palpable contradictions." Although he himself went through "a period of tormenting doubt," he finally decided that there were no contradictions with Darwinian theory in his work, and at that point he set about writing his book.

Fritz's first demonstration was the air-breathing adaptations of terrestrial crabs:

> It seems to be a necessity for all crabs which remain for a long time out of water . . . that air shall penetrate from behind into the branchial cavity. Now these [terrestrial] crabs, which have become more or less estranged from the water, belong to the most diverse families . . . and the separation of these families must doubtless be referred to a much earlier period than the habit of leaving the water displayed by some of their members. The arrangements connected with aerial respiration, therefore, could not be inherited from a common ancestor, and could scarcely be accordant in their construction. If there were any such accordance not referable to accidental resemblance among them, it would have to be laid in the scale as evidence against the correctness of Darwin's views.[59]

Darwin had written in *The Origin*: "In . . . cases of two very distinct species furnished with apparently the same anomalous organ, . . . although the general appearance and function of the organ may be the same, yet some fundamental difference can generally be detected. . . . [N]atural selection, working for the good of each being and taking advantage of analogous variations, has sometimes modified in very nearly the same manner two parts in two organic beings, which owe but little of their structure in common to inheritance from the same ancestor."[60]

Fritz showed that terrestrial crabs belonging to two families had different methods of exposing the gills to air out of water, although they were otherwise very similar to one another, and to their marine relatives, in a host of minute details. He asked:

> If, in the closely allied families of the Ocypodidae and Grapsoidae, the closest agreement prevails in all the essential conditions of their structure; if the same plan of structure is slavishly followed in every thing else, in the organs of sense, in the articulation of the limbs, . . . and in all the arrangements subserving aquatic respiration, even to the hairs of the flagella

employed in cleaning the branchiae, — why have we suddenly this exception, this complete difference, in connexion with aerial respiration?[61]

Fritz's answer was that the air-breathing adaptations had evolved independently in the two families and could not have been inherited from a common ancestor, since the common ancestor of the two species did not have such an adaptation.

A second example based on ancestor-descendant relationships dealt with the value of what are now called shared derived characters in determining evolutionary relationships, that is characters which have evolved fairly recently in a particular lineage and are not found in other lineages. In the amphipod genus *Melita*, five species share a highly asymmetric "clasp-forceps" on one of the second pair of feet, but one species, *M. Fresnellii* was said to lack a secondary flagellum on the anterior antennae and had consequently been placed in a different genus. Fritz presented two alternative patterns of ancestor-descendent relationship (Fig. 7) and argued that the upper pattern

**From the structure of the clasp-forceps:**

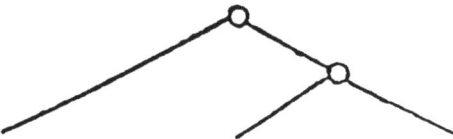

*M. palmata, &c. M. exilii, &c. M. Fresnelii.*

**From the presence or absence of the secondary flagellum.**

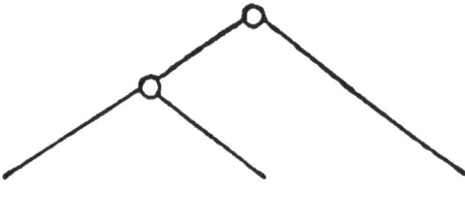

*M. palmata, &c. M. exilii, &c. M. Fresnelii.*

*Fig. 7. Fritz Müller's "cladograms" showing alternative interpretations of the evolutionary relationships among amphipod crustaceans of the genus* Melita. *Müller, 1869,* Facts and Arguments for Darwin.

showed the true relationship, because the clasp-forceps of the five species "is so unusual among Amphipods...that one must unhesitatingly regard [those species] as having sprung from common ancestors belonging to them alone among known species." In other words, the clasp forceps is a shared derived character, while the secondary flagellum is lost in many amphipods and therefore has no value in determining relationships among species of *Melita*. The alternative lower pattern gives the four species having the secondary flagellum a common ancestor not shared by *M. Fresnellii* and says that the clasp-forceps has evolved twice. The use of shared derived characters for showing phylogenetic relationships among living species was an innovation introduced by Fritz. His use of a branch diagram of the type now known as a cladogram,[62] so-called because it clusters organisms with common ancestry into clades, was a century ahead of its time.[63]

Darwin's theory of the mutability of species raised a question in many minds as to why species remain distinct in the face of "the accumulation of the smallest variations diverging in various directions"[64] and do not show the endless range of intermediates that Heinrich Bronn, in the additions to his translation of Darwin's *Origin*, thought ought to follow from mutability.[65] Darwin had answered the question himself, mostly in generalities, by showing how selection could favor extremes, for example in pigeon-breeding[66], or how transitions between species would have a high probability of extinction.[67] Fritz's answer had to do with discrete variation within species, for which he had a specific example in the dimorphism in reproductive characters in males of a member of the genus *Tanais*. Males resemble females until they reach sexual maturity, but after the last moult there are two male forms, one with large claws for grasping females during mating but with few sensory ("olfactory") filaments on the antennae, the other with small claws like those of females but many sensory filaments. Fritz thought that there were two optimal states, "claspers" and "smellers," with no advantage to intermediates, and he concluded that "only a few directions stand open in which variations are at the same time improvements and can therefore accumulate and become fixed; whilst variations in all other directions, being either indifferent or injurious, will go as easily as they come."[68]

127

In modern terms, he was suggesting that disruptive selection for two optimal states has been responsible for the persistence of the dimorphism, and by inference that the distinctness of species might have the same basis.

These examples dealt with patterns of variation within and among species, but the best known part of *Facts and Arguments* has to do with development and its meaning for classification and evolution.

In Fritz's time it was known that different crustaceans hatch in widely varying forms. Freshwater crayfish and some terrestrial crabs, for example, emerge looking like tiny adults, marine crabs and shrimps come out as a zoëa, usually with spines and some rudimentary limbs, while ostracods, copepods and barnacles hatch as a nauplius, the simplest crustacean larval form. Fritz discovered that a marine shrimp, *Penaeus,* hatched as a nauplius before passing through a zoëal stage, and he suggested that in crabs and other shrimps in which the zoëa was the first larval form the nauplius has been traversed before hatching.[69] Because he fished his *Penaeus* nauplii from the sea and never actually watched them develop to adult shrimps, his observation was not at first believed, and only by the time of Lang's comparative anatomy text in 1889 [70] was it accepted. His discovery of the *Penaeus* nauplius set him to thinking about variation in developmental pathways, and this was the principal topic of the last chapters of his book.

In his penultimate chapter, "On the progress of evolution," Fritz states his views on the significance of development for evolutionary history, that is, phylogeny.

Darwin believed that ideally the only possible natural system of classification would be based on descent, the genealogy of all organisms, and that embryonic structure would be better for that purpose than adult structure. Fritz, however, was less sanguine, perhaps because he was aware of a host of examples in which there were large differences in development even among species that on many other grounds were clearly closely-related. In his chapter "On the principles of classification" he enumerated a variety of patterns of metamorphosis in Crustacea and concluded: "we can scarcely speak of a general plan or typical mode of development of the Crustacea, differentiated according to the separate Sections, Orders, and Families."[71] In isopods and amphipods, for example, the number of legs is the same in adults but different in newly-hatched young of the two groups. In other cases development starts and ends similarly but diverges widely in mid-course, or the reverse may be true, as in barnacles and parasitic rhizocephalans, in which there "proceed different forms of Nauplius, these being converted into exceedingly similar pupae [=cypris larvae], and from the pupae again proceed sexually mature animals differing diametrically from each other."[72]

He sought to explain developmental diversity by natural selection and proposed two possible modes of developmental change in evolution:

> *Descendants . . . reach a new goal, either [1] by deviating sooner or later whilst still on the way towards the form of their parents, or [2] by passing along this course without deviation, but then, instead of standing still, proceeding still farther.*[73]

Mode [1] will predominate in groups having a common fundamental body plan, like birds, crabs or amphipods, where "the developmental history of the descendants can only agree with that of their ancestors up to a certain point at which their courses separate," and adult structure "will teach us nothing [about phylogeny]."[74] The reason is that in groups like these there are no species with adults that resemble immature stages of other species.

The idea that an organism might evolve by developing up to a point like its ancestors, but then diverging from the ancestral path, has been said to run counter to the conclusion reached around 30 years earlier by the pioneering embryologist Karl von Baer (1792–1876), but Fritz's Mode [1] seems much like von Baer's Third Law, which says: "every embryo of a given animal form, instead of passing through the other forms, rather becomes separated from them."[75] Von Baer's statement has been interpreted to mean that "different forms deviate from one another in development from the outset because they arise from eggs that are in essence, if not visibly, different,"[76] but that interpretation assumes that the separation occurs only at the very beginning of development, in which case no two species would share any embryological stages whatever. Von Baer seems to be referring to organisms having different body plans, like arthropods and vertebrates, rather than related species.

Mode [2] will characterize groups in which the adults of some animals resemble the immature states of others: In this case, "*the entire development of the progenitors is also passed through by the descendants, and, therefore, so far as the production of a species depends upon this second mode of progress, the historical development of the species will be mirrored in its developmental history.*"[77] How many groups of organisms might show Mode [2]? Fritz's only examples are of polychaete worms (annelids), and he is explicit about only one of them, a tube-dwelling fanworm of the genus *Serpula*, where it seems unexceptionable. The operculum which closes the tube when the adult retreats into it develops from a modified gill-filament by stages resembling those of adults of related species (Fig. 8).

The concept described here is recapitulation, where descendants repeat the development of their ancestors and then add something to it. The idea is identified with the "law of parellelism," that "embryos of higher organisms advance through the adults stages of lower

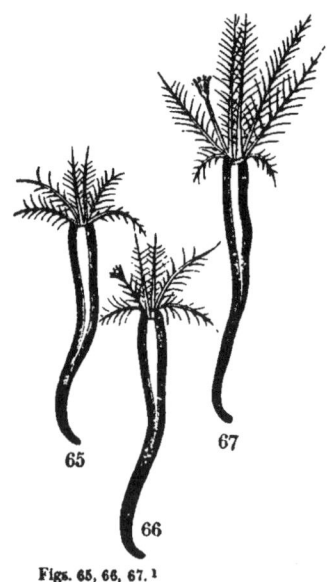

Figs. 65, 66, 67. [1]

*Fig. 8. Fritz Müller's example of "recapitulation" in the development of the operculum of a tube-dwelling annelid worm. "Fig. 65, without operculum,* Protula-*stage; Fig. 66, with a barbate opercular peduncle,* Filograna-*stage; Fig. 67, with a naked opercular peduncle,* Serpula-*stage." Müller, 1869,* Facts and Arguments for Darwin.

130

organisms."[78] Von Baer attacked that concept in his Third Law (above) and in his Fourth Law, which states: "...the embryos of higher forms never resemble any other form, but only its embryo."[79] That refutation of the law of parallelism was lost on Fritz (and on Darwin), but as Churchill points out, although Fritz "encouraged the confusion," with his Mode [2] of the evolution of development, it was Ernst Haeckel who ultimately codified the confusion with his biogenetic law. In 1897 Haeckel asserted that Fritz had "firmly established and explained" the law of parellelism "by the theory of descent."[80]

It is curious that Fritz missed von Baer's conclusions, since Johannes Müller had endorsed them 30 years earlier, before Fritz became his student. In his *Handbuch der Physiologie*, published in the 1830s, Johannes Müller wrote:

> Not long since it was supposed and seriously affirmed by many naturalists that the human embryo previously to arriving at its perfect state passed through the different stages of development which are permanent conditions of other animals. This was a very bold hypothesis, and one that is by no means correct. Its falsity was well demonstrated by Von Baer. The human embryo in fact, at *no* period resembles a radiate animal, or an insect, a molluscous creature or a worm. [Man being a vertebrate and having a vertebrate plan, could at most resemble other vertebrates.] But it is not true even that he resembles at one time a fish, at another time one of the amphibia or reptiles, and at another time a bird; he merely bears the same resemblance to a fish which he does to a bird or reptile, namely, the resemblance which all vertebrate animals bear to each other.[81]

Later in Chapter 11 Fritz emphasized the importance of adaptation as it affects the reliability of developmental pathways as guides to phylogeny. "*The historical record preserved in developmental history is gradually EFFACED as development adopts an ever straighter course from the egg to the adult animal, and it is frequently FALSIFIED by the struggle for existence which the free-living larvae have to undergo.*" Variation in adult stages and in the timing of developmental processes allows natural selection to operate on both. The "straighter course" is expected in cases where adult and larvae have similar modes of life and is exemplified by freshwater shrimps that hatch from the egg in essentially adult form. The record may be "falsified," for example, where ecological conditions offer the immature stages sources of food different from those of the adults, as in bottom-dwelling marine species that have free-swimming or drifting pelagic larvae. In that case the larvae might evolve specialized adaptations. Fritz recognized that complex metamorphosis might evolve into direct development, or the reverse, depending on whether the modes of life of juveniles and adults are similar or not. For example, a female with a given amount of material (nutrients) at her disposal might produce a few richly-endowed eggs and therefore more fully-developed hatchlings. Or she might spread the same amount of material among a larger number of small eggs, in which case the hatchlings would pass through more of their development after coming out of the egg. Had anyone previously recognized that sort of "trade-off"?

Fritz concluded that such variations in life history would affect our ability to make out the phylogeny. "The primitive history of a species will be preserved in its developmental history the more completely, the longer the series of juvenile states through which it passes by uniform steps; and the more faithfully, the less the mode of life of the young departs from that of the adults, and the less the peculiarities of the individual juvenile states can be perceived as transferred back from later ones to previous periods of life, or as independently acquired."[82]

In 1866 Ernst Haeckel introduced the biogenetic law in two of his "ontogenetic theses" on the causal connection between phylogeny and ontogeny, Nos. 41 and 42, which may be summarized: The ontogeny, or development, of an individual organism is the brief and rapid recapitulation of phylogeny, or the evolutionary history of the lineage to which that organism belongs. In short, "ontogeny recapitulates phylogeny."[83] He appended two theses, Nos. 43 and 44, that qualified the "law," lifting them from *Für Darwin* without attribution and even using many of Fritz's words. Only in 1872 did he acknowledge his debt.[84] The parallel statements are arranged and italicized below to emphasize the similarities, with identical German words yielding identical English.

| Fritz in 1864:<br>(pagination in *Werke*) | Haeckel in 1866 II:300: |
|---|---|
| In [a] short period . . . the changing forms of the embryo and larvae will pass before us, a more or less complete and more or less true picture of the transformations through which the species, in the course of untold thousands of years, has struggled up to its present state. (p 249) | 42. The organic individual repeats during the swift and brief course of its...development the most important of those changes in form which its ancestors passed through during the slow and long course of their paleontological development. . . . |
| The historical record preserved in developmental history is gradually *effaced as development adopts an ever straighter course* from the egg to the perfect animal. . . . (p 250) | 43. The complete and true repetition of phyletic [historical] development by biontic [individual] development is *effaced and shortened by secondary condensation, as ontogeny adopts an ever straighter course.* . . . |
| The primitive history of a species will be preserved...the *more completely, the longer the series of immature stages through which it passes.* . . . (p 252) | Thus the repetition is *more complete* the *longer the sequence of successive juvenile stages passed through.* |
| The...record is frequently *falsified by the struggle for existence.* . . . (p 250) | 44. The...repetition of [phylogeny] by [ontogeny] is *falsified and changed by secondary adaptations.* . . . |
| The primitive history...will be preserved...the *more faithfully, the less the mode of life of the young departs from that of the adult.* . . . (p 252) | Thus the repetition will be *more faithful,* the *more alike the conditions of existence under which the individual and its ancestors developed.* |

There is an irony in Haeckel's use of theses 43 and 44, since they "blunt the certainty of recapitulation," as Frederick Churchill pointed out.[85] Perhaps Haeckel's principal debt to Fritz should have been for the idea that selection could modify developmental patterns. Recapitulation itself was not a new idea in 1864.[86]

Fritz never seems to have taken the biogenetic law very seriously or used it in his own research. He wrote approvingly to Haeckel about nearly all of his books but made no use of Haeckel's new vocabulary, and apparently only once, in 1880, did he write about Haeckel's biogenetic law, his example being the steps in regeneration of lost limbs in a shrimp.[87] As Stephen Jay Gould recognized, Fritz's interest was not so much in reconstructing phylogenies as it was in natural selection as the driving force in the evolution of adaptations, including life histories.[88] In using Fritz's statements as the basis of the biogenetic law, and then switching the emphasis from the variety of developmental patterns and the importance of adaptation, to a "rule," Haeckel, as William Montgomery put it, "very nearly undermined Müller's original purpose."[89]

One hundred twenty years after its original publication in German, *Facts and Arguments* was still being misread. In 1984 an historian of science took Fritz's statement that descendants might reach a new goal by passing along the developmental path of their ancestors and then proceeding still farther — his Mode [2] — and characterized it as "derived more easily from Lamarckism, where evolution proceeds from efforts of the adult organism, than from Darwinism, where random variation more easily can be seen as a deviation in the growth process."[90] Fritz never implies anything about "effort," which is often erroneously thought to be a Lamarckian idea, but stresses instead the role of natural selection, which is certainly not Lamarckian. As for random variation, Fritz recognized its essence when he spoke of the "few directions . . . in which variations are . . . improvements . . . and can therefore accumulate and become fixed; . . . whilst in all others, being either indifferent or injurious, they will go as lightly as they come."[91]

Fritz lost no chance to press Darwin's case on any doubting correspondent, but the fullest such exchange on record is the one with Alexander Agassiz, Louis's son, who accompanied his father in the move from Geneva to Harvard in 1846 and began studying marine zoology in 1859.[92] Early in 1863 Fritz received a reprint from Agassiz on jellyfish development and responded with a detailed letter, admitting that for a long time his work on Crustacea had pushed aside his own studies of jellyfish.[93] After a response from Agassiz, Fritz began urging Darwin's ideas on him, summarizing in September 1863 several of the arguments that would appear the following year in *Für Darwin*, and for more than three years they tussled over the evidence and implications of Darwin's theories. Fritz was strongly opposed to Louis Agassiz's views, but his letters to the son always ended with cordial greetings to the father, even after he had mocked the elder Agassiz in print, and he envied the Agassizes as "the realization of what I have already dreamt of as the perfect model for my old age — father and son in joint research."[94]

In 1864 Alexander Agassiz thought it "... a salutary thing for science to have a skillful skeptic attack its most religiously received dogmas," but he was not cordial to Darwin's theory, which he felt was "... only bringing up the same arguments as those used by Lamarck, only backed by greater research and greater knowledge," and would ultimately be destroyed by the same objections that had been raised to Lamarckian theory. "Far from having been drawn to the Darwinian Theory," Agassiz wrote, "all my studies and all my experience thus far has led me in the opposite direction." And he called on embryology in his support:

> Why should there not be nowadays going on what Darwin urges has taken place formerly. Does a crab ever lay eggs from which anything but something identical with it does come forth. Does a starfish ever lay eggs from which an Ophiuran [brittle star] is developed. Darwin must show greater changes to have taken place than those of domestication if he wishes us to hold to his theory with any sort of adherence. The idea that a plan pervades the animal kingdom must first be disproved and what is far more important he ought to be able to show in the geological record the traces of these changes. I only ask for the traces of these changes. But far from this he makes a sweeping assertion of the imperfections of the geological record and expects us to take that for the truth. Let him take any of the well studied beds . . . in all of which not a link is wanting and let him then see what he can say about the imperfection of the record and the gradual transformation of one species into another.

To Agassiz the "most damning point" was geographical distribution: "If there is *anything* in geographical distribution, there is *nothing* in Darwin and vice versa." Agassiz was evidently thinking here of

Darwin's "faunas," distinct sets of species occupying different geographic regions. It was not differences in physical conditions that caused them to be distinct, because each region had a similar range of climates, but rather the common ancestry of many organisms living in the same region and the barriers that had prevented mixing: in other words, an evolutionary explanation. Darwin mentioned the marine faunas of the western Atlantic, the eastern Pacific, and the western Pacific in this connection and referred specifically to fishes, molluscs, and crabs. Agassiz, judging from the magnificent collections at Harvard, thought that many marine invertebrates with which he was familiar lapped over the ranges usually given to a fauna. Fritz told Max Schultze about Agassiz's idea and added his opinion that even the great collections were not yet complete enough to draw serious conclusions about distribution. He himself had been walking his beach for eight years, he said, and was still turning up new organisms of every class.[95] Agassiz thought it in vain to theorize on the origin of species before more was known of the "development and physical laws" affecting animals. "The principle of the coincidence of geological succession and of embryonic development as well as of complication[96] is by far a more suggestive one than Darwin's theory. . . ."[97]

Fritz[98] objected to Agassiz's characterization of Darwin's theory as a mere repetition of Lamarck's views: "specifically the argument about the 'struggle for existence' and 'natural selection' deriving from it, seems to me to be something peculiarly new and to be the really crucial point of the whole theory." And while conceding that there was much to be learned about development, geographical distribution, and the rest, Fritz quoted with approval the view of the astronomer Johann Mädler that there are "questions whose answers must still be deferred for centuries, perhaps thousands of years. . . . But this should not prevent us from dealing with such a task, while the possibility of the slightest provisional solution presents itself."[99] He cited recent evidence from paleontology that he felt supported Darwin, including "Loew's experience with the Diptera of amber, of which he said that their genealogical connection with modern species could not be denied."[100] And he mentioned the example of the shrimp nauplius in his forthcoming book. "It is certain that no one — before Darwin's theory — had considered the possibility or likelihood that Decapods could leave the egg in the form of a nauplius."

Agassiz received Fritz's book early in 1865,[101] and in March he wrote, "I have read very carefully your 'Für Darwin' and I was much pleased to see the first beginning of an attempt to test 'Darwin' by facts especially by facts applied to Embryology. It had always appeared to be a great oversight in the supporters of Darwin not to take hold of Embryology," where they would find "much more substantial evidence than the conclusions thus far drawn from different breeds under the influence of man." With respect to Fritz's evidence of common ancestry based on the nauplius larvae of shrimps and parasitic barnacles, Agassiz admitted his unfamiliarity with crustacean metamorphosis and referred to "Radiates" (echinoderms) instead. Pointing out the close similarity of the young forms of brittle stars and sea urchins, on the one hand, and of those of star fish and sea cucumbers, on the other, Agassiz draws a non-evolutionary conclusion:

> According to Darwin or rather "your interpretation of him" for I do not think that your ingenious application of his theory has ever entered the head of any Darwinian, you would see in this the fact that Ophiurans [brittle stars] and Echinoids [sea urchins] come from the same ancestor as much as that Starfishes and Holothurians [sea cucumbers] showed us in their larvae the unmistakable sign of their community of parentage. To me it is simply the expression of the plan upon which the animals are all built modified in such a way as to produce in one case an Ophiuran, in the others Starfish, Echinoids, Holothurians.[102]

What troubled Agassiz was the lack of fossil evidence of transitions between echinoderm classes. Fritz responded optimistically that some fossil echinoderms were placed in different classes by different echinologists and might be transitions between present day groups, and he pointed out that as long as zoologists merely described new species and did not study their morphology, development, and what we now call ecology, intermediates between seemingly sharply-divided groups would go unnoticed.[103] Fritz makes clear, however, the sharp division between Darwinian and anti-Darwinian viewpoints:

It seems to me that he who thinks at all logically about the questions that Darwin has stimulated anew has a choice between only two points of view, your father's and Darwin's. The dissection of a single animal, the observation of the marvelous linkage of its life with its environment must, it seems to me, immediately convince one of the impossibility that it could arise as it now is and lives from a mere combination of physical and chemical forces.

If one is not willing, with Darwin, to have the present organic world develop gradually from the simplest beginnings and to have species emerge from one another and be perfected by the struggle for existence among themselves, there remains, it seems to me, for those who find contentment in empty words, no choice but to interpret them as the incarnate thoughts of the creator, who with infinite wisdom arranged the infinitely complicated relationships of internal structure and the external relations of species to species.

The strongest factual considerations against this last view appear to me to be in rudimentary, seemingly useless organs. I do not see how one can bring these into harmony with the infinite wisdom of the creator. The excuse that they belong to a bauplan [body plan] of the class as it was once drawn up does not hold water; for one often finds, close to those animals in which an organ is atrophied and apparently already completely useless, others which lack it entirely, and that shows that it is not indispensable even for the "common bauplan." If it could be shown that an organ were itself really without function for the whole life of an animal, its derivation from an "infinite wisdom" would be disproved. Unfortunately, we are still so ignorant of the conditions of life even of the best-known species, that such a demonstration is scarcely possible.

Fritz then tells a cautionary tale about "how careful one must be when declaring any organ to be useless:"

You are familiar with the small pencil-shaped appendage which *Squilla* [a mantis shrimp] carries on the last three pairs of thoracic feet. It always seemed to me a completely superfluous appendage, and through repeated observations of living animals I was unable to find any use for it. Now that von Hensen's excellent "Studies on the auditory organ of Decapods"[104] has induced me to look over the "hearing hairs" of various crustaceans, I have found that the aforementioned appendages have the most magnificent hearing hairs and are thus the auditory organs of *Squilla*.[105]

Agassiz remained unconvinced and in his next letter raised still another objection to the Darwinian view, namely that the transformation of one body plan to another would require either "an infinite number of forms or an infinite time for infinitesimal changes." Using mathematical formulae to describe body plans, he could transform the plan of radiate animals to that of bilaterally symmetrical ones like molluscs only though an infinite number of steps, yet the earth clearly had a finite age and there had been a finite number of species.[106] Fritz, however, would have none of it. Conceding the finitude of the earth and its inhabitants, he objected:

> in order to use this as an argument against Darwin, it would have to be shown that the gap existing between different organic beings is really infinite, or following your illustration, for example, that the "organic equations" of molluscs and radiates are really such that one can be transformed into the other only by an infinite progression. . . . That proof is lacking from your considerations.

Fritz also pointed out that the eggs of coelenterates and molluscs are extremely similar and yet give rise to completely different adult animals; there cannot be an infinite gap between the adults because they "arise from nearly identical primary forms (eggs)." And lastly, in an argument like that against Zeno's paradox, Fritz says "An arc of a circle becomes a straight line if $r = \infty$ ; but a curved tentacle does not on that account require infinite time to be straightened."[107]

In his response in November 1866,[108] Agassiz grants the objections but repeats his belief that Darwinian theory leads "naturally to the producing of organic out of inorganic, working during an infinite times and through infinite forms." And he inverts Fritz's argument about the divergence of adult animals arising from similar eggs by asking why "we never see these eggs developing into *different* classes from the animals which laid them," as Darwin's theory would predict.

It was the same point he had made nearly three years earlier, in January 1864.

In March 1867 Fritz returned to an early point of disagreement between them, the relationships of Echinoderms and Coelenterates (including what are now separated as comb-jellies). Louis Agassiz stood with Cuvier in placing both groups in the Radiata, while Fritz believed that Echinoderms were not radiate animals, since they had bilaterally symmetrical larvae.[109]

Fritz wrote to the zoologist Wilhelm Keferstein in 1869:

> The unity of the Radiata received its first blow with Joh. Müller's discovery of bilateral Echinoderm larvae. [Louis] Agassiz rightly appreciated the significance of this fact and made every possible attempt to put the larvae of Echinoderms back in the radiate type. "The larvae of Echinoderms are never bilateral, they only appear to be so," he told me in a letter. You know that Alexander Agassiz holds the same view in his splendid Embryology of the Starfish. I do not think it indiscrete of me to tell you that this brilliant investigator is now beginning to have serious doubts [as he wrote]: "I begin to have very serious doubts concerning the existence of types.... The embryology of Echinoderms and of some of the Annelids certainly is pointing out coincidences and affinities which the study of the mature animals was far from showing."[110] If someone who knows Echinoderms so well, and is also such a resolute opponent of Darwin's views, says such a thing, we may surely discard the echinoderm type as something sharply circumscribed.[111]

Alexander Agassiz's letter of November 1868, quoted above, was his first to Fritz in nearly two years, during which time he had been away from Cambridge managing the family copper mines near Lake Superior.[112] Considering Agassiz's earlier resistance to Fritz's arguments, it is surprising that within a year he seems to have come round to accepting at least some of Darwin's theories. Fritz reported to his brother Hermann in February 1870:

> A recent letter [lost] from Alexander Agassiz, who is now journeying through Europe to recover his health, has given me great surprise and joy. We have corresponded rather actively and have argued much about Darwinism, and I now hear that A. Agassiz is well on his way to becoming a Darwinian. He has

even visited Darwin and was completely charmed by him. Darwin wrote me about him: "We like him very much. He is a great admirer of yours, and he tells me that your book and correspondence first made him believe in evolution."[113]

By the time Fritz received the letters from Agassiz and Darwin, however, he had left Desterro and marine zoology and was once again a pioneer farmer in the forest of the Itajaí valley.

# 8

# Botany and the Return
# to the Itajaí Valley, 1867–1872

Even before he left Desterro in 1867, Fritz expanded his interests into botany, largely in response to Darwin's publications and letters. "Since I last wrote you," he reported to Max Schultze at the end of 1865, "I have been in active correspondence with Darwin and have already had three letters from him (August, September and October), as well as his orchid book and articles on dimorphic plants."[2]

Scarcely had Darwin's paper on climbing plants[3] reached Desterro, than Fritz searched his vicinity for local examples. On 12 August 1865 he wrote to Darwin:

> A few days ago I received your article on Climbing Plants. . . . I have read it with the greatest interest and am very pleased that my attention has been directed to these remarkable plants, which are so extraordinarily common in our flora. After reading your work, in a couple of days I collected in the vicinity of Desterro the following genera of climbing plants . . .

and there follows a list of over 40 genera classified by their methods of climbing.[4] Over the next few months Fritz sent further observations on climbing plants to Darwin, who submitted them to the Linnean Society as Fritz's first paper in English[5]. Even his children observed climbing plants with their father, as they had earlier fished with him in the sea. And in doing so, Rosa, who was then eleven years old, made the original observation that the tip of the stem of a flax plant had a characteristic revolving motion, following the sun.[6] Darwin's book on orchid pollination reached Brazil the same year, and again Fritz followed the directions in which it pointed. He devoted years of work to orchids, although he published very little on them, and sent many observations to his brother Hermann and to Darwin, who used some of them in the second edition of the orchid book.[7]

Fritz shared the excitement of his research by regular letters to his brother Hermann and encouraged him to respond. "At one o'clock in the morning let me ask you in conclusion to write more regularly; the more often we correspond the more we will have to write about, and with our equally keen interest in Darwin's theory I think that a more frequent exchange of ideas would be beneficial and stimulating."[8] He urged his brother to work on pollination biology, the subject for which Hermann Müller became famous. The relationship of insects to the pollination of plants, he wrote to Hermann, is:

> a subject for which you would be particularly well qualified, having been as much occupied with entomology as with botany. For there is certainly still an immense amount to be discovered. I have sent a note to the *Botanische Zeitung* about one example, a member of the Rubiaceae (*Martha* or *Posoqueria*), which may now be already in print and have reached you.[9] Darwin, to whom I wrote about it, and who is experienced in this field, pronounced this case to be "one of the most extraordinary, that I have ever read."[10] As strange as it may sound, I believe that it surely shows that we owe all the colorful displays, abundant forms and sweet scents of the world of flowers to insects, and that, on the other hand, the bright colors of insects are due in no small part to the flowers on which they spend time.[11]

Fritz's observations on *Posoqueria* started when he was out walking and encountered "a shrub adorned by white flowers with a marvelous scent" but with no pollen in the anthers. He soon found out that *Posoqueria* had a mechanism for avoiding self-pollination, a story that Darwin called "as wonderful as that of the most wonderful orchid:"

> The stamens . . . are irritable, so that as soon as a moth visits a flower, the anthers explode and cover the insect with pollen; one of the filaments . . . then moves and closes the flower for about twelve hours, after which time it resumes its original position.

143

Thus the stigma cannot be fertilised by pollen from the same flower, but only by that brought by a moth from some other flower.[12]

Although Darwin's letters to his far-flung network of correspondents could seem badgering in their quest for facts, the ones he wrote to Fritz were frequently in a different spirit, perhaps more like those from Darwin to his friends and allies in Britain, where he "was unwilling to appear quite so exploitative."[13] Of course Darwin queried Fritz on his sub-tropical experience, but he also shared results or asked Fritz's opinion of his latest book or idea, an opinion that he valued more highly "than that of almost anyone," even when it was unfavorable.[14] Fritz's letters contained a wide-ranging wealth of observations and experimental results, sometimes illustrated in pencil or watercolor (Figs. 9 and 10), or enclosing pressed flowers or butterfly wings. Before he thought about publishing a new discovery he often wrote to his friends and offered it to them for publication.

*Fig. 9. Letter from Fritz Müller to Charles Darwin, 1 April 1867, p. 1, with attached watercolor of crab. MS. DAR. 110.B:111-112. Courtesy of the Syndics of Cambridge University Library.*

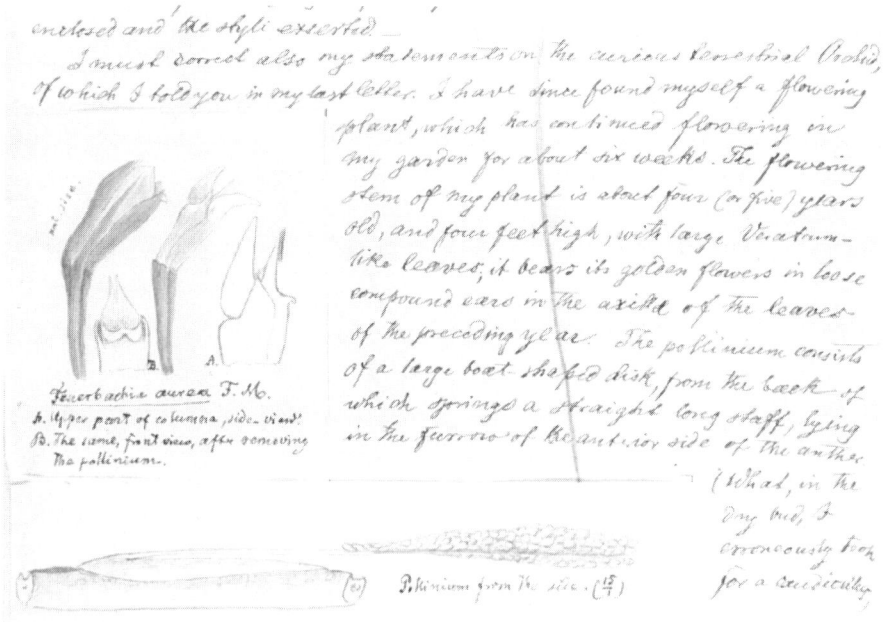

*Fig. 10. Letter from Fritz Müller to Charles Darwin, 2 June 1867, p. 1, with attached watercolor and pencil illustrations of an orchid flower. MS. DAR. 110.B:113-114. Courtesy of the Syndics of Cambridge University Library.*

Hence many of his observations were published by others, including Max Schultze, Hermann Müller, Friedrich Hildebrand[15] and Friedrich Ludwig[16] in Germany; Henri Milne-Edwards in France[17]; Raphael Meldola[18] and, of course, Darwin in England. Fritz's name was probably always mentioned, but when Alfred Möller republished his collected writings in the *Werke* in 1915, he had great difficulty locating everything that had come from Fritz. Perhaps no other naturalist of Fritz's stature has ever shown less interest in personal fame or been so unconcerned about priority, although he was evidently delighted by the recognition of his peers.

Letters to and from Europe took several weeks to reach Fritz in Brazil. He noted the date of receipt on most of the letters from Darwin; they took an average of seven weeks to arrive, and even his usual immediate reply would rarely have completed the exchange in

145

less than four months. Books, journals, and articles probably took as long, so it is not surprising that he sometimes repeated a discovery already reported by someone else.

He treasured his correspondence but clearly missed personal contacts with like-minded people. The odd visit by a traveling naturalist was a festive occasion. The first one to call was Friedrich Gerstäcker (1816–1872), a German traveler who sailed round Cape Horn from Chile and spent a short time in Desterro in September 1861. In November 1862 several Spanish naturalists, who were completing a trip around the world in the frigate *Triumfo*, came for a fortnight's stay. "After having been for fully ten years the only 'sensitive soul' among the larvae (N.B., taking 'larvae' literally and not referring to the good citizens of Desterro[19]), you can imagine my delight in walking the shore with zoologists once again."[20]

Fritz returned in 1867 to a changed Blumenau. Fig. 11 shows the center of town as it appeared around that time.[21] Although there were few houses in the town itself, the settled part of the colony extended a good day and a half's march upstream and half a day's downstream, along the Itajaí and its tributaries, and other German settlements were scattered downstream as far as the town of Itajaí, at the mouth of the river. There were about 7000 German settlers in the Blumenau colony in 1867, but their dispersion prevented much in the way of community life. The colony already had 300 kilometers of roads and plenty of bridges, all of them the responsibility of the provincial government, and newly-arrived colonists could earn good wages in public works. The diversion of so much labor from agriculture may not have been favorable for the long-term development of the colony, but the income from lumber cut in local sawmills, and public money for roads and bridges, generated a temporary prosperity, and inns and small shops were built all over the colony.

There were all sorts of associations in Blumenau, including social clubs, choruses and a sharp-shooters club, but most of them led a tenuous existence because the settlers came from such a motley assortment of social and cultural backgrounds. The Cultural Society,[22] had more serious aims: the improvement of agriculture through instruction and exchange of collective experience, the introduction of suitable cultivated plants and domestic animals, and the thorough

Blumenau.

*Fig. 11. Blumenau, Santa Catarina, 1867. The sharp bend of the Itajaí River flows from left to right, with Garcia Brook, by this time bridged a little above its mouth, entering from the left. Velha Brook, on which the Müller brothers first settled in 1852, enters from the left just out of sight upstream. Tschudi, 1868–69,* Reisen durch Südamerika *III. Courtesy of the Syndics of Cambridge University Library.*

exploration of the region. Since Fritz's new official position as a provincial naturalist entailed most of those functions, it is no surprise that he and August Müller were among the Society's most active members, although August complained in the late 1860s that out of a hundred members only about a dozen usually attended its monthly meetings. August Müller's letters were Alfred Möller's principal source of information about agriculture and commerce in the colony at that time, but none was published and all have been lost. August recognized that Blumenau's ultimate independence would depend on its productive soil and the health of its inhabitants; saw-timber was sparse in the virgin forest and would soon be exhausted, and govern-

147

ment subsidies for road building were transient. Through his teaching in the Cultural Society and by his own family's example, he stressed agriculture as the only sure source of prosperity. It would feed the colony and furnish exports, chiefly sugar, tobacco, butter, lard, bacon, poultry, and eggs. Blumenau's isolation, however, was a continuing problem, and it would be years before its exports could make it to the markets of Rio de Janeiro or São Paulo.[23] A steamboat connected Blumenau with Desterro and other coastal towns, but it came up-stream only to the edge of the colony's territory. An expedition by the engineer Emílio Odebrecht[24] had shown that a road to the cattle-breeding highlands of the province was feasible and that there was still room for a thousand settlers on the arable land stretching westward from Blumenau to the foot of the Serra Geral, the escarpment that formed the divide with the great inland rivers. German immigration, however, was relatively slight. Italians were then arriving, and larger numbers would come later. Fritz was uneasy about the prospects:

> The southern part of the country, Rio Grande do Sul, Santa Catarina and Paraná, could become predominantly German, if the German government would promote emigration, rather than place every possible hindrance in its way. Unfortunately the topic cannot be discussed in the press; and of course we cannot speak openly of the prospect that a large German influx would become the dominant force in southern Brazil and would eventually displace the degenerate Latin element. I have not the slightest doubt that some day, though certainly not in our lifetimes, the Teutonic race will prevail in extra-tropical Brazil; it could be Germans, if Germany so wishes; unfortunately it is more likely to be English or Yankees.[25]

In 1874 Thomas Belt, viewing the indolent inhabitants of Nicaragua, made a similar prediction, that Central America would eventually be dominated by energetic North American immigrants.[26] German and other European immigrants have had an impact on the southern Brazilian states, but, like Belt's optimistic hope for North American immigration in Central America, Fritz's pessimistic fear that "Yankees" would eventually dominate southern Brazil has never been realized.

Fritz, the "old '48er" (a veteran of the Revolution), seldom revealed his German prejudices as clearly as he did in hoping for German culture to take over southern Brazil, but during the Franco-Prussian War (1870–71) he did so again in his enthusiasm over the flush of German victory. He had sent money to Hermann for the purchase of books but asked him to redirect the funds to aid wounded soldiers.[27]

The condition of the schools remained a sore point in the development of Blumenau. More than twenty private schools had been established across the colony by the Cultural Society, but suitable teachers were hard to find, since most of the colonists valued teachers far less than day laborers and were prepared to pay accordingly. Hermann Blumenau insisted on secular schools when he founded the colony, and in the 1850s there was one teacher recognized by the provincial government,[28] but August Müller ran a small private school himself for many years. Fritz educated his own daughters, as he had in Desterro, though often pressed for time to do it.

Fritz thus returned in 1867 as a provincial official to a Blumenau differing in many respects from the young settlement that he had left eleven years before. He now rented a house for his family near the center of town while deciding on a permanent home:

> My own land, like August's, lies on the north bank of the Itajaí, which lacks a land route, while there are good roads on this side as far as the colony extends up and downstream. We are therefore far more isolated over there than here on the south bank and depend constantly on our canoe, which is not very convenient, especially when the river is high and running strongly. Chiefly for the children's sake, I would like to find a suitable piece of land to buy on this side of the river.[29]

By September 1867 he had found the land, a farm of 16 or 20 hectares about twenty minutes downstream from the center of town on the right bank, with a small house on high ground offering a lovely view of the Itajaí. The proceeds from the sale of his former homestead covered the price of the new property, where he lived for nearly 30 years, until just before his death.[30] Until the mid-1870s, while he still felt himself to be a settler on the river in the virgin forest, most of his letters carried the address "Itajaí." With increasing frequency after 1875, and regularly from 1878 on, he wrote "Blumenau," suggesting that development along the road had by then connected him with the town.

Not much of his new property was immediately productive when he acquired it in 1867. The arable land lay in narrow strips between the road and the river, while across the road were hills covered with virgin forest. Hence Fritz, who was now 45, turned once again to the work of a pioneer, with all the hardships with which he was familiar. The hands that had dissected tiny crustaceans under the microscope and so expertly depicted orchid flowers for Darwin now took up axe and spade once more. In December 1867 Fritz wrote to his parents:

> Since the beginning of October I have had my hands full preparing more land for our most essential crops, but I was still able to get maize, yams, manioc, tajá (*Caladium*), sweet potatoes, gourds, cucumbers, and others, in the ground at the right time, and even planted a number of bananas. Happily, I am far stronger than I expected after eleven years of inactivity; I can handle an axe all day without much fatigue. Just now, with the help of two men, I have built a fence around a piece of pasture so that I can keep a cow. We had to bring long tough palm trunks, which we split for palings, down a hillside through thick forest: not especially easy or pleasant work. Sometimes we had to climb twenty times up and over a tree trunk which had driven itself into the ground or under a fallen tree at one end, or been jammed between two trees at the other.[31]

Natural disasters wiped out much of Fritz's work. In November 1868, twenty-two centimeters of rain fell in 15 hours, destroying some of his crops and sweeping away a piece of gently sloping fertile land on the riverbank and leaving a steep drop from the house to the river. It also wiped out a patch of *Alisma* (water-plantain) in which he had made observations on peduncle movement[32] and in which he hoped to extend those observations during the coming summer.[33] "Since everyone is busy on his own land, there are no laborers to be had, and after waiting fruitlessly for outside help I have had to clear a piece of forest myself in recent weeks."[34]

Observing nature was in Fritz's blood, as Alfred Möller noted many years later; whatever else he was doing, however carefully and conscientiously, seemed only an annoying interruption. He was perfectly cordial when talking with friends or neighbors, but as soon as the conversation turned, he almost unconsciously stepped aside to look at some insect, leaf, twig, or other natural object within reach. Even when at hard manual labor he looked around during every resting moment, his memory preserving images to be brought together later. Only by this kind of organization could he have produced such a volume of scientific work; subsistence alone would have occupied anyone else's life, especially in the first few years after the return to Blumenau, but of course he was also fulfilling his obligation to the Province to study the natural history of the region.

In April 1868, for example, he undertook a long botanical excursion to Boa Vista, a prairie-covered mountain top in the highlands of southern Santa Catarina. Accompanied by his nephew Johannes, he walked barefoot, as was his custom, down the coast to Desterro and thence inland on the Lajes road through the colony of Theresopolis (now Queçaba). It was autumn, and his attention was often drawn to plants in fruit, and especially to mechanisms of seed dispersal. The following excerpts are drawn from his account of the trip, written to Hermann in June 1868 and published in *Flora* the following year:

> We set out at daybreak on 27 April to walk to the mouth of the Itajaí. The way led partly through pasture land, partly through plantations of sugar cane or manioc, rarely through a piece of virgin forest.
>
> The pastures were surrounded by palm lath fence or hedges of prickly acacias, and we could usually recognize the nationality of the owner with fair certainty by its condition: a clean, smooth grassy expanse meant that it belonged to Germans, while on Brazilian land the grass was often completely overgrown with a yellow-flowered member of the mallow family (mata pasto, pasture-killer) and with all sorts of brush, especially *Cassia* [senna]. Farther downstream we frequently encountered a climbing plant (*Chamissoa*; Amarantaceae) with ripening fruit. The flowers are in large open panicles, and when the floral

sheaths later turn vivid red the plant becomes a real hedge ornament, still more so when the seeds ripen, as we found on the way home: they then look like white pearls on red panicles. (The seed is black but covered with a white aril.)

28 April. [Between the Luís Alves River and the mouth of the Itajaí] the route soon turned away from the river across a broad marshland toward the foot of the hills, and then back through the marshland to the river again.

We frequently encountered the delicate climbing fern *Lygodium*, a marsh-lover. It is remarkable how the few genera that are placed in the [fern] family Schizaeceae because of the form of their sporangia (*Aneimia, Schizaea, Lygodium* — I am not familiar with the fourth genus *Mohria*) differ from one another in appearance more than any two species among the thousands in the Polypodiaceae. Both the geographic dispersion of the group and the great diversity among the few species hint at the same cause, an enormous extinction of intermediate species.

The Itajaí River widens above its mouth into a broad harbor separated from the ocean by a narrow flat tongue of land projecting from the north. On the rugged rocky southern shore the little town of Itajaí presents a cheerful sight with its white buildings, which are mostly warehouses, but the surroundings are rather bleak and lack fresh water, which must be brought from the northern shore. On the way from the Little Itajaí ["Itajahý mirim" in Map 3] to the town we found ripe fruits of a common woody-stemmed climbing plant (Dilleniaceae, probably *Curatella*, locally called "cipó pão") [more likely *Dolicarpus*, according to Alfred Möller] whose fruits open in a characteristic way. They split along a meridian line about 3/4 of the circumference, then the husk disengages to about the middle of the receptacle and each of the two valves cracks from top to bottom. In this way are formed two wide scarlet-red wings, the end of each of which bears seeds enclosed in a succulent snow-white sheath.

29 April. About an hour beyond the Cambriú River [now Camboriu] we came to the foot of Morro do Boi (Oxen Hill), which is notorious for its bad road. Rainy nights and drizzly days had made the red clay immensely slippery, and the climb

up the steep road, with numerous stones, potholes and over-
hanging banks, was anything but pleasant. But the descent on
the even steeper southern slope was still worse. Mules and horses
had made a characteristic kind of staircase, as is usual on muddy
roads: each animal steps in the hoofprints of its predecessor and
in that way deep transverse muddy holes gradually develop,
separated by transverse ridges of more resistant clay from which,
in wet weather, it is easy to slip into the mud holes. We had to
watch our footing too closely to be able to look around very
much at the virgin forest; yet at the top of the hill we did find a
splendid specimen of a *Catasetum* that we hid behind a palm
trunk for our return journey. The orchid had a spike more than
a foot long with rather well-developed buds which we could
already recognize as male, but there was as yet no sign of the
serpentine appendages of the column (Darwin's "antennae") that
are characteristic of the male flowers. [The genus *Catasetum*
then included only male plants; the females and hermaphrodites
of the same species were assigned to other genera.[35]]

1 May. During my previous trips through this swampy shore
land, which were always in the summer, I had repeatedly found
a member of the Hippocrateaceae [now Celastraceae] in bloom.
Now we finally encountered it in fruit; the large round berries
enclose seeds covered with sweet mucilage and by themselves
distinguish this genus, *Salacia* (or *Tontelea*), from *Hippocratea*,
which has dehiscent capsules and winged seeds. The distinction
is similar to that between some genera of the Sapindaceae,
*Paullinia* on the one hand, and *Serjania* and *Urvillea* on the
other, which are absolutely identical in vegetative characters and
floral morphology. In these instances the devices for seed
dispersal, on the one hand by birds, on the other by the wind,
are evidently of comparatively recent origin, and that seems on
the whole to be a common situation. It is remarkable that even
in the family Compositae, which has long possessed a pappus
that is unsurpassed for wind dispersal, one genus, *Wulffia*, has
started to go in for berry-like fruits. ["The one species of *Wulffia*
that I have seen grows in the virgin forest, and here dispersal by
birds is certainly preferable."[36]]

7-10 May. In Theresopolis I looked up some acquaintances,
the Colony engineer Heeren and the Catholic priest Roer, a
farmer and close acquaintance of Anton Karsch, my Greifswald

university friend now in Münster. The priest is keenly interested in the natural sciences and visits me whenever he is in Desterro, even though he had been warned on the sea voyage from Europe that I was a dreadful godless man who had not even had his children baptized.

11 May. [On a side excursion in the Theresopolis colony, they ascended the Capivaras river three hours further] to Busch's inn, which we reached around 3:30 P.M. A friendly, strapping chatty woman soon filled our empty stomachs with solid Westphalian fare, and until nightfall we strolled along the riverbank and in the vegetation nearby. We were surrounded by a world of plants differing greatly from that on the Itajaí, no doubt due more to the higher elevation than to the lighter sandy soil. Except for a few fine cedars (*Cedrela*, a commercial mahogany), the palm-less broadleaf forest was shorter than it is here on the Itajaí, and the stately araucarias, which are completely lacking here, rose to twice the height of the broad-leaved trees. I have seen our araucaria several times figured in German children's books, but always from conical greenhouse specimens with branches starting right at the bottom of the trunk. Young trees are in fact like that, for example the two which stand in front of my house and are perhaps six years old. But an old *Araucaria brasiliensis* looks just like a Latin T; sometimes the trunk has a few additional branches which form similar Ts at different heights. On the upper Capivaras, araucaria replaces the juçara palm, which provides us with posts, beams and lath, and the uricana palm (*Geonoma*), whose leaves furnish the roof of the settler's first cabin. Houses on the Capivaras are built of araucaria timbers, walls clad with araucaria planks and roofs covered with araucaria shingles.

15 May. In the afternoon, accompanied by the engineer Heeren, we set out from Theresopolis to S. Isabel, I with my big vasculum, Heeren and Johannes each with a thick red wool blanket for the cold nights that we expected. We crossed the Cubatão River on a bridge under construction and followed the right bank of Cedar Brook which we then forded in order to enter a small tributary valley. That valley is still uninhabited, so we walked in the shade of a beautiful virgin forest in which there was a common tree fern with its trunk covered by a thick black mat of rootlets. At the top of an imposing mountain we reached

the boundary of S. Isabel Colony, to the center of which we descended in twilight. On the way, we met our friend Reusing, who wished to accompany us to Boa Vista, and who introduced us to his bachelor household. Our evening meal concluded with boiled araucaria seeds, the staple of Indians and peccaries. To me they tasted excellent, something between potatoes and chestnuts. We then fixed our sleeping place of reed matting with a few skins of "lions" and "tigers," as they call pumas and jaguars around here.

17 May. We followed the Rio Taquaras, climbing slowly and wading from left bank to right, and in scarcely an hour we reached the foot of the mountain of Boa Vista. Here began a rather difficult climb. At first there were a few places with the familiar steps where mules had trampled deep mud holes. We then went steeply up a stony track trampled by innumerable herds of cattle. The blackberry bushes often detained us, not because of their thorns but rather the abundance of fruit. Among them bloomed *Fuchsia* and the gorgeous melasto-mataceous *Pleroma*, whose large flowers open snow white and gradually turn dark reddish-purple. The bushes are thus simulta-neously adorned with white, pink and dark purple flowers. Some twenty feet below the mountain top, sandstone replaced the shale that had accompanied us till now. When we stepped onto the summit we had before us a broad nearly level grassy expanse (campo) of about two square miles, broken here and there by small isolated bits of low forest, so-called capões. The treelessness of the campo is not caused by elevation, because westward one can see even higher well-wooded mountains, and there is a smaller campo at Invernadinha, significantly lower than Boa Vista. Perhaps trees do not thrive on it because the nearly horizontal sandstone strata are covered at most with such a thin layer of soil. The plant life has altogether special charac-teristics, the grasses with tough narrow leaves, the other gener-ally low plants with small thickly-crowded leaves. Unfortunately we found almost nothing in bloom: only a few blue *Polygala* looking like the German species, and a little *Lobelia*. I collected seeds of a fragrant labiate [mint] and of two small shrubs of the [heath] family Ericaceae scarcely nine inches tall: a *Gaylussacia* with little yellowish berries and (probably) an *Andromeda*. Of the Ericaceae here I am otherwise familiar only with a *Vaccinium*

that grows close to the coast, gets quite tall and bears beautiful red flowers and blue fruits ("camarinhas") that taste like blueberries.

We settled ourselves at the edge of a capão, after clearing the vegetation with our machetes so as to be safe from snakes, and ate our breakfast of corn bread and hard cheese. While Reusing and Johannes rested in the grass, I roamed through the capão with Heeren; the low gnarled trees were mostly Myrtaceae (probably *Eugenia*). They were covered with lichens and mosses, and there were also orchids, among them a species new to me (by appearances perhaps an *Oncidium* or a *Gomezia*). The ground was for the most part thickly covered with prickly bromeliads.

We strolled across the campo for a few hours to enjoy the prospect, for in truth this campo fully deserves its name "beautiful view." The sky cleared by midday, and the view opened in nearly all directions: to the west the steep jagged crest of the Serra, through which the road to the highlands ascends; far to the north Morro Bahú, a hill on the Luíz Alves in the region of the lower Itajaí. All around us lay a confusion of dark wooded mountains and valleys, and not a sign of human settlement. The mountain of Boa Vista is said to be completely isolated and to drop off steeply into all of the surrounding valleys.

We returned from Boa Vista to our previous night's lodging, which we reached by 4 o'clock.

18 May. We . . . soon reached the vicinity of the Rio Antas, roaring below us in the valley. The forest was nearly without understory; besides tall trees, which were not growing very thickly, and the common tomentose tree fern, the ground was almost entirely covered by a tall bamboo. Here we found a splendid fruiting umbel of a *Bomarea* (a climbing *Allstroemeria*; Amaryllidaceae), with more than thirty 20-centimeter pedicels at the end of each of which, by the dehiscence of its three valves, the fruit forms a graceful little basket full of beautiful spherical red seeds. This excursion introduced me to four plants in which the brightly-colored seeds do not fall after the dehiscence of the fruit, and to date I know more than twenty families in which such plants occur.

28 May. From Morro do Boi we took with us our *Catasetum*, now blooming and equipped with long "antennae."

1 June. Returned home in a drizzle.[37]

In July Fritz made a short excursion up the Itajaí River in the company of August, who wanted to look at a piece of land, and later in the week as he was writing up the journey he sent Hermann a report:

> On Sunday evening August came by, shod and in a heavy blue wool shirt, an oar in his hand, a Mühlberger sack (sent by Father) with provisions, and a musket on his shoulder, and announced to me that his neighbor Seiffert[38] would call for us early next morning in his big canoe. My own preparations were quickly made: a *mate* walking stick[39], machete, fire lighter, shirt and pants, in addition to my vasculum, in which was packed a piece of bread and some cold roast pork, and everything rolled up in a red blanket.
>
> The next morning between 3 and 4, just as coffee was ready, the shoemaker Seiffert appeared, a cheerful and active little man of 60 years, with his two oldest sons, powerful fellows of 20 and 22. We traveled upstream by moonlight to the vicinity of the salto [the waterfall at the top of navigation on the Itajaí] where we disembarked opposite the mouth of the Itoupava and continued our journey on foot. By daybreak we were at the inn of our compatriot K. His house is nearly the last one up river with a tile roof; farther on the roofs are of uricana palm leaves. After a brief rest for breakfast somewhat below Encano Brook, we marched on without delay to the last inn, which we reached around midday. Where the path led through forest, it was frightfully bad in places on account of the recent rains. About an hour beyond the inn we reached what is now the last settlement on the Itajaí River, here called the Rio Morto (Dead River) because of its gentle current. We walked through the forest on a newly-made road about another half hour to an imposing stream, the Warnow, named by the first settlers after their river at home [Rostock in northern Germany]. Here a piece of virgin forest had already been felled, and we found a party of twenty road-builders lodged in a large shelter. We ourselves took up quarters in a small shelter in which the forest cutters had stayed.

Such a shelter is very easily built: two upright posts carry a palm trunk, and the latter a roof of uricana leaves; the side walls and floor are of palm leaves. At dusk we lit a big fire in front of our shelter, brewed coffee and chatted away the evening with the overseer of the road crew. I slept pretty well on the palm-leaf bed, rolled up in my blanket with my vasculum as a pillow.

The next morning we crossed the Warnow and went on upriver. Our destination was not far and would have been reached in an hour at most on a good road, but after a few minutes the road ended, and our route was full of lianas, criss-crossed by tree trunks. We had to clamber through two clearings in which fallen trees lay every which way in confusion. Our way then led along a steep mountainside and across several deep ravines; at nearly every step we had to grasp a bush or a liana to avoid falling. Seiffert's sons, who were to supply us with game for the midday meal, led the way. The first thing they saw was a howler monkey, which hid itself so cleverly among the branches of a tall tree that they could not shoot it down. Not so lucky were two jacutingas (*Penelope*), which the brothers shot shortly afterwards out of the same tree. August and I took a bird apiece to pluck as we walked.

Our destination was a piece of land which one of our neigh-bors had cleared in a level spit; he had recommended the adjacent land to August, and Seiffert also wished to look over the land upriver where his sons had a mind to settle. We found a cooking-pot and some mugs and spoons in a shelter there, and after a fire was made and one and a half jacutingas were in the pot (no more would fit), August roamed the forest with the boys, while the old man tended the fire and I climbed over fallen trees after orchids. When our comrades returned and the birds were well done, we took the latter out of the pot and mixing manioc meal to a stiff dough (pirão) in the greasy broth, each took a piece of meat in his left hand, sliced off bites with the knife in his right hand and helped himself to pirão. Coffee followed our tasty lunch, after which we started back. It was nearly dark when we reached the inn. Soon an immense dish of excellent manioc and a generous serving of smoked paca meat [spotted cavy, *Agouti paca*] were steaming on the table. The former is the tastiest of all the starchy roots, the latter the most delicious game that I had eaten in fourteen years.

158

Wednesday, like the two previous days, brought us fine weather, and we were home in the afternoon in good time. My vasculum was crammed with orchids. As big as it is, it scarcely held a half-dozen specimens; a fine example of *Gongora bufonia*, which has one of the most curiously shaped flowers, was too heavy for me on such a long march, and I left it in the care of a casual acquaintance along the way. If the weather remains as nice as it has been this week, I am thinking of going back up to the Warnow again next Monday to search at my leisure over the many trees hewn down along the new road and in various clearings. I expect with ease to collect a wagon-load, which, excepting what I do not yet have myself, ought to go to Kew.[40]

During the two years after he returned to the Itajaí in 1867, Fritz communicated regularly with J. D. Hooker at the Royal Botanic Gardens, Kew.[41] They exchanged seeds, and Fritz sent 483 plant specimens to Kew for identification.[42]

Although Fritz evidently had time for excursions like these after moving back to the Itajaí, the work of being a pioneer kept him for a time from starting any major scientific projects. His submissions of manuscripts for publication had dried up two years before he left Desterro, and in the two years after his return to Blumenau in September 1867 he sent off only four articles, the two longest of which, on marine ostracods and parasitic isopods, were reports of observations made earlier on the coast. An additional four were published by his correspondents. His letters were also scarcer between 1868 and 1870 than before or after. Nevertheless, the arrival of Darwin's orchid book[43] and his papers on heterostyly in *Lythrum* and *Linum*[44] late in 1865[45] stimulated Fritz to look at pollination in the local orchids and at the phenomenon of heterostyly. Heterostyled plants are those in which there is polymorphism in floral characters, with two or three forms differing in the relative positions of the anthers and the stigmatic surface at the top of the style where pollen germinates, and perhaps also in the size of pollen grains and the structure of the stigma. Although a difference in style length and the height of the anthers is a conspicuous feature of heterostyled species, Darwin emphasized in his *Forms of Flowers* that the ultimate criterion was "finding that pollen must be applied from the one form to the other in order to ensure complete fertility,"[46] and he recognized that heterostyly therefore prevented self-fertilization.

When the 4th English edition of *The Origin* arrived from Darwin in October 1866, Fritz picked out heterostyly as the most interesting among the "mass of new material missing in the first German edition," as he wrote to Hermann:

> The most important novelty seems to me the discussion of dimorphism and trimorphism in plants, wherein is removed the last mainstay of the usual species concept, namely that species produce sterile hybrids while varieties give fertile ones. According to D's careful studies over many years, the illegitimate offspring of dimorphic and trimorphic plants behave in all respects exactly like hybrids between different species.[47]

Fritz had in the meantime been looking for dimorphic plants himself and reported to his brother ten examples in a variety of families. His letters to Darwin begin to contain notes on dimorphic plants and to include dried flowers, many of which Darwin cut out and filed separately for later use. Of the seventeen heterostylous genera in the Rubiaceae that Darwin described in *Forms of Flowers*, nine were from Fritz's specimens, including one of the most remarkable, a species of *Faramea* in which the pollen grains and stigmas of the two forms of flowers differ in size and morphology. Darwin tells the story from Müller's paper:[48]

> The pollen-grains [of the short-styled form] are to those of the [long-styled] form as 100 to 67 in diameter. But the pollen-grains of the two forms differ in a much more remarkable manner, of which no other instance is known; those from the short-styled flowers being covered with sharp points; the smaller ones from the long-styled being quite smooth.[49]

Fritz also pointed out a difference in floral behavior in the two forms, and showed it to be another example of an adaptation not yet perfected by natural selection, as Darwin relates:

> the stamens . . . rotate on their axes in . . . the short-styled [form], in order that their pollen should be brushed off by insects and transported to the stigmas of the other form. In the long-styled flowers the anthers of the short enclosed stamens, do not rotate on their axes but dehisce on their inner sides, as is the

common rule with the Rubiaceae; and this is the best position
for the adherence of the pollen-grains to the proboscis of an
entering insect. Fritz Müller therefore infers that as the plant
became heterostyled, and as the stamens of the short-styled form
increased in length, they gradually acquired the highly beneficial
power of rotating on their own axes. But he has further shown
. . . that this power has not as yet been perfected; and, consequently, that a certain proportion of the pollen is rendered
useless, namely that from the anthers which do not rotate
properly.[50]

Fritz, who never lost an opportunity to taunt creationists, added
in his own account that this "weakness . . . will seem disturbing and
inexplicable to those who, with Agassiz, see species as the embodied
thoughts of the 'Creator.' Does it not look as though the 'Creator'
understood the right way but could not accomplish it — as though
he had the desire but not the ability?"[51] In this, as in many other
cases, Fritz echoed Darwin's own argument, that the small variations
from which adaptations were fashioned by natural selection made no
sense as things foreordained. Darwin had written to Charles Lyell in
1861:

> If you say that God *ordained* that at some time & place a dozen
> slight variations should arise, & that one of them alone should
> be preserved in the struggle for life, & that the other eleven
> should perish in the first, or few first, generations; than the
> saying seems to me mere verbiage. — It comes to merely saying
> that everything that is, is ordained.[52]

Fritz also reacted to Darwin's account of Bates's "wonderful
observations of Amazonian butterflies," which first appeared in the
4th edition of *The Origin*, and suggested that a previously puzzling
similarity between the flowers of two unrelated shoreline plants, a
bindweed and a legume, might be a mimetic resemblance.[53] If the
flower color of one species was "a well-recognized signal to the local
insects of a good nectar meal," any member of the other species with
similar color "could easily deceive the insects and attract them as well
and in this way would the first similarly-colored flowers be more fully
pollinated."[54] This is Fritz's first reference to mimicry, a phenomenon

about which he was already "beating his brains out," and which would occupy him increasingly over the decade of the 1870s.[55]

Fritz's receipt of Darwin's orchid book while he was still in Desterro sent him immediately into the field, and in letters to the botanist Friedrich Hildebrand, and especially to his brother Hermann and to Darwin, he reported observations and experiments on pollination and other aspects of orchid biology. He left his orchid collection behind when he moved back to the Itajaí in 1867 but soon began building a new one, and he ultimately accumulated a mass of material on orchids, including pencil and watercolor sketches, some of which he sent to Darwin and many of which were found among his papers after his death. From the care with which he had preserved those notes and drawings it was clear that he had at one time considered publishing his orchid material as a separate book.[56] In 1871 Hermann asked his brother, "How stands it with the publication on orchids that you once had in mind? Must your many interesting observations, which even Darwin confidently assumes you will publish in a special work, be lost to our contemporaries and descendants?"[57] Fritz's preoccupation with being a pioneer once again in the late 1860s may have kept him from working up the orchid material, but he also evidently agreed with Darwin that "observing is much better than writing," a sentiment in English attributed to him by Alfred Möller. Darwin had written to Asa Gray, "what much better fun observing is than writing,"[58] though both Fritz and Darwin managed to do a good deal of the latter.

Fritz was among the first to study pollination in epiphytic orchids in their native habitats. With respect to previous studies of the effects of self-pollination, for example, Darwin wrote in the 2nd edition of *Variation*:

> As these orchids had been grown under unnatural conditions in hot-houses, I concluded that their self-sterility was due to this cause. But Fritz Müller informs[59] me that at Desterro, in Brazil, he fertilised above one hundred flowers of the above-mentioned *Oncidium flexuosum*, which is there endemic, with its own pollen, and with that taken from distinct plants: all the former were sterile, whilst those fertilised by pollen from any *other plant* of the same species were fertile.[60]

Darwin reported that Fritz had repeated these experiments on a large scale and on several other species, and he also wrote of another "highly remarkable" observation:[61]

> namely, that with various orchids the plant's own pollen not only fails to impregnate the flower, but acts on the stigma, and is acted on, in an injurious or poisonous manner. This is shown by the surface of the stigma in contact with the pollen, and by the pollen itself, becoming in from three to five days dark brown, and then decaying. The discoloration and decay are not caused by parasitic cryptograms [Darwin intended "cryptogams"], which were observed by Fritz Müller in only a single instance.[62]

These observations were first published in 1868 as excerpts from a letter from Fritz to Hildebrand in 1867.[63] Two subsequent discursive letters to Hildebrand, and one to Hermann Müller, also appeared in the *Botanische Zeitung*[64], and Darwin used these and his own letters from Fritz as sources of information for *Orchids* and for *Variation*. One observation scattered over these various sources and reported briefly in the 2nd edition of the orchid book[65] touches on Fritz's interest in the role of natural selection in molding variation, in this case favoring an evidently ancestral character. From the Itajaí, Fritz wrote to Hildebrand and to Hermann:

> There is a rather common species of *Epidendrum* on the island of Santa Catarina which develops three fertile anthers. The two lateral ones serve for self-fertilization, the middle one, as in other *Epidendrum* species, can be removed only by insects, which seems to occur extremely rarely. Here on the Itajaí there is an *Epidendrum* which is so similar to that triandrous species that it would scarcely be considered more than a variety of it, and this one is monandrous. The triandrous species, or variety, is nearly scentless, the monandrous one has a very strong spicy scent. Lateral anthers have of course been observed occasionally in other orchids, though they are usually missing. The reason that natural selection has again made them a permanent feature of the Sta. Catarina species may be that it was visited by few or no insects and that self-fertilization was therefore of advantage. It is after all most remarkable for two almost indistinguishable forms to differ in the number of anthers, when that number serves to separate the two principal groups of the family.[66]

In any case the monandrous form from the virgin forest is the original one; the appearance of lateral anthers is a throwback to a long lost character which in a region almost completely lacking virgin forest was apparently maintained by natural selection because the necessary pollinating insects were lost with the virgin forest, and the self-pollination that was once eliminated would once again become advantageous. On [the island of] Sta. Catarina many orchids that depend on insects, for example the common *Oncidium flexuosum*, hardly ever produce seed, far fewer than here. . . . It is also remarkable that the need for insect pollination is lost together with the scent.[67]

Aside from these examples, nearly all of Fritz's observations of orchids are recorded only in letters unpublished at the time, and in the documents left at his death but now lost.

On 30 January 1868, the date of publication,[68] Darwin sent to Fritz a copy of *The Variation of Animals and Plants under Domestication*, and wrote, "I sh^d very much like to hear what you think of 'Pangenesis,' tho' I fear it will appear to everyone far too speculative."[69] Darwin hypothesized pangenesis as a process by which all the cells of the body in each stage of development produce gemmules which aggregate to form the sexual elements (eggs and sperms) and therefore give rise to progeny through fertilization and subsequent development.[70] Fritz received the book on 1 April[71] and the letter on the 6th, and he replied on the 22nd:

> You must permit me to begin this letter by expressing my sincere and cordial thanks for the great pleasure, which I have derived from the lecture of your admirable work on Variation under Domestication. You say, that the greater part is not meant to be read; but I have read, with increasing interest, the whole work from the first to the last page. [Averaging 45 pages a day, not bad for a farmer in harvest season.]
>
> As to "Pangenesis", on which you wish to hear my opinion, my first impression, when for the first time I rapidly read your exposition, was the very same, which I formerly had at the first lecture of your "Origin of species", viz. that it was a fanciful speculation; but you know, that notwithstanding this first impression I am now fully convinced of the truth of the views maintained in the "Origin". The hypothesis of "Pangenesis"

would certainly account for, and connect several great classes of facts hitherto isolated and unexplained; it can also hardly be doubted, that eggs, spermatozoa, ovules of plants and pollengrains, notwithstanding their minute size and apparent simplicity, must be highly complicated structures, containing, as it were, a photograph of the whole organisation, from which they are derived. But I think, it will be better to delay my objections, till I shall have reflected more maturely on the subject.[72]

Fritz apparently never sent his more mature reflections on pangenesis to Darwin, but, although he thought that Darwin "had it fundamentally right,"[73] he remained unconvinced. In 1876, on receiving Haeckel's book on "perigenesis,"[74] he responded to the author with a long critique of the idea and added that he could as little reconcile himself to it as to pangenesis.[75] Haeckel derived perigenesis from an earlier theory that "the vibrations of an external stimulus are transferred to the nervous system and hence to all other organs, especially to the developing gametes."[76] He defined it as "the periodic generation of waves by the atoms of life or plastidules."[77] Fritz complained to Hermann:

> I cannot like perigenesis any more than pangenesis, which it is supposed to replace. It seems to me arbitrary to liken the periodic appearance of reproductive phenomena to a "wave motion." One might as well call it "cyclic," "cycloidic," "spiral," etc. Mathematical relationships like that have the evil of spreading the false appearance of scientific certainty. In other respects the basic idea of perigenesis is far more plausible than that of pangenesis, but far less useful, it seems to me, for explaining specific hereditary phenomena.[78]

Nevertheless, he kept his eyes open for evidence of pangenesis, as he reported to his brother Hermann and to Darwin early in 1869:

> Last year I harvested an ear of maize which had six dirty bluish-green kernels among its pale yellow kernels. I planted yellow and bluish kernels separately; on the ears coming from the former scarcely 1/1000 bluish kernels developed, on those of the latter they were more than 1/5 of the total.[79]

On the hypothesis of Pangenesis the facts might be explained
by assuming that in the seeds from an individual flower the
gemmulae derived from this flower are more numerous than
those from any other flower on the plant, and that therefore in
the offspring flowers of the same kind are more numerous, than
in the mother-plant. Do you think, that this will hold good as a
general rule?[80]

Fritz was of course unaware of transposable elements in maize,
which may have accounted for his variably-bluish seeds, but their
initially controversial recognition by Barbara McClintock was over a
century away.[81] He also did not know about the inheritance of seed
color (endosperm) in maize, in which the female parent contributes
two sets of genes, the male parent one.

Fritz suggested how what we would call "neutral" variation
might become distributed among allied species:

I now intend, as soon as I have time, to start experiments with
plants which produce two sorts of flowers, for example, 4-parted
and 5-parted, which occur in many Rubiaceae and
Melastomataceae, to see whether plants growing from seeds of 4-
parted flowers pollinated by pollen of a similar plant, for
example, always produce more numerous 4-parted flowers than
the mother did. Were this the case, if a plant produced two sorts
of flowers with no advantage over one another in the struggle for
existence, and if one sort of flower was more numerous, then it
would be easy to show that the other sort must decrease more
and more in each succeeding generation. And that would
explain very simply the odd, seemingly perverse way in which
4-, 5- and 6-parted flowers are distributed among species and
genera in the families mentioned.[82]

Fritz was also experimenting on self- and cross-pollination in
plants other than orchids and was finding self-sterility to be common
even in species without heterostyly. In April 1868, for example, just
after receiving the first edition of *Variation* from Darwin, he sent off
the results of recent experiments on self-sterility in a *Bignonia* species:
there were three plants growing close together, and Fritz self-pollinated twenty-nine flowers of two of them and effected no fertiliza-
tions. He cross-pollinated thirty flowers of the same two plants, using
pollen from all three plants in three combinations, and obtained two

capsules of seed. Lastly, he pollinated five flowers of one of the three plants with pollen from a fourth plant growing some distance away, and all developed capsules. Darwin's account of these experiments in *Variation* is not quite correct in the details, and he overstates Fritz's conclusion: "Fritz Müller thinks that the three plants which grew near one another were probably seedlings from the same parent, and that from being closely related, they acted very feebly on one another."[83] He is probably referring to Fritz's letter of 14 March 1869,[84] for Fritz hedged in his published discussion of the *Bignonia* species:

> Were the three plants growing close to one another possibly seedlings from the same mother plant, perhaps having even sprouted from seeds in the same fruit and therefore infertile because of their close relationship? Or have they, by growing in the same place under the same conditions, become so similar to one another that the pollen of one of them has scarcely more effect on another one than its own pollen does? Or on the other hand, are they merely shoots of one individual that have acquired a small degree of reciprocal fertility by growing independently for years? Or lastly, was it a mere accident that in crosses with a neighbouring vine only two out of 30 flowers set fruit, whilst all of those pollinated from distant flowers did so? For the moment I dare not call any of these possibilities the more likely.[85]

In September 1868 he reported to Hermann that he was again occupied with Gärtner's book on plant hybrids.[86] He thought the author's style deadly dull and criticized him for paying insufficient attention to the fatal consequences of close inbreeding and of self-sterility. After listing the few European species which Gärtner said are self-sterile, Fritz suggested that "it would be interesting to determine if these plants are equally fertile with all other individuals of the same species," because "it seems more likely that this will not be the case, but that they will be fertilized more easily and fully by certain plants than by others. I intend to pay particular attention to these self-sterile plants and to carry out experiments on dimorphic and trimorphic plants and on hybrid pollination."[87]

The winter months of 1869–72 were taken up with studies of self- and cross-pollination in *Abutilon*,[88] a genus of self-sterile species in which Fritz intended to learn for himself about plant hybrids and to test Darwin's speculation in the 4th edition of *The Origin* with respect to Gärtner's statement that the fertility of species hybrids declines in succeeding generations: "I believe in nearly all these cases," wrote Darwin, "that fertility has been diminished . . . by too close interbreeding,"[89] rather than by hybridity itself. Fritz made an immense number of pollinations (over a thousand, he wrote to Hermann in September 1872), involving six native species and their complex hybrids, and by crossing hybrid plants of various sorts with their siblings and with other more distantly related individuals or with unrelated hybrids he showed that inbreeding was the important factor in reducing fertility and happily offered the evidence in support of Darwin's speculation.

The wide range of Fritz's interests at the time is revealed in three letters in early December 1868. To Ernst Haeckel on 7 December he sent his manuscript on the movement of the peduncles of *Alisma*,[90] referred to an article on crustacean morphology that he was preparing,[91] and commented on the reception of Darwinism in England and Germany, on self-sterility in orchids, on pangenesis, and on Kovalevsky's recent discovery of similarities in the development of ascidians and *Amphioxus*.[92] The ascidians are the largest group of tunicates, which together with *Amphioxus* and the vertebrates make up the phylum Chordata, but until Kovalevsky's papers of 1866–71 (see for example, the notice in the 1876 *Annals and Magazine of Natural History*, 19:69-70), their relationships were not recognized. Fritz had himself noticed the similarity of the tail of the tunicate *Clavelina* to that of a tadpole, and of the gills of ascidians to those of *Amphioxus*, suggesting the relationship of ascidians and vertebrates, "which I thought so fantastic in many respects that I did not venture to express it."[93]

The paper on *Alisma* related the daily movements of the peduncles of this aquatic plant to similar movements by which certain climbing plants wind around their supports: "The tip of the peduncle described a circle . . . and moved just like a young shoot of a bindweed, bean, or any other plant winding to the right." Fritz's object was to aid Darwin in the question of how the movements of climbing plants first arose: "It was a serious difficulty for Darwin's theory of the origin of species that hitherto these sorts of movements had been observed only in climbing plants, that they seemed to be a character-istic limited to them."[94] Now it was clear that such movements were widespread in non-climbers. Fritz added that similar movements had gone unnoticed even in common European flax until his daughter Rosa observed them in his garden several years earlier.

On 8 December Fritz sent his congratulations to Oscar Schmidt on becoming a Darwinian, and discussed some sponges (Schmidt's specialty) which he was dispatching.[95] And on the same day he wrote to his brother Hermann about extra-floral nectaries in orchids and the relationships between insect pollinators and flowering time, floral morphology, scent and nectar production. He also asked his brother to look for parasitic barnacles on a European shore crab.[96]

Casual comments in Fritz's letters show what a tenacious natural-ist he was in the face of daily distractions. His letter to Hermann, for example, closes:

> Today I harvested the first fruits from the bananas that I planted only last December. I now have my hands full planting maize, manioc, and yams, [but as soon as that is done] I plan to make a long journey up river and perhaps spend a couple of weeks in the forest with an engineer [Odebrecht].[97]

# 9
# Termites, Ants, Bees, and Sambaquis, 1871–1876

Before completing the *Abutilon* hybridizations in 1872, Fritz began to shift his attention to termites, which were common on the Itajaí but whose biology was then scarcely known. He was familiar with papers on termite systematics by Hermann Hagen (1817–1893), who had been brought by Louis Agassiz to Harvard's Museum of Comparative Zoology from Prussia in 1867 to be curator of entomology, and in 1869 he had already written Hagen the first of the thirty-five letters that survive:

> At the risk of offering you something long known — you would not hold it against me in this case, as a peasant in the wilderness, to be ignorant of the literature — I take the liberty of sending you a short description of a peculiar underground termite nest that we often find here in hard clay soils on hillsides.[2]

Fritz described a nest about eight inches high and two or three inches thick, suspended in an underground chamber and divided into twelve to fifteen horizontal compartments with connecting passages large enough for winged individuals but not the queen to pass through. He illustrated it in the letter and published a similar drawing in a paper on termite nests submitted three years later,[3] and it proved to be far from "something long known." When Hagen read a translation of the description at a meeting of the Boston Society of Natural History in January 1870, later published in the Society's *Proceedings*, he commented that "no such description of white ants' nests like this has ever been given before."[4]

Fritz also asked Hagen for a copy of the latter's monograph of the termites,[5] for "these animals are so frequently encountered here that I would like to learn more about them." Until Hagen's monograph arrived two years later, Fritz said nothing further about termites to his correspondents, but in October 1871 he wrote to his brother Hermann that since his *Abutilon* fruits were ripening and butterflies had not started flying, he had:

> taken up another subject that I had long wanted to study, the biology of our termites. Until now I have lacked the requisite literature, but I recently received Hagen's monograph and see from it that there are still quite a few things about them to be cleared up. [According to Hagen] no locality is known to have more than nine species. I already know of a dozen around here, and I believe that we have at least 20 or 30 species, based on my experience in other classes of animals in comparing what I found at first with what I actually discovered. The reason that others have found so few, and for the most part only winged males and females, is that they did not carry an axe or did not know how to use one. Apart from the few nest-building species, soldiers and immature stages are unobtainable without an axe. Yesterday I gave a popular lecture on termites to our Cultural Society, to acquaint my friends with these animals and especially so as to be able to say to them on my excursions, without a long explanation: "give me an axe and let me go termite-hunting on your land."[6]

Fritz sent the lecture with his letter, and also drawings of the soldiers of several species (Fig. 12).

With the impetus of Hagen's monograph, Fritz began gathering observations and submitted four publications on termites over the next three years. In July 1872 he sent off an article on termite dwellings, justifying it by Hagen's comment that almost nothing was known about the nests of many species.[7] In addition to the underground nest that he had described in 1869, he described those built in trees, on the ground, and among the roots of cabbage palm (palmito). "The most serious enemies of this last species are armadillos," he wrote:

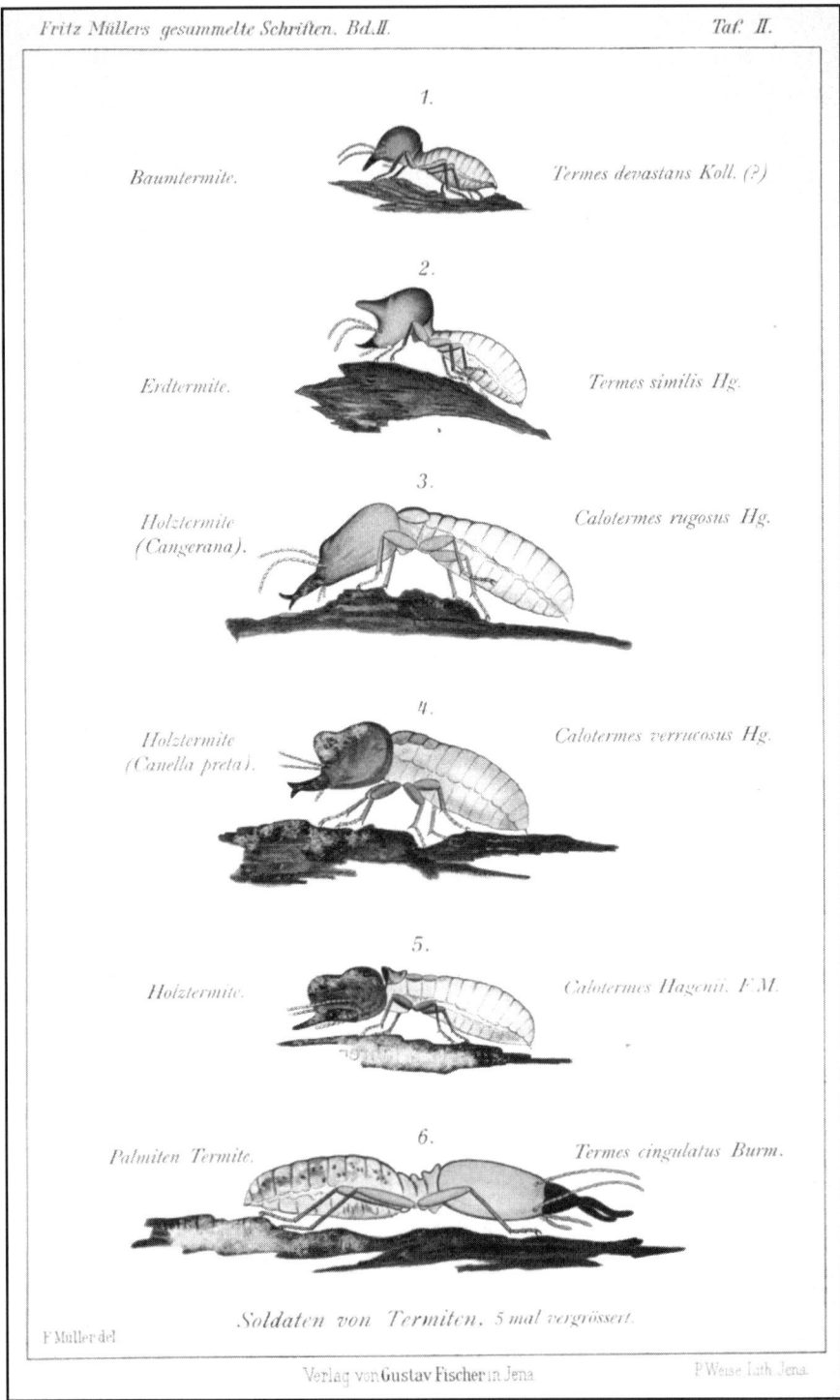

Fritz Müllers gesammelte Schriften. Bd.II.                                        Taf. II.

1.
Baumtermite.                                    Termes devastans Koll. (?)

2.
Erdtermite.                                     Termes similis Hg.

3.
Holztermite                                     Calotermes rugosus Hg.
(Cangerana).

4.
Holztermite                                     Calotermes verrucosus Hg.
(Canella preta).

5.
Holztermite.                                    Calotermes Hagenii. F.M.

6.
Palmiten Termite.                               Termes cingulatus Burm.

Soldaten von Termiten. 5 mal vergrössert.

F. Müller del.

Verlag von Gustav Fischer in Jena.                    F Weise Lith. Jena.

Sooner or later, when the palm roots decay, most nests fall victim to their attacks. One often sees cabbage-palm trunks in the forest with an opening on one side made by the powerful claws of an armadillo, and sometimes with fragments of the termite nest scattered about. Although such a raid certainly costs the lives of a large part of the colony, the royal pair at least is saved by the thick tough walls of its chamber. The first queen of this species that I saw actually came from such a hard core of a destroyed nest that I found loose in the forest.[8]

Accompanying his first termite paper, which he submitted through Haeckel in July 1872, Fritz wrote of how little was known even of the numbers of termite species, let alone the various castes of any one species, and:

> sadly it seems still to be the case with what we know of their life histories. With the exception of Bates, who with Wallace is in every way far superior to the usual sort of "traveling naturalist," none of the many collectors of beetles and butterflies who have roamed Brazil have thought it worth the trouble, in comparison with those colorful little objects, to pay more than passing attention to the inconspicuous termites.

Fritz went on to complain that the Handbooks simply repeated statements that were untrue, and he closed by asking Haeckel to send reprints of his termite papers to Darwin, Bates, Lespès (one of the few observers of termites in nature)[9], A. Agassiz, Hagen, Gerstaecker, and his brother Hermann.[10]

Fritz's belief that there was more to learn from a few living animals than from a host of "impaled corpses" in museums was vindicated in Robert McLachlan's review[11] of his first three termite papers in the *Zoological Record* of 1873:

> An exceedingly valuable contribution to the natural history of White-ants, showing (from personal observations in the province of Santa Catharina, Brazil) that many of the popular and scientific ideas on important points are pure misconceptions, and, in the main, upholding the assertions of Lespès,[12] many of which had been called into question.[13]

---

*Fig. 12. Termite soldiers drawn by Fritz Müller to accompany a popular lecture in 1871. A. Möller, 1921,* Briefe, *Plate II.*

Fritz summarized his principal discoveries in a letter which Darwin received early in 1874 and sent to *Nature:*

For some years I have been engaged in studying the natural history of our Termites, of which I have had more than a dozen living species at my disposition. The several species differ much more in their habits and in their anatomy than is generally assumed. In most species there are two sets of neuters, viz., labourers and soldiers; but in some species (*Calotermes*) the labourers, and in others (*Anoplotermes*) the soldiers, are wanting. With respect to these neuters I have come to the same conclusion as that arrived at by Mr. [Henry Walter] Bates, viz. that, differently from what we see in the social Hymenoptera, they are not modified imagoes (sterile females), but modified larvae, which undergo no further metamorphosis. This accounts for the fact first observed by Lespès, that both the sexes are represented among the sterile (or so-called neuter) Termites. In some species of *Calotermes* the male soldiers may even externally be distinguished from the female ones.

I have been able to confirm, in almost all our species, the fact already observed by Mr. Smeathman[14] a century ago, but doubted by most subsequent writers, that in the company of the queen there lives always a king. The most interesting fact in the natural history of these curious insects is the existence of two forms of sexual individuals, in some (if not in all) of the species. Besides the winged males and females, which are produced in vast numbers, and which, leaving the termitary in large swarms, may intercross with those produced in other communities, there are wingless males and females, which never leave the termitary where they are born, and which replace the winged males or females, whenever a community does not find in due time a true king or queen. Once I found a king living in company with as many as thirty-one such complemental females, as they may be called, instead of with a single legitimate queen.[15] [In his own published paper Fritz had written: "Instead of a royal palace in which a king lives in chaste union with his queen of equal birth, I had before me a harem in which a sultan diverts himself with numerous paramours."[16]]

Fritz pointed out that it would "save an extraordinary amount of labour" if termites produced only a few wingless females and males and not the vast swarms of winged individuals which disperse and are mostly lost. But recognizing the strength of Darwin's arguments for the importance of intercrossing, he concluded, "the wingless individuals would of course have to pair always with their near relatives, whilst by the swarming of the winged Termites a chance is given to them for the intercrossing of individuals not nearly related."[17] In the full German paper published in 1873 Fritz had compared termites with plants that have both cross-pollinated and self-pollinated (cleistogamous) flowers, quoting from chapter 17 of Darwin's *Variation*: "that the crossing of animals and plants which are not closely related to each other is highly beneficial or even necessary, and that interbreeding [we would now say inbreeding] prolonged during many generations is highly injurious."[18] Darwin thought "the analogy with Cleistogene flowers . . . wonderful. The manner in which you refer to my chapter on crossing is one of the most elegant compliments which I have ever received."[19]

At that time no one had yet captured a pair of mating termites, although it was thought by some that mating followed the characteristic "promenade," in which a female walks in front with a male close behind, often grasping her abdomen with his mandibles. Fritz showed experimentally that the promenade was not a mating ritual and suggested that the pair was merely moving to a new home. In a footnote he corrected some of the "misconceptions" to which McLachlan referred and showed his disdain for unobservant naturalists:

Only Ménétriés[20], in a marvelous mixture of fact and fancy, says that this promenade ends in mating. I simply do not believe it, any more than I believe his statements that termites . . . defoliate trees and carry the leaves to their nests (probably a confusion with leaf-cutting ants), that males have stronger mandibles than females, that females lay their eggs immediately in the first two or three days after arriving in a new home (other species are quite immature at this time) and are then driven from the nest, that everywhere in Brazil roasted manioc roots are the principal food of the inhabitants, and so forth. During five years of travel in various provinces of Brazil in which termites are just as abundant as here in Santa Catarina, Ménétriés "never found termites in real virgin forest." A dozen species live in my own piece of virgin forest.[21]

Through his farming activities Fritz had also been keeping an eye on some of the local ants which were (and still are) major agricultural pests. In 1869 he told his brother Hermann about leaf-cutting ants and in that letter suggested, apparently for the first time, that they were cultivating fungi for food, a conclusion confirmed more than 20 years later by his cousin Alfred Möller during a period of research with Fritz in Blumenau. "The most destructive ant in our settlements," he wrote to Hermann:

> is *Atta*, which cuts the leaves of many plants into pieces and forms immense colonies. The decaying leaves which they carry home are completely penetrated by mycelium and form in the center of their nests, traversed by innumerable labyrinthine passages, a loose grey-white substance like a sponge which undoubtedly serves as food for the ants and their brood. Some of that fungal substance is carried along when they form a new colony. The worst of the *Atta* species, *A. cephalota*, seems to be spreading continually southward but fortunately has not advanced as far as Santa Catarina.[22]

Early in 1874 Darwin had a copy of Thomas Belt's *Naturalist in Nicaragua*[23] sent to Fritz and asked him to "look at what [Belt] says about the leaf-carrying ant storing the leaves up in a minced state to generate mycelium, on which he supposes that the larvae feed. Now, could you open the stomachs of these ants and examine the contents so as to prove or disprove this remarkable hypothesis?"[24] In April Fritz responded:

> I was much surprised to learn from Mr. Belt's book how closely the far-distant province of Chontales resembles by its vegetation and animal life our own of Sta. Catharina. . . . As to leaf-cutting ants, I have always held the same view which is proposed by Mr. Belt . . . though I had not yet examined their stomachs. Now I find that the contents of the stomach are colourless, showing under the microscope some minute globules, probably the spores of the fungus. I could find no trace of vegetable tissue which might have been derived from the leaves they gather; and this, I think, confirms Mr. Belt's hypothesis.[25]

Fritz also picked up on Belt's observations of ants living in the hollow stems of *Cecropia* trees, on which they cultivate scale insects for honey-dew. Belt believed that those ants benefited the trees by repelling leaf-cutting ants but thought that the case was not like that of the ants that he had discovered in Nicaragua that protected bull's horn acacia trees, "where the tree has provided food [=the Beltian bodies] and shelter [the hollow swollen thorns] for the ants, but rather one where the ant has taken possession of the tree, and brought with it the [scale insects]."[26] Fritz wondered why ants would so assiduously protect the imbaúba (*Cecropia*) if it was only providing shelter in its hollow stems, and he soon found the reason:

> there is a wonderful contrivance by which, as in the case of the "bull's-horn acacia," the attendance of the ants at the right time and place is secured. At the base of each petiole there is a large flat cushion, consisting of most densely-crowded hairs, and within this cushion a large number of small white pear-like or club-shaped bodies...are successively developed, which, when ripe, emerge at the surface of the cushion, like asparagus in a bed, and are then greedily gathered by the ants to be carried away to the nest.[27]

"As a rule," Fritz wrote, "it is nectar glands that attract protecting ants," but he thought that these "Müllerian bodies," as they were later called, were predominantly proteinaceous, judged by the chemical tests to which he subjected them. The scale insects provide the ants with sugar, he said, and "thus, while we obtain our nitrogenous food principally from animals and our non-nitrogenous food from plants, in the imaúba ants it is just the other way round."[28] Fritz was misled by his test for protein. The Müllerian bodies are not proteinaceous but contain glycogen, a complex starch indistinguishable, however, from that found in animals.[29]

Fritz wrote a pedagogical verse about ants as a dialogue between leaf-cutting ants and the farmer whose crops they were destroying. The ants begin:

> You spiteful man, what cause for blame,
> Why pursue us with poison and flame?
> Though on the *Cecropia* trunks those things
> May have pricked you with their noxious stings,

177

> Yet we are a quiet peaceful throng,
> Who never did you any wrong.
>
> Early and late, from dawn to dark,
> Industriously toiling, hard at work.
> We have leaves to cut, no time to tarry,
> Trails to make, and loads to carry,
> To feed our young and build our nest . . .

and the ant wonders why the farmer is so vindictive. The farmer replies that he doesn't mind seeing the ants carrying their loads, but why not raid the weeds on the river bank rather than his crops?

> I sow and plant and tend the soil.
> But vainly do I sweat and toil,
> For scarcely has a tiny leaflet started,
> Then chewed it is right off, and off it's carted.
>
> I planted out a little tree
> And its fresh growth delighted me,
> But now, as I approach, I see
> A nearly leafless little tree.
> I've wasted all that trouble and care,
> Save one small twig the sapling's bare.
> And look, upon the twigs are you,
> To bite the juicy leaf in two
> And take the pieces on your back
> And carry them off.
>
> You would destroy the plants I cherish,
> So without mercy you shall perish.[30]

In the summer of 1872-73, chiefly at the instigation of Hermann, Fritz began the systematic observations of stingless honeybees that took up the whole of 1873 and most of 1874. Apart from his notes on orchid biology, these observations are probably the largest body of Fritz's unpublished material, and they represent the first major investigations of the biology of stingless bees. He had first written to Hermann about them in the winter of 1872:

> When I was recently at August's, his boys were intending shortly
> to empty out the bees' nests that they knew of in his woods.
> They know many species, and I instructed them to keep a few of
> each for me. Most seem to collect their honey in irregularly

piled-up round cells (the size of a walnut in one little black species). The brood-comb is made up of six-sided cells, but there is only a single layer, not two as in *Apis melifica* [hive bees]. None seems to sting, but one of them produces a sharp burning sensation and even blisters on the skin, probably by squirting out its venom; for that reason it is called cagafogo [fire-shitter].[31]

Hermann asked Fritz in May 1872 whether the nests of any of the local stingless honeybees had yet fallen into his hands and suggested that now that he had started his termite studies with such grand results he should turn his attention to the lives of the local stingless bees which:

> stand in no less need of detailed study by a naturalist living in virgin forest and acquainted with an axe. I see from Frederick Smith's papers that for many, perhaps, most species only the workers are known. You would certainly be successful in moving nests close to your house and in your spare time making observations of the greatest interest on these animals' lives.[32]

Fritz sent specimens of the bees and other Hymenoptera to Hermann, who forwarded them to Frederick Smith at the British Museum for identification, and he established an apiary for observing the local stingless bees. In October 1874 there were still seven bee-hives next to his house with five species of bees under constant observation. Fritz sent a letter that Darwin submitted to *Nature* on 11 February 1874, in which Fritz wrote that he had turned his attention from termites to:

> a still more interesting group of social insects, viz., our stingless honey-bees (*Melipona* and *Trigona*). Although a high authority in this matter, Mr. Frederick Smith, has lately affirmed, that "we have now acquired almost a complete history of their economy," I still believe, that almost all remains to be done in this respect. I think that even their affinities are not yet well established, and that they are by no means intermediate between hive- and humble-bees, nor so nearly allied to them, as is now generally admitted. Wasps and hive-bees have no doubt independently acquired their social habits, as well as the habit of constructing combs of hexagonal cells, and so, I think, has *Melipona*. The genera *Apis* and *Melipona* may even have separated from a

common progenitor, before wax was used in the construction of the cells; for in hive-bees, as is well known, wax is secreted on the ventral side; in *Melipona* on the contrary, as I have seen, on the dorsal side of the abdomen; now it is not probable, that the secretion of wax, when once established, should have migrated from the ventral to the dorsal side, or *vice versa*. . . . Some of our species are so elegant and beautiful and so extremely interesting, that they would be a most precious acquisition for zoological gardens or large hot-houses . . .[33]

Fritz sent his brother a "popular lecture" on the local honeybees which he had delivered to the Cultural Society of Blumenau in March 1874, once again educating his fellow-farmers:

In the forests of warmer America, from southern Brazil to Mexico, live many species of wild honeybees. About a hundred have been described, and their number will certainly not be exhausted for a long time. Even around here these bees are represented by diverse species, and you have surely all become acquainted with one or another of them, be it in the forest, at your sugar evaporator, or on the young shoots of your orange trees which one of the species loves to gnaw. You know that the most palpable difference between these local bees and those brought from Europe is that the former do not sting. They also differ widely from stinging bees in the characteristics of their hives, their habits, all their domestic arrangements. . . .[34]

Fritz continued with details on the number of local species (sixteen), the differences between them and European honeybees, and variation among them in structure, scent, and habits. He was particularly interested in comb-building and wax secretion, and he described how he had discovered that these bees secrete wax between the segments on the dorsal surface of the abdomen rather than the ventral surface, as hive bees do:

A French naturalist, Lepeletier de St. Fargeau [1770–1845], concluded years ago from the lack of the toothed processes [on the hind legs] with which European honeybees lift out the little wax plates [from the underside of the abdomen] that the stingless honeybees must in this respect be quite aberrant and peculiar. And he was right. One day [while watching individuals of one species, gurupú, outside its hive] I noticed on the back of

the abdomen a thin white fringe contrasting sharply with the
dark brown background along the margins of several segments. I
caught the animal and as a result several thin white crescent-
shaped sheets of wax dropped out from between the dorsal
sclerites of the abdomen. I have seen the same thing many times
since, and upon closer examination have found that not only
gurupú, but also other species and apparently all stingless
honeybees, secrete wax on the dorsal side of the abdomen rather
than the ventral side, although on the same segments from
which European honeybees secrete it.[35]

Stingless honeybees mix various substances with their wax for
comb construction, and they wall up the entrances to their nest holes:

> with earth or with various resinous, rubbery or other plant
> materials. [Five of our species] are often found in moist places
> gathering mud which they carry as they do pollen, in the little
> baskets on their hind legs. The little stingless honeybee (mirim)
> seems to prefer a very sticky black rubbery material of which it
> builds up copious reserves in its burrow. I have also seen it
> collecting copaiba balsam that was exuding from a newly felled
> copal tree (*Copaifera*), though certainly not for the same purpose
> for which our physicians prescribe it [which was as a nasty
> treatment for gonorrhea]. The larger mandaçaia is often seen
> returning home with enormous "breeches" of a fragrant snow-
> white resin, and one often finds huge quantities of this resin in
> old nests. After the tree decays these resinous lumps can be
> found loose on the ground, and you may recall how years ago a
> large such lump of resin was brought to the scholars of the
> colony in perplexity and was even declared to be a meteorite.[36]

Fritz's letters to Hermann between June 1872 and June 1875 are
full of observations on the bees. Few of them were published, but
Hermann, who was interested in bees himself, used many of them in
a long article based on his brother's communications.[37]

When Fritz was intent on a subject he could be single-minded,
as, for example, in October 1873 when he gave Hermann a detailed
account of comb-building in the "little bee," *Trigona mirim*, one of
the species in his apiary. He followed the construction of fifty-nine
cells over several days, waking one night and going to his bees with a
light to watch their progress, since "cell construction seems as a rule

to proceed more rapidly at night," and witnessing the queen laying eggs and covering cells with such speed that he realized why he had never seen the process before, despite ten days of intensive watching.[38] Hermann was enthralled, and regretted that for fear of being tedious his brother might have omitted some details, for he believed that there would be absolutely no finer evidence for explaining the colossal gap in hive construction and social instincts between bumblebees and European honeybees than the details from stingless honeybees, which might show the steps by which the elaborate behavior of honeybees had evolved. "Since Réaumur [who wrote on bees in the 1740s], there has been scarcely any discovery more interesting than yours in the natural history of bees."[39] Fritz apparently did not comment on Hermann's suggestion, but since he believed that hive bees and stingless bees had evolved social behavior independently[40] he would not have followed Hermann's logic.

Fritz's reluctance to submit manuscripts on stingless honeybees for publication may have been fueled by his belated discovery of a book by the Cuban naturalist Felipe Poey y Aloy (1799–1891) who had preempted all of his "discoveries, and had even seen the little wax plates on the back of the abdomen."[41] He called Poey's work "by far the best on the natural history of stingless honey bees" and abstracted Poey's information on a Cuban species of *Melipona* for a European audience that had scarcely noticed the work since its appearance in 1851.[42] Despite the wealth and originality of Fritz's observations on stingless honeybees, most of them remained unknown to European naturalists, and in 1910 the author of the article on bees in the *Encyclopaedia Britannica* knew so little of them that he wrote only: "The habits of the Brazilian species of [stingless honeybees] have been described in detail by H. von Ihering [1903], who points out that their wax glands are dorsal in position, not ventral as in *Bombus* and *Apis*."[43] Hermann von Ihering[44] was a friend of Fritz's, 28 years his junior, but by 1903 even Fritz's rediscovery of Poey's observation on the position of the wax glands had been forgotten.

On other occasions Fritz submitted manuscripts without having seen all of the pertinent literature, notably in May 1875 when he described with excitement a new freshwater crab brought to him from the highland streams of Santa Catarina by his friend the engineer

Odebrecht, for whom it was named *Aeglea odebrechtii*. Fritz was aware of only one closely-similar crab, a marine species from Chile, and he wondered how that species had gotten from the Pacific Ocean to his mountains.[45] At first he had only a juvenile male, but in September 1875, when Odebrecht brought more specimens, he confirmed that the species had no metamorphosis but hatched as a tiny crab, unlike marine crabs in closely related genera which hatch as zoëae.[46] In October 1875, however, he learned of a freshwater species of this genus already described from Chile and told Haeckel, the editor of the journal to which he had sent his paper, that his own description was therefore not worth publishing.[47] Despite his retraction, the paper appeared unchanged early the following year.

Fritz's publications and letters during the 1870s suggest a life almost wholly devoted to scientific research, but there were in fact many distractions. After returning from Desterro he had first to reestablish a homestead, and in 1871 and 1872 he was so preoccupied by the illness of his youngest daughter and a long life-threatening illness of his wife that he was then "as good as dead to the world."[48] 1873 brought wearisome civic duties. As a juryman he often had to undertake the trip to the town of Itajaí on the coast. Appointed Justice of the Peace for the settlement, he had to hold an open session weekly and was pestered almost daily with all sorts of gossip and petty affairs.[49] The chairmanship of the Cultural Society also took up time, and in 1873 he had to build a roomier house for his growing children. But his priorities were clear in a letter to his parents in April that year; according to Alfred Möller, two lines are given to house construction and the rest to stingless honeybees.

In February 1870 Fritz's brother August bought a new piece of property about an hour upstream from the center of town, and thereafter the two brothers saw less of one another. They had already been separated by the river after Fritz's return from Desterro, but their children covered the distance in less than half an hour by canoe and the brothers saw one another regularly, at least on Sundays when August brought his produce to market. According to Alfred Möller, Fritz, who was the more outgoing of the two and enjoyed talking with his younger brother, lost more by that change of residence than did the taciturn August, who took pleasure in a day's dull practical work.

At Christmas 1873 came news of his father's death, for which Hermann's letters had prepared him. Whatever differences Fritz and his parents may have had were by then long forgotten:

> To see father again has always been my silent wish; I could have realized it but postponed it from year to year until it is now too late. To have had parents like those allotted to us is rare fortune and a blessing for one's whole life, and the image of father along with that of our unforgettable mother will surely live on in all of us, gratefully and unclouded by discord, until the end of our days.[50]

In January 1874 Fritz suffered another loss in the death of Max Schultze, his close friend from Greifswald, and at his death a famous microscopist in Bonn. Schultze had been an important contact and source of literature when Fritz was a lonely figure in Desterro. "For years my correspondence with Max was all that kept me in touch with scientific doings in the old country," he wrote to Haeckel soon after.[51] Schultze had been one of those who hoped that his friend would return to Germany, and indeed Fritz wrote to Hermann at the same time that "The desire to see Father and Max Schultze kept me always in mind of a visit to Germany. But that is all over."[52]

The visit to Germany that Fritz had grudged himself he made possible for his daughters. A stay in his homeland would be a precious memory for his children for the rest of their lives and a stimulating educational experience irreplaceable in Brazil, and through his children he would reestablish relations with his siblings. His eldest daughter Anna went first, at age 22, traveling in April 1874 in the care of a family of friends and being welcomed in Hermann's house. Fritz always valued Anna's assistance in the field; the day before she left the Itajaí she showed him what proved to be a large nest of one of the stingless bees on a branch 14 meters off the ground. And she took with her a culture of jatí, another of the stingless honeybees, which Hermann kept alive in Lippstadt until the winter and on which he repeated many of the observations that he had known about only from his brother's detailed communications. In 1876 the next two sisters, Rosa and Agnes, set out across the ocean on a journey that would end in Rosa's tragic death three years later.

The insecurity of his official position with the province was exceedingly worrisome for Fritz, though its tiny monthly stipend of 50 milreis (then about $23) made his scientific work possible. The Jesuit College had not lasted long in Desterro, despite the elimination of its competition, and when a new school, the so-called "provincial Athenaeum," was established by a new President in 1874, Fritz was asked to be professor of mathematics:

> According to the law which abolished our former professorial chairs, I was not obligated to take up a position that was not agreeable to me. I was so much at home on the Itajaí, where I had been working hard and happily for six or seven years at the tasks that I set myself, that I would have declined the offer of the chair. But my former Director wrote me that the President would suspend our stipends if we did not sign up as teachers. And even if one so clearly has right on his side, can he bring it to bear against the whim of a Minister or President?
>
> Reluctantly, I went to Desterro, while my family remained on the Itajaí. A minor inflammation in my left ear became worse there with the change in climate, and I was therefore in a most unpleasant mood, and did not conceal it when Ladislau Netto, the Director of the National Museum in Rio de Janeiro[53], sought me out on his return journey from Rio Grande do Sul and offered to secure for me a post as a "Traveling Naturalist" of the Museum. "You can live on your land on the Itajaí in the company of your family and devote yourself completely to your scientific work. You submit articles to me for the *Archivos do Museu Nacional* and send to the Museum what you find noteworthy on your excursions. You no longer have to deal with the President of the province and his whims, but only with me, etc." I need hardly assure you that I accepted happily and with heartiest thanks. In the event, since everyone in Brazil has time to wait, it took nearly two years for Netto to fulfill his promise and notify me of my appointment as "Naturalista Viajante" under the date of 2 October 1876.[54]

For the present there was no alternative to moving to Desterro, but Fritz returned to his family for the holidays in October 1874 and also stayed home after Christmas. "Unfortunately I am still uncertain about the shape of my future," he wrote to Hermann in January 1875:

> My holiday ends at the end of the month, but for the present I will not return to Desterro. The loss to my income will be more than made up by what I save on the sojourn in Desterro. When the provincial legislative assembly meets in March, I will try to assert to it my established right and claim against the arbitrary and illegal interference of the President. Whether I will succeed is of course an open question.
>
> That uncertainty keeps me from regular work. As soon as it is past (in a way that permits me, as before, to use my time pretty much as I wish; for I may not be able to get out of the Athenaeum except by a sacrifice that compels me to spend all my time and strength working for bread), I will turn enthusiastically to completing my apiary, so as to bring my observations on how those [stingless honeybees] keep house to at least a temporary conclusion as soon as possible.[55]

Fritz lost nearly all of 1875 in that crippling uncertainty. A ministerial crisis in Rio de Janeiro nearly wiped out his expected appointment from the Museum, and in October Fritz wrote resignedly to Haeckel:

> My own scientific activity is probably over forever. Last year, through the arbitrariness of the then provincial President, I was wrenched from a position which allowed me to devote a large part of my time completely at my discretion to natural history. To no avail I have tried to urge my rights against that willful act and still have for the future a scant hope that it will succeed. Brazil is a scarcely half-civilized country, where Due Process is an empty phrase to which one appeals in vain. Meanwhile the Director of the Museum in Rio de Janeiro offered me with the firmest promise a position of an entirely different kind, one that would also have given me the opportunity and the spare time for scientific observations and investigations. But a change in the Ministry seems also to have brought that prospect to naught. And so in the future my botanical activity will probably not go beyond the felling of trees and the cultivation and weeding of my maize and manioc plots, and my dissections may be limited to cutting up a pig for the pot.[56]

The provincial treasury not having paid his stipend since July 1874, and the prospect of his appointment as "Traveling Naturalist" gradually dwindling, Fritz decided in November 1875 to go yet again to Desterro to press his claim in person. The journey might have been fatal. A torrential rain near Porto Bello had opened up a way through the dunes for little streams that usually had no outlets to the sea, and while fording one of these Fritz lost his footing and saved himself only by swimming twenty paces to the other bank.[57] But a pleasant surprise awaited him in Desterro, where once again a new President was in charge. He was required to teach at the Athenaeum for one day only, and then by order of the President to return forthwith by steamer to the mouth of the Itajaí in order to accompany two young scientists, Charles Wiener (1851–1913) from Paris and Carl Schreiner from the Museum in Rio, on commission from the government to investigate the shell mounds, or sambaquis, of Santa Catarina.

These "hillocks of shells accumulated by the former inhabitants of our coast," Fritz wrote to Darwin:

> exist in great number, and some of them are now to be found at a distance of several miles from the sea-shore, though originally they were, of course, built near the spot where the shells lived. Some are of considerable size; we were told that a sambaqui on a little island near San Francisco had a height of about 100 meters, but the largest I have seen myself did not exceed 10 or 12 meters.[58]

The sambaquis were as notable for their shells as for the human bones and stone implements that were found in them. Fritz saw that some mounds contained shells of species still living in the area, while others were almost exclusively composed of a thin-shelled burrowing clam of the genus *Corbula*, which was no longer found anywhere on the coast. Having found in the same mound another clam that he knew to live in brackish waters, he surmised that "when the lowlands of the lower Itajaí and some of its tributaries were as yet beneath the level of the sea, they would have formed a large estuary, and here probably the Corbulae lived."[59]

The first visit was to the shell mound on the Luís Alves, a lower tributary of the Itajaí. In December he met the two scientists in Desterro for further excursions near the town, and they then undertook a longer expedition to a large shell mound at Armação da Piedade on the mainland north of Desterro:

> We had a large boat manned by nine sailors from a warship, which with a good wind could take us there in 1½ to 2 hours. In the event, unfortunately, we had nearly gale-force contrary winds and finally reached the lime kiln after 11 hours, whence Schreiner and I continued on foot, the others in a little whaler. Despite the long day, we only reached our destination after dark.
>
> The next morning, with a number of laborers for doing the excavating itself, we proceeded to the shell mound, which had accumulated on a little hill right by the open ocean. It consisted of many different species of shells, all of which now live in the vicinity. Remarkably, there were among them no mussels, which are attached in enormous numbers to the rocks nearby and are eaten nowadays by the coastal inhabitants. We made a good haul, especially of stone axes. Human bones were also common, but unfortunately no complete skull; the skull bones lacked the incredible thickness of those on the Luís Alves. This sambaqui, however, is much younger than that on the Luís Alves; *Corbula*, the shells of which make up the latter exclusively, apparently no longer lives here.
>
> Those who have found human bones in sambaquis always speak in wonderment of their gigantic size. Our workers were also unanimous in their amazement over the enormous length of a shinbone and a femur that we found, until I laid the latter against my own leg and so demonstrated before their eyes that its former owner was not only no giant, but probably had a span less than mine. The case is probably much the same with the giants in other sambaquis; it is a common illusion that a bare bone looks longer than one with muscle and skin.
>
> My companions made the return journey by water, I by land; I have the peculiarity of not sweating very easily, which is estimable for foot travel in this country and is often envied by my traveling companions, but on that trip I had scarcely a dry stitch. I blame a long steep hill that I had to climb, mostly in full sun and without a breath of air moving, and I found out later that 11 December had been the hottest day in Blumenau for many years as long as records had been kept, and that the

temperature climbed to 38° C in the shade. By land it was a 10-hour walk, and I only arrived back in Desterro the next morning. I stayed there until the 17th, when I made my way home on foot, and after a very tiring journey on account of the hot weather, and because at the end the way was nearly impassable from rainstorms, I reached home once more on the 21st.[60]

The incidental comment that his companions returned by water, but Fritz by land, signals his preference to travel by his own two feet. Nearly everyone in Blumenau rode, but Fritz almost never mounted a horse, just as in later years when the roads in the colony were better he rarely climbed into a vehicle if he could avoid it. Water transport was acceptable but foot travel the best. Alfred Möller surmised that Fritz enjoyed the close observations that were possible while walking, and also that he disliked the sort of casual conversation that would spring up in a conveyance.

In January 1876, at the charge of the provincial President, Fritz completed a work on the climate, flora, and fauna of the region around Desterro. It cost him time, gave him little satisfaction and was subsequently lost or buried in the Desterro archives, but he felt obligated to the President, as he wrote to Hermann early in 1875:

> for the opportunity of the delightful and instructive excursion with Wiener and Schreiner, and because I cannot be indifferent to his kindness to me in asserting my rights in my claim against the provincial treasury, which now amounts to nearly a conto (1000 milreis, about $450). The President has already recognized in an official letter that I still have the commission for which I have received no stipend since July 1, 1874, and I may therefore hope, perhaps from the next provincial assembly in March, to be paid the stipends that have been withheld and to have them guaranteed for the future.[61]

The provincial assembly also recognized his claim; Fritz once again received his 50 milreis monthly stipend and could continue to live on the Itajaí in his former style. "Moreover I shall have the gratification of back pay for the last two years, depending of course on the condition of the provincial treasury, which is often debilitated! I therefore hope soon to be able to resume my excursions and my zoological and botanical pursuits."[62] In fact he had to wait until the following year, 1876, for the payment of the stipends in arrears since 1874. Although the provincial assembly recognized the obligation by law and the President approved it, the treasury official who had to make the payment refused to do so, a move characteristic of many governments over the years.[63]

Those two years of insecurity allowed Fritz a practical test of the meaning of Brazilian sayings that under other circumstances he would have imparted in jest: "de vagar se vai ao longe" (make haste slowly); "depois de um dia vem um outro, não ha cousa mais barata" (there's nothing cheaper than one day following another).

In October 1876 Fritz finally received through Ladislau Netto his appointment as a Traveling Naturalist of the museum, which had been reinstated in July at a monthly stipend of 200 milreis ($90). The duties of the Traveling Naturalists were vaguely defined in the original law: they were simply to "render services assigned by the Director General,"[64] and as long as Netto was in that position the job description was interpreted liberally. The first four Traveling Naturalists included two anthropologists, Domingo Soares Ferreira Penna and Carlos Schreiner, the botanist Wilhelm (Guilherme) Schwacke, and Fritz. Fritz's friend Karl Friedenreich was added in 1880, and another friend, Hermann von Ihering, together with Gustav Rumpelsberger in 1884, bringing the number to seven. No more were added up to the last listing of Traveling Naturalists in the *Archivos* of 1887. The income was useful to Fritz for acquiring books and journals, and from then until he was dismissed by the museum in 1891 he subscribed to *Nature*. And the new position was exactly to his liking, "for I can use my time as I wish for scientific excursions in the province and even beyond, or I can occupy myself with scientific work right here at home."[65]

# 10

# Traveling Naturalist: Insects, Honors, and Tragedies, 1876–1881

Fritz began his profession as a Traveling Naturalist in high spirits by realizing a long-cherished dream to accompany his friend the engineer Emílio Odebrecht on an expedition up the Itajaí River to the highlands of western Santa Catarina (Map 3). Odebrecht had the reputation of spending most of his time traveling, returning to Blumenau only to sire the next child or to be there at its birth,[2] and he had led many such expeditions prospecting for a road between Blumenau and the highlands. Fritz's obligations had allowed him to accompany Odebrecht only once before on a brief excursion, but an extensive trip like this one was now completely within his range of duties. It would be easier to make one's way through unexplored forest with a party than as a solitary naturalist, and Fritz gladly set out with Odebrecht for the highlands on 25 October 1876. They ascended the west branch of the Itajaí and then the Taió River and climbed the escarpment to an area of campo (grassland). The ascent of nearly 1000 meters brought a marked change in climate and ecology, and Fritz was in for new experiences.

On his return in late December he wrote to his sister Rosie:

Up there is a completely different world, a different climate, far cooler and drier than here and thus far more agreeable in summer; a world of completely different plants, fir forests (though little resembling German ones) and broad rolling grassy plains; completely different people and customs. Among the plants are large numbers of violets and forget-me-nots which remind me of Germany, although both are white rather than blue, and the former odorless. German fruit trees, which do not survive here because of the warm damp summers and the lack of winter dormancy, grow splendidly there, and after twenty-five years I have once again eaten my fill of damsons. As pleasant as the trip was, however, I was happy in the end to return safely home, where I could once again eat at a table and sleep in a bed.[3]

Fritz's brief impressions of the flora of that highland region in the headwaters of the Uruguay River drainage were published the following year. The vegetation, he wrote, was:

completely new to me, a marvelous mixture of Brazilian species, others that were deceptively like German species and seemed to have migrated from the northern hemisphere, still others that may have come from the south, for example a common member of the genus *Drimys*, a shrub with beautiful flowers and very aromatic bark.[4] The most distinctive and conspicuous plants of that region are *Araucaria brasiliensis* [the "fir" in the letter to his sister], several giant bamboos that sometimes form nearly impenetrable thickets in the largely araucaria and broad-leaved forests, and an extremely common tree fern called xaxim ("shashíng"), *Dicksonia sellowiana*, whose trunk is upholstered with a thick brown blanket of aerial roots. One of them, for example, was 45 cm in diameter but had only 9 cm of actual trunk, the rest being the blanket of roots. These ferns are sometimes used for fencing; they are planted close together and the layers of "felt" on the adjacent trunks fuse, forming a single continuous wall.[5]

The campos are rolling grassy plains, broken by hills and forest, often swampy in low places with a covering of sphagnum moss, and either treeless or set with more or less abundant araucarias. Originally they were for the most part araucaria forest intermingled with bamboo. Every seven or eight years, after flowering, the bamboo dies back and can be burned off, and a different grass appears in its place. The campos themselves are usually burned every other year, which ever enlarges them as the fire advances into the neighboring forest; in this way of course all of the plant cover of the campos has been changed completely from what it used to be. The araucarias die back little by little; it is really sad to see a prairie on which still stand only the tall limbless trunks of those splendid trees.[6]

Fritz declared the trip "rewarding and enjoyable," and despite its exertions his brother August found him on his return "as vigorous and cheerful as I have seen him in years."[7] Nevertheless, the season in the highlands in November was still not far enough advanced for the butterflies with which Fritz was then occupied, and he decided to accompany Odebrecht once again in February 1877, returning 23 March. This time his entomological friend the veterinarian Friedenreich went along.[8] Even though the yield of butterflies was better this time, the exertions of the march were considerably greater than on the first trip:

> 24 February. Several streams that we had to ford were full on account of recent storms, at times overflowing their banks and giving cause to many amusing scenes. Trouserless, we looked for a ford, built a bridge of nearby logs, climbed across with our oddly overstuffed baggage on tree trunks that had fallen across the stream, or waded through the water up to the navel, probing carefully ahead with a stick.

> 25 February. Up and down hill, through woods and grassland, by largely unused ways to the last uninhabited piece of campo. Except for Friedenreich, the cook and me, our fellow travelers had borrowed horses from laborers on the Campo de Justo, and our luggage had also been loaded on a mule. I reached our tent dead-tired. In the first place I hadn't slept at all the night before, as sometimes happens to me if I am disturbed when I first fall asleep, and then one of my boots began rubbing early in the day and I had to go barefoot from then on. Barefoot is still my favorite way to walk, even in the forest, but not under araucarias, which strew the path with dry branches so that one literally walks on needles, and still less so in bamboo thickets, where even with the greatest care one's feet may be cut to ribbons.

Around noon the next day they reached their goal, the house of an old settler friend near Curitibanos, where they received a hearty reception:

> The house is situated at the edge of a high plain, offering a wide and lovely panorama of valleys and hills, meadows and woods (predominantly araucarias, rarely broad-leaved trees). In front of the house are several high-fenced cattle pens. The fences are built in the usual local manner: the posts of the most durable wood possible, the rails of split araucaria trunks. Behind the house is a fine looking orchard with plums, peaches, figs and a large vineyard; a few walnut trees bore this year for the first time. The peaches and grapes were just ripening and we re-freshed ourselves especially with the latter during our stay. Our old friend's principal means of livelihood are breeding horned cattle, which are, however, of little use for milk. About three times a week as many milk cows as can be found (there were some hundred calves produced this year) are driven home and the calves confined overnight in the pen; the next morning after the calves have been suckled the cows are milked and the milk made into cheese.

Back in the Itajaí valley the going continued to be rough:

> 19 March. At the end of today's journey we found ourselves, as on the previous day, covered with various species of ticks which cause an itching that lasts all day. I immediately shed my clothes and got in the river as quickly as possible to free myself of the pests, at the same time building a bridge of a few tree trunks so as to get the baggage across. The forest here, as along the whole of the South Branch of the Itajaí, is thickly grown with bamboo and most of it is frightfully dull. There is not a flower or butter-fly to be seen, not a bird to be heard, hushed silence all round.[9]

Conversation around the campfire in the highlands commonly turned to the legendary giant worm, the minhocão, which was said to dwell in bogs and to dig underground tunnels that diverted rivers from their beds and toppled the toughest araucaria. On his return from the second expedition to the highlands Fritz wrote to Darwin:

> On the campos of the southern provinces of Brazil (S. Paulo, Paraná, Sa Catharina, Rio Grande do Sul) there seems to be a

general belief in the existence of a gigantic subterranean animal, which they call "minhocão" (i.e., huge earthworm). Most of the accounts given of it are truly fabulous; it is said to be "as big as a house," six metres in diameter and sixty metres long! — It would have its skin covered by thick hard scales, like a Tatú [armadillo], etc. From the various accounts, I have been able to collect during my last excursion, I have come to the conclusion, that it is highly probable, that some very large animal (about 1 metre in diameter) probably some cousin of Lepidosiren and Ceratodus [lung-fishes], lives as yet in the large swamps which accompany the course of many of the smaller tributaries of the rivers Uruguay and Paraná.[10]

The reports of that as yet undiscovered monster were so frequent and sometimes so well attested to that Fritz collected them for publication, adding, however, that "the sketchy and unreliable accounts of the animal leave us completely in the dark about its shape and even its size."[11]

Despite the hardships, Fritz, now 55 (Fig. 13), clearly enjoyed those trips, by which he got to know the remoter parts of the province. In August 1877 he went on another long excursion, to the coast near São Francisco and Joinville, in March 1878 still farther, to São Bento in the northern highlands of the province, and in May 1878 he went with his friend Friedenreich on butterfly excursions that figure in the next chapter. Further trips were planned, but his duties as a delegate for choosing deputies to the provincial legislature took him several times to the town of Itajaí, and after he was reluctantly appointed justice of the peace late in 1878 and again in 1879, longer absences from home became impossible. He found plenty to occupy his time close to home, however, and in the late 1870s his correspondence with Hermann Müller reached its peak, with monthly reports to his brother.

In 1877 he also began corresponding with Ernst Krause (pseudonym Carus Sterne), the editor of *Kosmos*, a new journal that announced its founding "in conjunction with Charles Darwin and Ernst Haeckel, as well as a range of leading research workers in the area of Darwinism," to present a "unified view based on the theory of evolution." Krause asked Fritz to contribute to the journal and received a delighted reply, but not without its hesitations:

Of course I will gladly comply as well as I can with your complimentary invitation for me to be a contributor; but I must first beg you to lower your expectations of my assistance to the most modest level. Living a full quarter-century in the land of the sloth, one gradually assumes something of the qualities of that creature, whether as a result of example or climate, or perhaps chiefly of a lack of intellectual stimulation. Add to this that I can get access only to the scantiest fragments of the literature and am therefore falling far behind the rapid onrush of science and may scarcely dare say anything. In addition, I will hardly be able to make any progress in a larger coherent project; I shall probably seldom be home for any length of time, but will be occupied instead in expeditions around our province. Detailed investigations are out of the question on such trips into the country, because one often has to give up table and chair, bed and house, for weeks at a time, and one's scientific apparatus consists only of a magnifying glass, a pocket knife and a pencil.[12]

Despite these protestations, Volume 1 of *Kosmos* saw the appearance of the first part of Fritz's "Observations on Brazilian butterflies"[13] together with a short note on the hygroscopic awns by which the seeds of the grass *Aristida* drill themselves into the ground, and he published in every volume of the journal until it lapsed nineteen years later at the end of 1886. Ernst Krause resigned the editorship in 1882 but remained one of Fritz's most valued correspondents, especially after Hermann Müller's death the following year.

Fritz was never much influenced by the ways of the sloth, but those early years as a Traveling Naturalist, when he was free from worry over his daily bread, were his most productive. Between 1877 and 1879 he had over fifty publications, including about twenty-five major papers. He felt duty-bound to publish in the *Archivos* of the National Museum, which was his source of support and whose Director, Ladislau Netto, had solicited his contributions. These of course had to be in Portuguese, and Fritz therefore turned to a language in which no one had yet written on the subjects with which he was dealing. "As familiar as Portuguese is to me," he wrote to Hermann:

it is still a foreign language in which I must first find the references and turns of phrase for the subject in question. That

*Fig. 13. Fritz Müller around 1877.
A Möller, 1920,
Fritz Müllers Leben.*

is difficult for a foreigner, as much as he may have tried to enter into the spirit of the language. Those articles cost me a great deal of time and are far more wooden than if I had written them in German. Besides, their publication will probably not be exactly quick, and as far as Europe is concerned will be as good as no publication at all. Nevertheless, the Director seems to consider these articles important. Because I eat the Museum's bread I also have to work for it, and anyway, this sort of work is infinitely more pleasant than mere collecting, for which I have little motivation or aptitude.[14]

The publication of the *Archivos* started punctually in 1876, and its second volume carried four pieces by Fritz reporting various discoveries in the Lepidoptera. One of them dealt with the function

197

of color change in flowers in relation to butterfly pollination. "Observations which could explain the biological significance of versicolored flowers have been very scarce until now," Fritz wrote:

> Corolla color is even today generally scorned by modern botanists, as Brotero said that it was nearly a century ago.[15] There are otherwise excellent botanical textbooks which do not devote a line to flower color.

Fritz cited the unique observations of his contemporary Giacomo Delpino,[16] on the significance for insect pollinators of change in flower color, and Delpino's conclusion that

> in certain cases the change in flower color by plants with versicolored flowers has a causal connection with pollinating insects, advertising in this way the appropriate moment for an effective visit.[17]

In Fritz's garden there was a *Lantana* convenient for observation, and for three weeks in the spring of 1877 he watched butterflies of a dozen species visiting its flowers. The flowers of this *Lantana* species are borne in heads and last three days, during which they change color: yellow on the first, orange on the second, and violet on the third day, and almost without exception the butterflies probed only the yellow flowers, which had nectar, and avoided the nectarless orange and violet flowers. Among three individuals of a species of pierid butterfly, however, Fritz reported one that did not distinguish yellow and orange flowers, while the other two were highly discriminating. He watched one of the latter for a long time:

> on an inflorescence with seven flowers in a circle, six yellow and one orange; it nectared at a yellow flower next to the orange one, then circled around the inflorescence to the second, third and so on to the sixth yellow flower, avoided the seventh (orange) flower and tried again on the first and second before going off to another flower head. . . . The benefit which the plant thereby derives is obvious. If the flowers dropped off at the end of the first day their number would be diminished by day three; the flower head would then be far less conspicuous and far less suited to attract the attention of the butterfly.[18]

Beyond confirming Delpino's opinion, Fritz was also suggesting that the persistence of orange and purple flowers that were no longer sexually active would enhance the attractiveness of the whole inflorescence to pollinators. That hypothesis was finally tested in another species with versicolor flowers late in the twentieth century, with the conclusion that "Fritz Müller was right over 100 years ago!"[19] Fritz also wondered what motivated a butterfly to visit only the day-old flowers:

> Is it perhaps some sort of instinct, some inherited and inborn habit by which it avoids orange and violet flowers and visits only yellow ones? Or might each individual have to learn through its own experience that only yellow flowers reward with sweet nectar that service which is essential for the transfer of pollen from one flower to the stigma of another? The variation observed among individuals of a species argues in favor of the second supposition.[20]

This supposition was also recently experimentally confirmed, nearly a century after Fritz's death.[21]

Apparently during the Brazilian winter of 1869 Fritz first looked at the local caddis flies. On 12 June he wrote to Hermann that he had been to the back of his property to gather aerial philodendron roots for repairing a fence and found in the stream a caddis fly case shaped like a snail shell. "It reminded me," he wrote:

> that you told me a long time ago of the probability that Lepidoptera arose from the Phryganidae [caddis flies] and alluded to the similarity of the larval cases of Phryganidae and Psychidae [a family of moths], which is indeed often amazing. But what seems most remarkable to me is that the different forms of phryganid cases are repeated by the psychids. We have, for example, a large psychid whose larval case is a couple of inches long and is made of plant stems laid crosswise, just as in several large phryganids; another has an equally long smooth naked larval case which it spins itself, and even the marvelous snail-shaped case of the phryganid *Helicopsyche* is repeated in *Psyche helix*. This is a lovely instance, not easily explained, of "analogous or parallel variation," [English in the original[22]] and all the more striking because the larvae of one family live in water, those of the other in air.[23]

In 1878 Fritz's treatise on the caddis fly cases of Santa Catarina appeared in the third volume of the *Archivos*, illustrated with three plates.[24] The aquatic larvae of each species build cases in a different shape, from tiny pebbles, plant fibers, or fragments of twigs, or from material secreted by their silk-glands, and they usually attach them on or under stones in fast-flowing streams or on waterfalls. What most fascinated Fritz was the variety and ingenious construction of the cases, and he was also attracted by the thrill of being able to make discoveries in an untrodden field. "The three plates that I drew for those observations," he wrote to Hermann, "please me every time I look at them. It has seldom been possible to offer so many remarkable and for the most part utterly new forms in a short article."[25]

Fritz was familiar with the pools formed in the leafy rosettes of forest bromeliads. In 1878 he recalled his first experience with bromeliad pools many years before, and described a new caddis fly that he had just found living there, "an aquatic animal in the forest crown," he called it:

> On a hot summer day more than 25 years ago [i.e., when he first arrived in Brazil] I stood with a friend under a forest tree against whose iron-hard trunk we had been swinging our axes for a good hour. Being still little used to that work my arm was growing tired, and we let our axes fall for a moment's rest. Suddenly to our surprise heavy drops began falling around us from the tree's high crown. "The tree is starting to weep," called my friend, "here it comes." And scarcely had he dealt it a few last blows when the proud trunk slowly began tilting with loud groans, and then with an accelerating fall came crashing to the ground. How often since that day have I greeted the tears with which a forest giant laments its impending downfall!
>
> The branches of nearly all our larger trees are thickly grown with banana-like plants (Bromeliaceae) among whose prickly and often convex-based leaves rainwater collects. These reservoirs are never completely dry, but when full to the brim their overflow gives first notice of the otherwise imperceptible shift of the tree from its equilibrium position.[26]

Fritz had already found many kinds of aquatic animals living in the water collected at the leaf bases, and having by this time become acquainted with caddis fly larvae in the streams nearby, it occurred to him one day that there might be species living in the bromeliad pools. He immediately took a machete into his woods and had scarcely hacked down a dozen bromeliads when he found the first peculiar caddis fly case. Not surprisingly it was built of dead leaves, and Fritz conjectured that its builder lived exclusively in the tree tops and that it was descended from a rare species found nearby in streams that also used leaves for its cases:

> if a caddis fly whose larvae built their cases with leaves should by chance lay its eggs in a bromeliad pool, its offspring could persist more easily there than those of other species having different habits, and over time it would become adapted still more closely to its new circumstances. Such an emigration would be impossible for most of our species, the larvae of which grow only in fast-flowing clean water.[27]

The bromeliad caddis fly had another peculiarity related to its way of life. Typical caddis flies leave their cases as pupae and swim with the aid of a fringe of hairs on their legs to the water's surface, where the adults emerge. Although Fritz knew that the placement and quantity of the fringing hairs varied among species, he also knew that no stream or pond species lacked them. But the bromeliad caddis fly did, and he suggested that it was of no disadvantage, rather that the "appearance of unfringed legs was caused or favored by the altered conditions of life. Unfringed legs sometimes appear in other caddis flies as a throwback to a long-lost age, but in those species pupae incapable of swimming must die without progeny. In the bromeliads, on the other hand, there will be no selection against such a throwback [because the pupa is not at the bottom of a body of water], and the unfringed ancestral form of the legs can gradually in this way achieve absolute supremacy." Fritz did not suggest how a mere "throwback" could sweep through a population; failure of selection to eliminate it is not sufficient, but "that it happened so, is proof that the pupae have been living for a long time in places where there was no disadvantage in being unable to swim."[28]

Fritz described two examples of "instinctive" behavior in caddis fly larvae. Two local species of the genus *Grumicha* spun their tapering horn-like tubes of a shiny black material. The larger end of the tube has a cover of the same material with a narrow linear or bowed opening, and there is another opening, this one circular, at the narrower end of the tube. Fritz pointed out that water flows through the tube for the pupa's respiration, and he found that as closely as he could measure them, the areas of the two openings were just alike:

> As in the construction of honeycomb, here would be another occasion to marvel at the instinctive clairvoyance or the mathematical genius of the little builder, who despite the difference in the shapes of the two openings knows how to give them the same size. But in fact the matter may be a rather simple: One would expect the larva to know when it is bathed by a steady stream of water. If one of the openings were smaller, water would pass through it more quickly, and toward that opening the current in the tube would be accelerated, or from it the current slowed, according to whether it is the entrance or exit.[29]

His other example was of a piece of "inappropriate" behavior:

> To whom has it not happened that he mechanically performs an action which has been habitually evoked on certain occasions when it is without purpose or even inappropriate? The larva of *Macronema* (?) provides a striking example that it is no different with the inherited habits of animals, Hartmann's "unerring instincts."[30]

This species usually hollows out a twig for pupation, partially shielding the open front end of the tube thus formed with a pebble, and gnawing a small lateral hole through the wall behind it, ahead of the pith which closes off the tube at that end. The silken case spun within this tube has sieved ends through which water can flow, and:

> the larva, and later the pupa so confined, keeps up a steady stream of water solely for respiration; this enters through the anterior sieve and exits through the posterior sieve of the pupal case into the space behind the pupa and from there through the lateral hole. That hole is therefore of the greatest importance for the inhabitant of the tube. If the larva takes possession of a completely hollow twig, it secures itself against the attack of an enemy with a pebble at its rear, attached either at the end of the twig, or more often, inside the twig near the posterior sieve of its pupal case. Now, even in this instance, with an open tube

behind it and no use for the habit, it does not fail to gnaw the usual hole through the wall.[31]

While looking for caddis flies Fritz discovered a mysterious immature insect clinging to rocks in rushing water which he eventually recognized as a midge larva of the family Blephariceridae, a "true marvel," he wrote, with only six segments. He described its remarkable metamorphosis into a twelve-segmented pupa, but its further transformation into the adult insect yielded another surprise: there were two female forms with completely different mouth-parts, one equipped to suck blood, the other, as in males, to take nectar. Fritz likened the dimorphism to that known in certain swallowtail butterflies:

> in which there are two females differing completely in color and pattern, and sometimes even in wing shape, with no intermediates. Wallace described and illustrated with his well-known mastery one such example (*Papilio memnon*) in his work on the Malay Archipelago.[32] Last year I became acquainted with a similar dimorphism in the females of a fly to which my attention was drawn by its most peculiar larvae. The two kinds of females differ in the size of their eyes as well as the structure of their mouth parts and feet, that is in those parts which have been ascribed the greatest value in the classification of insects, and which have also been used in the dipterans to which this fly is related in distinguishing genera and even higher groups. The differences are so fundamental as to lead to the conclusion that the females have completely different ways of life. In the butterflies one group of females is usually far more like the males in every respect; not so in our fly. One group of females is almost exactly like the males in the structure of its mouthparts but has completely different feet. The second group, on the other hand, has feet like those of the males but completely different mouthparts.[33]

Fritz explained the differences by selection for different life styles in the two female forms. Although he never saw the flies feeding, he deduced from the structure of the mouthparts (the lack of mandibles) that the males and one of the female forms fed on nectar, while the other female form, with mandibles, was predacious, sucking "blood" (body fluids) probably from insect prey, a distinction already familiar in male and female mosquitoes, where males feed mostly on nectar and females have piercing-sucking mouthparts for securing blood. The resemblance of the long tarsal claws and large eyes in the blood-sucking females and males was related to similar necessities in the two: blood-sucking females have to find their prey, catch it and hold it, just as the males have to find, catch and hold females for mating. But the nectar-feeding female form, with mouthparts like the males, has no special problem in locating the flowers on which it feeds, and small eyes and small tarsal claws were adequate.

Baron Osten-Sacken[34], the expert on Diptera at the time, had difficulty accepting the female dimorphism, and Fritz had to explain that he had sexed the flies properly and that he had reared many flies from pupae and had always met with:

> two sets of females, and never more than one set of males. The two sexes seem to occur in equal numbers. One day from 70 pupae I extracted 20 males and 20 females, and of those 13 had small eyes, short claws and no mandibles, whereas 7 were provided with mandibles and had large eyes and long claws.[35]

In July 1879, in the midst of this wealth of observations, Fritz received the news of his daughter Rosa's suicide in Germany, the first of several setbacks.

After his eldest daughter Anna had returned home from her successful European trip, Rosa and Agnes followed her example in 1876. They were warmly received in Regensburg by their Aunt Rosine and her sister, the widowed Luise Pfeifer, and continued their education in a high school for girls. Rosa did well and decided to remain in Germany for the time being and to take the teachers' examination in Berlin. Agnes studied music and hoped to return to Blumenau and to find a job there as a music teacher. The fourth sister, Emma, had incurable congenital malformations and was mentally retarded; Fritz's medically trained view was perfectly clear on that point, but members of his wife's family thought that Emma might find a cure in Germany, and so in May 1878 Fritz reluctantly sent her there in the care of her oldest sister Anna to join the other two. They met Rosa in Berlin, where she had lived since August 1877, and where after a further half year's study she had also taken the teachers' exam. Emma was taken to

her aunts' in Regensburg and was left there by her sister Agnes, who
returned to Blumenau with Anna toward the end of the year. Rosa's
hopes of finding a teaching position in Berlin were dashed, and she
had only a few temporary school jobs or private lessons in families of
friends. She took her sister Emma into her place in Berlin in January
1879 in the vague and impossible hope that doctors there could help
her, but her hopes of success in Germany and of a cure for Emma
gradually sank. A heroic effort to become independent through
further study and writing brought no results, and living with her
ailing and often bad-tempered sister increased the pressures on her. In
her letters home she never mentioned the failure of her plans but had
recently discussed her prospects as a teacher in Blumenau, and Fritz
had no idea of the crisis to which his favorite daughter would suc-
cumb. On 12 June 1879 in deep depression she threw herself from
the window of her third floor room and died instantly on the pave-
ment beneath. Emma was there with another boarder but was unable
to avert the disaster and was carried out in a faint, only later to learn
of Rosa's death in the home of Fritz's eldest sister Charlotte in Bavaria.

The news reached Fritz on 22 July, as he wrote his sister Rosine:

I do not know how to get over the dreadful blow, which was so
completely unexpected. Only a week before her death Rosa had
written to Anna and Thusnelda and seemed in a very cheerful
mood, and now this terrible news follows today. From the first
years of her life, when she was a wonderfully sweet child, I doted
on that daughter and sometimes reproached myself for that
unintentional favoritism. In later years I found again in Rosa, in
so many ways, my own character.[36]

"All our thoughts," he wrote to Hermann:

are contained in two words: Rosa and Emma, sadness and
worry. The more I awaken from the first numbness, the more I
feel that this blow has shattered me forever. Since [Rosa] had a
more reserved manner than Anna, you will scarcely have gotten
to know her well enough during her fleeting visits to your house
to understand just how fond I was of that one child above all the
others, and how I had linked all my hopes of a serene and happy
old age with her homecoming and my association with her. That
has now ended in so terrible a way.[37]

In September 1879 he wrote further to his brother about his plans for a work on the natural history of Santa Catarina:

> With Rosa's death has gone all my pleasure in life. I collect, observe, sketch, describe, without much desire or enjoyment, but only to supply my regular submissions to the *Archivos* of our Museum. How happily I dreamt of spending the twilight of my life in the company of my Rosa, as a substitute for the son that I was denied. I had planned, after Rosa's return, to offer my friends over there as a surely welcome gift, a set of illustrations of the riches of nature here. I would have supplied the data from nearly thirty years of experience and taken responsibility for their correctness, and Rosa with her keen understanding of nature would give the illustrations the fresh bloom of youth and embellish them with her skillful hand. That too is now gone.
>
> I have given up my plan to travel to São Paulo or Rio Grande do Sul next summer. My principal aim, which was to look about for a suitable place for Rosa, after which we would also have moved, no longer holds, and becoming acquainted with the flora and fauna of another part of Brazil, which even a short time ago still seemed highly desirable, now no longer entices me.[38]

Darwin's last letter to Fritz reiterated his suggestion of such a book: "I remember once suggesting to you to write a journal of a naturalist in Brazil or some such title, & give in it a resume of your endless & most interesting observations; I wish that my suggestion would bear fruit."[39] Fritz's response, which reached Down House after Darwin's death in 1882, was:

> for many years I hoped that my daughter Rosa, to whom I would have passed on all my miscellaneous observations of general interest, would write such a book with my help. But now that I have lost her, I think the book will remain unwritten. I have just now read once more Thomas Belt's "Naturalist in Nicaragua" and am once again convinced that I would simply not be in a position to write such an interesting book.[40]

After the sadness of the winter months following Rosa's death, Fritz began to recover his enthusiasm for natural history with the coming of spring. In October 1879 he sent Hermann the drawings to accompany a paper on a recent and surprising discovery: an ostracod living only in bromeliad pools. It had a dorso-ventrally flattened shell, unlike any "living ostracod," but was adapted to the habitat, for whereas marine species climb on slender strands of algae, this one moves about on broad leaf surfaces. It resembled in shape a Silurian species, *Elpe pinguis*, from which came Fritz's generic name *Elpidium*. He looked in vain for it in all other habitats in which he had found ostracods; this one was restricted to bromeliads and was common between Blumenau and coast, as Fritz found during a mid-October walk.[41]

How did the ostracods get from one bromeliad to another?

*Elpidium* is almost the only one of the visitors and inhabitants of bromeliads that is born and dies there. Many animals visit bromeliads for shelter, to feed on the organic matter which accumulates among the leaves, or to lay their eggs. Those visitors are very diverse, among them planarians (*Geoplana*), isopods (*Philoscia*), spiders, millipedes, many insects, leaf frogs and even snakes. Other species live there as larvae which leave their place of residence after transforming, for example the leaf frogs, various damselflies (Agrionidae), mayflies, caddis flies, water beetles (Dryopidae) and dipterans (mosquitoes, crane flies, syrphid flies and others), Neither for the visitors nor for those larvae is there any difficulty in explaining their presence in the bromeliads. For *Elpidium* it is otherwise. How is it possible for these tiny ostracods to form new colonies when they cannot move from one bromeliad to another, let alone from one tree to another? They will be able to make the necessary journey only if they attach to the body of some visitor to the bromeliads. Nevertheless their chance of emigrating seems to be as regular as that of pollen which is carried by insects from one flower to another, as witness the fact that there is almost no bromeliad without its *Elpidium* colony.[42]

Fritz was dissatisfied with the production of the text and plates for his last two articles for the Museum in Rio de Janeiro. The figures in the *Archivos* of the ostracod and of *Paltostoma*, the fly with two female forms, were so different from those published in *Kosmos* that he had to explain that the wood-cutter for *Kosmos* had reproduced his drawings exactly, but that he had not been so lucky with the lithographer for the *Archivos*. Moreover, he could never make corrections for the *Archivos* and was therefore utterly powerless against it. After volumes 4 and 5 were published in 1881, however, the *Archivos* lapsed, and Fritz's further submissions to the National Museum remained unpublished for more than a decade.

The work on which those later papers was based was done, however, in the spring of 1879 and brought Fritz back to a favorite topic, crustacean development, and specifically to the loss of complex metamorphosis in freshwater species. In November 1879 he told Hermann that he was just then going after aquatic shrimps and crabs, which were breeding in the streams nearby. At that time only land crabs were known to lack complex metamorphosis. "All marine crabs whose development is known are born not as crabs but rather as zoëae, lacking the five pairs of legs to which the name Decapoda refers," Fritz wrote in a paper published only years later in the *Archivos*, but knowing that other freshwater crustaceans, for example crayfish, hatch out as tiny adults, he wondered how freshwater crabs developed:

> I sought an answer to that question for many years in vain until recently I had the satisfaction of securing an egg-laden female of a crab (genus *Trichodactylus*) from a small tributary of the Itajaí. The unusual size of the eggs showed at a glance that the young must develop in the egg beyond the zoëa stage, and in fact when after a few weeks they were born, they appeared so like their parents that they had almost all of the distinguishing characters of the genus to which they belonged. They were born not only as crabs but in fact actually as *Trichodactylus* . . . . The female whose young I studied was caught, as I said, in a small brook. It carried about 120 eggs attached to its abdominal appendages, a very small number compared with the thousands which marine crabs usually produce. In *Carcinus maenas*, which is not much larger than *Trichodactylus*, van Beneden estimated the number of eggs at 200,000.[43]

Having added freshwater crabs to the previously known examples of abbreviated metamorphosis in river crayfish and land crabs, Fritz turned to the shrimps living in the Itajaí and its tributaries. In a

German abstract of the longer paper submitted to the *Archivos* but published only a dozen years later, Fritz wrote:

> For the freshwater shrimps that I am familiar with I can say that the species living in the navigable Itajaí leave the egg as zoëae. These include the small *Atyine*, a *Leander* and a few *Palaemon* species. In contrast, a rather common *Palaemon* (*P. potiuna* F.M.) in the rocky beds of brooks offers a remarkable example of abbreviated metamorphosis. Instead of about 1200 eggs, which I counted in a *Palaemon* of similar size in the Itajaí (*P. potiporanga* F.M.), the female of the brook-shrimp seldom carries more than 20, sometimes only 6-8. In exchange they are all the larger: about 2 millimeters long by 1.5 millimeters. The young are at hatching some 5 millimeters long and reach sexual maturity at 25 millimeters. The mother provides nourishment for her brood which suffices until they have developed completely into shrimp, although this is achieved only at the fourth stage of development after leaving the egg. The young moult three times before their mouthparts are suitable for feeding. The first moult comes at the most within a few hours of hatching, the second moult two days, and the third one four days after hatching. The young behave from the start like shrimp, running about on the substrate, whirling about with their abdominal appendages, darting backwards and forwards in enormous dashes, exactly like the adults, while the young of *Leander potitinga* F.M. from the nearby river, for example, resemble the zoëae of other palaemonids and are fond of hanging with head down close to the water surface on the side of the glass closest to the light.
>
> I will add only a few words about the conditions in which this species lives. Our brooks are mostly deeply entrenched in gorges in which they rush to the valley over a great many smaller and larger falls. The quieter pools at the foot of the waterfalls are the favored habitat of the shrimps. If their young swam about like the zoëae of their river-dwelling congeners, most of them would of course be "swept away in the swirling waves of the rushing torrent" after every violent thunderstorm.[44]

"These two closely-related species of *Palaemon*," Fritz wrote to his brother, about *P. potiuna* and *P. potiporanga*, "provide an especially nice confirmation of what I said about the loss of metamorphosis in my book *Für Darwin*."[45]

In his last major paper on freshwater crustaceans Fritz reiterated his belief in the power of natural selection, and in the value of studying living organisms in their habitats for an understanding of their structures. He described a shrimp from the Itajaí River which fed on the slimy layer of organic material that accumulated on the leaves of aquatic plants. This shrimp, to which he gave the generic name *Atyoida* [now *Macrobrachium*], differs from related species in several characters, including the appendages which it uses for cleaning its gill chambers, the brush-like structure of the feeding feet, and the structure of its carapace or shell. In the conclusion to the German abstract of the longer paper which he sent to the *Archivos* in 1879 but which did not appear until 1892, Fritz wrote:

> Just as *Atyoida* deviates from the usual structure of shrimps, (*Palaemon, Hippolyte, Alpheus* etc.), in a whole series of characters, so indeed do species, genera and families generally differ from their relatives and ancestors not by any single character but by a great many characters. Since causal connections are usually not recognizable among these various characters, for example between the structure of the claws and that of the posterior maxillae, or in the difference between the sexes in the armoring of the carapace, would one scarcely suspect them merely by dissecting dead specimens of *Atyoida*. As soon as one observes the activities of this little shrimp in life, however, its food habits clarify the structure of its claws and mouthparts and its habitation on plants, and the latter explains the multiramous fingers of its walking feet. Furthermore, the form of its claws, which are unsuited to cleaning the gill chamber, is related to the shape of the posterior maxillipeds which are adapted to that function and to the completely different way in which the first pair of swimming legs is borne. And so too the lack of defensive weapons in the males explains their small size, and that in turn the juvenile form of their carapace, and so on. In short, at a stroke all of its various characters are shown to be intimately related to one another, and so one may therefore hope that in many other cases, through careful observation of living animals, various structures seemingly unrelated to one another and now explained by some mysterious correlation of parts, will be recognized as having achieved their interrelationships by natural selection.[46]

In the meantime, Fritz's research activities as a naturalist were beginning to be recognized by academic honors. The first had come in August 1868, when the medical faculty of Bonn University, through its dean and Fritz's friend Max Schultze, conferred an honorary M.D. on him for *Für Darwin* and for his many contributions to botany and zoology. Fritz evidently never mentioned it in any letter, nor did Alfred Möller hear of it from him during their three years together in the 1890s, and if Möller himself had not later seen the diploma, the honor would have been completely forgotten.

The Sociedad Zoologica Argentina in Buenos Aires appointed Fritz a corresponding member in the year of its founding, 1874, and in the same year Tübingen University made him an honorary Doctor of Natural Science at their 400th jubilee.

An increasing number of European scientists were sending him their publications, which kept him apprised of developments and pleased him even more than did the honors. "The post," he wrote in 1887, "brought from Paris a splendid quarto volume, richly illustrated: *Contributions à l'étude des Bopyriens* by A. Giard and J. Bonnier, which the authors have dedicated to me. It was a completely unexpected Christmas present from afar."[47] The dedication reads

> To Fritz Müller . . . we dedicate this work in token of our admiration for the author of "Für Darwin" and of "Bruchstücke zur Naturgeschichte der Bopyriden."

The reference to Fritz's paper on bopyrid isopods acknowledges the correctness of his observations on *Entoniscus porcellanae*, a parasite of crabs and crayfish, reported 25 years before but doubted by other investigators because of their oddity.[48]

On the 22nd of September 1880, just after Fritz had finished the drawings for the *Atyoida* paper, an enormous flood swept the Itajaí River, the worst in the 28 years of the colony. The river reached 14.6 meters above its usual level, two meters higher than it had in 1855, and because it rose in little more than 24 hours many residents barely escaped with their lives. Fritz's house was under water to half the height of the rooms. Four days after the flood he wrote to his brother:

> We too had to vacate our house and stay with a neighbor a kilometer away; now the house is empty again, but full of mud;

tables, cupboards, chairs, bedsteads, lie in complete disarray. I got off very lightly in comparison with others and believe that the water damage will not exceed 2 or 3 thousand marks. As far as I now know I have lost no books of value. I had carried the lower shelves of the bookcase to the attic, but of those that I deemed to be safe one shelf still got in the water. Carus Sterne's *Werden und Vergehen*[49] was at the binder's and has floated off to the sea with his entire house; I had already given it at least a cursory reading. My wife was perfectly all right; in our exodus a neighbor carried her through chest-deep water. Agnes lost her balance in the deep water, but luckily she can swim; neither that swim, nor much splashing through mud and water has caused her any harm so far. I too was in wet clothes until midday of the 23rd, often up to my chest in water, and I caught only a slight cold. Good thing that I had previously inured myself to that kind of thing while catching caddis flies, shrimps, etc.[50]

Fritz's personal hardship was aggravated by worry about Anna, who was now married and awaiting the birth of her first child, and who lived with her husband on much lower ground in the center of town. "The poor thing, with her husband and a younger sister, had to let off shots from the attic and call for help for four hours until a canoe came to rescue them. And she was then lodged in a church for two days with hundreds of other refugees, in wet clothes without a bed and with scanty rations, fortunately without damaging her health."[51]

"I am sick of the Itajaí after this recent flood," he wrote to Hermann three weeks later:

and have a good mind to move completely to Rio Grande do Sul. In fact it is more than likely that I will not live to see another like it, unprecedented for perhaps a century, but one is never safe. When I was at the mouth of the Itajaí during the high water of 1855, I saw an old man driven from his deathbed by the flood being carried away in a boat on the raging current in torrential rain. That made a frightful and indelible impression on me. My house lies high enough that the water would not have reached it in 1855, and I thought that I had a place where I could die in peace. That is quite certainly not the case, as we learned in recent weeks. Had the inundation come two months sooner, during my wife's serious illness, it would surely have been the death of her; had it come a month later, Anna might have had to give birth on the roof of their house, as we thought at the first news of the flood, and as actually happened to another woman. Such possibilities can spoil the pleasure of one's home, even if one has grown fond of it; it is, for example, still pretty cheerless, although certainly convenient, to be able to walk through the walls from one room to another, in parts of my house.[52]

Although his family reoccupied the house toward the end of September, it was only at the end of November that Fritz could take possession of his work room once more. The relief committee to which the President of the Province had appointed him also took up time, but there was soon a bright spot, in the birth of Anna's child, as Fritz wrote to Ernst Krause in January 1881: "In recent weeks I have started once more to take some joy in life, and I owe that to my first grandson, a really splendid boy with whom my eldest daughter has presented me."[53]

The news of the flooding in Blumenau reached the outside world, and the descriptions of the devastation brought sympathy and help. Bridges, roads, sawmills and flour mills had been destroyed or badly damaged, great numbers of cattle, horses, pigs and chickens had drowned, and large stores of planks and building timbers, of sugar, rice and other produce, had gone with the waves. Homesteads were destroyed along a broad stretch of the river. A later estimate put the direct damage to the colony at more than half a million marks [$140,000], of which a fifth was made good by subsidies and contributions[54], but Blumenau recovered comparatively quickly.

In late November Darwin heard the news and wrote an offer of help to Hermann Müller:

> I also had a letter from Dr. Ernst Krause by this post telling me of the dreadful risk from a flood which your admirable brother, Fritz, has barely escaped from with his life. I rejoice that none of his family were lost. Has he lost many of his books, microscope, apparatus or other property? If he has suffered in this way, nothing would give me so much pleasure as to be allowed to send him £50 or £100. Do you think he would permit me to do so? The money would be sent solely for the sake of science, so

that science should not suffer from his loss of property. Pray have the great kindness to advise me. Nothing would grieve me so much as to offend your brother, and nothing would please me so much as to be able *slightly* to assist him in any way. Please let me hear soon.[55]

Hermann Müller conveyed the offer to Fritz, who responded on New Year's Day 1881 that he really had no need of help and wrote to Darwin himself the following week:

I do not know how to express [to] you my deep heartfelt gratitude for the generous offer, which you made to my brother on hearing of the late dreadful flood of the Itajaí. From you, dear Sir, I should have accepted assistance without hesitation if I had been in need of it; but fortunately, though we had to leave our house for more than a week and on returning found it badly damaged, my losses have not been very great.[56]

"I am extremely glad that the inundation did not so greatly injure your scientific property," Darwin replied in February:

though it would have been a real pleasure to me to have been allowed to have replaced your scientific apparatus. I do not believe that there is anyone in the world who admires your zeal in science and wonderful powers of observation more than I do. I venture to say this, as I feel myself a very old man, who probably will not last much longer.[57]

In October, before his life was back to normal, Fritz received a letter from Paul Mayer (1848–1923), an entomologist in Naples, reporting discoveries about the wasps that pollinate figs, and despite the distractions of the moment he replied with enthusiasm:

The information about caprification in figs[58] was of the greatest interest to me, and if at all possible I will look into the subject here as well and send you any material that I can obtain for you to work up. Because there are many *Ficus* species here, and some are among the commonest trees of the virgin forest, it will surprise you that I say "if possible." But their crowns are so high in the forest that the fruits are completely inaccessible. The trees are usually giants; once in my early years, for example, it took me two full days to fell such a "figueira."[59]

A month later he had found some of the native figs and wrote his brother Hermann:

A few weeks ago I received a letter from Paul Mayer, who is studying the caprification of figs as a zoologist, together with the botanist Solms-Laubach[60], and who would like contributions from me. What he tells me of the subject is so remarkable that I will transcribe the passage in question, of course only for you until he himself publishes it.[61]

"[The wasp] *Blastophaga grossorum* [=*psenes*] . . . is remarkable in having wingless males that never leave the [capri]figs. They gnaw out of their particular achenes[62], chew a hole in the achenes where the females reside, and mate with them by inserting their long white abdomens. Every female that emerges from the [caprifig] ovary already has sperm in its *receptaculum seminis*. After emerging from the . . . inedible caprifig, it enters another fig, either a caprifig of the next generation or an edible one, and lays its eggs in the immature ovaries; but because of the nature of the ovaries its eggs can be properly accommodated only in the caprifig, and there only can it reproduce. The wasps have three or four generations a year. There is moreover a remarkable convergent adaptation in an ichneumonid wasp that lives in the figs, apparently at the expense of *Blastophaga*; it too has wingless males and winged females, and its mating and other behavior is just as in *Blastophaga*. Furthermore a nematode lives in the figs, developing there from the egg and when the female *Blastophaga* works its way out of the fruit conceals itself in a deep furrow in the membranous integument at the base of her ovipositor (that is on the outside of the animal), in order to be carried from one fig to another. What do say you to that adaptation?"

That sounds completely different from the earlier accounts from Aristotle through Delpino. Isn't it remarkable, by the way, that there is not a word about caprification in any of the recent botanical texts that I can consult, for example Sachs[63], while the old Portuguese botanist Brotero devotes several pages to the topic in his *Compendio de Botanica*[64] published a century ago?

In the past few days I have had the opportunity to confirm many of Paul Mayer's statements in one of our local figs. I have found the two kinds of Hymenoptera, with wingless males of the most marvelous appearance, and on one occasion already the tiny nematode. The fig has protogyny as extreme as any yet known; the male flowers mature only as the seeds are ripening! The interior of the fig is then like a flour barrel, full of white pollen in which the females of *Blastophaga* or the ichneumonids crawl about. It is striking that around here *Blastophaga* is very scarce relative to the ichneumonid; in most figs, I have found none of the former at all, while the latter swarm. I am sending you females and males of both species. I am curious whether each of our rather numerous fig species has its own pollinator; I think it probable, because if the same species of insect visited different figs, pollen would often be carried to an alien species.[65]

Fritz reported to his brother at the end of December:

I have been giving special attention to figs during the past month and have become acquainted with the inhabitants of four species. In two species of figs there are three different Hymenopterans, all with wingless males; in one fig I encountered at least five different females! With at least a dozen kinds of figs growing here, I see the prospect of a rich harvest, though not easily to be reaped. The principal question about the figs-dwellers has to do with their mutual relations: are all the other species parasites of *Blastophaga* and of no use in pollinating the figs, or do some of them live independently in the seeds of the figs and serve as a pollinators? Probably the latter; at least I have repeatedly failed to find dead *Blastophaga* in unripe figs, and when they are present they are usually very conspicuous. *Blastophaga* is the only one to force its way into the figs, but the other species could effect pollination with pollen grains adhering to their ovipositors. The resolution of this and other questions is complicated by the impossibility of easily obtaining fruits in every stage of development. In the forest one depends on birds feeding on the ripe fruits knocking down the unripe ones; the ripe fruits that fall are already empty of female wasps. Of the only two trees with accessible branches that I know of now bearing fruit, one is six kilometers, the other nine, from home. The latter is as gigantic a tree as I have known in all my years in Brazil, but only one of the lower branches of its enormous crown has half-developed fruit, another one completely immature and as yet unpollinated figs. I sent you in my last letter in alcohol the wingless males of two species; almost more marvelous is the third species, of which I here give you a hasty sketch.[66]

Solms-Laubach thought that the edible fig had arisen from the caprifig, in cultivation. Fritz pleaded the case that they were, respectively, the female and male of one species and had evolved together by natural selection before cultivation,[67] a view which Solms-Laubach later accepted.

# 11

# Traveling Naturalist: Butterfly Scent and Mimicry, 1876–1884

Even before Fritz took on the post of Traveling Naturalist of the National Museum in the summer of 1876, he was shifting his attention from the stingless honey bees and termites that had occupied him during the 1870s to the rich lepidopteran fauna of Santa Catarina. He had sent butterfly wings to his brother Hermann for identification by Karl Gerstaecker in 1871 and had commented in letters to his brother and to Darwin that year on mimicry, butterfly systematics, and the role of butterflies in pollination, but it was only in April 1875 that he submitted a paper on the evolution of mimetic *Dismorphia* butterflies, and a year later that he began to write in earnest on his discoveries in butterfly biology.

The first of these discoveries was his recognition of the function of specialized "scent-scales" on the wings of butterflies. In April 1876 he sent to Haeckel for publication a revolutionary paper, "On hair-tufts, felted patches, and similar structures on the wings of male Lepidoptera," which appeared the following year.[2] In it Fritz suggested for the first time that the many modified scales and other structures that had been known in male butterflies for years, but without explanation, actually functioned in courtship and defense. After describing a variety of such structures gleaned from the literature and his own experience, he concluded that "scattered as these patches and tufts are through the most widely separated groups of diurnal Lepidoptera, whatever they possess in common must be considered as an adaptation to some similar purpose, since they can scarcely be traced back to a common origin." Adding that "as far as I know, what that purpose is has not even been conjectured," he then described how the idea occurred to him that they were scent-producing structures:

> I had caught a freshly emerged male of *Callidryas* [*Phoebis*] *argante*, and in order to show a friend the mane-like pubescence of the hind wings I drew the fore and hind wings apart. I then perceived a distinct, somewhat musky scent and convinced myself that it came from the hairs which stood on end as the wings were parted.

Fritz was not the only one who could smell butterfly scents. "On a male of *Prepona laertes* I found a not very strong, but still unmistakable scent arising from the tuft on the hind wings. Several of my children not only perceived the same scent, which they (very appropriately, I consider) spoke of as bat-like, but they also pointed to the same spot as its source." E. B. Poulton,[3] writing 35 years later in his introduction to the English translations of Fritz's papers on the subject, commented that many of Fritz's observations "still remain unique and unconfirmed. The power of distinguishing the scents emitted from particular organs on the wings, legs, or body of Lepidoptera, a power which Fritz Müller and his children exhibited in so remarkable a degree, has hitherto only rarely been possessed by other naturalists."[4] In 1878 Fritz reported that on his excursion to the highlands near São Bento he had collected a swallowtail, *Papilio scamander*, "the wings of the male of which exhaled a strong and so delicious an odour that one might use it as indeed we did as a nosegay."[5]

"Having therefore demonstrated by actual observation," Fritz wrote:

> that the purpose of the patches and hair-tufts in the males of [several] species from widely differing families is to exhale scents which are probably agreeable to their females and entice them to pair, I am led to infer that this is the meaning of all similar structures on the wings of male Lepidoptera, not only because of the unmistakable similarity amidst such great diversity, but even

more on account of the . . . peculiarities which render them especially suitable for such a purpose. They are usually sheltered from exposure to air, enclosed between the fore and hind wings or in some other manner, or at least while at rest concealed between the closed upright wings. Thus the scent is not diffused at the wrong time and so wasted, but collects between the densely packed scales, among the hairs, brushes or manes. One could hardly find a more effective method of employing any odoriferous substance than that of saturating with it the hairs of a brush, and then suddenly opening them out in all directions so as to provide an enormous surface for evaporation.[6]

Fritz had written August Weismann[7] about his forthcoming paper in August 1876, but before the paper appeared in April 1877 he wrote again to report that in the meantime he had:

learned of such a mass of new and to some extent highly surprising examples for the opinion expressed in my article . . . that the peculiarly formed scales of male butterfly wings are organs for producing and dispersing scent, that it seems to me now to be completely beyond doubt. As the finest example, I enclose a *Papilio protosilaus* male: the inner margin of the hind wing is turned over on the upper side, and if the wings are pulled well forward the fold is opened and there appears standing up a tuft of thick black hairs which gives off an extraordinarily strong smell.[8] . . . The male of *Daptoneura lycimnia* is remarkable in bearing peculiarly shaped scales over the whole upperside of the wings.[9] . . . I believe that I have already indicated in my article on the subject that sometimes in related species the male of one carries the scent organ on the wings and the male of the other on the abdomen. On that point I recently became acquainted with another fine example. Nearly all the genera of Morphidae seem to have very well developed scent organs on the wings of the males. Only the genus *Morpho* lacks them. I found that the male of one *Morpho* . . . everts on the sides of the abdomen two hairy and very strongly smelling protrusions. In some cases the scent organs of the wings seem to be vestigial and functionless, while effectively the same organs have developed on the abdomen, as in the males of [*Biblis hyperia*[10]]. . .[11]

Always alert to examples of evolutionary convergence, to which he had called attention in many papers since *Für Darwin*, Fritz described in 1878 the scent structures on the wings of the butterfly *Antirrhaea archaea,* which were remarkably like those of *Epicalia* [*Catonephele*] *acontius* that he had described the year before. In the males of both species there is a mane of hairs in the same position on the underside of the fore wing where it overlaps the hind wing, and a scent-patch facing it on the upperside of the hind wing. "Now all this would be very simple, and would be very easily explained," Fritz wrote:

> if the two species belonged to the same, or to allied genera, for then all the characters in which their scent-organs correspond might have been derived from a common ancestor. So far from this being the case, however, they are of two very different sub-families, *Antirrhaea* being claimed by the Satyrinae and [*Catonephele*] by the Nymphalinae[12], while even the nearest relatives of both are destitute of similar organs. They are completely wanting, for instance in [*Catonephele*] *numilia.* . . . The two organs are not "homologous," but simply "analogous," and they furnish a most notable example of "convergence," to use the modern term for a resemblance caused not by inheritance, but by adaptation to similar circumstances. I know of no other case which proves so clearly and irrefragably, and attests with such force, the truth of a principle which should never be lost sight of in morphological studies, viz.—when in two species certain organs which serve the same function, are found in the same place, are composed of the same parts occupying the same relative positions, and exhibiting similar forms—all this by itself constitutes no sufficient proof that these organs are homologous, nor does it give ground for placing the two species in the same family.[13]

In a long paper in the *Transactions of the Entomological Society,* Fritz recognized two classes of sexual odors: those which "give notice to the opposite sex of the existence of, and lead it the way to, the odoriferous animal, [which] must exist in many female moths which attract the males from great distances;" and those which "do not serve as a guide, but as an excitement to the opposite sex, [which] appear to be far more frequent in the males, though occurring also in some females. Odours of both classes will of course be agreeable to the attracted or allured sex: but in the first class the odour of the female is agreeable to the male because it is the odour of his female, while in the second class the odour emitted by the male is agreeable to the female, males with that peculiar odour having been preferred," the odors in other words having evolved by sexual selection. He also recognized protective scents, which "appear to be in most cases equally strong in both sexes, or sometimes stronger in the females."[14] Fritz was a pioneer in all of these distinctions.[15]

Fritz was also interested in possible parallels between the relationships among butterfly larval food plants and those of the butterfly species themselves. In April 1878 he wrote to Darwin about his recent attempts to raise caterpillars from eggs extracted from female butterflies:

> The main difficulty consists in finding a proper food-plant for the young caterpillars, but generally the caterpillars of nearly related butterflies feed on the same or on nearly related plants. Thus, knowing that the caterpillars of *Anartia Amathea*, *Victorina* [*Siproeta*] *Frayja*, and *Eresia* [*Phyciodes*] *Langsdorffii* live on the same Acanthaceous plants, I gave the same plants to a young caterpillar of *Junonia Lavinia* [*evarete*] and they were not rejected. The caterpillars of those four species resemble each other so perfectly, that in a system of caterpillars they would no doubt be united into a single genus.
>
> Some time ago I found on the leaves of *Passiflora* [a passion-flower] . . . eggs of a butterfly, which evidently belonged to some Heliconius or any allied species. The young caterpillars died — (to my great surprise, for I had raised plenty of Heliconinae from the egg) — one after the other without touching the leaves, on which the eggs had been found. At last, when only one survived, it occurred to me that their mother might have deposited her eggs on a wrong plant. For, though based on a more solid ground, than that of the pope, the infallibility of butterflies also is not absolute. In consequence I placed before the starving caterpillar leaves of various other species of Passiflora at my disposition and before long it began to feed on one of them. By the choice, it made, I immediately supposed, that it would be a caterpillar of *Dione vanillae* and this afterwards proved true.[16]

Fritz's best known work is undoubtedly his explanation of the sort of mimicry that now bears his name — Müllerian mimicry. He published the idea in 1878 but had begun thinking about mimicry a dozen years before, when he read about "Batesian" mimicry.

Bates returned from South America in 1859 with a mass of specimens and observations from eleven years on the Amazon. He had found butterfly species almost identical in color and markings, flying together, yet belonging to different genera, subfamilies, or families, and after reading *The Origin* he recognized the resemblances as mimicry. In 1862 he explained how mimetic patterns would evolve in palatable species by natural selection because their resemblance to unpalatable 'models' would reduce predation on them.[17] It was a triumph of Darwin's theories. Until then, many of those deceptively similar species, models and mimics, were taken to be close relatives *because* of their similar colors and markings.

Fritz learned of Bates's explanation of the resemblance between a palatable mimic and its unpalatable model — "Batesian" mimicry — from Gerstaecker's review journal *Jahresbericht*, although he never saw Bates's paper itself[18], but he evidently absorbed it only when he received from Darwin, on 25 October 1866, the 4th edition of *The Origin*, in which Darwin first introduced Bates's ideas. Fritz was then working principally on plants, and his only known response to Darwin's account of Batesian mimicry is a comment to his brother about an observation made eight or nine years before: the similarity of flower color in a scarce legume and a common bindweed growing together, which he now thought might be an example of mimicry:

> I explain the matter thus: one of the species was regularly visited by insects, the color being a well-recognized signal to the local insects of a good nectar meal. Now if the other produced somewhat similarly colored flowers, it could easily deceive the insects and also attract them, and in this way the first more similarly-colored flowers would be more amply pollinated, etc. This explanation, which was still rather doubtful, has now become far more probable to me because of Bates's observations on mimetic butterflies in the new edition.[19]

Fritz does not mention a potential objection to his explanation, namely that two plant species that attracted the same pollinators would suffer from inappropriate pollinations, but a similar hypothesis was proposed more than a century later, the objection was answered for mimetic hummingbird-pollinated flowers, and Fritz's story thereby achieves respectability.[20]

In March 1870, thanking Darwin for the German translation of Wallace's *Malay Archipelago*,[21] Fritz first mentioned butterfly mimicry, with an example of a common local species of "white" (Pieridae) and three or four rarer species with similar wings, and in a letter to his brother in May he described other local examples of mimicry. He also raised the question of sexual selection as a possible cause of butterfly mimicry, an issue that continued to occupy his mind for several years. Fritz often commented on the preferences of different kinds of butterflies for particular flower colors, [*Catanephele*] species, for example, visiting red flowers, the transparent ithomiines white flowers, etc., and he thought it "not improbable that a butterfly endowed with a highly-developed sense of color found the pretty males or females of another species more to its taste than those of its own species" and thus by sexual selection "gradually acquired a raiment similar to that of its favourites."[22] The following month he presented Hermann with evidence for the role of sexual selection from two observations: the species that are mimicked are brightly colored and would "generally attract pursuers rather than protect against them; but brightly colored species could be forced upon others as models by sexual selection"; and often only the upper side of the model is mimicked, "and therefore the mimic resembles its model only in flight, while, at least in quick flyers, similarity at rest would be most important for protection from pursuit [and many species rest with wings closed]."[23] Fritz also wrote on the subject to Darwin on 5 July 1870 in a letter now lost.[24]

In his first observation Fritz had not yet recognized that the bright colors of models might be warning coloration and that predators would more easily learn to associate them with unpalatability precisely because of their boldness. This concept of warning, or aposematic coloration, as Poulton later called it,[25] was given by Wallace as an explanation for the bright colors of conspicuous caterpillars, in a letter that Darwin quoted in *The Descent of Man*,[26] and

Darwin suggested to Fritz that it might also apply to conspicuous butterflies.[27]

The importance of Fritz's second observation, that butterflies resting with wings folded are at risk from predators and that both surfaces of a butterfly wing should be subject to natural selection, is still not often acknowledged,[28] and it is usually only the upper surfaces of the wings of models and mimics that are compared.

In the Brazilian summer of 1870-71 Fritz's attention was:

> particularly attracted by "mimetic butterflies." We are rather rich in such species here; as on the Amazon, nearly all our *Leptalis* [*Dismorphia*] imitate other species, though they use not only *Heliconius* but also whites and the very common *Acraea* [*Actinote*] *thalia* as models. There is a nice demonstration of how perfectly the mimics resemble their models in Prittwitz's copious catalogue of the butterflies of Rio de Janeiro in the Stettiner Entomological Journal.[29] There are no *Leptalis* or *Euterpe* [*Archonias*] species among them, in fact not one "mimetic species," although it is highly probable that scarcely any of our local species is absent.[30]

Fritz himself overlooked some local mimetic butterflies, for example the polymorphic kite swallowtail *Eurytides* (*Mimoides*) *lysithous*.[31] He described a pupa of this or a related mimetic species in a letter to Hermann Müller,[32] and even though he was not a collector, it is surprising that he missed the adults in his ramblings. Many a lepidopterist, however, has had the experience of confusing models and mimics in the rich butterfly fauna of a place like Santa Catarina.

One of the problems in mimicry theory was how mimetic resemblances could evolve. In 1871 Fritz wrote to his brother about Darwin's *Descent of Man*, commenting especially on butterfly mimicry and on Darwin's perceived problem of "how the first steps in the process could have been effected through natural selection,"[33] but with an odd suggestion about the role of sexual selection:

> Darwin seeks to remove the difficulty by the assumption "that the process probably has never commenced with forms widely dissimilar in colour."[34] But in cases where the model species is mimicked by species of four or five widely different families [Fig.14], or where on the other hand members of one genus

Aus Kosmos Bd.X.1881. Verlag von Gustav Fischer in Jena. Lith.Anst.v.K.Wesser,Jena

[*Dismorphia*] mimic models of such different color and shape as whites [Pieridae], [*Actinote*] *thalia*, and *Mechanitis lysimnia*, such an assumption is scarcely permissible. The difficulty would vanish completely if mimicry were viewed as something truly conscious, with a preference by sexual selection for individuals similar in any way to the model. The resemblance need not have been deceptive in any way from the beginning. If you compare *Eresia* [now *Phyciodes*] *langsdorfii*, for example, with the gorgeous *Heliconius phyllis* [*erato*], you could take the former for a very imperfect attempt so far at mimicking the latter, though an insectivore would surely never confuse the two.[35]

When Alfred Russel Wallace heard of Fritz's last example, he protested that *E. langsdorfii* was not "too imperfect and that its red patch, whatever the tint, is very conspicuous against a green or other contrasting background,"[36] and I agree from my Brazilian experience.

Fritz made the same points in a long letter to Darwin on 14 June 1870, adding another example of mimicry that might have sexual selection as its basis, and Darwin asked in his response if he might give:

some such sentence as follows: "F. Müller suspects that sexual selection may have come into play, in aid of protective imitation, in a very peculiar manner, which will appear extremely improbable to those who do not fully believe in sexual selection. It is that the appreciation of certain colour is developed in those species which frequently behold other species thus ornamented."[37]

---

*Fig. 14. Wings of butterflies from Santa Catarina. 1.* Lycorea cleobaea *(Danainae), 2.* Mechanitis lysimnia *and 3.* Melinaea ethra *(Ithomiinae), 4.* Heliconius ethilla *and 5.* Eueides isabella *(Heliconiinae). 6.* Protogonius hippona *(Nymphalinae) and 7.* Dismorphia astyocha *(Pieridae). Fritz Müller considered 1–5 to be unpalatable Müllerian mimics, and 6 and 7 to be palatable Batesian mimics. 8.* Lycorea ilione *(Danainae) and 9.* Thyridia megisto *(Ithomiinae) are the original Müllerian mimics. The wings of 1–7 are black, orange (intermediate shade), and yellow (palest shade). 8 and 9 have pale yellow transparent areas with black borders. A. Möller, 1915,* Gesammelte Schriften (Werke) *Plate 62, from Müller, 1881/82.*

Darwin never used such a sentence, and Fritz's thoughts on sexual selection and mimicry remained largely in private communications to his brother and in circulation among Darwin, Wallace, and Meldola. Wallace called it "a very wild supposition,"[38] and Meldola, wrote to Darwin that he would use Müller's facts but would not "dare to publish" his hypothesis on sexual selection.[39] Fritz mentioned the hypothesis only once in his publications on mimicry.[40] The suggestion that sexual selection might be responsible for some examples of butterfly mimicry was an idea that Darwin called "a strange speculation,"[41] although he added that it was not "as incredible as it may at first appear," and he told both Meldola[42] and Fritz[43] that the same idea had occurred to him "in quite different cases, viz. the dullness of all animals in the Galapagos Islands, Patagonia, etc." Walter Blandford,[44] however, quoted Darwin's proposed sentence in his obituary of Fritz and added "Granted that this was a somewhat fanciful speculation, it is at least significant that it should have presented no improbability to the mind of an observer before whom the insects concerned were constantly present as a living reality."[45]

In a letter to Darwin of 14 June 1871, Fritz acknowledged the receipt of *The Descent of Man*, and treated the principal difficulties in mimicry theory:[46] the first steps in the evolution of mimicry; the relative abundance of models and mimics; and the fact that mimetic patterns were often limited to females. He enclosed some sets of butterfly wings to demonstrate some of his points:

> One of the most interesting of our mimicking butterflies is *Leptalis* [*Dismorphia*] *melite*, [Fig. 15, Nos. 2-13]. The female alone [Nos. 10-13] . . . is imitating one of our common white Picridae [No. 14], which she copies so well, that even her own male is often deceived, for I have repeatedly seen the male pursuing the mimicked species, till after closely approaching . . . he suddenly returned.[47]

---

*Fig. 15. Butterfly forewings sent by Fritz Müller to Darwin, June 1871. (1) non-mimetic* Dismorphia thalia, *(2–9)* Dismorphia melite *males and (10–13) females, (14)* Melete *(or* Daptoneura*) lycimnia. MS. DAR. 142:58. Courtesy of the Syndics of the Cambridge University Library.*

Fritz noted that the two sexes differed both in wing shape and coloring and that the males were similar to another species of *Dismorphia* which he believed to be non-mimetic (No. 1), and he also commented that both sexes were highly variable, as his specimens showed. But he then limited his discussion to sexual selection.

Fritz's first publication on mimicry, in 1876, no longer mentioned sexual selection but used these butterflies to demonstrate the "first steps" in the evolution of mimicry with an emphasis on natural selection by predators. His paper was an answer to those who objected that a potential mimic would already have to be somewhat like its model at the outset if natural selection were ever to be able to improve the mimicry. Although Darwin and Bates both thought it probable that mimetic resemblances would have to start that way, it was Oscar Schmidt[48] and Eduard von Hartmann whom Fritz was answering. In 1872 Hartmann had written:

> Only when the ancestral form . . . is already so similar to the model that predators are confused . . . can natural selection perfect the resemblance. . . . But because that is true only of some examples of mimicry now known, other yet unknown causes must have been acting in the remaining cases.[49]

For the examples that Bates had presented, von Hartmann continued, there was no question about mimicry, but how could a mimetic pattern [in *Dismorphia*, a member of the family Pieridae] evolve from an "ordinary white pierid" by natural selection of "random individual variations," when intermediates between the ancestral and mimetic patterns would have no advantage in the presence of sharp-eyed predators like birds? Fritz argued first that protective coloration in general could evolve from any starting point, so long as it rendered its possessor even slightly more successful at avoiding predators than the original form had been, and he extended this argument to incipient mimicry of one butterfly species by another:

> from any starting point whatever, natural selection could bring an animal to the point of vanishing from an enemy's sight among a great swarm of another species, perhaps a white pierid among a host of colored Ithomiae [the models]. If the first trifling deviations from the original white coloration served only in reducing the distance at which their possessors attracted the

attention of an inattentive enemy flying by, they would still be useful . . . and could consequently serve as the basis of the gradual evolution of a resemblance which would be able to deceive even the sharp eyes of birds foraging for prey in a swarm of Ithomiae.[50]

The benefit of poor mimicry when there was as yet nothing better was recognized as an important point by the reviewer of Fritz's paper in the *American Naturalist*,[51] but it remained a sticking point in discussions of the evolution of mimicry for many years.

Despite his belief that mimicry could evolve from "any starting point whatever," Fritz adduced evidence from among the local species of *Dismorphia* that the ancestor had not been an "ordinary white pierid," as von Hartmann had supposed, but probably had a black and yellow pattern from which the various mimetic *Dismorphia* species could have evolved. His reasoning was that a mimetic species should stand between its ancestor and the model in wing shape, coloration, and other mimetic characters, and that since mimicry was often better expressed in females than in males, the females should be closer to the model and the males closer to the ancestral pattern. Hence "in a mimetic species with appreciable sexual dimorphism there will be the following series: ancestral form, male and then female of the mimetic species, model species."[52] Fritz arranged the pertinent species in a series by hind wing shape, from a non-mimetic *Dismorphia*, through the male and the female of a mimetic species, to the model, and then to an "ordinary white pierid." Because the mimic stood between the non-mimetic relative and the model, rather than between the "ordinary white pierid" and the model, Fritz believed that the ancestor of the mimetic species resembled the non-mimetic *Dismorphia* and not the "ordinary white pierid" which lay at the other end of the series. The comparison of fore wing patterns led to the same conclusion. In Fig. 15, the series runs from the non-mimetic No. 1 through the male (No. 3) and female (No. 10) of the mimetic species to the model (No. 14). Fritz emphasized the tremendous variation in the mimetic species and suggested that mimicry was still evolving.

A second issue in mimicry theory was the relative abundance of models and mimics in natural populations. Bates's principal criterion

for telling mimics from models was that the former showed "a departure from the normal style of colouring of their congeners, whilst the
other are conformable to their generic types,"[53] but he added that
mimetic species were usually scarcer than their models, the latter
flourishing because "they enjoy by some means immunity from
effective persecution."[54] At the end of his discussion he cautioned,
however, that "a mimetic species need not always be a rare one,
although this is very generally the case; it may be highly prolific, or its
persecution may be intermitted when the disguise is complete."[55] Fritz
was not aware of Bates's caveat, having read only Darwin's account,
which stressed the abundance of models and the rarity of mimics, and
he often returned to this point when he found variation in the relative
numbers of presumed models and mimics on his travels in Santa
Catarina. In a letter to Hagen in 1871, however, he struck on the fact
that little was known of what determined the abundance of any
species:

> The model is not in every case more common than the mimic.
> For example, the splendid *Parides nephalion* [an unpalatable
> *Aristolochia*-feeding swallowtail] is a rather rare butterfly here,
> far rarer than *Euterpe* [*Archonias*] *tereas* [a pierid and probably
> palatable] which, aside from being smaller, mimics it to perfec-
> tion. . . . However, before reaching a final decision we must have
> far more detailed knowledge than I yet possess of the habits of
> the species in question and of the conditions which promote or
> check their increase.[56]

In 1878, after returning from a butterfly-collecting excursion to
São Bento in the northern coastal mountains of Santa Catarina, Fritz
touched on relative abundance again:

> On the Itajaí we have three species of *Eueides*, viz., *E. pavana*,
> *isabella* and *aliphera*; all of them are rare, and *E. pavana* ex-
> tremely so. This last species closely resembles *Actinote thalia*; *E.
> isabella* resembles *Mechanitis lysimnia* and *Heliconius ethilla*,
> while *E. aliphera* mimics *Dryas julia*. I, therefore, formerly
> thought that the three rare species of *Eueides* mimicked the three
> common species of *Actinote*, *Mechanitis* and *Dryas*. Afterwards,
> after finding that the several species of *Eueides* possess a very
> strong and repugnant odour, I had become somewhat doubtful,
> and at São Bento I found that *E. aliphera* was extremely com-

mon, so common indeed that repeatedly I caught as many as eight specimens in the net at once, whereas *D. julia* was so rare that I have only seen two or three specimens together. Thus judging by their relative abundance, an observer on the Itajaí might consider *E. aliphera* to be a mimic of *D. julia*, while an observer at São Bento might take *D. julia* to be a mimic of *E. aliphera*.[57]

The later obsession with the idea that Batesian mimics were always scarcer than their models was probably due to Wallace's strong statement in 1889 "that the imitators are always less numerous in individuals,"[58] but even now Bates's and Müller's words are rarely read and the error persists.[59] The question which is the mimic and which the model, applied only to Batesian mimicry. It lost much of its force with Fritz's explanation of the convergent resemblance of several unpalatable species, "Müllerian" mimicry, which was published soon after that letter to Darwin.

A third issue in mimicry theory was that mimetic patterns are frequently expressed only in female butterflies. This sex-limitation was explained by Belt in 1874 as a consequence of sexual selection by females for conservative (ancestral) male patterns, which prevented the latter from acquiring mimicry. Belt used as evidence the fact that males of *Dismorphia* species in which both sexes were mimetic still retained a "primordial" white patch on the upper hind wing in an area usually covered by the fore wing. Belt believed that the patch was displayed in courtship to "gratify a deep-seated preference for the normal [white] color of the order to which the [*Dismorphia* species] belong."[60]

Fritz had made a similar suggestion in his letter to Darwin in 1871 but supported it with a different observation. His example was [*Dismorphia*] *melite*. The female, he believed, mimicked a white pierid, *Daptoneura lycimnia*, while the male was brightly colored and non-mimetic. "As in this case," Fritz wrote:

the male is more brightly coloured than the female, it may be asked, whether the plain dress acquired by the latter through natural selection has been transmitted exclusively or almost exclusively to the same sex, or whether being transmitted to both sexes the transmission has been checked and the bright colouring preserved in the male through sexual selection . . .

> [T]hat part of the lower surface of the fore-wings, which is covered by the hind-wings and where consequently the transmission of the white colour of the female to their male offspring could not be checked by selection, is indeed white in the male also.[61]

Of the wing surfaces which overlap, Belt chose the *upper* surface of the male hind wing, where a "primordial" white patch would be revealed by a courting male and thus be preserved by sexual selection in a species in which both sexes had mimetic patterns; Fritz chose the *under* surface of the male fore wing, which carried the mimetic character of the female but would not be revealed in courtship and would therefore escape sexual selection.

In February 1878, at the height of the Brazilian summer, Fritz made his first excursion into the coastal mountains of northern Santa Catarina (Map 3). He was principally seeking butterflies, and he had a satisfying take "not of new or rare pinned specimens, but rather of observations aimed at various general problems."[62] While at the foot of the mountains, he repeatedly caught *Ituna* [now *Lycorea*[63]] *ilione*, a milkweed butterfly (Danainae) with a pattern of black bands across otherwise transparent wings, and he also caught one specimen of the scarcer ithomiine *Thyridia megisto*, which he wished to compare with *Ituna* because of its remarkably similar appearance (Fig. 16). On this excursion he seems to have gathered the observations that finally stimulated him to his explanation of what we now call Müllerian mimicry. He also recognized that he had a mimetic resemblance between two unpalatable species. Bates had also recognized mimetic resemblances among species all of which appeared to be unpalatable,[64] but he did not pursue the topic. Writing to Weismann in June, Fritz said that he had submitted to *Kosmos* in late April a paper, "*Ituna* and *Thyridia*," in which he "discussed the sort of mimicry hitherto scarcely noticed, between species equally well protected by nasty smell and taste."[65] That paper did not appear until May 1879[66] and is dated "Itajaí, September 1878" but was evidently completed before June. It contains a full discussion of the deceptive similarity of *Ituna* and *Thyridia*, Fritz's evidence that the two genera should be assigned to different families (or subfamilies), and a presentation of a mathematical argument supporting his explanation of how two species both

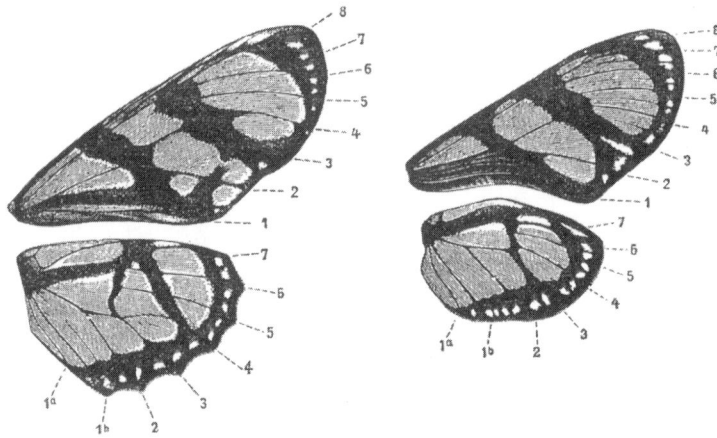

*Fig. 16. Fritz Müller's original example of "Müllerian" mimicry; left,* Ituna *(now* Lycorea*) and right,* Thyridia, *showing how a similar pattern is achieved independently in two unrelated species. The wing veins are numbered for comparison. Wallace, 1889,* Darwinism, *from Müller, 1879a.*

protected from predators by their unpalatability could evolve a mimetic resemblance to one another. Without prior mention to his correspondents, Fritz had already submitted an abstract of the mathematical explanation of such mutual resemblances, which appeared in July 1878,[67] and in it Fritz suggested how suddenly the idea had come to him after long gestation:

> It is remarkable how one racks one's brains over a problem the solution to which is so simple that it is scarcely conceivable how one could have found it so difficult only a moment before. So it was for me with mimicry in butterflies; danaines, ithiomiines, acraeines, heliconiines, all appear to be equally well protected by unpleasant smell and taste, and yet there are many mimetic species among them. The smell of *Eueides* species is particularly strong, and yet *Eueides pavana* is a mimic of *Actinote thalia*, *E. isabella* of *Heliconius ethilla* or *Mechanitis lysimnia*, and *E. aliphera* resembles *Dryas julia* except in size. Now, what advantage can a species which is protected by a disgusting smell have in mimicking another equally protected? If its enemies avoid this

species by instinct, none; if on the other hand, and that is certainly more probably, its enemies must first learn of its unpalatability by experience, then the scarcer it is the greater the advantage. The advantage which two unpalatable species gain from their resemblance is inversely related to the square of their individual numbers. Instead of a general deduction, which is in fact very simple, I give an example. Suppose that two unpalatable species live in a certain region, 10,000 of one and 2,000 of the other. Each year predators in the same region eat 1,200 individuals of an unpalatable species before they learn its unpalatability. If the species are different, each one loses that many; if they are so similar that experience with one is as good as with the other, then the first species will lose 1,000 and the other 200 individuals, the former thus gaining through the resemblance 200 (or 2% of its total numbers) and the latter 1000 (or 50% of its total numbers). It follows from these considerations that in most cases (e.g., *Thyridia* and *Ituna*) the question, which is the original species and which the mimic, is probably an idle one. Each had an advantage in becoming similar to the other; they could have converged.[68]

Fritz's fuller treatment of the subject[69] appeared in *Kosmos* in May 1879 and was sent by Darwin to Meldola, who translated it and presented it at a meeting of the Entomological Society of London.[70] He reported to Darwin that it was severely criticized by several members, "the majority of whom are, as you know, nothing more than species describers. In fact, I do not think anyone grasped the line of argument through inability to follow the simple algebraic reasoning which Fritz Müller has adopted."[71] Bates himself:

> whilst acknowledging the great value of the numerous facts adduced from his own personal observations by Dr. Fritz Müller, could not agree with him in his proposal to separate, as a distinct family, *Ituna* and *Lycorea* (with *Danais*) from *Thyridia* and the remainder of the *Ithomia* group . . . With regard to the still incompletely solved problem of mimicry, he could not see that Dr. Müller's explanations and calculations cleared up all the difficulties.[72]

But Bates was "then somewhat past the reception of new ideas."[73] Jean Gayon has recently claimed that the entomologists at the meeting in 1879 failed to appreciate Fritz's hypothesis because it "implied a hardening of the concept of natural selection, [that is] a clearer rejection of alternative hypotheses." By way of explanation Gayon adds, "As Meldola pointed out [in 1895[74]], by a strange route Müller's hypothesis underlined the importance of acquired characters [in the Lamarckian sense]."[75] But Meldola says no such thing, and Gayon misunderstands Fritz's use at the time of "acquired" (*erworbene*), meaning "derived," and "inherited" (*ererbte*), meaning "ancestral." Meldola's assessment explains why Fritz's idea was resisted.

Fritz published again on mimicry theory in 1881/82,[76] treading some familiar paths but chiefly criticizing Wallace himself, who, in an address entitled "By-paths in the domain of biology" delivered in 1876 but only published two years later, attributed the resemblance of protected species as well as unprotected ones, to unknown "local causes." With respect to South American examples, Wallace wrote:

> in the three subfamilies Danainae, Acraeinae, and Heliconiinae, all of which are specially protected, we find identical tints and patterns reproduced, often in the greatest detail, each peculiar type of coloration being characteristic of separate geographical subdivisions of the continent. . . . The resemblances thus produced between widely different insects is sometimes general, but often so close and minute that only a critical examination of structure can detect the difference between them. Yet this can hardly be true mimicry [i.e., Batesian], because all are alike protected by the nauseous secretion which renders them unpalatable to birds.[77]

Wallace suggested in an accompanying essay that the cause might be "the presence of peculiar elements or chemical compounds in the soil, the water, or the atmosphere, or of special organic substances in the vegetation."[78]

Fritz had already[79] attacked von Hartmann with a touch of sarcasm for suggesting "unknown causes" of mimicry, but he now had more examples at hand, a theory of his own, and a target whom he deeply respected as a fellow Darwinian. He covered the ground again carefully and laboriously, pointing out, among other things, that a single genus might be represented by several different mimetic patterns in any one locality, while different genera were represented by a common pattern; and that mimetic resemblances often depended on corresponding pattern elements that were located in different parts of the wings of different species.

Wallace responded[80] by agreeing with the arguments and repudiating "unknown local causes." In addition he gave Fritz the palm for his original theory, which he had not of course seen when he put together his essays in 1878, and he extended Müllerian mimicry to include species differing in degree of unpalatability, anticipating modern arguments that many butterflies are somewhat distasteful and that mimicry is mostly Müllerian.

The principal criticism of Fritz's theory was the lack of proof that insectivorous birds and other predators had to learn about unpalatability by experience. Fritz thought learning to be essential for his theory: if predators avoided each distasteful species because of instinctive recognition, there would be no selective pressure for change in any of the species. Meldola also had doubts that predators had instinctive recognition[81], and Wallace felt it necessary to respond to the critics by pointing out the improbability of predators having instinctive recognition of the many different color patterns displayed by distasteful butterflies.[82]

In August 1882 Fritz sent to Meldola a specimen of *Heliconius*, an unpalatable butterfly, with evidence that a bird had seized it and let it go,[83] By April 1883 he had completed for *Kosmos* a manuscript of additional observations bearing on the question whether or not predators had an instinctive knowledge of unpalatable species, and he laid his cards on the table:

> it is no secret that my entire explanation [of Müllerian mimicry] stands or falls on one assumption, which although highly probable has not yet been proven, that a certain number even of unpalatable butterflies will be destroyed by young inexperienced birds.[84]

On the same day he wrote to Meldola. He had spent the previous week looking for bird-damaged wings of the unpalatable species *Actinote thalia* and had caught 38 such specimens out of a few thousand, and he enclosed as many specimens as he had room for in his letter, in the hope that they would "suffice to convince anyone that even distasteful butterflies are attacked by birds and that therefore the birds are not born with any "instinctive" knowledge of them.[85] He chose *Actinote* because it was very common at that season, not at all shy, and easily observed nectaring on the flower heads of a shrubby composite in his neighborhood. One individual had apparently been attacked three times by birds, lost enough of three wings to be incapable of flight, and yet had not been eaten. Fritz reasoned that the attacker had recognized the nastiness of the butterfly from its juices and had rejected it. The fraction of damaged individuals surprised him at first:

> You can count on one among a few hundred intact animals being mutilated in this way. That is certainly no less than is found in edible species, according to casual and therefore very unreliable observations. And yet it is conceivable that proportionally even more individuals of unpalatable species than of palatable ones would be flying about with bitten wings. For in the latter, a good bite out of the wing is generally followed by being eaten, while in the former the first bite betrays the unpalatability of the prey and if not fatal, allows the cripple to live.[86]

Fritz's belief that a potential predator's experience with a distasteful butterfly was more important than any inborn aversion was strengthened by an anecdote that he wrote to Krause in 1884:

> The caterpillars of *Papilio anchisiades* usually sit during the day in large groups thickly crowded on the trunks of orange trees, and when disturbed give off from their everted [osmateria] a strong smell, which has given them the name "stink caterpillars." I tell you this because of a strange experience. As children we always loved to eat carob and I never knew of any schoolmates to be averse to it. Once years ago I had carob pods sent from Germany in order to plant the seeds, and offered them to my children as a special delicacy, but none would taste it, any more than would my nieces and nephews or others who grew up here. They all rejected it and declared unanimously and quite independently of one another that it smelled like "stink caterpillars." The odors are in fact quite similar. A nice example of my point that aversion to certain smells, or pleasures, are not innate, as Jäger's theory of the mind claims, but that far more often, indeed as a rule, learning plays a very large role.[87]

239

Fritz's observations on bird-damaged butterflies were noted in the *Transactions of the Entomological Society of London* in 1888, but Roland Trimen,[88] speaking to the Society in 1897, discussed the lack of evidence for bird predation on butterflies, listed several anecdotal accounts, and prefaced his remarks: "Considering that there is no record of any naturalist's having seriously taken up the investigation of the matter in the field. . . ."[89] But he never mentioned Fritz's work.

Bates on the Amazon, Wallace in the East Indies, Trimen in South Africa, and Müller in Santa Catarina were the pioneers in the study of butterfly mimicry, but only the last two tackled the major questions with experiments and observations designed for the purpose. By the time that Bates had published his Darwinian explanation[90] and Wallace his first paper on the subject,[91] both were back in England. Before returning to England from South Africa, Trimen had recognized the remarkable polymorphic Batesian mimicry of the swallowtail now called *Papilio dardanus*[92] through a breeding program that he organized, but only Fritz continued to live in the midst of mimetic species. He had published on the evolution of mimetic patterns, the behavior of predators, and the question of sex-limitation, and was able to discuss most of the critical questions as a field naturalist. The value of that approach was reflected in Blandford's comment after Fritz's death in 1897 that, "since Müller's work, little progress has been made on the study of mimicry by observations on living forms."[93]

England was the principal land of mimicry theory well into the twentieth century, and Fritz's German was no barrier to understanding, because nearly all of his writings on mimicry were published in English or were noted or excerpted in American or English journals. Hence the irony that his papers remained largely unknown to the principal theorists, although his evidence of bird predation and the steps by which mimicry might evolve should have caught their attention. R. C. Punnett, in his influential attack on mimicry theory in 1915 [94], disregarded Fritz's views on these topics and cited only the English translation of the Müllerian mimicry paper of 1879, but by 1915 even Meldola, Fritz's English champion, was gone and could no longer spring to his defense.

# 12

# Traveling Naturalist: Visitors, Losses, and Dismissal, 1881–1891

On New Year's Day 1881 Darwin's book *The Power of Movement in Plants*[2] arrived in Blumenau. Fritz read it with fascination in ten days. "It could not have come at a better time," he wrote to Ernst Krause:

> Who would not immediately want to become acquainted on his own with the existence and significance of the various movements of plants? It seems a shame to have to read that splendid book in a heated room, knowing that the plant life all around you was dormant and buried under snow and ice. Here it is just the season of most luxuriant growth. Any plant seeking protection from bright light by paraheliotropic movements [turning the edges of its leaves toward the sun] is going to be doing it now, when at noon the sun is nearly at the zenith. So these days I have been rambling about a good deal under the vertical midday sun, as well as in the evening with a lantern, in order to see just what could be seen without any special equipment.[3]

Fritz reported his findings to Darwin, adding in response to the book that "since I observed the spontaneous revolving movements of *Alisma*,[4] I have seen similar movements in so many and so different plants that I felt much inclined to consider spontaneous revolving movements or circumnutation as common to all plants and the movements of climbing plants as a special modification of that general phenomenon. And this you have now convincingly, nay superabundantly, proved to be the case."[5]

Darwin, with his son Francis, had shown in England that the sleep movements of leaves protected them from the chilling effects of radiation to a clear night sky, and that the movements were sometimes different in related species. To Darwin's single example of sleep movements in a grass, where the leaves rose vertically at night, Fritz added a second grass species whose leaves instead sank vertically.[6] Some of the species in which Fritz reported sleep movements also had paraheliotropism under intense sunlight, but, as Darwin wrote in his letter to *Nature* reporting Fritz's findings, "F. Müller doubts whether so strongly marked a case of paraheliotropism would ever be observed under the duller skies of England; and this no doubt is probably correct, for the leaflets of *Cassia neglecta*, on plants raised from seed formerly sent me by him, moved in this manner, but ever so slightly that I thought it prudent not to give the case."[7]

The arrival of the book on plant movement renewed the contact between Darwin and Fritz after a hiatus of nearly two years, and over the following year the two exchanged accounts of their observations and experiments on plant movement and heterostyly in a score of letters. During Darwin's last years he was in touch with scarcely any other naturalist in the field, and he queried Fritz repeatedly. In April 1881, for instance, he asked about the movements of leaves in the rain:

> I think that I told you that my experiments had led me to suspect that the movement of the leaves of *Mimosa*, *Desmodium* and *Cassia*, when shaken and syringed, was to shoot off the drops of water. If you are caught in heavy rain, I should be much obliged if you would keep this notion in your mind and look to the position of such leaves. You have such wonderful powers of observation that your opinion would be more valued by me than that of any other man.[8]

It had been raining for five hours when Fritz received the letter, and he immediately went into his garden and sent off the pertinent observations. Darwin, whom one feels was hungry for any news from the real world of nature, shot back:

Your kindness is unbounded, and I cannot tell you how much your last letter (May 31) has interested me. I have piles of notes about the effect of water resting on leaves, and their movements (as I supposed) to shake off drops. But I have not looked over these notes for a long time, and had come to think that perhaps my notion was mere fancy, but I had intended to begin experimenting as soon as I returned home; and now with your *invaluable* letter about the position of leaves of various plants during rain . . . I shall be stimulated to work in earnest.[9]

Fritz had scarcely finished Darwin's book on the movement of plants when Hermann Müller's book on insect pollination in alpine flowers arrived,[10] stimulating a profusion of observations which he sent to his brother in the letters of 1881 to 1883. He began making short excursions again, searched the streams in his neighborhood for caddis flies, and returned to the shell mounds on the Luís Alves in May and June 1882.[11] Observation continued to remedy his sorrow over Rosa's death and his letters gradually lengthened and became livelier. Curious about the Lucretian epigrams that Ernst Krause had used as chapter headings in his evolution text *Werden und Vergehen* [Origin and Disappearance][12], he asked Hermann for a copy of Lucretius,[13] and he also requested Polish and Russian grammars and dictionaries in order to read publications that he had received, and because he always enjoyed languages.[14]

Three of Fritz's daughters had married in quick succession, and he followed his grandchildren's first attempts at speech and the development of their color sense with delight. At Christmas 1881 he decorated a "splendid araucaria" as a Christmas tree for two grandchildren, and on his 60th birthday (31 March 1882) he reported to Hermann that his little favorite, the year-and-a-half old eldest son of Anna, had been around him all day.

He wrote to Hermann that he was still not particularly tired after a 40-km march on shadeless paths under a cloudless sky, although he was reminded, by rheumatism after wading around for hours among the rocks of a waterfall, that he could no longer expect of a 60-year-old body what a younger one had been able to do without damage.[15] Even in physical discomfort his appetite for observation continued:

I have been harboring a parasitic oestrus larva[16] in my upper
right arm for the past two weeks, for the first time since I had
eight of them at once more than 30 years ago. It usually causes
little hardship, and sometimes you don't notice it all day; only
now and then when it becomes restless does the animal cause a
most unpleasant racking pain. I would like to raise the fly from
it, but I doubt that my stoicism is up to it.[17]

The larva, however, kept him awake so much that it had to be
removed.

The news of Darwin's death on 19 April 1882 reached Fritz
within a few weeks. "And now," he wrote to Ernst Krause in early
May:

what affects me above all, the death of our Darwin! He spoke of
it even a year ago, saying that he felt very old and would probably not live much longer, but at the same time his letters
continued to show the old intellectual vigor and his keen
interest in everything; even his last letter (of 4 January), in
which he told me of Balfour's personal circumstances and of his
own investigation of ammonium carbonate, and spoke of some
notes that I had made on *Pontederia*, etc., was written so much
in his usual manner that the news struck me completely unpre-
pared. It is an altogether irreplaceable loss for me, perhaps more
than for anyone else. For many years I was accustomed to telling
him all my little natural history adventures and to receiving his
stimulating and instructive suggestions. The splendid qualities
of his character, his freedom from petty vanity, the gentleness of
his opinions, the ungrudging and often too willing acknowledgment of others, won him everyone's sympathy. To me he was
always so cordial, and showed, as I learned after our flood, such
selfless goodwill, that in him I may well say that I mourn a
second "father."[18]

"Since Darwin's death," Fritz later wrote to Krause, "I have no
one besides my brother and you from whom I may expect an interest
in all those remarkable things that my surroundings offer me; otherwise, I can speak to one person only of Crustacea, to another only of
Lepidoptera, to a third of plants, etc."[19]

Soon after the news of Darwin's death, Fritz heard that his half-
brother (Gustav) Wilhelm Müller, born after Fritz emigrated and 35

years younger, wished to come to Blumenau for an extended visit to work jointly on zoological subjects. Although Fritz would have been glad to see him at any time, his visit was especially welcome just then. "I hope that we shall become close friends as brothers and naturalists," Fritz wrote to Krause, "and that he will fulfill my cherished wish, to find in a young friend a substitute for the son whom I lost on the day of his birth."[20]

A room was added to the house, and Wilhelm arrived at the end of June 1883. Fritz's hopes were realized, as he wrote to Hermann in September:

> In the morning each of us usually attends to his own work in his room, in the afternoon we wade about in some stream or go into the forest with axe and machete, hunting for termites, etc. In doing so I take renewed and doubled pleasure in our natural treasures, always regretting only that you too cannot be with us. Wilhelm is now completing an article on his studies of our aquatic Lepidoptera, with which he has been thoroughly occupied and which have yielded many very nice and, it seems to me, important results.[21]

Hermann Müller never received that letter, the last of Fritz's 286 letters to his brother. He had died of a pulmonary thrombosis on 25 August 1883, at age 54, while on an alpine journey in the South Tyrol, and was buried in Prad (now Prato allo Stelvio, in a corner of alpine Italy) below the Ortler, surrounded by the mountains that had long been his favorite research area.[22]

For years the brothers had discussed the idea of Hermann's emigrating to Blumenau, or at least coming for a visit. When Hermann first showed signs of a chronic lung ailment, Fritz hoped that he would abandon his strenuous schedule, seek a cure through a sea voyage and a stay in the healthy climate of Blumenau, and fulfill Fritz's desire to see him again. But that was not be:

> In Hermann I lost not only a brother who was my particular favorite from his earliest childhood, but also the last of my friends in the old country who stayed in close correspondence with me over the years. I have exchanged a few letters with Hermann nearly every month for the last two decades, as we

never waited for the answer to our last letter before writing again.[23]

"The rest of my life lies pretty bleakly before me," Fritz wrote to Krause:

Fortunately for me, I now at least have Wilhelm here; our daily excursions keep me busy, and I have someone to talk with about the things that interest me, although of course it is no substitute for the correspondence with our late beloved and unforgettable brother that has been my necessity for decades.[24]

Various botanical topics which I had planned to take up this summer, mainly those dealt with in Hermann's last paper, still remain, because whatever the results of my observations, their disposition was to be decided by him. I miss Hermann constantly, and the more so as time goes by; botany, especially, has lost nearly all fascination, for my botanical observations were really nothing but raw material which gained value and significance only through him.[25]

A round of scientific honors came in 1884: the Sociedad Nacional de Ciencias in Buenos Aires named him as a Corresponding Member, the Kaiserlich Leopoldinisch-Karolinische Akademie der Naturforscher as a Member, and the Entomological Society of London as an Honorary Member. Of the last, he reported to Ernst Krause:

an honor has come my way which has delighted me and which I really do not deserve; the Entomological Society of London named me to its honorary membership, which by statute has no more than ten. The Society could probably have chosen no one who would do more poorly on an examination in entomology than I, and that pleases me no end and not at all out of vanity; for if the Society passes over a hundred famous describers of beetles in order to take to its bosom someone who has produced only a few fragments from the world of insects, it shows that all that wretched species rubbish is no longer considered the main point.[26]

Fritz and Wilhelm undertook expeditions in August 1884 and early in 1885 to Armação da Piedade, on the mainland opposite the northern tip of Santa Catarina Island, the site of a shell mound which

Fritz had visited in 1875, where at low tide a sheltered bay offered a rich bounty of marine invertebrates.

The most interesting of their discoveries was a huge new species of acorn worm, *Balanoglossus gigas*, at that time of uncertain taxonomic relationship but now considered a member of a small phylum allied to the chordates. The brothers collected specimens of this burrowing worm-like animal a meter and a half long, and Fritz confirmed anatomical details that had been in dispute, commented on its strong iodine smell (which a chemist friend of his in Blumenau determined to be iodine itself), and observed its nocturnal phosphorescence. Fritz wondered whether light-production in subterranean tube-dwelling worms like *Balanoglossus* and some annelids was a warning of their unpalatability, but he concluded from the cryptic dwelling places of these animals that the facts were against it.[27]

Wilhelm Müller returned to Germany in May 1885 with a completed work on South American nymphalid caterpillars[28] and a variety of collections and observations. From Blumenau he had written Ernst Krause an appreciative letter about his working conditions:

> Free from tiresome worry over room and board, in a natural world teeming with more interesting things worth doing than I can accomplish, with a guide who instructs me not only in the lay of the land, but also in the current status of a scientific problem and has saved me time-consuming preliminary work, and in daily communication with my brother: who could ask for more?[29]

After Wilhelm's departure, Fritz sought by increased work to overcome the feeling of isolation that would now often depress him. He conscientiously recorded his daily observations in reports that he transmitted to the Museum in Rio quarterly or semi-annually without a break from September 1884 to December 1889. These were written in Portuguese and illustrated with his drawings, and they were a continuation of the series of his larger papers that had appeared in the *Archivos* of the Museum. But because he rightly recognized that the Museum in Rio was not a safe depository for those manuscripts, he saved the drafts and entrusted them shortly before his death to his daughter Anna with the suggestion that they might eventually be published in the *Revista* of the Paulistan Museum in São Paulo. That journal published only the observations on *Balanoglossus* and other invertebrates, a fragment of the total, and the remaining reports appeared only when Alfred Möller brought them out in German translation in the *Briefe* in 1921. The drawings and the fair copies of the reports themselves had been lost in the National Museum when Ernst Ule, then an official of the Museum, searched for them after Fritz's death.[30] With Wilhelm Müller's help, Alfred Möller also found among Fritz's papers the drawings to accompany the reports on caddis flies of 1885–1888, and they were included in the 1921 publication.

The reports of the years 1887 to 1889 were taken up with Fritz's observations on the irregularities of flowers, which he recognized as examples of the sort of ubiquitous individual variation from which natural selection could form races and species. In 1886 he reported, for example, that races and species differed only in degree because "without fixed boundaries and with many transitions, the oddest and most striking deviations from the norm form a continuum with the most insignificant." He was so fascinated with floral variation in an introduced species of *Alpinia* that he finally made an end to his thousands of detailed observations only by rooting the plants out of his garden. In this member of the ginger family, in which a single stamen is the rule and the flowers are three-parted, Fritz found flowers with two functional stamens and others with a four-parted ovary and four "sepals" and "petals." Among 2639 flowers that he inspected in 1887 and 1888, more than 300 deviated from the normal structure in these sorts of ways,[31] and similar studies of a common weedy yellow-eyed grass *Hypoxis decumbens* (Amaryllidaceae) and a cultivated *Cypella* (Iridaceae) added huge numbers of examples of deviations in floral structure.

In 1886, a year and a half after his brother Wilhelm's departure, Fritz's loneliness was broken by the short visit of two young botanists from Bonn, A. F. Wilhelm Schimper and Heinrich Schenck.[32] They were following up subjects that Fritz had studied years before: Schimper the mutualism of *Cecropia* trees and their ant protectors, as well as epiphytic plants, and Schenck the biology and anatomy of climbing plants, and both produced major works based on their Brazilian experience after they returned to Germany.[33] Not long after:

in April and May 1887, unfortunately only briefly, we had here the members of the Xingú Expedition, first [the geographer] Peter Vogel from Munich, the expedition's astronomer, then [the ethnologists] Karl von den Steinen [1855–1929] and Paul Ehrenreich [1855–1914]. An outbreak of cholera in Argentina and Matto Grosso had interrupted for a month the steamer connection with Cuiabá [whence the expedition would cross the watershed into the Xingú River drainage of the Amazon], and they used that unwelcome delay to examine the shell mounds (sambaquis) in our Province. Because I was also familiar with several of those sambaquis from my own observations, we immediately had a great deal to talk about, since at first our opinions about them were miles apart. You have surely read von den Steinen's book about his first journey to the Xingú.[34] I found it doubly interesting for having personally known the author, who is recognizable in every line of the book, as well as for the memories which it called to mind of many of my own little adventures in the virgin forest or in dangerous rapids.[35]

Fritz had given a souvenir photograph, showing himself as a cheerful, barefoot man of the forest, to Schimper and Schenck. Peter Vogel later wrote a piece about Fritz for *Die Gartenlaube*, a popular German weekly of science and the arts, and reproduced the portrait shown in Fig. 17.

These occasional visits by scientific colleagues were supplemented by the move to Blumenau in 1886 of Ernst Ule, who accompanied Fritz on many excursions, although they had little research interest in common. Two years later Ule moved to the southern part of the province, but the two of them corresponded for the rest of Fritz's life.

The political situation in Blumenau during the 1880s was unsettled and greatly affected Fritz's life, for although he only rarely and unwillingly took part in party squabbles, he would not stand aside in the face of notorious injustice. August Müller's letters to his brother Hermann, now lost except for extracts in the *Leben*, described the situation. Blumenau received substantial appropriations year after year from the State treasury, principally for roads and bridges, and these effectively subsidized new settlers. August had long before pointed out the danger that those gratefully accepted government

*Fig. 17. Fritz Müller, characteristically bare-footed. After a photograph taken as a souvenir of the visit of Schimper and Schenck, 1886. Vogel, 1892, in* Die Gartenlaube. *By permission of the British Library, shelfmark P.P.4736.ib.*

subsidies would lure labor away from the export agriculture on which the community's independence depended. There were hard times for everyone when the government funds failed, and struggles over the irregular trickle of money began to shake the colony's tranquility. Between 1864 and 1866, when the long drawn-out war between Brazil and neighboring Uruguay and Paraguay had exhausted Brazil's already debt-ridden finances, Blumenau had already learned that the national treasury did not always pay promptly or with any surety. When resources increased, spiteful or incompetent officials perpetrated extravagant waste, forcing more conscientious civil servants into excessive economy when times got harder. After the "emancipation" of Blumenau in 1880, that is its conversion into an independent "Município" no longer needing state aid for its colonization, money was so scarce that commerce returned for a time to the barter system.[36] Had it not been for the flood of 1880, however, the colony would have been strong enough to weather the crisis. That disaster struck such a serious blow to the prosperity of Blumenau that government assistance was unavoidable, despite emancipation. Government funds flowed again, and the danger that August had foreseen became a reality. "At the end of 1880," he wrote to Hermann in April 1882:

> the government sent a Commission of engineers to repair damaged bridges and roads, and the considerable sum of 400 contos de reis (about $225,000) was set aside for the purpose. The Commission, consisting only of Brazilians, spent the public money in the usual Brazilian way on favoritism, offering a chance to enrich one's supporters far more than to serve the public interest. There was a riot among the colonists last December when the workers' wages were being paid, as a consequence of incompletely kept records but especially because of the bungling of one of the engineers. No serious excesses were committed, and despite the mendacious report of the engineers, the Chief of the Military Commission demanded and got a criminal investigation which concluded that nothing had been started by the colonists. To preserve the honor of the Commission, however, several persons were nevertheless prosecuted and punished with stiff penalties, 12, 6 and 3 years in prison. The most distinguished residents of the colony immediately came out strongly against the Commission, while on the other side

those who had done well in the affair and for the most part still had claim to payment, did not join in. The strongest attack was now directed against the latter people, and indeed in such a grossly offensive way that it caused a deep rift in the local community that will be difficult to heal.[37]

Fritz was among those "most distinguished residents" and took up the cause against the Commission and its followers publicly and with sharp words. He felt obliged to intervene because he was at the time a justice of the peace, and also because he was outraged by the Commission's conduct. Alfred Möller thought, however, that Fritz probably regretted his participation in the dispute, because it got him into intense personal quarrels with many fellow citizens with whom he was otherwise on cordial terms, fulfilling August's prediction of a lasting rift in Blumenau society. An intense and disagreeable newspaper war dragged on for several years, especially after the Commission began publishing the *Immigrant* to attack the opposition. Among Fritz's fiercest enemies in the conflict were Bernardo Scheidemantel, editor of the *Immigrant*,[38] a broadly educated and highly respected member of the community with whom Fritz became friends again later, and Paul Schwarzer,[39] who delivered the eulogy at Fritz's grave. Through his struggle against the Commission, Fritz was also dragged into a terrible political fight between the Conservative and Liberal parties, which:

> are less taken up with fighting over political principles — that is an important secondary consideration — than over places at the trough. Every position from provincial president right down to policeman is occupied by men of the party — excepting only teachers if they have served for a certain time, and clergy — and everyone tries as far as possible to make use of the time for feathering his nest as quickly as he can; for as soon as the opposition party comes to power it is all over.[40]

The trivial party squabbles into which Fritz was now repeatedly drawn against his will and inclination embittered him for a long time, as he wrote to his friend von Ihering in Rio Grande do Sul:

> I hope that our wretched political situation will soon clear up somewhat, though probably not without a dissolution of the chamber and new elections. Here a society of the lowest riff-raff

plays at being rulers in the most insolent way, and one cannot but be disgusted at their actions; before we can be rid of the rabble and finally breath clean air once again among decent human beings we have to long for the downfall of the so-called Liberal Party. I have to say, however, that nothing in either of the old parties inspires me with much confidence; they are both moribund. But is it even possible for the country to regenerate itself?[41]

The result of the conflict, however, was that Fritz made implacable political enemies among the Brazilians, who did not rest until he was finally dismissed as Traveling Naturalist in 1891 and deprived of that means of support. Beginning in 1884 his position became incresingly insecure, a situation which, when added to all of his other sad experiences, dampened his enthusiasm for research:

Early in 1884 I received completely unexpectedly from Ladislau Netto the word that I was dismissed from my position, no reasons given. And although I was never in doubt about those whose scheming I had to thank for that dismissal, I am to this day completely in the dark over the means by which they accomplished it and what role Netto played in the affair. Yet as soon as that notice reached me the dismissal had already been reversed (by the Emperor's intervention as I have been credibly assured), and the official newspapers even tried to deny it. All of the German, French and English newspapers, and even a few Brazilian ones, for example the *Gazeta de Notícias*, had come out against my dismissal, and most pointedly and resolutely a highly talented young French naturalist, Couty, who unfortunately died prematurely.[42]

"Were I a dozen years younger," he wrote to von Ihering, "or had I not a sizable family around me, I would turn my back on this country, where a civil servant is exposed to every intrigue of an anonymous foe and every ministerial whim."[43]

Four years later, in 1888, he was threatened again but learned of it only a year later through a letter from von Ihering, who had also been threatened with dismissal from his post as a Traveling Naturalist. The same enemies were at work, and Fritz wrote back that "for the present we have nothing more to fear except to remain uncomfortable. The older one becomes, the more everlasting insecurity there is in these Brazilian civil service posts."[44]

In November 1889 the liberal monarchy of Dom Pedro II was overthrown, the emperor sent to Portugal, and a provisional military government installed which promised a Republican constitution.[45] The National Museum was an object of the provisional government's "reforms," however, and in June 1890 Fritz read in the *Gazeta de Notícias* that the Traveling Naturalists' positions had been cut. There was still no official notice, and the Director of the Museum answered his query with a telegram: "your position maintained." That state of affairs, however, was short lived. On 4 June 1891 Fritz received from Ladislau Netto, who was still the Director, an official letter:

> The Minister and Secretary of State for Public Instruction, Post, and Telegraphs has decided that henceforth the Traveling Naturalists of the National Museum are no longer to reside outside the capital and are to be subject to the rules of the Museum, their excursions therefore having to be directed to the service and the development of the Museum. I inform you this so that you may proceed to Rio de Janeiro. Your income will henceforth no longer be paid from the Treasury of the State of Santa Catarina, but from the National Treasury, and will in fact be paid in the amount of 3 contos de reis annually [about $1690], matching the emoluments for Traveling Naturalists already in the direct employment of the Museum.[46]

Ladislau Netto must have realized that his official letter was equivalent to a dismissal. Fritz answered without hesitation on the following day:

> The Minister and Secretary of State for Trade, Public Instruction, Post and Telegraphs having decided that Traveling Naturalists may no longer reside away from the capital, according to official communications received by me yesterday, I must from today consider myself dismissed because I cannot move my residence to Rio de Janeiro. Health and brotherhood. Blumenau, 5 June 1891. (signed) Fritz Müller.[47]

Netto responded on 31 July 1891:

> In view of the statements in your communication of 5 June, in which you declared to me that you prefer dismissal as a Traveling

Naturalist to the obligation to live in the capital in order to
devote your service to our unit there and to submit yourself like
the other officials to the law that now prevails there, which
statements I brought to the attention of the Minister, you were,
to my deep regret dismissed. You would have been able to render
the Museum distinguished service if you had fulfilled the terms
to which you would not assent, and which because they place
the interests of the Museum in the closest association with the
presence of its employees, would thereby eliminate serious
failings. Be that as it may, I have to thank you for your contributions to our *Archivos*, in which your articles will still continue to
appear in the future.[48]

Fritz viewed his fate calmly, writing to von Ihering on the same
day that he had responded to the ultimatum from Rio: "After all that
I lived to see in more than 30 years as a Brazilian civil servant, I was
not especially surprised by my recent dismissal and have easily gotten
used to it. Of course it is no pleasure to see oneself stranded at age 70.
Under Dom Pedro that would have been impossible. The only thing
that is affected by the great loss in earnings is, to my regret, that I will
have to give up the scientific journals that I receive and some of
which, like the English *Nature*, I have become fond of over the
years."[49]

Fritz's quick response to Netto's ultimatum probably astonished
the authorities in Rio and gave them no alternative to immediate
dismissal. Hugo von Ihering let his official letter lie unanswered, but
that possibility probably never crossed Fritz's mind. "I had already
been dismissed by the end of June (1891)," he later wrote, "while
Ihering still had no official notification of the ministerial order in
September and was still drawing his salary in December. He received
the telegram containing his dismissal precisely as he was lighting up
his Christmas tree."[50]

# 13

# Heredity and Variation:
# Agreements and Arguments with
# Weismann, 1885–1888

August Weismann endorsed Darwin's *Origin* in 1867 in the first of his published lectures at the University of Freiburg, "On the correctness of Darwinian theory,"[2] but there is no evidence that Fritz was aware of this kindred spirit until 1875, when Weismann began sending copies of his publications, including his first major work, "Studies on the theory of descent"[3] which appeared in 1875–76. In five letters written between August 1876 and June 1878 Fritz responded warmly to Weismann's ideas about the evolution and development of lepidopteran caterpillars, pupae, adult wing patterns, and sexual dimorphism. He sent many observations of Brazilian species to correct and amplify Weismann's points and told Weismann of his discoveries of scent structures in butterflies and of his impending explanation of "Müllerian" mimicry. Although the correspondence may have continued after 1878, the existing letters begin again only in 1885. By then Weismann had developed his major contribution to evolutionary biology, the theory of the continuity of the germ plasm as a key to the puzzle of heredity, and how that continuity rendered impossible the inheritance of acquired characters, that is, characters acquired by the parents as a result of some stimulus during their development.

Weismann believed strongly in the power of natural selection, but he recognized, as Darwinians had for a long time, that its efficacy depended on the existence of heritable variation. Where that variation came from was the puzzle. There were many examples of environmental stimuli that could alter the appearance or physiology of an individual during its development, and it was then a short step to the idea that variation acquired as a result of such things as use and disuse could be passed from parent to offspring. Darwin's hypothesis of pangenesis[4] was an attempt to explain how those acquired characters could be inherited. But Weismann became convinced that only the nucleoplasm (contents of the nuclei) and cell bodies of sperms and eggs passed from parent to offspring, and that the former, which he called germ plasm, carried the determinants of development and was preserved during individual development in certain cells that would eventually develop into germ cells. Those cells would not be affected by the action of use and disuse as body cells (somatic cells) might be, and they would therefore not transmit acquired characters to the offspring. Weismann was also convinced that the reason that the somatic cells in most animals differentiated during development was that they had "simpler" nucleoplasm, which unlike "germ plasm" had lost some developmental information and was capable only of promoting the formation of some specialized cell type and not a complete individual:

> [T]he molecular structure of the germ-plasm in all higher animals must be excessively complex, and, at the same time . . . this complexity must gradually diminish during ontogeny as the structures still to be formed from any cell, and therefore represented in the molecular constitution of its nucleoplasm, become less in number.[5]

If the germ plasm were preserved in a few cells and passed on intact to the next generation through eggs and sperms, there would be no way in which modifications in the body of an individual could feed back into the nucleoplasm of their germ cells, as Darwin proposed in pangenesis, because those modifications would have affected cells that would never form germ cells. Weismann recognized, however, that in most animals there were many generations of cell division before the gonads were formed: "It is therefore clear that all the cells of the embryo must for a long time act as somatic cells, and none of them can be reserved as germ-cells and nothing else."[6] But if this were so, how could some of those "somatic" cells be transformed back and regain the complete germ plasm to be passed on into germ cells? It was clear to Weismann that there could be no such re-transformation. Having backed himself into a corner, Weismann resorted to special pleading: it is not the germ cells that are immortal but only the "undying part of the organism — the germ-plasm,"[7] which they contain, and since that substance does not always affect a cell which carries it, it may persist cryptically in certain somatic cells. These particular somatic cells would then be destined to give rise to germ cells and would carry along the complete germ plasm. Although their destiny might be revealed by such behavior as migrating in the embryo to the site of gonad formation, the ultimate criterion for whether they carry the complete germ plasm is whether they will eventually differentiate into germ cells.

Eduard Strasburger[8] pointed out that some plants could be propagated by pieces of somatic tissue, including leaves. How could a leaf composed of differentiated somatic cells give rise ultimately to germ cells if those somatic cells had lost something of the complete germ plasm? Simple, said Weismann, with some circular reasoning: in plants that can be propagated from leaves certain of the leaf cells contain a small amount of complete germ plasm, whereas in those plants that cannot be propagated from leaves there is no such admixture of germ plasm in the nucleoplasm of the leaf cells. The former are adapted for propagation by leaves, the latter not.

Weismann's belief in the continuity of the germ plasm led him to reject the possibility of the inheritance of acquired characters, an idea that he attacked repeatedly after 1883 in its many manifestations. Curiously, however, Weismann placed the origin of heritable variation in the unicellular ancestors of complex organisms, where there was no distinction between "body cells" and "germ cells," and where "the ultimate origin of hereditary individual differences lies in the direct action of external influences upon the organism."[9] He therefore accepted the inheritance of acquired characteristics in unicellular organisms. The variations arising in those ancestral unicellular organisms would be passed on through evolution into their more complex multicellular descendants, and sexual reproduction would then form all sorts of combinations of those variations, perpetuating the heritable variation on which natural selection could work. In fact Weismann believed that sexual reproduction was the *only* cause of such variation in complex organisms.

Fritz's experience with plant variation led him to criticize Weismann on both points: the impossibility of the inheritance of acquired characters, and the unexceptionable role of sexual reproduction in generating the variation on which natural selection could work.

By "acquired characters" Weismann meant those which an individual expresses as a result of influences on its development, and the term has been used in that sense ever since. Fritz's earlier usage, in *Facts and Arguments* or in writing about mimetic butterflies, had been in a different sense. For him, "acquired" characters were those that had evolved, like the mimetic patterns that distinguish a Batesian mimic from its non-mimetic relatives. In current usage they would be called "derived" characters. In contrast, Fritz's "inherited" characters were "ancestral" characters like the wing venation that might be shared by mimetic and non-mimetic relatives. Beginning in 1886, when he was corresponding with Weismann, however, he usually used "acquired" in Weismann's sense.

After receiving reprints of Weismann's lectures on the continuity of the germ plasm and the non-inheritance of acquired characters sometime in 1885, Fritz wrote to Weismann, in a letter now lost, the results of experimental crosses in *Abutilon* that suggested the inheritance of an acquired character. He had found a few hexamerous (6-parted) flowers on a hybrid between two species in which he had never seen anything but the normal pentamerous (5-parted) flowers of *Abutilon*, and after pollinating both kinds of flowers with pollen from a wholly pentamerous plant, he saved seed separately from the hexamerous and pentamerous flowers of his hybrid and compared the flowers produced by the resulting plants:

> For three weeks I examined all the flowers from a plant grown from [seed from a hexamerous flower], finding 145 pentamerous, 104 hexamerous, and 13 heptamerous [7-parted] flowers. I examined similarly the flowers of another plant derived from seed obtained from pentamerous flowers of the same parent plants. There were 454 pentamerous and 6 hexamerous flowers,

and hence only 1.3 per cent. of the latter kind [compared with 39.4% hexamerous flowers in the first case].[10]

Fritz believed that the condition of having six-parted flowers was a character acquired by the buds that produced those flowers, and that the tendency toward six-parted flowers was passed on to the offspring through gametes from those flowers. Weismann incorporated Fritz's comments in an appendix to his lecture "The significance of sexual reproduction in the theory of natural selection," which he was preparing for publication late in 1885,[11] explaining that there must have been hexamerous tendencies in the embryo from which the plant in question developed, "either as a spontaneous change in the germ-plasm or through the combination of the two parental germ-plasms — a combination which may lead to the appearance or the reality of a new character."[12]

But he did point out that Fritz's observation seemed to be in opposition to the continuity of the germ plasm. "If a single flower can transmit to its descendants special peculiarities which were not possessed by its ancestors, we seem to be driven to the conclusion that the ancestral germ-plasm has not passed into the flower in question, but that new germ-plasm has been formed, inasmuch as the new characters are derived from the flower itself, and not from any of its ancestors." Weismann's interpretation was, however, that "a specimen of *Abutilon* with many hundred flowers is not a single individual, but a colony consisting of numerous individuals which have arisen by budding from the first individual developed from the seed,"[13] and he then discussed for the first time how the origin of bud-variations could be explained within his theory of the continuity of the germ plasm. Bud-variations are new characters that appear on individual shoots of a plant, as many apple varieties have done.

Weismann's argument was that the germ plasm in the bud contains not only germ plasm from the earliest stage in development (that is, the complete set of instructions for development), but also "*this substance altered* so far as to correspond with the altered structure of the individual which arises from it—namely, the rootless shoot which springs from the stems or branches."[14] Weismann is saying that the "persistent" germ plasm may be changed as it passes through generations of cell division in the somatic plant tissue, so that when the latter eventually give rise to shoots and ultimately to germ cells, these may carry an altered hereditary potential. The fact that Fritz's control cross (pentamerous x pentamerous) produced a plant with a few of the rare hexamerous flowers was taken by Weismann as evidence that even normal pentamerous flowers developed on shoots which had some potential for hexamerous flowers in their persistent germ plasm. Weismann seemed uncomfortable about applying his germ plasm theory to plants, and in this case appeared to accept the inheritance of acquired characters.

Fritz received a copy of Weismann's lecture on the significance of sexual reproduction, and its appendices, early in 1886, and in his response he expressed complete agreement with everything in the first nineteen pages.[15] But he had misgivings:

> about the non-heritability of acquired characteristics, of which I can still even now not be convinced. From the fact that "the germ-plasm is not formed anew in each individual," that "[the individual] only forms, as it were, the nutritive soil at the expense of which the germ-plasm grows,"[16] it does not seem to me to follow that its condition must be independent of the individual; it seems to me on the contrary scarcely to reject the hypothesis that the condition of the nutrient medium must have an influence, even if only a small one, on the germ plasm growing in it. Of course the transferability of acquired characteristics from the parents would not necessarily follow; it would follow only that the descendants vary, as Darwin claimed, as a consequence of external influences to which the parents were subjected.[17]

Fritz was not insisting that a character acquired by a parent during its development would necessarily be heritable, only that germ plasm might be altered as it passed through the parent, and that this could be a source of variation in the offspring. We would call those alterations "mutations," and that seems to be the sense both of Weismann's explanation of the ultimate origin of heritable variation and of Fritz's explanation of the influence of "the nutrient medium" on the germ plasm, but in 1886 the concept of mutation was still years away.

In reference to Weismann's explanation of the *Abutilon* case, Fritz wrote:

> The six-parted flowers may of course be considered as "inherited," though not without doing violence to previous usage, according to which one cannot inherit from one's parents what they do not possess. However, they are not to be treated as "acquired" in the sense that they were caused by external conditions which affected the hybrid in which they first appeared.[18]

In Fritz's last known letter to Weismann in 1888 he acknowledged the soundness of Weismann's objections to his interpretation of the *Abutilon* case, but returned to the subject again, making a distinction between characters that were latent in the parent but expressed in the offspring ("inherited") and those that were the result of something that happened in the offspring itself ("acquired"), saying that he had:

> again become confirmed in the view that such deviations in structure of single leaves or flowers are to be considered in a sense as acquired, not as inherited characteristics, above all from the fact that most of the time the very rare deviations in the usual structure, which occur once in many thousands if at all, usually appear together in most cases.[19]

It seems that what Fritz meant by the "inheritance of acquired characteristics" was not like the supposed inheritance of piano virtuosity which a parent develops and passes to his children, as Weismann relates in his lecture.[20] He meant merely that *variation* induced in parents might be inherited:

> Even if the possibility of all of the later-appearing developmental deviations must already be present in the embryo, yet it still seems that particular outside influences must contribute to whether this or that developmental deviation actually forms, and in this respect, as contingent on external influences, such deviations in structure would be considered as "acquired."[21]

As to Weismann's second point, about the significance of sexual reproduction, Fritz agreed that it could "produce the material of individual differences,"[22] although he thought that it was at least as important because of "the crossing that it permits between individuals, the beneficial action of which Darwin's experiments show . . . in all the arrangements of flowers."[23] But he disagreed principally with Weismann's insistence that *only* sexual reproduction could generate the individual differences on which selection could act. From his experience with selection in vegetatively propagated plants, Fritz wrote:

> If sexual reproduction were the only cause of individually inherited differences, then unquestionably the processes of selection would be "an impossibility in species propagated by asexual reproduction,"[24] and since, on the contrary, they are a possibility, then sexual reproduction is not the only source of variability. Let me remind you in this connection of a passage in Darwin's "Animals and plants under domestication": "To my surprise, I hear from Mr. Salter that he brings the great principle of selection to bear on variegated plants propagated by buds, and has thus greatly improved and fixed several varieties, etc."[25] Why should natural selection not be able to do the same? I believe that most of the numerous kinds of bananas originated after the banana had abandoned sexual reproduction; I myself obtained a new and very fine-tasting sort by asexual means and wrote a short communication[26] to "Nature" about it some time ago.[27]
>
> According to your interpretation, the atrophy of parts that have been superseded could occur only through sexual reproduction, not through vegetative propagation. But how else, if not through disuse, can one explain the loss of fertility, the disappearance of sexual parts and finally the loss of flowering ability in so many plants that are propagated continually by asexual means? (compare Darwin, Animals and plants under domestication, II:169). As examples, I have among our cultivated plants sugar cane, arrowroot (*Maranta arundinacea*), *Dioscorea* [yam] species, *Colocasia* [taro], . . . etc. Asexual reproduction itself can hardly be the cause; self-fertile plants which continue to operate sexually (potatoes, manioc) show no such atrophy despite hundreds of years of asexual propagation.[28]

Fritz came to accept the continuity of the germ plasm after reading Weismann's paper on the subject in 1886, but he "was ever less able to be reconciled to its constancy and to the origin of variability being limited to sexual reproduction."[29]

Fritz's reading of Francis Galton[30] on inheritance, and his own experiments on the subject, stimulated another rejoinder to Weismann's "significance of sexual reproduction." Weismann had written:

> Sexual reproduction can also increase the differences between individuals, because constant cross-breeding must necessarily and repeatedly lead to a combination of forces which tend in the same direction, and which may determine the constitution of any part of the body. If, for instance, the same part of the body is strongly developed in both parents, the experience of the breeder tells us that the part in question is likely to be even more strongly developed in the offspring; and that weakly developed parts will in the same manner tend to become still weaker.[31]

Fritz objected:

> Your argument for the intensification of inherited variation through continual crossing of two individuals does not actually seem to me quite correct. If the same body part is strongly developed in both parents, for example exceeding the average measurement by $a$ in the father and by $b$ in the mother, then in the children it must rise above the average by $(a+b)/2$, as far as it is dependent on the mixing of parental germ plasms; but $(a+b)/2$ always lies between $a$ and $b$. Because grandparents, great-grandparents, etc. are involved, however, the children would have to be even closer to the average, and as far as I know the average of children agrees empirically with that expectation. You are certainly familiar with Francis Galton's statistical studies of human stature. Some breeding experiments in maize that I undertook years ago (and am now sending to *Kosmos* for publication) are in complete agreement with his results. If individual children differ still further from their parents, it seems to me that it cannot be as a consequence of the mixing of parental germ plasms, but rather despite it.[32]

Fritz's selection experiments in maize, which he had started immediately upon returning to the Itajaí in 1867, were aimed at increasing the number of rows of kernels on the ear. His original conclusion from the experiment, stated in a letter to Hermann Müller in 1872, had been that selection could move the mean of a population. At that time he wrote:

As soon as there is selection in a variable species in a certain direction, there will be as a result of that selection, and quite apart from external conditions, a progressive change in the same direction from generation to generation. In that way of course the transformation to new types is much facilitated and is accelerated.[33]

After giving Hermann his maize results and two examples from his *Abutilon* crosses, Fritz explained that:

each species seems to possess the characteristic of varying within certain limits; so long as there is no selection in a certain direction, the crossing of different individuals maintains the mean at the same point, with deviations around it and thus the persistence of the extremes. But if one direction is favored by natural or artificial selection the mean is displaced to that side, and with that the extreme forms also move beyond the original limits in the same direction.[34] [Fritz added that the explanation did not serve for all cases, but what followed was omitted from the published letter and has been lost.]

Starting in 1867 Fritz had selected ears of maize with higher than average numbers of kernel rows and planted groups of seeds from ears with the same number separately, so as to avoid crossing between them. The progeny ears were harvested and the selected seed planted the next year, and so forth. For example, seeds from a 16-rowed ear planted in 1867 yielded 385 ears ranging in row-number from 10 to 20 with a mean number of 14.08 rows. Seed from 18-rowed ears of that harvest planted in 1868 yielded 262 ears ranging from 10 to 22 rows with mean row-number 14.39; and the 1869 planting of seed from those 22-rowed ears yielded 373 ears ranging from 12 to 26 rows, mean 16.15 rows. In his notes Fritz gave the complete distributions of row-number in each generation. The efficacy of selection was obvious, as he pointed out in summary:

It appears generally that the higher the row-number in the seed-ear, the greater the decline among harvested ears of those with a lower number than that of the mother ear, the greater the increase of those with higher row-number, and what is more, that there appear ears with a row number higher than that of the mother ear and actually higher than that found in the whole harvest from which the seed ears were gathered.[35]

Fritz submitted the results of his maize experiments for publication only in 1886, after reading Francis Galton's lecture on heredity to the anthropological section of the British Association at its 1885 meeting.[36] Fritz saw the published lecture in his copy of *Nature* and thought it "among the best that has been said on this subject since Darwin."[37] Galton was most interested in human inheritance, but in his lecture in 1885 he first restated the preliminary conclusion that he had reached in 1877 from experiments on the inheritance of seed size: "offspring did *not* tend to resemble their parent seeds in size, but always to be more mediocre than they [closer to the population mean] – to be smaller that the parents, if the parents were large; to be larger than the parents if the parents were very small." He called the phenomenon "filial regression," because the offspring tended to regress from the size of the parents toward the population mean. He now reported the results of a similar investigation into human stature, using a large set of measurements of parents and children, and concluded that the same was true of the inheritance of that trait. The apparent generality of the phenomenon led him declare it the "law of regression."

Fritz attributed the lack of agreement among those interested in the nature of heredity to "the fact that most observations on heredity for which horticultural and market gardens, poultry houses, dovecotes, etc. everywhere offer ample opportunity, are not suited to quantitative expression, and that the resulting uncertainty carries over to the opinions which are based on them." He now recognized that his selection experiment confirmed Galton's "law," and because the German Darwinians with whom he was familiar had never produced those sorts of quantitative results, Fritz decided to publish his 16-year-old observations. But he now emphasized their relevance to Galton's hypothesis rather than to selection, as he had in 1872. After presenting the 1870 data, he concluded:

> I will add only that the law established by Francis Galton about
> 10 years ago for the size of plant seeds and recently for human
> stature, according to which the offspring of parents who deviate
> in any direction from the "type" of their race, far from continu-
> ing in the same direction, approach on the contrary more closely
> the mean of the type and differ from their parents all the more

the farther the parents deviate from the mean,— this law is confirmed without exception by the facts just reported.

The "typical" [most common] row number of maize grown here lies between 10 and 12. The study of 7358 ears of maize . . . yields the following results bearing on the Galtonian law:

| Row number of parents | Mean row number in progeny | Reduction in number from parents |
|---|---|---|
| 14 | 12.61 | 1.39 |
| 16 | 14.08 to 14.15 | 1.85 to 1.92 |
| 18 | 14.90 to 15.57 | 2.43 to 3.10 |
| 20 | 15.76 | 4.24 |
| 22 | 16.15 | 5.85 [38] |

In each generation the mean row number in the progeny was less than that of the parents and closer to the "population" mean, and the farther the parental row number from the "population" mean, the greater that difference became. All of these experiments used row numbers greater than the local mean, but Fritz had also planted seed from 8-rowed ears, and although the yield was small on account of bad weather there were more 10- and 12-rowed ears than 8-rowed, "in conformity with the law."[39]

In 1965 Alfred Sturtevant wrote, "The question has been raised: Would any biologist have appreciated Mendel's work if he had seen the paper before 1900? My own candidate for the most likely person to have understood it is Galton, because of his interest in discontinuous variation, his mathematical turn of mind, and his acceptance of Weismann's view that the hereditary potentialities of an individual must be halved in each germ cell."[40] Fritz apparently never commented on the last point, but he accepted most of Weismann's ideas, and with his mathematical approach to biological problems he is also a candidate for Sturtevant's hypothetical nineteenth-century Mendelian. Fritz was critical of the vaguely quantitative approaches of Darwin's pangenesis and Haeckel's perigenesis of the plastidule,[41] which placed their authors in an intellectual framework uncongenial to Mendel's results, and, unlike Galton, he had a background in experimental crosses of varieties and species and might have appreciated the meaning of Mendel's ratios. But of course we shall never know.

# 14

# Birthday Honors, Civil War, and the Last Years, 1891–1897

On 24 September 1890, Alfred Möller arrived in Blumenau for three years of research on the local fungi. He had been trained by the mycologist Oskar Brefeld[2] at the Forestry Academy in Eberswalde and wrote that he:

> had worked out a plan with Brefeld to use his methods for studying tropical fungi, about which very little was then known. As a suitable place for such studies I naturally turned to Blumenau, which by all accounts combined tropical vegetation with a healthy climate, the opportunity to live among German countrymen, and above all the expectation of Fritz Müller as an experienced and obliging guide. Only then did I introduce myself to him by letter as a relative. [Alfred Möller's paternal grandmother and Fritz's mother were Trommsdorff sisters.] He responded with joyful assent and gave me all the information that I needed for the trip, especially about establishing the laboratory which I set up in the center of town in the house of Fritz Müller's oldest daughter, Anna Brockes. He visited me there several times a week and made it extraordinarily easy for me to start my own research by guiding me through the forest and introducing me to the local plants, of which there was an overwhelming abundance of species new to me. He rarely came empty-handed, almost always bringing some remarkable object with him: a peculiar bignoniaceous fruit or a bunch of cassia flowers; Lepidoptera with scent organs or a non-poisonous coral snake confusingly similar to the poisonous one; palm fruits or

lianas with marvelous structures in their woody tissue; the magnificent flower of the parasite *Lophophytum mirabile* and its remarkable tubers associated with the roots of its host, a leguminous tree of the genus *Inga*; a section of *Cecropia* stem with the workings of guardian ants, or one of the ingenious soil nests of *Termes lespesii*. I induced leaf-cutting ants to build and tend their gardens in artificial nests open to observation, and as the mysteries of the underground fungus gardens of the ants were gradually revealed in my laboratory, including the discovery of the completely unexpected large hat-shaped fruiting body of the fungi that they cultivated, I was often encouraged by Fritz Müller's reminder, which I can still hear: "You must not hold anything impossible a priori."[3]

Alfred Möller's classic elucidation of the underground fungus gardens of leaf-cutting ants[4] finally confirmed Fritz's belief, first expressed in a letter to his brother Hermann in 1869, that the ants were cultivating the fungi for food.

Fritz's property, which he had acquired in 1867, was half an hour's walk down the Itajaí River from the center of town along the road to the coast. From the steep hillside above the road, Alfred Möller reported, one looked down over a cattle pasture with a cowshed. Across the road the roof of Fritz's half-timbered house showed through the dense verdure of the enclosed garden, and beyond it at the bottom of the property flowed the Itajaí River:

> When the sun beats down on the dusty road and the cow takes refuge from its scorching rays at the edge of the woods or under the shed, it is a pleasure to enter the well-tended garden. Tall fan palms shade a spacious fore-court, and on the trunks of these and other trees there is a choice collection of orchids and bromeliads from the depths of the forest. On one tree the long panicles of an *Oncidium* arch out from the midst of a thick bushy *Miltonia* in bloom. On another, *Cattleya*s delight us with their splendid rose-red petals, and at the foot of the trunk in deep shade we spy the marvelous great flowers of a *Stanhopea*. In this botanic garden, however, the orchids are not chosen only with a view to the worth of their flowers. There are also insignificant representatives of many species of *Epidendrum* and *Pleurothallidia*, and the colors and shapes of these small orchid

flowers delight the eye of the attentive observer just as much as
do those of the larger species.

The bromeliads to which Fritz was then devoting most of his
attention were even more richly represented than the orchids. Nearly
all of the fifty-odd species that he had found in the forest around
Blumenau were in his garden, each in its natural position on a tree or
on the ground:

> Huge specimens of *Hohenbergia augusta*, their leaves more than
> a meter long, were fastened to suitable crooked branches, and
> the curious big flowery nests of *Nidularium* and *Canistrum*
> could be seen on the ground. The beautiful red flower heads of
> *Vrisea* shone in the distance, *Bilbergia* displayed its delicately
> colored blue and rose inflorescences, and some *Aechmea* species
> delighted the eye with the richly colored patterns of their leaves.[5]

> Fritz Müller welcomed me into his garden and led me around
> in what could really be called his laboratory. Early every morn-
> ing he observed and took notes, and since he liked to have in his
> garden the plants with which he was occupied, he gradually
> established a collection which reminded him of the stages of his
> work over the years. But the garden was also decked out with
> other particularly striking and beautiful plants, including those
> grown from seeds sent by his many friends abroad. In one bed
> next to the house grew members of the ginger family which had
> successfully made the voyage via Europe from the botanic
> garden in Buitenzorg (Java). *Cycas revoluta* was cultivated by
> many colonists on the Itajaí, but in the whole valley there was
> no grander specimen of this cycad than the one in his garden. A
> huge *Araucaria* overshadowed the house.

Compared with his spacious and practical outdoor laboratory,
Fritz had only a tiny work space in his house:

> A sharp observer once noted that the size and opulence of a
> laboratory is often inversely related to the significance of the
> work carried out in it. I recalled that expression every time I saw
> the little Blumenau study from which so many fertile ideas had
> been sent out round the world. The room was scarcely three
> meters square. A simple table stood by the window, equipped
> only with the most essential apparatus, including an old
> Hartnack microscope. A bookcase stood against the wall, and

271

with the addition of a bed and dressing table there was scarcely space in the room for a chair. I doubt that in the whole world any scholar who deserves the name has been satisfied with more modest equipment.

Fritz recognized the value of museum collections and was always ready to lend them support, but he could do completely without a personal collection as long as he could rely on his memory. He said that his own observations of living plants or animals remained forever in his memory while things of which he had only read were easily forgotten, and he formed his opinions only on the basis of his own observations, never on what he learned only from the illustrations or descriptions of others [an echo of the motto at the head of his Ph.D. dissertation of 1844].[6]

Alfred Möller reported that Fritz had only two book shelves and rarely kept reprints except those useful for his ongoing research; there was simply no room in the house for the mass of printed material that had arrived over the years. But he read everything that came to him touching his interests, and even without a library had a remarkable command of the literature. He also saved few of his own drawings and publications and had no reprints of most of his works. When Ernst Krause asked him to draw up an index of his publications, he responded that he had more exciting things to do with his time.[7] He must have produced an enormous volume of notes and diaries during his many active years, but he kept only a few of them, including sketches of orchid flowers, observations of stingless honey bees, and the manuscripts of his reports to the National Museum in Rio. Among letters, he kept only those from Darwin and from his brother Hermann.

In 1892 Alfred Möller asked Hermann Blumenau to donate a piece of nearly virgin forest which he owned across the river from the town for an experiment station. The property had not yet been divided into lots, but Blumenau was resistant, both because he could see no source of funds to open and operate such a station, even for a planned existence of only four or five years, and because it would interfere with future development as immigrants continued to arrive. In addition, as he wrote to his agent in Blumenau: "The celebrated scientific works of Dr. Fritz Müller have brought him much-merited fame, but they have had no practical effect on the development of Brazil and its inhabitants, especially those of the Itajaí Valley."[8]

Roland Trimen urged the desirability of terrestrial tropical research stations a few years later in his Presidential Address to the Entomological Society of London. After pointing out the necessity for field work to answer important biological questions, Trimen said:

> Admitting gratefully the good work of this kind which has been carried out in Europe, and especially in our own country [Britain], one cannot but regret that from tropical regions, where alone the abundance, complexity, and incessant activity of life afford full prospect of the adequate reward of such research, we have little more than isolated notes and unconnected and incomplete observations, mere indications — precious as they are — of the rich harvest that lies unreaped for lack of resident workers devoted to the task.[9]

Trimen was evidently not familiar with most of the "rich harvest" that Fritz had already reaped, but he was prescient about the value of the sort of research station that Alfred Möller had proposed. His views and those of Hermann Blumenau, however, were at opposite poles.

Alfred Möller was in Blumenau in 1891 when Fritz lost his post as Traveling Naturalist, and also at Fritz's 70th birthday the following year, when indignation over the dismissal swelled the outpouring of birthday congratulations. Möller learned about the dismissal almost incidentally, Fritz being reluctant at first to tell him the exact circumstances. He immediately reported it to Ernst Krause and other friends in Germany, and through them the *Vossische Zeitung* in Berlin carried the first account in Europe.[10] The news was followed by a nationalistic appeal from the editors of the journal *Die Natur* in October 1891:

> Given such facts, the idea suggests itself to us that the German people should respond in accord with the honor of the Fatherland. We believe that is best done by presenting the venerable scholar from Thuringia on his 70th birthday with a gift that would make his last years secure. Consequently, we turn to our readers with the request that they would assist us in doing so. It would be the first reward for a German naturalist like those often given to German poets and artists, but we believe that the

naturalist carries no lesser qualities. We will gladly accept
contributions to such a national expression of thanks, and Prof.
Dr. Henry Lange [1821–1893] . . . , the well-known geographer
of Brazil, has declared himself ready to do the same.[11]

The appeal was well supported in European scientific circles, and
Fritz soon heard of it and immediately asked Alfred Möller to forestall
its good intentions: Fritz Müller sends thanks, is glad to hear of the
general expression of sympathy, but asks you to refrain from giving
him money, because his dismissal has not driven him into such need
that he cannot continue his accustomed modest existence as before.
He did, however, have to give up cigars.

Fritz wrote in the same vein to Haeckel, who had intended to
place the means of a private foundation at Fritz's disposal, and added
that:

> the purpose of the Ritter Foundation for Zoology is far better
> served by giving its resources to a younger, vigorous worker than
> to an old man already in his 70th year from whom little more is
> to be expected. Moreover, I have turned almost completely from
> zoology to the world of plants and have become almost com-
> pletely disaccustomed to the microscope.[12]

Fritz's personal circumstances may not have been seriously
affected, but he was demoralized by the wholesale sacking of other
Traveling Naturalists and employees of the museum:

> With v. Ihering's dismissal, the last of the scientifically trained
> naturalists in the National Museum has gone. The first to be
> dismissed during the Republic were [the ornithologist] Göldi[13]
> and the excellent North American geologist Derby.[14]. . . Finally,
> I and Ihering. "There is much gloom in the Museum," a friend
> recently wrote from Rio, with many officials doing absolutely
> nothing . . . , and the Republic has cut the work of [the man]
> who has done more than anyone else on the *Flora Brasiliensis.*

> But enough about our so-called Republic, a disgusting mix of
> military despotism and anarchy. Difficult to say what will
> become of the chaos, whether the former Emperor Dom Pedro's
> grandson will return or not. If so, Santa Catarina might unite
> with Rio Grande do Sul and Uruguay. The language would be

no problem, since Portuguese and Spanish differ no more than High and Low German.[15]

On 21 March 1892 Fritz celebrated his 70th birthday in excellent health and delighted over the congratulations that were arriving:

> The one good thing about my dismissal from the Museum has been to realize how universally and how highly I am respected by zoologists and botanists. My 70th birthday would have passed unnoticed without that dismissal; instead, from the ends of the earth it brought me congratulations that were as much condemnations of the Brazilian government: Australia (Baron Ferdinand von Müller[16]), Siam (Director Haase of the Siamese Museum[17]), La Plata, Chile, etc. Even from San Francisco in California a newspaper clipping was sent me with my picture (taken from *Die Gartenlaube*) and an article entitled "A German Naturalist, a Government's Ingratitude." In Brazil, as you know, it was only foreign naturalists who wished me well, among them French, English, North Americans, Swedes, etc.[18]

Fritz was most pleased by congratulations from those foreigners, twenty-four of whom presented him with a document commending him for a life "free from selfishness and scholarly pettiness" which "offered us a shining example in an intellectual oasis of his own making, far from the wrangling of modern society." The signatories included Derby; Friedenreich, veterinarian, entomologist, and friend from the early days in Blumenau; von Ihering; Carl Schreiner, his companion on the first expedition to the shell mounds; and other botanists, geologists, geographers, meteorologists, and physicians.[19]

Further honorary appointments arrived: Corresponding Member of the Senckenberg Scientific Research Society in Frankfurt am Main; Honorary Member of the Association of Natural Scientists of Hamburg, of the Botanical Society of the Province of Brandenburg, and of the German Botanical Society; and a greeting from the German Zoological Society recognizing the naturalist's approach to the study of organisms in nature as a "proper task for science . . . in an age all too often inclined to look upon work with scalpel and microscope as the only proper sort of research."[20]

Fritz's cousin Hugo Trommsdorff sent an album of pictures and photographs from Thuringia, among them the graves of his parents in

Mühlberg, the old Swan Pharmacy in Erfurt, and others recalling memories of times past and struggles overcome.

The journal *Die Natur* had suspended its appeal for donations after Fritz's refusal of aid, but there were already contributions from 117 people representing all the sciences and including those "from Darwinian and anti-Darwinian camps." The money was now used for a different purpose, an immense album prepared by an arts and crafts workshop in Berlin to contain photographs of Fritz's friends in Germany. "Its front cover," the journal reported:

> is artfully tooled in leather, with silver corners, and ornamented in the middle panel by an allegorical figure of science, surrounded by four panels with representations from the world of tropical plants and animals.[21]

The heavy packing case containing the album arrived in Blumenau in October 1892. Alfred Möller helped Fritz haul it in pouring rain up the sodden garden path into the house, where it was "soon delighting the honoree and his family, although the great silver-sheathed object did contrast oddly with the modest surroundings."[22] After Fritz's death, Anna Brockes sent the album to Alfred Möller, who gave it to Haeckel's Phyletic Museum in Jena. It is now in the Ernst-Haeckel-Haus of the University of Jena.

Several admirers, led by Professor Henry Lange, had opened up an account with the Berlin bookseller R. Friedländer & Son through which Fritz could acquire literature. And, as he wrote to Krause, having "missed the scientific journals that I had to give up . . . it has been rich compensation to have several scientific societies (Jena, Freiburg, Frankfurt, Hamburg) send me their publications, as well as to have the publishers of the *Zeitschrift für wissenschaftiche Zoologie*, the *Archiv für Naturgeschichte, Zoologische Jahrbücher*, and the *Biologische Zentralblätter* send their journals, so that I am really swimming in a sea of literature."[23]

Early in 1892 the paper *Jornal do Comércio* reported on an article about Fritz's dismissal in *Nature* (London) in which the Republican government was the subject of some unflattering remarks. A long article in the *Jornal* a few days later sought to vindicate the government. It said that Brazil had shown Dr. Fritz Müller charity by appointing him to the lycée in Desterro and then as naturalist of the province of Santa Catarina, his civil service position from the time he returned to the Itajaí until he became a Traveling Naturalist of the National Museum, and that he had also been "given" a beautiful piece of land in Blumenau. Müller, the article continued, had not fulfilled his contractual obligations, there was no trace of the required reports to the province in the public records of Desterro, and his position had been merely a sinecure.

The newspaper's attack continued with charges that Fritz had failed in his obligations to the National Museum as its Traveling Naturalist, claiming that although he had at first "fulfilled his obligations punctually, . . . the beginner's zeal lasted only a few years, and his contributions gradually failed to appear . . . ." Fritz in fact stopped contributing to the *Archivos* of the Museum only after it ceased publication in 1881, and his manuscripts on the crustaceans *Trichodactylus, Atyoida potimirim, Palaemon potiuna,* and *Janira exul* lay for more than a decade in Rio de Janeiro before a new director decided to publish them.

Fritz disregarded the article and declined several requests from his friends to speak out publicly in his own interest, and when his autobiographical sketch appeared in *Ausland* in October 1892,[24] he described his experiences in Brazil objectively and without ill-will. But he felt badly used, as he wrote to von Ihering two years after losing his position as Traveling Naturalist:

> I had thought of giving the German newspapers an account of our dismissal and a refutation of the lies and slander of Netto in the Rio press. But that has seemed to me long since superfluous. If necessary, there would be people after my death who would defend my good name from the dirt, for example my brother Wilhelm, who was here for two years and witnessed my first dismissal, and my cousin Alfred Möller, who has already been here more than two years and has seen the second.[25]

"The National Museum," he wrote to Ernst Krause in 1895:

> seems to be in a permanent state of decay, the *Archivos do Museu,* of which four issues should appear annually, died away years ago. When at last a new director had a new volume published in 1892, he found not a single piece of work by the present officials but had to fill it with papers by foreigners dismissed

under the Republic (Göldi, v. Ihering, and myself). So finally, after ten or more years of repose, four of my articles have been printed. The present Museum officials naturally have no idea that science advances over such a long period. They have taken the trouble neither to ask me whether I wish to see my articles published, and if so, whether in their old form, nor even to give the date of submission of each article. They haven't even sent me a reprint.[26]

Alfred Möller did set the record straight. He found the notebook in which Fritz had recorded the dates of submission of reports, articles, and even seeds of native plants to the provincial government between July 1867 and January 1877. He also had the drafts of manuscripts submitted to the Museum while Fritz was a Traveling Naturalist, and in the biography he detailed and refuted with indignation the charges laid out against Fritz by the government press in 1892.[27]

In spite of his harsh view, however, Alfred Möller recognized gratefully that Brazil had aided Fritz's independent pursuit of natural history for nearly twenty-five years.

When Möller left Brazil in 1893, the continuing deterioration of the Republic was about to break into civil war. He said good-bye to Fritz on 6 June:

Our farewell was brief and wordless, just a hearty handshake. We were both too moved to be able to say what we felt, for we knew that we would never meet again and would be left only with correspondence. There were several well-known Brazilian politicians on the little steamer *Progresso* which took me to the coast, and I can still he hear their repeated assurance, "Saímos em boa hora": we are getting out just in time. And how right they were.[28]

In 1890, a year after the overthrow of the emperor Dom Pedro II, a national congress met to formulate a new constitution modeled on that of the United States of America. The provinces became states and the country a republic, the United States of Brazil. But the authoritarian and increasingly corrupt military government of General Floriano Peixoto,[29] who succeeded to the presidency in November 1891, attracted active opposition, culminating in September 1893 in a naval rebellion in Rio harbor led by Admiral Custodio de Mello. After negotiations, he withdrew, set up a provisional government in Desterro, and joined forces with the leader of a long-simmering rebellion in Rio Grande do Sul for a march on the Republicans in Rio. Until de Mello and the rebel leader had a falling out in 1894, they fought successfully north through Santa Catarina, sweeping the area with conflict. The rebellion ended in 1895, but "the greatest barbarities were practiced upon those who, although they had taken no part in the insurrection, were known to have desired the overthrow of President Peixoto."[30]

The first fighting broke out near Blumenau just as Alfred Möller was leaving, putting Fritz's life in danger, as he related to his botanical correspondent Friedrich Ludwig more than a year later:

> 4 June 1893, when your delightful letter arrived, was an un-settled time here in Blumenau; soon after, a battle took place scarcely a kilometer from my house, and six badly wounded men were quartered here. I myself was locked up with eight rabble from Blumenau and threatened with execution. Why? Probably not one of those who howled for our blood would be able to say. During that imprisonment I remembered both of my grandfathers who, after the battle of Leipzig, when Erfurt was in the hands of the French, were imprisoned as hostages with ten other prominent citizens of that city. [Only grandfather Müller was among the hostages; grandfather Trommsdorff was saved by a trick of his wife's.[31]] A little later, when the fleet under Custodio de Mello had rebelled against President Floriano Peixoto, we had no postal communications for months, even within the colony, and only once by chance found a shipment of mail going your way.
>
> Being so unused to writing letters, I take up the pen again only with difficulty, and the more so because there is only unpleasantness to report. The livestock belonging to residents along the main road suffered especially from passing soldiers; seven horses and mules were seized from my neighbor and a number of cattle slaughtered. Because I had only a single horse they could not rob me of more than one, and like most of the milk cows, mine was spared.

Around Christmas time [1893] my wife was laid up for several weeks seriously ill; on the morning of 24 March 1894, her 68th birthday, she died in the arms of myself and my daughter. With that, my house and my whole life have become completely empty.[32]

In November 1894 Fritz wrote to Ludwig:

With the loss of my faithful wife, the year now coming to an end has been one of the saddest of my life. I feel myself becoming all the more isolated because I now have to get along without my cousin's company [Alfred Möller], to which I had become accustomed in the course of three years, and because everything outside the house has become most unpleasant due to the civil war.[33]

"You would have found endless material here for snapshots during the war," Fritz wrote to Möller late in 1894, appreciating the irony:

the barefoot gauchos, often pantless and barely clad in a poncho, armed only with lance and bolas, with their various primitive tents (perhaps a couple of branches with a cowhide covering); or a great general, barefoot, helping Fritz [his grandson] drive the cow down from the hill.[34]

Unfortunately the disputes of the Brazilian political parties contending for influence in the country did not unify the German inhabitants of Blumenau, who were enlisted only too easily to this side or that in hopes of immediate or future gain. Once, in 1892, Fritz felt duty bound to urge peace and order against increasing public insecurity and disorder, and without naming names he had spoken sharply about perceived improprieties. There was a flood of invective by anonymous writers in a local newspaper,[35] but Fritz's fault was only in defending the principles of truth and justice in a society in which everyone to whom he spoke sought influence or gain of some sort for himself or for a friend, and to whom Fritz's viewpoint was as unwelcome as Hecuba's. He had criticized the Brazilian Commission in the same way when it singled out scapegoats following the flood of 1880, and with similar results.

"Were it not for my grandson Fritz, for whom I would like to live a few more years," he wrote to Alfred Möller in 1895:

> it would be quite all right with me if my life came to a close. You wouldn't believe how the mutual flattery of our Republicans and the servile tail-wagging of our German country folk disgust me. Two years ago (that is 1893), shortly after we ninepins escaped the bullets with which we were threatened — even the next morning, when the telegram liberating us arrived from Desterro, the noble "rabble" of Blumenau shouted: "No! Blow their brains out!" — we were invited by [our opponents] to a little gathering where those gentlemen admitted that the blame for the mutual enmity of the Blumenauers was to be assigned only to the Brazilians and to the undue influence that was granted them. In the future it would be different. We took the hand offered to us; our adversaries, after all, intended well. At the next opportunity (an election), however, none of us was invited to the preliminary discussions, and our dear Blumenauers once again dance to the Brazilians' tune.[36]
>
> As to the political situation in the state of Santa Catarina, and in the whole of the Republic, one can only say with Prutz: "the ruins fall in ruins, and things go from bad to worse."[37]

Despite adversity, Fritz's spirits rose with the rearing of two grandsons and his return to natural history. In 1892 he had taken into his house his daughter Thusnelda's sons, Hans and Fritzie Lorenz, 11 and 9, whom he educated and who were his regular companions in the forest. Fritzie stayed with him nearly until his death five years later, while Hans soon moved to an apprenticeship in Curitiba, in the neighboring state of Paraná. In March 1893, before the political situation seriously deteriorated, he described to Friedrich Ludwig the pleasures of having the two boys around:

> Of course my grandsons have to forego snowmen and sledding here; nevertheless the huge woody boat-shaped floral sheaths of the palms in front of my house (*Arecastrum romanzoffianum*) furnish them with a sort of sled in which they sail down the steep grassy hill behind the house.[38]
>
> Your boys would enjoy being able to roam with my grand-children through the woods around here, which are completely

different from any German forest, although of course our forest also has its dangers. On an excursion to Caeté Brook, Fritzie nearly stepped on a jararaca (*Bothrops*) lying in the path but saw it in time and killed it. We found on cleaning the skull that one of its 9 mm-long fangs had broken some millimeters from the tip but that a substitute was already in place. Behind each fang there were three replacement teeth, the longest of which was already fully grown. Jararacas are not uncommon here; only a few days ago I killed one not far from my house. But a non-poisonous snake indistinguishable from it in color and pattern seems to be more common. I do not know if the resemblance is based on protective mimicry of the jararaca, or if the coloration was acquired independently by both snakes as a protective resemblance to dead leaves and the like. A few weeks ago I was looking for bromeliads in my woods with Fritzie; out of the corner of my eye I saw a flowering nest-bromeliad on a fallen tree with its inflorescence apparently covered with dead leaves. I was about to brush them off with my hand when I felt some-thing cold, and a snake resembling a jararaca slid quickly away.[39]

He also wrote to his sister Rosine about the boys:

It is taken here almost as a matter of course that Fritzie, like Hans and both of Anna's youngsters, would be an excellent hunter; but it might surprise you that without hesitation I let the four youngsters go hunting together in the forest. Hunting accidents are common even here, but never among young people who were born here and learned how to handle firearms when they were small.[40]

From the early 1890s until his death, Fritz studied mostly bromeliads, of which a previously unsuspected number of species were discovered near Blumenau, and his grandson Fritzie was an inseparable and nearly indispensable companion on his excursions. Fritz studied their systematics and natural hybridization, and their pollination biology and germination as adaptations to life in the tree-tops, and by the time he heard on 14 December 1894 that the University of Berlin had renewed his Ph.D. of 1844 with congratulations on his publications, his promotion of Darwinism, and his generous aid to so many zoologists and botanists, he was deep in bromeliad research.

He now saw a use for the support offered by the Ritter Foundation which he had rejected before. In November 1894 he wrote Alfred Möller:

> A very profitable excursion which I made with Fritzie to the mouth of the Itajaí, and several lovely bromeliads new to me which Anna brought back from Victoria (Espírito Santo) and from Iguape (São Paulo), have contributed significantly to my change of mind.[41]

In an enclosed letter to Ernst Krause, he explained what he would now do with the money:

> For a long time I have been occupied with a project that I have lacked the means to pursue as I wished . . . . It is our bromeliads to which I have devoted myself almost exclusively for the past few years, and it seems to me increasingly that even after Schimper's pioneering work in this field there is still a rich harvest of facts to be reaped, not only on new problems, but also on more general questions.[42] Even our knowledge of the species in the family and their classification is still in a sad state. For one thing, much can be worked out only incompletely and with difficulty from herbarium hay, and for another collecting the plants themselves is especially difficult. Schimper, for example, who was particularly attentive to bromeliads, overlooked nearly all of our largest and most beautiful species. For collecting these plants, one needs not only a very sharp and practiced eye to distinguish species which are often confusingly similar, especially without flowers high in the tree tops, and to recognize new species among them immediately; one also needs an uncommon climbing ability in order to bring down what one has seen. I pride myself on neither the one nor the other; but, as my cousin [Alfred Möller] can testify, my 11-year old grandson Fritz Lorenz, who is growing up in my house, possesses them both to a rare degree. Here is but one example of the sharp-sightedness with which he surprised me a few weeks ago: amidst a truly remarkable variety of leaves he picked out quite confidently a *Nidularium* whose flowers were invisible from below as a "new hybrid", and he proved it so when he brought it down. Incidentally, that was already the fifth hybrid bromeliad that he had found, and he recognized all of them immediately as such, although, despite the discovery of the first one, we had thought

that there were no natural wild hybrids around here. As far as I know, they have not yet been found elsewhere in Brazil. To be sure, he and his brother had already tried all possible and impossible crosses in my garden. With the help of those grandchildren I will now have a nearly complete collection of the bromeliads growing in my immediate surroundings. And those will offer material enough for observation and experiment the rest of my days. But that abundant yield in such a limited area entices me to further excursions, first in the Itajaí region, then across the state of Santa Catarina, and if possible at least to the coastal regions of the subtropical neighboring states, Paraná and São Paulo.

Now, with reference to my young companions, I think that I might accept assistance for such excursions from the Ritter Foundation. It would really be a shame to pass up the opportunity offered by my grandchildren of a bromeliad hunt that promises results. Even for the "species people" there would certainly be much that was new: there are several undescribed species even among the conspicuous and common ones that we brought back at the end of August from the mouth of the Itajaí. In the course of two days there my grandchild observed twice as many species as Schimper had seen during two months around Blumenau in a region no less rich in bromeliads.

Physically I feel hale enough for such trips. I am not out of practice in scrambling through trackless virgin forest or in rocky forest streams, and I have also been on several long walks recently. Whether I still possess the necessary intellectual vigor to work up the collected material and to render it useful to science is of course another matter, which I myself naturally cannot judge.[43]

Fritz still seemed pretty fit in 1895, at the age of 73:

This month I traveled with Fritzie up the Beneditto River for several days, the second day of which could serve as proof that my legs are still in good shape; we walked from 5:30 in the morning until 6:30 in the evening, and the last few hours at a precipitous pace in order to reach an inn before nightfall, and in all we rested scarcely an hour or an hour and a half. Of course the weather was as favorable as could be, overcast skies and some light drizzle, which was merely refreshing. The next day was showery, so we did not go as far up the Santa Maria (the river next the Beneditto) as we had intended. As far as we went the flora was not strikingly different from that here. We found a new *Aechmea* [a bromeliad], which was, however, of little value to me because its only merit was as a *nov. sp.* [new species]. The scenery is very beautiful, with the upper Beneditto dashing wildly among blocks of stone. As we were told by a man with whom we walked for a while, the poor people who settled high up the Santa Maria have good land but are without roads or bridges; the paths go steeply up and down hill and are often so narrow and overgrown that a snake can hardly slither through. For that reason many have abandoned their land. On the way home we traveled in the man's cart from Engelke to Blumenau. On jumping down from it I stepped on a sharp stone or something of the sort; I hardly bled and was able to get home without difficulty, but I then found a really serious wound which is now at last nearly healed. It still keeps me from long trips, however, and from putting on my shoes, so that to my great regret I shall not be able to participate tomorrow in August's 70th birthday.[44]

Besides studying bromeliads, Fritz returned in the 1890s to questions that still bothered him about the inheritance of acquired characters and the significance of sexual reproduction. He had done many pollinations in *Abutilon* in the 1870s, and after his dismissal from the National Museum in 1891 he started similar experiments with two species of *Ruellia* (Acanthaceae), the stigmas of which he dusted simultaneously with their own pollen and that of the other species. The results were pure offspring like the female parent as well as hybrids between the two species, but of particular significance to Fritz was the discovery that reciprocal hybrids showed regularly recurring differences, depending on which species had been used as the female or male parent, and that the differences were hereditary, as he was able to establish in 1895. He argued that the reciprocal hybrids should be identical in their inheritance of germ plasm, and that any differences between them could therefore be due only to a different influence of the female parent on the developing seeds, an influence that must act sometime between fertilization and seed maturation. Such differences were therefore acquired characters in Weismann's sense, and he showed that they were inherited, contrary to Weismann. Fritz's iconoclastic delight was cut short, however, by the arrival in 1895 of a new botany text whose authors included his friends Schimper and Schenck,[45] from which he learned that in the fertilization of seed plants chloroplasts are inherited only from the female parent. Fritz realized that the chloroplasts might have caused the difference between the reciprocal crosses *A* female x *B* male and *B* female x *A* male, making his conclusion inadmissible. He then suggested that seed plants might have a symbiosis comparable to that of lichens, with the green photosynthesizing chloroplasts playing the same role as the algae in lichens, and the germ plasm acting like the fungal component of the lichens. He compared the difference between his reciprocal *Ruellia* hybrids with that between two lichens that Alfred Möller had studied, both of which had the same fungal species but differed in appearance depending on which of two completely different algal species accompanied it. He let the short article on this discovery first go only to a small circle of friends and doubted that it should be published, and it appeared only after his death.[46]

Fritz was still full of creative energy as he approached his 75th birthday during the summer of 1896–1897, and his last two papers were typically polemical. He returned first to his disagreement with Weismann in 1886 over the significance of sexual reproduction as the sole source of variation for the action of natural selection, when he had referred to horticultural varieties that arose as bud-variations and had been propagated asexually for years. In 1897 he now had an example from nature, a white-flowered species of *Marica* (now *Neomarica*, in the iris family) that was completely self-sterile and occurred in widely separated clones, spreading from the rootstock and also by rooting at the tip of the flower stalk, which was far longer than in related sexual species and bent to the ground before flowering. Under these conditions, he wrote:

> pollen is useless — it is vestigial; and furthermore it is useless to have the flowers standing above their surroundings to attract [pollinating] visitors. On the other hand, it is advantageous for the young shoot to distance itself from the mother plant as far as possible and to become rooted and independent as soon as possible — the flower stalk has lengthened and lies on the ground before the flowers open.

It is as though nature had itself carried out an experiment expressly to test the two culminating sentences in Weismann's book on the significance of sexual reproduction: "Selective processes . . . are not possible in species with asexual reproduction," and "in parthenogenetically reproducing species useless organs will not become rudimentary."[47] One might object that these plants did not first acquire their deviant characteristics gradually in their present localities, but rather that the first seeds to have reached this remote place already had them. Against that view, remember that as long as sexual reproduction was possible, atrophied pollen as well as the premature bending down of elongate [flower stalks] would have been detrimental, so they could not have been acquired by sexual means.

I would not deny, for the sake of these exceptional and probably very rare cases, that sexual reproduction is of great importance in plants in making more varied progeny available for natural selection. But it may be of still greater significance that the crossing of different stocks produces more vigorous progeny, as Darwin had already shown ten years before Weismann's book, from a decade of experiments on species of the most diverse families (*Cross and self fertilisation*, 1876).[48]

At the end of March 1897, seven weeks before his death, Fritz submitted his last paper, on the effects of double pollination, where a flower is simultaneously dusted with pollen from two other species. He had always wanted to decide for himself about the subject, never fully trusting Gärtner's compendium on plant hybrids,[49] and he started his paper by summarizing the possible results:

1. One kind of pollen might be effective, the other completely ineffective, with only one kind of hybrid being produced. "This is probably by far the commonest case, and one can therefore often employ double pollination to decide which of two species has the greatest [sexual] affinity for a third," Fritz wrote, but he added that the paucity of evidence for that conclusion in the writings of Kölreuter[50] and Gärtner "does not justify without new experiments its elevation to the status of a general law for the entire plant kingdom, a law that is still being passed like an 'everlasting disease' from text to text." "Besides, the wide distribution of self-sterility in flowering plants would have to make one cautious."

2. Both kinds of pollen might be effective, some ovules being fertilized by one, some by the other. Gärtner had considered this possibility, and Fritz realized it in his *Ruellia* crosses, although in that
   case one of the pollen parents was of the same species as the female
   parent.

3. Both kinds of pollen might be effective in the same ovule.
   Kölreuter and some of his predecessors had believed that pollinating a flower with a mixture of two kinds of foreign pollen could
   yield not only pure hybrids, but also offspring with characteristics
   of both pollen parents, a "tinting" of the hybrid with characters of
   the other foreign species. These "tinctures" were dismissed as
   nonsense in 1849 by Gärtner, who insisted on the basis of his own
   experimental crosses that each pollen grain acted independently
   and that each fertilization involved only one pollen grain.[51]

Fritz, who had advised Alfred Möller never to "hold anything
impossible a priori," was not impressed by Gärtner's evidence, which
came from a small number of crosses in two genera and which was
even then weakened by an exceptional plant "which can scarcely be
interpreted other than having been 'tinted'. . . in Kölreuter's sense."
"Kölreuter's term 'tinctures' has been silenced to death, solely, it seems
to me, on the basis of Gärtner's opinion, and without any new experimental test. I do not recall even having read the word in any recent
book."[52]

After his 70th birthday Fritz therefore had started double pollinations with three species of *Neomarica*. He had now made all six
possible reciprocal crosses with these species and was thoroughly
familiar with flower color and the seasonal and daily timing of flowering of the species, of their hybrids, and of some of the backcrosses to
one or other of the parents. The flowers of *Neomarica* have two
stigmatic branches, and using species B (blue sepals) as the female
parent Fritz applied separately to the two stigmatic surfaces pollen
from species W (white sepals) and T (yellowish sepals, strongly
scented). He obtained one fruit with 23 viable seeds, from which he
had fifteen plants in bloom by early 1897. He knew that hybrid BW
was very close to W in flower color, while hybrid BT was close to B,
and all of the products of double pollination were closer to BW than

to BT, suggesting that the W pollen was more successful. Nevertheless, Fritz thought that he detected an influence of T pollen in some of the progeny. For example, he knew that species T flowered earliest in the day, followed by BT, W, BW and B in that order, but the putative "tinctures" always flowered earlier than BW, sometimes as early as hybrid BT. On 14 February 1897 the sixteenth plant flowered for the first time, and its flowers resembled those of the BW hybrid in the pale color of the sepals, but those of BT in their abundant dark blue spotting and in having the strong scent of species T, again suggesting that both W and T pollen had been involved in the hybrid.

Fritz believed that others would have to reconcile his conclusion about "tinctures" with prevailing views of the process of fertilization in flowering plants, but he was keenly delighted by his discovery. "If I publish my observations, there will be a general shaking of heads. I can hear Professor X already, saying 'Ahem, ahem' and then 'second class,'" he wrote to Ludwig on 27 February 1897.[53]

The pollen tube contributes two sperm nuclei in the process called double fertilization, one to the embryo and one to the nutrient endosperm, and there is modern evidence that two pollen tubes may both contribute their fertilizing nuclei to the same embryo sac, with a sperm nucleus from one pollen tube entering into embryo formation and a sperm nucleus from the other entering into the formation of the endosperm. But the possibility that DNA from two different sperm nuclei might enter into the formation of one embryo is dismissed and seems never to have been tested directly, and the possibility of "tinctures" is as dead an issue now as it was at the end of the nineteenth century.

Fritz entrusted Alfred Möller with the publication of this final work[54] in what was probably his last letter, 23 March 1897: "With this article I conclude my literary curriculum vitae; I am certainly old enough for that, and in any case too old to plan a new 'experiment station' for myself."

This last observation referred to his impending change of residence. In 1895 his daughters had advised him to move to Anna's house in town. "I vacillate," he wrote to Möller:

> whether to remain living on my land or to sell it and move, as
> Anna and Agnes advise me. I would find it very difficult to be

away from my garden, which continues to provide rich material for observations and where every plant is an old acquaintance, and I cannot say that the center of Blumenau much attracts me. But on the other hand, housekeeping without a wife, and with only young Fritz and a servant girl, is pretty disagreeable.[55]

The decision to move was postponed again and again, perhaps because Fritz felt that his days were numbered and that it wasn't worth the trouble. He often thought of the approaching end of his life. Most of the comrades from his pioneering days were already gone. "Seckendorf, one of the few survivors from 1852, died suddenly last evening." he wrote in December 1896. "In the afternoon he was still working cheerfully in his garden. A fine way to go, as I would wish it myself."[56] He was also worried about the fortunes of his children and grandchildren. His daughter Selma, with a hip ailment from childhood and serious emotional problems, had gone to Germany with her sister Agnes and against Fritz's will had entered a sanatorium from which he expected no improvement.

"In consequence of that and many other recent events, I have fallen into such a gloomy mood," he wrote his sister Luise in January 1896, "that I often wish, as I did a few times after my wife's death, to follow her soon."[57]

Fritz's domestic life briefly took a turn for the better when his daughter Agnes came to live with him for a few months after her return from Germany. But she soon had to find employment and looked to Curitiba, where three of her sisters already lived. Young Fritz Lorenz also moved to Curitiba, where he was apprenticed to a mechanic, and where his brother Hans and a cousin had already gone, and Fritz seriously considered moving there as well. His oldest daughter Anna Brockes, however, lived in a comfortable house in the center of Blumenau where he would be well cared for, and there was no one in Blumenau who better appreciated him than she. It was difficult leaving his residence of 30 years, still more difficult leaving his garden, and most difficult of all being separated from Fritz Lorenz, his beloved grandson and pupil, his "little eyes," as he called him. Despite Fritz's dissuasion, his grandson carried two canoe loads of his finest bromeliads to Anna's garden so that he could continue his daily observations; but he would never take them up again.

On 20 April 1897 Fritz moved into Anna's house. She described the ensuing events to Alfred Möller:

> On the very first day after the move he developed a pain in the thigh, at first only slight but enough to keep him from walking and soon confining him to the house. A hard place on the thigh remained unchanged and became very painful, and the wormwood liniment and iodine ordered by the doctor brought no improvement; after a few days the rest of the leg began to ache and swelled up down to the foot. His appetite dwindled, and 8 days before his death fever set in, at first weak and for only a few hours, but soon staying with him. From 17 May his strength ebbed noticeably and his fever increased. In his delirium he was intensely occupied with his bromeliads, on which he had not been able to complete this or that observation because Fritz Lorenz was no longer there to help. He also eagerly awaited the arrival of the mail for news of how his latest paper (on double pollination) had been received in Germany.[58]

August Müller hurried from his residence on 18 May at the news of his brother's illness and found him lucid and without fever, but resolutely rejecting any hope of recovery. When he came back on 21 May, his brother was much weaker and the doctor thought the end imminent. Fritz gradually lost consciousness, and about 3 o'clock that afternoon he died so quietly that the onlookers could not tell the actual moment of death.[59] On 22 May he was buried in the Blumenau cemetery in the presence of many friends, admirers, and acquaintances. The shops had closed their shutters for the afternoon and German and Brazilian flags were lowered to half mast. Paul Schwarzer, at one time an antagonist but now a friend, spoke at the grave. He mentioned Fritz's scientific accomplishments, the significance of which, of course, scarcely anyone in Blumenau could appreciate; then his modesty and character, which were known to all the older residents of Blumenau from first-hand experience:

> He will live on in all our memories as we have so often seen
> him, in plain settlers' garb, barefoot, with a staff in his hand,
> even as he was immortalized a few years ago in *Gartenlaube*, a
> man of the greatest imaginable simplicity and modesty and with
> the most princely intellect.[60]

Bernardo Scheidemantel, editor of the *Immigrant* for many years and also Fritz's former adversary, conveyed to Alfred Möller what he believed many people in Blumenau to have felt at that grave side:

> that your late cousin in his unassuming way has contributed more to widening the intellectual horizons of the whole colony, not to mention those of his close circle of friends, than all the so-called educational establishments together. That may surprise you. But having had personal dealings with him for nearly a generation, I think that I may be allowed the opinion that even as great a scholar as he was, as keen, perhaps as unique, an observer, he was a greater teacher. He had mastered the difficult art of making his scholarship easily accessible, and it is precisely in that respect that Blumenau is so much in his debt.[61]

Obituaries appeared around the world in scientific journals and newspapers. Ernst Haeckel took his as an opportunity for some self-congratulation,[62] but others reflected the warmth and affection with which Fritz was known by those who had never met him.

Walter Blandford, secretary of the Entomological Society of London, summed up Fritz's contributions in *Nature*:

> Although . . . his natural modesty and self-effacement left him indifferent to his own fame, it has long been recognized that the qualities of observation and interpretation which drew from Darwin the title of "prince of observers," have earned him a position as one of the greatest and most original naturalists of the century.
>
> If his name is not associated with any marked advance in thought, except on one or two special questions connected with natural selection, it is because he found his intellectual faith in the theory which he set himself to developing and strengthening. He was content, in fact, to assist in the building of the structure of which another was architect, and in this task his services have been great. It may be questioned whether any other naturalist, save Darwin himself, has given the world so large and original a mass of observations of the kind by which natural selection has been most strongly supported.[63]

Ernst Krause, writing in a Berlin newspaper, gave the same point a romantic flourish:

> Our Nordic ancestors always laid particular stress on the generosity of their princes; they called their ruler *Geber der Ringe* (giver of support) because a prince can do no better for his able subjects than support their endeavors. In this respect Darwin's characterization of Fritz Müller as "prince of observers" is doubly nice, embracing as it does his outstanding trait: selfless assistance from someone striving for the same goal.[64]

# Locations of Fritz Müller's Correspondence

In 1897 Alfred Möller began borrowing Fritz Müller's correspondence from as many recipients as he could locate. He copied the letters, translated some of the English ones, returned the originals, and in 1921 published about 20 per cent of their contents in the *Briefe*.[1] I list the locations of existing letters and record the losses below.

**Charles Darwin:**
There are at least parts of 50 letters from Fritz Müller to Charles Darwin (1865–1882) in the following locations:

The Darwin manuscripts collection, Cambridge University Library (DAR), has 21 complete or partial letters, plus a memo of additions to the translation of *Für Darwin*. I found two additional pages of one of those letters in 1993 in the J. D. Hooker file at the Royal Botanic Gardens, Kew.

The Linnean Society of London has two, one of them (14 March 1869) not recorded in the *Calendar of the Correspondence of Charles Darwin*.[2]

The Oxford University Museum of Natural History (OUMNH) has two, one of them a copy by Raphael Meldola.

The *Briefe* contains 19 German translations and one draft in English of letters not in the DAR. Three of those 19 letters in German translation are represented by non-overlapping portions in Müller's publications. The *Briefe* also contains German translations of missing parts of three, and drafts in English of missing parts of four, of the 21 letters in the DAR.

Five letters are known only in published papers.

The curiosity of the Müller-Darwin correspondence is that the contents of the unique 19 letters and parts of three letters in the *Briefe* (in German translation) are mutually exclusive of those of the letters in the DAR. In 1921 Möller wrote: "Fritz Müller's letters to Darwin were all written in English, but only some of them exist. Those letters which remain were made available to the Editor some years ago by Mr. Francis Darwin. Translations of them were prepared, and only those were available when the present volume was published."[3] Möller had borrowed the letters from Francis Darwin in 1898[4] and apparently returned them, as he did others. Because Charles Darwin often cut up letters and filed the parts separately for different purposes, however, it is likely that Francis Darwin sent Möller only certain letters and portions of letters, and furthermore that those that Möller borrowed were lost after their return.[5] Anna-K. Mayer has recently discussed these curious non-overlaps.[6] Ten letters from Müller to Darwin have been completely lost. Their contents were acknowledged in letters from Darwin, and Fritz Müller annotated the dates of dispatch of eight of them on letters from Darwin.

Alfred Möller reported that the only letters that Fritz Müller kept where those from his brother Hermann and from Darwin.[7] There are 58 letters from Darwin (1865–1882), most of them numbered and dated on receipt by Müller. They were intended by Alfred Möller to go to Haeckel's Phyletic Museum in Jena,[8] but the Müller family kept them in Brazil, and in 1928 Henry Fairfield Osborn[9] learned of their existence and purchased them for $500 as a gift to Down House on the occasion of its opening as a Darwin museum the following year.[10] They are now on permanent loan to the British Library, and many of them have been published.[11]

**Hermann Müller:**

Alfred Möller had in his possession at one time over 280 letters from Fritz Müller to his brother Hermann Müller (1854-83), and he preserved much of that side of the correspondence by publishing at least parts of 165 of them in the *Briefe*. There must have been a comparable number of letters from Hermann to Fritz, for the two corresponded regularly for 30 years, but Alfred Möller published parts of only 11 of them in the *Briefe*. Osborn wrote in 1929 that "one of the Müller heirs had successfully carried out his intention of taking all the Müller correspondence to Germany some time ago,"[12] and since the Darwin letters were not included, the major component would have been the letters from Hermann to Fritz. Unfortunately Osborn did not say who took the letters to Germany, nor when they were taken. That "hidden treasure," as Hermann Müller's great-grand-daughter described it to me, remains a major loss, especially to any-one interested in the development of Hermann Müller's ideas.

### Ernst Haeckel:

Among the first letters that Alfred Möller obtained were those to Ernst Haeckel, which he returned to Haeckel on 18 November 1898.[13] There are 26 letters from Fritz Müller (1876–1897) in the Ernst-Haeckel-Haus, of which parts of 17 were published in the *Briefe*, but none from Haeckel to Müller has been found.

### Alexander Agassiz:

Alfred Möller published at least parts of eight letters from Fritz Müller to Alexander Agassiz (1863–1888) in the *Briefe*, but the originals are lost. I found a ninth, previously unrecognized, in the Ernst Mayr Library of the Museum of Comparative Zoology, Harvard (MCZ). There are ten letterpress copies of Agassiz's letters to Fritz Müller (1863–1888) in the Agassiz Letter Books, Houghton Library, Harvard, some in poor condition and difficult to read. All of the letters are on microfilm in the MCZ, and some were published.[14]

### Hermann Hagen and Robert McLachlan:

Thirty-five letters from Fritz Müller to Hermann Hagen (1869–1881) in the MCZ comprise the largest archive of Fritz Müller's surviving letters. They contain observations on insects, including termites, caddis flies and solitary bees, and many are illustrated with drawings. The OUMNH has ten letters from Fritz Müller to Robert McLachlan (1878–1889), principally about caddis flies but including Müller's drawings illustrating the homology of wing venation in Trichoptera and Lepidoptera. Although Alfred Möller knew that Müller had corresponded with Hagen and McLachlan, he apparently never saw these letters.

None of the other letters published in *Briefe* and *Leben* are known to exist in original form. Among important losses are those from Fritz Müller and his brother August to their friends and family in Germany, and nearly all of the personal portions of Müller's scientific correspondence. It is odd that so many letters from such a prominent biologist as Fritz Müller were lost after Alfred Möller published them. These include 41 to Max Schultze in Bonn (1858–1866), 19 to Ernst Krause in Berlin and Eberswalde (1877–1895), nine to Paul Mayer in Naples (1880–1886), 23 to Friedrich Ludwig in Greiz (1884–1896), 16 to Wilhelm Müller in Greifswald (1885–1895), and 18 to August Weismann in Freiburg i. Breisgau (1876–1888), as well as those between Fritz and Hermann Müller. Three letterpress copies of letters from Weismann to Fritz Müller in the Universitätsbibliothek, Freiburg in Breisgau, are nearly illegible.

The huge archive that Alfred Möller gathered was evidently still in his possession in Eberswalde at this death in 1922, after which it disappeared. In 1917 Alfred Möller had written a tantalizing suggestion to Haeckel:

> When my work is finished I would like to send all of the material on which it is based, a full cabinet, to the Phyletic Museum [Haeckel's museum in Jena], which would certainly be the best place for its preservation.[15]

The archives in the Phyletic Museum were ultimately transfered up the hill to the Ernst-Haeckel-Haus, but the cabinet full of documents was not there[16] and seems never to have been sent to Jena. I have searched German libraries and archives and found a few minor letters, but nothing that would have been in that collection. There is no Möller archive in Eberswalde either. Perhaps the cabinet remained after his death in the *Pilzhaus*, Möller's wooden laboratory in the experimental forest at Eberswalde, but that building, adjacent to the graves of Möller and his widow, was destroyed by Russian troops in 1945.[17]

There are eighteen unpublished letters from Fritz Müller's parents to his mother's brother Hermann Trommsdorff and wife, now in the Staatsbibliothek zu Berlin, Preußischer Kulturbesitz, and the Trommsdorff Familienarchiv/Meilen.[18] Alfred Möller was evidently not aware of them.

Important documents pertaining to Fritz Müller's problems with graduation from his medical course in 1849 have recently been discovered in the Greifswald University archives and published.[19]

# Abbreviations

*ADB*: *Allgemeine deutsche Biographie.* 1875–1912. Reprint 1967-71. Berlin.

AMNH: American Museum of Natural History, New York.

*Archivos*: *Archivos do Museu Nacional*, Rio de Janeiro.

*BE*: *Brockhaus Enzyklopädie.* Stuttgart: Brockhaus.

BL: The British Library.

*Briefe*: Möller, A., ed. 1921. *Fritz Müller. Werke, Briefe und Leben. Vol. 2. Briefe und noch nicht veröffentliche Abhandlungen aus dem Nachlaß, 1854–1897.* Jena: Gustav Fischer.

*CAL*: Burkhardt, F., and S. Smith, eds. 1994. *A calendar of the correspondence of Charles Darwin, 1821–1882*, with supplement. 2$^{nd}$ ed. Cambridge: Cambridge University Press.

*CCD*: Burkhardt, F. et al., eds. 1985–. *The correspondence of Charles Darwin.* Cambridge: Cambridge University Press.

CD: Charles R. Darwin.

DAR: Darwin manuscript collection, University Library, Cambridge.

*DSB*: C. C. Gillespie, ed.1970-80. *Dictionary of scientific biography.* New York: Scribners

*EB*: *The Encyclopædia Britannica.* 1910-11. 11th ed. New York: Encyclopædia Britannica Co.

EHH: Ernst-Haeckel-Haus, Friedrich-Schiller Universität, Jena.

FM: Fritz Müller.

Houghton: Houghton Library, Harvard University.

*Leben*: Möller, A., ed. 1920. *Fritz Müller. Werke, Briefe und Leben.* Vol. 3, *Fritz Müllers Leben.* Jena: Gustav Fischer.

*LL*: Darwin, Francis, ed. 1887. *The life and letters of Charles Darwin, including an autobiographical chapter.* 3 vols. London: John Murray.

MCZ: Ernst Mayr Library of the Museum of Comparative Zoology, Harvard University.

*ML*: Darwin, Francis, and A. C. Seward, eds. 1903. *More letters of Charles Darwin: a record of his work in a series of hitherto unpublished letters.* 2 vols. London: John Murray.

*NEB*: *New Encylopaedia Britannica.* 1992. 15th ed. Chicago: Encyclopaedia Britannica Inc.

*Orchids*: Darwin, C. 1862 and 1877a. *On the various contrivances by which British and foreign orchids are fertilised . . . .* London: John Murray.

*Origin*: Darwin, Charles R. 1859 and later eds. *The Origin of Species.* . . . Various publishers.

OUMNH: Library, Oxford University Museum of Natural History.

Passmore Edwards: Passmore Edwards Museum, Stratford, London.

*Werke*: Möller, A., ed. 1915. *Fritz Müller. Werke, Briefe und Leben.* Vol. 1, *Gesammelte Schriften.* Jena: Gustav Fischer.

# Notes

## Chapter 1. Childhood and Early Education
## in Thuringia, 1822–1841

[1] An edited version of the first four chapters of *Leben* with additions by the author from unpublished letters of FM's parents to the Trommsdorffs.

[2] Müller 1892b. Johann Müller died in 1873, his wife Caroline in 1843.

[3] "My paternal grandfather, and my maternal great-grandfather (Hoyer) were clergymen." FM to Ernst Krause, 1884, *Leben*:2. Hoyer was pastor in Wandersleben, close to Mühlberg; his eldest daughter Martha married J. B. Trommsdorff.

[4] Rosenhainer & Trommsdorff 1913.

[5] See note 4.

[6] Letter from Lina Walther to Alfred Möller, 14 July 1897, *Leben*:1. Lina Walther, née Möller (1824–1907), was a daughter of Maria Dorothea (Trommsdorff), a sister of FM's mother. Her father was Friedrich Möller, who died in Magdeburg as a bishop in 1861. Lina Walther's family memories and some of her juvenile books and light works of fiction, including Walther 1882 and 1901, were important sources for the *Leben*.

[7] FM's siblings were:

    a. Charlotte, b. 1823, married the landowner Wilhelm Pfeifer of Wöllersdorf 1848, d. 26 January 1894.

    b. August, b. 24 November 1825, emigrated with FM to Brazil and was closely associated with him in Blumenau, Santa Catarina, d. 1900. "He began studying theology in Halle, and then, when intellectuals were forbidden any freedom of ideas in Prussia, became a nursery gardener and joined the Free Community in Quedlinburg. Like me, he was driven from his homeland by religious intolerance emanating from the 'capital of the intelligentsia' [Berlin]." (Müller 1892b:632)

    c. Rosine, b. (c 15 December) 1827, FM's favorite sister, unmarried, d. Regensburg, 5 May 1903.

    d. Hermann, b. 23 September 1829, a pioneer in pollination biology, secondary school teacher in Lippstadt, d. 25 August 1883 in Prad, on an alpine journey in the Tyrol. For his biography, see Krause 1883, 1884.

    e. Luise, b. 1832, married landowner Theodor Pfeifer in Thumsenreuth, Bavaria, d. 17 January 1905.

    f. Ludwig Theodor, b. and d. 1835.

[8] Rosine Müller to Alfred Möller, 1897, *Leben*:2.

[9] Lina Walther to Alfred Möller, 1897; address at the grave of Mrs. Caroline Müller, 10 February 1843; and Walther 1901, *Leben*:3.

[10] Ernst Biltz to Alfred Möller, 17 August 1897, *Leben*:3.

[11] *EB*, 22:916.

[12] Richard Mensing, FM's cousin and at that time often a guest in the Mühlberg parsonage, to Alfred Möller, November 1897, *Leben*:3.

[13] FM to Ernst Krause, 1 January 1883. *Leben*:3. Ernst Krause, pseudonym Carus Sterne (1839–1903), German botanist and popularizer of Darwinism, was editor of the evolutionary journal *Kosmos* for its duration, 1877–1883.

[14] Müller 1892b.

[15] Three hills northwest of Arnstadt, crowned with castles, are called the Three Gleichen ("The Three Identicals"). The name refers to the legend that all three castles were struck by lightning and set afire simultaneously during a storm in the Middle Ages. Two of the hills figure in FM's youth, the Mühlberger Gleiche with the Mühlburg on its summit, and the Wanderslebener Gleiche to the north, topped by Schloß Gleiche. Both castles have been in ruins since the seventeenth century. (Reiseführer, 1981.)

[16] J. F. Müller and Caroline Müller to Hermann Trommsdorff, 30 January 1828, courtesy of Dr. Wolfgang Götz.

[17] Walther 1901:65-6.

[18] Caroline Müller to Auguste Trommsdorff, 5 January 1838, courtesy of Dr. Wolfgang Götz.

[19] Caroline Müller to Hermann Trommsdorff, 2 February 1827, courtesy of Dr. Wolfgang Götz.

[20] Lina Walther to Alfred Möller, 17 July 1897, *Leben*:6.

[21] Walther 1901:69.

[22] Ernst Biltz to Alfred Möller, 17 August 1897, *Leben*:6.

[23] Rosine Müller to Alfred Möller, 20 June 1897, *Leben*:6.

[24] Rosine Müller to Alfred Möller, 20 June 1897, *Leben*:7.

[25] Walther 1901:67.

[26] FM to Rosine Müller, 13 July 1846, *Leben*:7.

[27] Walther 1901:21.

[28] Walther 1901:25-6.

[29] Walther 1882.

[30] Ernst Biltz to Alfred Möller, 17 August 1897, *Leben*:9.

[31] FM to Hermann Müller, 1 July 1866, *Leben*:9.

[32] FM to Hermann Müller, 14 June 1870, *Leben*:10.

[33] Müller 1892b.

[34] FM to Hugo Trommsdorff, 8 October 1892, *Leben*:10.

[35] Richard & Wilhelm Mensing to Alfred Möller, 1 November 1897, *Leben*:10.

[36] Ernst Biltz to Alfred Möller, 7 August 1897, *Leben*:10.

[37] Ernst Biltz to Alfred Möller, 17 August 1897, *Leben*:10.

[38] FM to Ernst Biltz, 9 February 1886, *Leben*:11.

[39] Rosine Müller to Alfred Möller, 3 July 1897, *Leben*:11.

[40] Ernst Biltz to Alfred Möller, 17 August 1897, *Leben*:11.

[41] A cathartic derived from the roots of certain Mexican species of morning-glories, esp. *Ipomoea purga*.

[42] FM writes "Moos," a pun on "moss" and "money." *Lactuca aurea*, a fictitious golden lettuce, replaces Fritz's *Adiantum aureum*, an equally fictitious golden maiden-hair fern.

[43] Quoted by Ernst Biltz to Alfred Möller, 17 August 1897, *Leben*:12.

[44] Caroline Müller's diary, 1839, present location unknown, *Leben*:12-13.

[45] Caroline Müller to Auguste Trommsdorff, 17 April 1840, courtesy of Dr. Wolfgang Götz.

[46] Wilhelm Daniel Joseph Koch (1771–1849), a physician and expert on the central European flora. ADB, 16:402-5.

[47] Karl Friedrich Wilhelm Wallroth (1792–1857), physician and botanist in Nordhausen, whose books on lower plants appeared in 1831 and 1833. *ADB*, 40:766-8.

[48] Ernst Biltz to Alfred Möller, 17 August 1897, *Leben*:14.

[49] FM to his parents, 3 October 1861, *Leben*:15.

[50] Quoted in *Leben*:15.

[51] FM to Ernst Biltz, 9 February 1886, *Leben*:15.

## Chapter 2. University Days in Berlin and Greifswald, 1841–1845

[1] An edited version of *Leben*, chapters 5-7, with information about the University of Berlin and unpublished letters added by the author.

[2] Paulsen 1895:65-6.

[3] McClelland 1980:131-2.

[4] Paulsen 1895:79.

[5] *ADB* 17:394-7.

[6] *DSB* 4:369-70.

[7] *DSB* 4:400-1.

[8] *ADB* 2:314.

[9] *DSB* 4:174-5.

[10] Paulsen 1895:187-8.

[11] FM to Rosine Müller, 5 December 1842, *Leben*:16-17.

[12] FM to Ernst Krause, 10 July 1882, *Leben*:17.

[13] Caroline Müller to Auguste Trommsdorff, 28 December 1842, courtesy of Dr. Wolfgang Götz.

[14] FM to Charlotte Müller, 14 February 1844, *Leben*:17.

[15] *DSB* 4:123-7.

[16] *DSB* 13:12-21.

[17] Originally a diverse assemblage of single-celled organisms that appeared in infusions of hay, the name was later restricted to ciliated and flagellated protozoans.

[18] *DSB* 4:288-91.

[19] *DSB* 11:539-40.

[20] FM to Max Schultze, 18 October 1860, *Leben*:19.

[21] Müller 1844a.

[22] *ADB* 16:395-8.

[23] FM to Hermann Müller, 24 September 1844, *Leben*:19.

[24] Müller 1844b.

[25] McClelland 1980:198.

[26] Translation partly from Friesen 1999-2000.

[27] *Leben*:20. The theses are not in FM's published dissertation. They were apparently to be defended when he was examined for the Ph.D.

[28] The peristome is a marginal ring of teeth around the opening of the sporangium of mosses. FM may be attacking single-character taxonomy.

[29] FM to Max Sagemehl, 12 July 1885, Senckenbergische Bibliothek, Frankfurt am Main.

[30] FM to Rosine Müller, 30 October 1845, *Leben*:20

[31] Quotation not identified.

[32] FM to Charlotte Müller, 14 February 1845, *Leben*:21.

[33] Richard Mensing to Alfred Möller, November 1897, *Leben*:21.

[34] Richard Mensing to Rosine Müller, 5 August 1845, *Leben*:21.

[35] FM to Rosine Müller, 23 August 1845, *Leben*:21.

[36] FM to August Müller, 5 August 1845, *Leben*:22.

[37] Their son, Fritz's half-brother, Gustav Wilhelm Müller (1857–1940) studied natural sciences, visited Fritz in Brazil, and became University Professor of Zoology at Greifswald.

[38] Hermann Müller's diary was seen by Alfred Möller but was subsequently lost.

[39] Referring to men like Gustav Wislicenus and Leberecht Uhlich, the founders of the Free Communities and the Friends of Light (see Chapter 3).

[40] FM to Wilhelm Mensing, 10 June 1845, *Leben*:23.

[41] FM to Rosine Müller, 23 August 1845, *Leben*:23.

## Chapter 3. Medical School, Freedom of Conscience, and the Revolution, 1845–1849

[1] An edited version of *Leben*, Chapter 8, with additions by the author on the Revolution of 1848 and on theological and political writers who influenced FM.

[2] FM to Rosine Müller, 5 November 1845, *Leben*:24.

[3] FM to Wilhelm Mensing, 4 December 1845, *Leben*:24.

[4] FM to Rosine Müller, 6 January 1846, *Leben*:24-25.

[5] FM to Rosine Müller, 3 December 1845, *Leben*:25.

[6] FM to Rosine Müller, 5 November 1845, *Leben*:25.

[7] Max Schultze (1825–1874), German biologist, Professor of Anatomy at Bonn and Halle, editor of *Archiv für mikroskopische Anatomie*, 1865–1874, and one of FM's important correspondents in his early years in Brazil. Eduard Oscar Schmidt (1823–1886), German zoologist, Professor of Zoology at Strasburg,

studied comparative anatomy and sponges. Anton Karsch (1822–1892), German zoologist, Professor at Münster.

[8] Johannes Iapetus Smith Steenstrup (1813–1897), Danish zoologist, Professor of Zoology and Director of the Zoological Museum, Copenhagen, known for work on alternation of generations.

[9] Steenstrup 1846.

[10] Steenstrup 1846: III-IV.

[11] FM's contribution, pp. 110-4 in Steenstrup 1846, was reprinted in *Werke*:36-9.

[12] Hornschuch also included an abstract of Quatrefages's *Studies on the genitalia of planarians* and comments by Creplin on hermaphroditism in intestinal flatworms: "Mr. Steenstrup denies the hermaphroditic nature of Trematoda (flukes) and Cestoda (tapeworms), which have long been thought to be hermaphroditic. He supposes that the organs which are considered testes in the former are partly accessory glands of unknown function, partly spermatheca of females.... Regarding those animals recognized as belonging to the Trematoda....we find invariably, adjacent to the female genitalia in the adult and fully-developed condition, organs which from their arrangement and contents cannot possibly be other than male genitalia." (Creplin, in Steenstrup 1846:110.)

[13] Müller 1885.

[14] Quoted by FM to Rosine Müller, 5 November 1845, *Leben*:26.

[15] FM to Hermann Müller, 29 October 1845, *Leben*:26.

[16] Oehlschläger to Alfred Möller, 1897, *Leben*:26.

[17] A shooting competition, also an occasion for much drinking.

[18] FM to Rosine Müller, 13 July 1846, *Leben*:27.

[19] Valentin 1930:44.

[20] Valentin 1930:46. Robert Eduard Prutz (1816–1872).

[21] Oehlschläger to Alfred Möller, 10 October 1897, *Leben*:27.

[22] David Friedrich Strauss (1808–1874), German philosopher and theologian.

[23] Ludwig Andrea Feuerbach (1804–1872).

[24] Gregory 1992:75-6.

[25] Gregory 1992:85.

[26] Strauss 1840:41, trans. in Harris 1973:134.

[27] Langer 1969:517.

[28] Gregory 1992:46.

[29] Harris 1973:140. Bruno Bauer (1809–1892), German theologian and politician who moved to the radical left in the late 1830s.

[30] Langer 1969:518. Max Stirner (1806–1856), pseud. of Johann Caspar Schmidt, German philosopher.

[31] FM's characteristic description of museum specimens.

[32] FM to Oehlschläger, 26 March 1893, *Leben*:27.

[33] Prutz 1845.

[34] Glaßbrenner (or Glasbrenner) 1845. According to Valentin (1930:49), Adolf Georg Theodor Glasbrenner (1810–1876), a liberal writer, "educated the people of Berlin in politics," was a popular figure, and ". . . despite the truly

radical, even social revolutionary slant that he occasionally showed, he was for the most part left in peace by the censor."

[35] Gervinus 1845. Georg Gottfried Gervinus (1805–1871), liberal theologian. "He zealously took up [in 1845] the cause of the German Catholics, hoping it would lead to a union of all the Christian confessions, and to the establishment of a national church." *EB* 11:908.

[36] Friedrich Theodor Vischer (1807–1877), German writer on the philosophy of art and active in the democratic movement of 1848–1849 (*ADB*). Lauterbach, 2000, identifies the publication as Vischer 1845. FM wrote of Vischer's critique: "He shows that every dogma, however arrived at and however liberal-seeming, must always have some exclusiveness, always give rise to intolerance and be in irreconcilable conflict with religious freedom." (FM to Hermann Trommsdorff, 19 Feb 1846, quoted in Lauterbach 2000.)

[37] Craig 1983:90.

[38] Langer 1969:126.

[39] Gustav Adolf Wislicenus (1803–1875), liberal German theologian.

[40] "Wislicenus," in *BE* 20:409.

[41] Friesen 1999-2000, gives a good summary of the fortunes of the Friends of Light.

[42] *ADB* 43:542-5.

[43] *Leben*:28.

[44] "Take any three doctors and two will be atheists every time." Gregory 1977:29.

[45] FM to August Müller, 2 January 1846, *Leben*:28-9.

[46] Gotthold Ephraim Lessing (1729–1781), German critic and dramatist, who took on theological controversy late in life and thereby secured "wider freedom for writers on theology." His play *Nathan der Weise* argued for the mutual tolerance of holders of different doctrines. *EB* 16:498. The quotation has not been identified.

[47] FM to Wilhelm Mensing, 16 February 1846, *Leben*:29-30. The lines by Prutz are the second stanza of his poem *Kriegserklärung* (Declaration of War) (Prutz 1843).

[48] FM to Wilhelm Mensing, 20 February 1846, *Leben*:30.

[49] FM to August Müller, 30 September 1846, *Leben*:30.

[50] Wislicenus 1846.

[51] Lauterbach 2000.

[52] Wislicenus had used Strauss's arguments and rejected Biblical authority when he took over the Friends of Light in 1844 (Friesen 1999-2000:48).

[53] Quoted in translation by Gregory 1977:5.

[54] FM to Wislicenus, 15 November 1846, *Leben*:31-2. Published as Müller 1846. The version given here differs slightly from the published one and may come from the original letter, now lost.

[55] Friesen 1999-2000.

[56] Bishop Möller to FM, 3 January 1847, *Leben*:32-3. The motto is not in Blumenbach, 1825, and the epigram in Linnaeus's 1st edition (1735) is actually Psalm 104:24, "O Lord, how manifold are thy works! in wisdom hast thou

made them all: the earth is full of thy riches." Johann Friedrich Blumenbach (1752–1840), German naturalist and anthropologist. Linnaeus (Carl von Linné) (1717–1778), Swedish naturalist and pioneering systematist.

[57] FM to Rosine Müller, 15 October 1847, *Leben*:33-4.

[58] FM to August Müller, 29 September 1847, *Leben*:35.

[59] Lauterbach 2000, which contains important documents relating to FM's "problem."

[60] The summary of the Revolution of 1848 comes principally from Langer 1969.

[61] Oehlschläger to Alfred Möller, 1897, *Leben*:36.

[62] FM to August and Hermann Müller, 21 October 1848, *Leben*:36.

[63] See note 62.

[64] See note 62.

[65] See note 59.

[66] *Leben*:35. No documentation of this rejection has yet been found.

[67] See note 59.

[68] McKinney 1974.

[69] FM to Wilhelm Mensing, 14 March 1849, *Leben*:35.

[70] Langer 1969:480-2.

# Chapter 4. Respite in the Country, 1849–1852

[1] An edited version of Chapter 9 of *Leben*, with additions by the author on Fritz's views on marriage and emigration, and on Hermann Blumenau's colony.

[2] FM to Hermann Müller, 28 November 1849, *Leben*:37.

[3] FM to Charlotte Pfeifer, née Müller, 23 February 1850, *Leben*:37.

[4] FM to Lamprecht, 20 November 1853, *Leben*:37-8. This and the following letters to Lamprecht were made available to Alfred Möller by Lamprecht's son Wilhelm, one of FM's pupils at Rolofshagen, who died in Eberswalde in 1917. Alfred Möller "often had the opportunity to speak with the old man. He remembered his teacher with gratitude, kept the letters to his father and the silhouette [Fig. 4], and placed everything at my disposal." (*Leben*:38n) Their present location is unknown.

[5] FM to Lamprecht, 23 March 1854, *Leben*:38.

[6] Macaulay, Thomas Babington (1800–1859), English historian. The German translation of his multi-volume *History of England* began appearing in 1849.

[7] Sue, [Marie-Joseph] Eugène (1804–1857), French novelist, dealing especially with the lower classes. *Les mystères du Peuple, ou Histoire d'une famille de prolétaires à travers les ages* began appearing in 1850.

[8] Proudhon, Pierre Joseph (1809–1865), French libertarian socialist and influential writer on anarchism. His book *Les confessions d'un révolutionnaire, pour servir à l'histoire de la révolution de février* [the Paris Revolution of 1848], "one of his two most important works," has never had an English translation. (*NEB* 9:744-5.)

9 FM to Hermann Müller, 25 July 1850, *Leben*:38. Adolph Kolatschek edited the *Deutsche Monatsschrift für Politik, Wissenschaft, Kunst und Leben* in Bremen.

10 Church records, Loitz, according to Alfred Möller, *Leben*:43.

11 Fröbel 1850.

12 FM to August and Hermann Müller, 21 October 1848, *Leben*:39.

13 Fröbel 1850 I:207-8.

14 Fröbel 1850 I:216.

15 Oehlschläger to Alfred Möller, 4 November 1897, *Leben*:39.

16 Friesen 1999-2000.

17 McKinney 1974.

18 Friesen 1999-2000:50.

19 FM to Hermann Müller, 27 December 1849, *Leben*:39.

20 FM to Hermann Müller, 30 March 1851, *Leben*:40. Most of the last paragraph is shown in Fritz's handwriting in Fig. 4.

21 Müller 1851a. "The holiness of God according to the notions of philosophy and of ordinary human intelligence." Fritz would have us seek the solution to the puzzle of life and science in ourselves and in a rational consideration of nature and human life, not in the Gods of philosophy or of the Church. Dr. Douai not identified.

22 Müller 1851b. "Nature as a moral standard for Man." Fritz believed that the mixing-up of science and morals would be detrimental, the former being turned back to physico-theology, the latter to a motley collection of more or less lame metaphors. Emil Adolf Rossmässler (1806–1867) studied theology as an undergraduate, but became a botanist and popular writer on natural history, and was Professor of Natural History in Dresden from 1848 until his dismissal in 1850 for political activities.

23 FM to Hermann Müller, 30 March 1851, *Leben*:42.

24 Blumenau 1850.

25 FM to Hermann Müller, 18 September 1851, *Leben*:42.

26 Fouquet 1950. In Portuguese translation.

27 Crofton 1972.

28 FM to Hermann Müller, 15 November 1851, *Leben*:42-43.

29 Crofton 1972.

30 Wappäus 1846.

31 Probably the Prussian "meile," 4.68 English miles, making it about 510 square kilometers (51,000 hectares), or a little larger than the area of Andorra.

32 Müller 1852.

33 FM to his parents, *Leben*:43-44.

# Chapter 5. Emigrant and Pioneer
# in Brazil, 1852–1856

[1] Largely an edited version of the documents published in Chapters 10 and 11 of *Leben*, with additions from letters in *Briefe* and from 20th C. historical works.

[2] *Leben*:45-8.

[3] The *Florentin* was a three-masted bark of 342 tons, 112.6 feet in length, 26.4 feet in breadth, and had been built in 1850. (Information courtesy of Wendy Schnur, G. W. Blunt White Library, Mystic Seaport Museum, Mystic, CT.) Compare the *Beagle*, 90 feet long, about 242 tons displacement, but carrying only 74 people (Browne 1995), less than a third of the *Florentin*'s load.

[4] An advertisement in Blumenau's brochure (Blumenau 1850) gives the price of cabin class passage from Hamburg to Brazil as 30 RG. Taking the value of the Reichsgulden or guilder as US$.40 (Chase 1856), that would be $12.00, surprisingly cheap compared with about $30.00 for second-class cabin passage on a rapid steamer from Hamburg to New York in the mid-1850s. (Information courtesy of Wendy Schnur, Mystic Seaport Museum Library.) Recall that the annual stipend for the pastor of Windischholzhausen around this time was 336 thalers (= 588 RG, or about $235).

[5] The temperatures in this account are in degrees Réaumur, an obsolete scale in which the freezing point of water = 0 and the boiling point = 80. Hereafter they have been converted to Celsius.

[6] FM gives prices in Brazilian currency, sometimes with German equivalents. For a comparison, in Blumenau in 1854, according to Tschudi (1868-69), a laborer might have earned 256 milreis ($138) per year, an artisan half again as much, while the annual cost of food was something over 70 milreis ($38). For a comparison with an item familiar to modern readers, the average price of a book at that time in the United States was about $2.

[7] Matthias Schneider, a fellow-settler, according to Ferreira da Silva 1931. He also helped the Müllers to build their cabins.

[8] Ferreira da Silva 1950:13.

[9] Fritz writes "farinha", flour or meal, but according to Müller's autobiographical sketch written many years later (Müller 1892b) it was manioc meal, not maize, although the latter was a common bread substitute in the backwoods of Brazil a few years later (Bigg-Wither 1878).

[10] "Continuation of the Notes on the journey for friends and acquaintances" by Fritz and August Müller, 25 August 1852, *Leben*:49. The date should be "28 August," according to internal evidence.

[11] FM to his parents, 29 August 1852, *Leben*:49-50.

[12] The first seventeen settlers arrived in Blumenau in 1850, nine bachelors and two men with wives and children. They included three farmers, two blacksmiths, surveyor, carpenter, joiner, tinker, butcher and veterinarian. Of these, two men left in 1851, although one of them returned and drowned in February 1852. The twelve families referred to here would have included the Müllers and perhaps Matthias Schneider (Ferreira da Silva 1950).

[13] August Müller to his parents and siblings, 30 October 1852, *Leben*:49-50.

[14] Tschudi 1868-69.

[15] "A generic term for any Indian, wild or otherwise, esp. certain Caingang of Santa Catarina." (Taylor 1970).

[16] FM refers to the settlers in the Indian attack as S. and T., but they are identified in an eye-witness account written by pastor Ostermann to Hermann Blumenau the day after the incident. (1957. "A bad Christmas present," *Blumenau em Cadernos*, I(2):38-9.)

[17] Ferreira da Silva 1959.

[18] FM to Rosine Müller, 6 January 1853, *Leben*:50-4.

[19] FM to his parents, 18 February 1853, *Leben*:54-5.

[20] FM to Hermann Müller, 28 August 1853, *Leben*:55.

[21] FM to Lamprecht, 23 March 1854, *Leben*:55-6.

[22] FM probably means araribá, genus *Centrolobium* of the pea family (Taylor 1970).

[23] Müller 1892b.

[24] See note 23.

[25] Friesen 1995-96.

[26] FM to his father, 25 July 1853, *Leben*:57.

[27] FM to his father, 18 December 1855, *Leben*:57-8.

[28] FM to Rosine Müller, 25 December 1853, *Leben*:58-9.

[29] FM to Lamprecht, 23 March 1854, *Leben*:59.

[30] FM to Hermann Müller, 31 August 1854, *Briefe*:1-7.

[31] Vogt 1851. Carl Vogt (1817–1895), German medical man and natural scientist, was exiled in 1848 because of liberal views, and became Professor of Geology at Geneva because the zoology chair was occupied. (*DSB*)

[32] Baruch Spinoza (1632–1677), Dutch philosopher. "The classical text of rational atheism is...the *Ethics* of Spinoza, who is considered to be the founder of modern biblical interpretation and demythologization." *NEB*, 2:261.

[33] Fröbel 1850.

[34] Bravais and Bravais 1838.

[35] FM to Hermann Müller, 14 January 1855, *Leben*:61.

[36] FM to Lamprecht, 14 January 1855, *Leben*:61.

[37] FM to Lamprecht, 3 July 1855, *Leben*:61-2.

[38] Paul Kellner, one of the original seventeen settlers who came to Blumenau in 1850 (Ferraz 1949; Ferreira da Silva 1950). The story of the Indian attack is mentioned by Tschudi (1868–1869), who calls him "Keller."

[39] Coutinho (1809–1870) was President of Santa Catarina, 1850–1859 (Tschudi 1868-69).

[40] Fouquet (1950) says the river rose 63 spans, about 14 meters, but he may mean closer to the mouth where the Little Itajaí enters it.

[41] FM to Lamprecht, 12 May 1856, *Leben*:62-4.

[42] Crofton 1972.

[43] "A Brazilian spiny club palm (*Bactris setosa*) whose fiber is used in hammock-weaving." (Taylor 1970)

[44] Tschudi (1868-69) says that the Indians raided in summer for lack of food. In the winter they stayed in araucaria forest in the hills, where they fed on the large seeds of *Araucaria brasiliensis*.

[45] FM to his parents and siblings, 6 April 1856, *Leben*:65-6.

[46] FM to Lamprecht, 12 May 1856, *Leben*:66-7.

[47] *Leben*:67.

# Chapter 6. Teacher in Desterro, 1856–1867

[1] Largely from the documentation in Chapter 12 of *Leben*. The author has added Fritz's views on Blacks, some of his correspondence with Haeckel, and information from reminiscences.

[2] Müller 1892b.

[3] FM to an unidentified correspondent, 31 March 1857, *Leben*:68-9.

[4] Taylor 1970.

[5] Taylor 1970, but FM may intend the form from which manioc meal is prepared.

[6] Alfred Möller does not identify the source of this description, *Leben*:71-2.

[7] FM to an unidentified correspondent, 31 March 1857, *Leben*:72.

[8] See note 7.

[9] R. Becker, a German, taught Latin; Dr. Hermogenes de Souza Miranda Souto, a young physician, taught French; Willington, a "little-educated" North American, English; FM, Mathematics. (Tschudi 1868-69)

[10] Tschudi 1868-69. Coutinho became Postmaster General in Rio de Janeiro in 1859.

[11] Müller 1892b.

[12] FM to Hermann Müller, 12 October 1857, *Leben*:73.

[13] FM to Hermann Müller, 28 March 1857, *Leben*:73.

[14] FM to unidentified correspondent, 10 February 1858, *Leben*:73.

[15] FM to Hermann Müller, 12 October 1857, *Leben*:73.

[16] A former pupil, Affonso Gama, told the story in an obituary of FM in the Rio newspaper *Gazeta do Povo*, 8 July 1897, *Leben*:74.

[17] Quoted by Alfred Möller from an otherwise unidentified colleague of FM's named Parucker, *Leben*:74.

[18] Hermann Burmeister (1807-92), German zoologist, traveled in Brazil, 1850s, emigrated to Argentina 1861.

[19] FM to Hermann Müller, 30 May 1860, *Briefe*:19. Burmeister's observations of blacks in Brazil are in Burmeister 1853; a chapter of Burmeister 1855, is also devoted to "The Black Man."

[20] Emma had congenital abnormalities, "a twisted face and incurable cutaneous irruptions." (*Blumenau em Cadernos* 3, 1960)

[21] FM to Max Schultze, 18 July 1858, *Leben*:74.

[22] FM to Max Schultze, 12 October 1862, *Leben*:74-5. There was one later birth, of stillborn twins with gross abnormalities. (*Blumenau em Cadernos* 3, 1960)

[23] FM to Max Schultze, 4 April 1862, *Leben*:75. Oesterlen (1856:823, n.1) cites Jeter (1854) that North American rattlesnake venom is just like bee venom and that multiple bee stings have the same effect as snake bite. *Bothrops* toxin is an extremely powerful depresser of blood pressure and was the foundation of the development of a treatment for hypertension. Irene Lauterbach, to the author, 6 September 2001.

[24] The author observed that German was still the first language of many children in rural Santa Catarina in the 1980s.

[25] Johann Wilhelm Hey (1789–1854), German theologian and fabler. His books of pictures and verses for children were first published in the 1830s but reprinted many times.

[26] FM to Rosine Müller, 20 August 1854, *Leben*:75-6.

[27] Six of these didactic poems were published in *Leben*. These and six more are in the Hamburg University Library, copied in unknown hands from a manuscript entitled "The little Brazilian songbook," which Fritz sent to the children of his half brother Wilhelm but which is now lost. A copy that evidently belonged to Fritz's daughter Rosa is in São Paulo (Friesen 1997-98, where all twelve poems are published), and there is apparently a copy with Fritz's sketches in Blumenau. Two pages of the latter were published in facsimile in Roquette-Pinto 1979.

[28] Found by Alfred Möller among FM's papers. The shapes and patterns of calculations are illustrated in *Leben*:81-2.

[29] After Coutinho's departure, FM thanked him for having made possible the spare time for his scientific work, and commemorated him with the name of a bryozoan *Serialaria coutinhii* in which FM demonstrated a colonial nervous system (Müller 1860).

[30] Francisco Carlos de Araújo Brusque (1822–1886), Brazilian lawyer, President of Santa Catarina 1859–1861.

[31] Müller 1892b.

[32] See note 31.

[33] FM to Hermann Müller, 5 April 1862, *Leben*:83.

[34] Ernst Heinrich Philipp August Haeckel (1834–1919), German zoologist, Professor of Zoology at Jena from 1862.

[35] FM to Hermann Müller, 1 July 1866, *Leben*:83-4.

[36] FM to Ernst Haeckel, 4 March 1866. EHH.

[37] Christian Konrad Sprengel (1750–1816), German botanist who recognized mechanisms for preventing self-pollination and showed the "close integration of floral structure with insect visitation." (*DSB*)

[38] FM to Ernst Haeckel, 17 December 1869, *Briefe*:166-7.

[39] *Leben*:68.

[40] FM to Hermann Müller, 31 May 1867, *Leben*:85.

[41] Müller 1892b.

# Chapter 7. Marine Zoology
## and the Defense of Darwin 1856–1869

[1] Nearly all of this chapter was written by the author, largely from FM's correspondence and publications.

[2] "Acalephs" then included coelenterates (hydras, jellyfish, sea anemones and corals) and ctenophores (comb jellies), not yet recognized as separate phyla.

[3] FM to Hermann Müller, 26 November 1856, *Briefe*:9-10.

[4] Schultze 1857.

[5] Darwin 1844a and b.

[6] Müller and Schultze 1856.

[7] FM to Max Schultze, 28 June 1861, *Briefe*:24.

[8] Müller 1862a.

[9] FM to Max Schultze, 4 April 1862, *Briefe*:34-5.

[10] Müller 1863b.

[11] See note 10.

[12] FM to Max Schultze, 17 December 1861, *Briefe*:30.

[13] Darwin 1860. Charles Robert Darwin (1809–1882), eminent English naturalist.

[14] *Leben*:87.

[15] FM to Max Schultze, 16 February 1862, *Briefe*:32-3.

[16] FM to Hermann Müller, 5 April 1862, *Leben*:87-8.

[17] Müller 1863a.

[18] FM to Hermann Müller, 16 December 1862, *Briefe*:40-1.

[19] FM to Max Schultze, 13 March 1864, *Briefe*:51-2.

[20] Müller 1864.

[21] Gerstaecker 1865.

[22] The Darwinian hypothesis. . . . 1865.

[23] See note 22.

[24] Bate 1865. Charles Spence Bate (1818–1889), English dentist and naturalist, interested in the development and morphology of Crustacea.

[25] Haeckel to Darwin, 26 October 1864, *CCD*, 12:381, 489.

[26] Darwin to Haeckel, 21 November 1864, *CCD*, 12:412.

[27] Cresy to Darwin, 30 May 1865, *CCD*, 13: 158.

[28] Darwin to FM, 10 August 1865, *CCD*, 13:212-13, *LL*, II:221-222 with slight alterations.

[29] FM annotated 43 of Darwin's 58 letters in English with date of receipt and/or response.

[30] Darwin to FM, 10 August 1865, *CCD*, 13: 212-13.

[31] Müller 1867.

[32] Darwin to FM, 17 October 1865, *CCD*, 13:271-2; also partly in *ML*, II:344-5.

[33] Darwin to FM, 20 September 1865, *CCD*, 13:234-5.

[34] FM to Darwin, 5 November 1865, *CCD*, 13:294-6; *Briefe*, 76-7, a German translation of the original draft found among FM's papers at his death, retranslated by DAW.

[35] Joseph Dalton Hooker (1817–1911), English botanist, Director of the Royal Botanic Gardens, Kew, 1865-1885.

[36] Darwin to Hooker, 31 May 1866, DAR 115:290.

[37] W. S. Dallas to Darwin, 22 February 1868, DAR 162. William Sweetland Dallas (1824–1900), English naturalist and translator.

[38] Darwin to Hermann Müller, 23 February 1868, DAR 146.

[39] Hermann Müller to Darwin, [after 23 February 1868], DAR 171.

[40] Darwin to FM, 16 March 1868. BL (Loan 10:22), parts in *LL*, II:269.

[41] Memo, FM to Darwin, 22 April 1868. DAR-CD Library, but incorrectly dated as "August 1868" in *CAL*. This passage includes the additions to Chapter XII of Müller 1869a:135-40.

[42] Müller 1869a:119 n.2. FM distinguishes the metamorphosis of shrimps, which he considers "inherited" (meaning what might be called a "shared primitive character"), from that of insects, which he calls "acquired" (meaning a "derived character").

[43] Charles Lyell (1797–1875). Scottish uniformitarian geologist, author of *Principles of Geology*, 1830–1833, an important source for Darwin on the *Beagle* voyage.

[44] FM to Darwin, 17 June 1868, *Briefe*:141-3, a German translation of the original draft found among FM's papers at his death, re-translated by the author.

[45] Darwin to FM, 17 August 1868, BL (Loan 10:25). *Für Darwin* was also translated into Russian by Nozhin (Müller 1865), and into French by F. Debray (Müller 1882/83) but without the footnotes that were added to the English edition. FM appears to have been unaware of these translations.

[46] W. S. Dallas to Darwin, 17 March 1868, DAR 162.

[47] 43. W. S. Dallas to Darwin, 27 November 1868, DAR 162.

[48] Darwin to J. Murray, 23 February 1869. John Murray Archives (Darwin:194-7).

[49] Ledgers, John Murray, Ltd. In June 1870 Darwin made up the difference between Murray's costs and the income from sales (£21.2s.3d) and reported to FM in September 1873 that sales had at last exceeded costs, but what with the "scandalous charges all English publishers make" he had received only £4.13s.1d. (Darwin to FM, 23 September 1873. BL (Loan 10:35)). Eventually, in response to FM's suggestion, he sent the balance to Hermann Müller (Darwin to FM, 13 February 1874. BL (Loan 10:37)). In 1882, at the time of Darwin's death, 247 copies were left, and in 1889 there were still 29 on hand.

[50] Darwin to FM, 18 March 1869. BL (Loan 10:28), *ML* I:312.

[51] Darwin 1871b.

[52] Lubbock 1869.

[53] Review of *For Darwin*. 1869.

[54] [Leifchild]. 1869. The reviewer was John Leifchild, according to the marked copy owned by the *New Statesman* (courtesy of Sue Holland, Athenaeum Indexing Project, The City University, London). Leifchild's famous review of Darwin's *Origin* appeared in the same journal in 1859.

[55] Agassiz and Gould, 1856. Louis Agassiz (1807–1873). Swiss-American zoologist and geologist, father of Alexander. Harvard professor 1847–1873.

[56] Müller 1869a:105-6. FM goes on to criticize those, like Louis Agassiz, who condemn classifications based on single characters and then construct them themselves. His examples are Agassiz's inclusion of Echinoderms in the Radiata, and the division of "true fishes" into Ctenoids and Cycloids "according as the posterior margin of their scales is denticulated or smooth, a circumstance the importance of which to the animal must be infinitely small, in comparison to the peculiarities of the dentition, formation of the fins, number of vertebrae, &c."

[57] Müller 1869a:97, n.2, referring to the passage: "Perhaps a sharper eye may be able, with Agassiz, to make out 'the plan established from the beginning by the Creator,' who may have written here, as a Portuguese proverb says 'straight in crooked lines.'"

[58] FM to Hermann Müller, 12 June 1869, *Briefe*: 157-8.

[59] Müller 1869a:8-9. Translation modified by the author.

[60] Darwin 1859:193-94.

[61] Müller 1869a:37.

[62] Craw 1992; Ghiselin 1996.

[63] Avise 1994:34-9.

[64] Müller 1869a:23, translation modified by the author.

[65] Heinrich Georg Bronn (1800–1862). German paleontologist, translated Darwin's *Origin of Species* (1860) and *Orchids* (1862). It was through Bronn's translation that FM first met *The Origin*.

[66] Darwin 1859:112.

[67] Darwin 1859:178-9.

[68] Müller 1869a:24, translation modified by the author.

[69] Müller 1863a.

[70] Lang 1891.

[71] Müller 1869a:97.

[72] Müller 1869a:105.

[73] Müller 1869a:111.

[74] Müller 1869a:111-2.

[75] Churchill 1991:11.

[76] Churchill 1991:19.

[77] Müller 1869a:111-2.

[78] See note 75.

[79] See note 75.

[80] Haeckel 1897.

[81] Johannes Müller 1842.

[82] Müller 1869a:121, translation modified by the author.

[83] Haeckel 1866, vol. 2:300.

[84] Haeckel 1872, vol.1:471.

[85] Churchill 1991:20.

[86] Gould 1977:esp. 63-8.

[87] Müller 1880/81a.

[88] Gould 1977:101. Stephen Jay Gould (1941–2002). American paleontologist, evolutionist, and science writer.

[89] Montgomery 1974.

[90] Bowler 1984.

[91] Müller 1869a:24. For misconceptions about Lamarck, see Mayr 1982:357.

[92] Alexander Agassiz (1835–1910). Swiss-American zoologist, Director of the Museum of Comparative Zoology, Harvard.

[93] FM to A. Agassiz, 11 February 1863, *Briefe*:41-2.

[94] FM to Max Schultze, 30 June 1863, *Leben*:90.

[95] FM to Max Schultze, 11 April 1864, *Briefe*:53.

[96] In the published letter (Agassiz 1913) "structure" was substituted for "complication."

[97] A. Agassiz to FM, 17 January 1864. Houghton *83M-38. Partly in Agassiz, 1913:48-51. A. Agassiz refers to his father's "'threefold parallelism' of embryonic growth, structural gradation, and geologic succession." (Gould 1977:66)

[98] FM to A. Agassiz, 27 June 1864, *Briefe*:53-5.

[99] Mädler 1858:30. Johann Heinrich von Mädler (1794–1874), German astronomer and director of the Dorpat observatory 1840–1865, best known for his moon-map.

[100] Loew 1864. F. Hermann Loew (1807–1879), German-American entomologist, interested in insects in amber.

[101] A. Agassiz to FM, 23 February 1865. Houghton *83M-38.

[102] A. Agassiz to FM, 9 March 1865. Houghton *83M-38.

[103] Recent opinion is that a similarity like that of the larvae of sea urchins and brittle stars "sheds little light on the interrelationships of living echinoderm classes" because "there is considerable convergence in the larval forms of different classes." (Barnes 1980:1014).

[104] Hensen 1863. Christian Andreas Viktor von Hensen (1835–1924), German physiologist and professor at Kiel.

[105] FM to A. Agassiz, 29 June 1865, *Briefe*:64-7.

[106] A. Agassiz to FM, 11 January 1866. Houghton *83M-38.

[107] FM to A. Agassiz, 30 August 1866, *Briefe*:90-3.

[108] A. Agassiz to FM, 16 November 1866. These sections of the letter are in Agassiz 1913:51-2. The unpublished parts in the Houghton Library, Harvard University, are almost undecipherable.

[109] Georges Cuvier (1769–1832), French systematist, comparative anatomist, and paleontologist, whose four *embranchements*, or body-plans: Radiata, Mollusca, Articulata, and Vertebrata, were defended by Louis Agassiz to the end of his life (see Gould 1977).

[110] Quoted from A. Agassiz to FM, 8 Nov 1868, in Agassiz 1913: 91-4.

[111] FM to Keferstein, 11 Feb 1869, *Briefe*:154-6. FM's reference to a letter from Louis Agassiz is unique; no such letter is known.

[112] Agassiz 1913.

[113] FM to Hermann Müller, 16 February 1870, *Briefe*:171-2. Darwin's letter of 1 December 1869, BL (Loan 10:31), *ML*,II:357-8, was received by FM on 23 January 1870. Two years later, however, Agassiz was still unhappy about the speculations of the Darwinians unsupported by facts: "The supporters of Darwin, who outdarwin Darwin himself, seem determined not to imitate their great leader, and attempt, in the most dogmatic manner, to crush any argument brought forward, not by showing its worthlessness, but by simply taking it for granted that discussion is no longer possible." His chief target was probably Haeckel, for he adds: "...when I am introduced to an archetype in a group where we have neither paleontological nor embryological evidence, or where I am asked to believe in a genealogical tree of which neither the roots nor the branches have ever existed, as far as we now know, I am no longer dealing simply with an hypothesis, but with the wildest speculation." (Agassiz 1872-74:753-4.)

# Chapter 8. Botany and the Return to the Itajaí Valley, 1867–1872

[1] The description of Blumenau and the narrative of FM's excursion to the Warnow in this chapter come from Chapter 13 of *Leben*. The author has added excerpts from FM's excursion to Boa Vista and the account of his correspondence with Darwin on the forms of flowers, pollination biology, orchids, and pangenesis.

[2] FM to Max Schultze, 12 December 1865. *Leben*:89. The orchid book is Darwin, 1862. Several papers by Darwin on the forms of flowers between 1862 and 1864 were the basis of Darwin 1877b.

[3] Darwin 1867.

[4] FM to Darwin, 12 August 1865, *CCD*, 13:215.

[5] Müller 1867.

[6] FM to Darwin, 10 October 1865, *CCD*, 13:266-7. *Briefe*:75, a German translation of the draft found among FM's papers at his death.

[7] Darwin 1877a.

[8] FM to Hermann Müller, 1 July 1866. *Leben*:86.

[9] Müller 1866. Uncertain that the species belonged in the genus *Posoqueria*, FM proposed as an alternative generic name that of his most recent daughter, who had just died in infancy.

[10] Darwin to FM, 9 & 15 April 1866, *ML* II: 261-3.

[11] FM to Hermann Müller, 1 July 1866, *Leben*:86-7.

[12] Darwin 1878:5.

[13] Browne 2002:12.

[14] Darwin to FM, 3 June 1868, *ML* II:82-3.

[15] Friedrich Hermann Gustav Hildebrand (1835–1915), German botanist in Bonn and Freiburg.

[16] Friedrich Ludwig (1851–1918), German botanist, taught at the Greiz Gymnasium, 1875–1918. Ludwig 1897 contains a full bibliography of FM's botanical papers, including those which Ludwig himself published.

[17] Henri Milne-Edwards (1800–1885). French zoologist, Professor of Entomology and Zoology, Muséum d'Histoire Naturelle, Paris.

[18] Raphael Meldola (1849–1915). English industrial chemist and entomologist, Professor at Finsbury Technical College.

[19] FM may be playing on the double meaning of the German "Larve", which can also mean a mask, as of someone's true nature.

[20] FM to Max Schultze, 15 December 1862, *Leben*:90.

[21] The woodcut was published in Tschudi, 1868-69 and reproduced in *Leben*:91 from "a sheet of note-paper" of 1867.

[22] According to Tschudi (1868-69), it was founded by Karl Friedenreich, veterinarian, amateur entomologist and later Director of the colony.

[23] Crofton 1972.

[24] Emilio Odebrecht (1835–1912), Brazilian engineer, traveler, and naturalist. His maps and articles on the Itajaí valley appeared in the journals of the Berlin Geographical Society, for example Odebrecht 1875.

[25] FM to Hermann Müller, 26 July 1871, *Leben*:93.

[26] Belt 1874.

[27] FM to Hermann Müller, 13 December 1870, *Leben*:93.

[28] Crofton 1972.

[29] FM to Hermann Müller, 12 September 1867, *Leben*:93.

[30] FM's half-timbered brick house is now a museum.

[31] FM to his parents, 17 December 1867, *Leben*:94.

[32] Müller 1870b.

[33] FM to Ernst Haeckel, 7 December 1868, *Briefe*:150.

[34] FM to Hermann Müller, 8 December 1868, *Leben*:94.

[35] See Darwin, 1862, on this remarkable group of orchids.

[36] FM to Darwin, 17 June 1868, *Briefe*:141-3, a German translation of the lost original.

[37] Müller 1869b.

[38] FM calls him "S," but he was a shoemaker (see below) and therefore Friedrich Seiffert, who had settled in Blumenau with the Müller brothers in 1852 and lived near them on the Garcia (Ferreira da Silva 1950:13).

[39] Mate, pronounced máhteh or mátcheh, is a small tree (*Ilex paraguayensis*) the leaves of which furnish Paraguay tea.

[40] FM to Hermann Müller, 10 July 1868, *Leben*:97.

[41] Correspondence file, Royal Botanic Gardens, Kew, vol. 215: letters 168-74.

[42] Herbarium Plant List, Royal Botanic Gardens, Kew, vol. 10: 73-8, 80-1, 83-4.

[43] Darwin 1862.

[44] Darwin 1864; 1865.

[45] FM to Darwin, 5 November 1865, *Briefe*:76-7, a German translation of the lost original. Part of the original letter was included in Müller 1867.

[46] Darwin 1888:245.

[47] FM to Hermann Müller, 29 October 1866, *Briefe*:94-8.

[48] Müller 1869d.

[49] Darwin 1888:129-30. Baker (1956) believes this plant to be *Rudgea jasminoides*.

[50] Darwin 1888:130-1.

[51] Müller 1869d.

[52] Darwin to Charles Lyell, 21 August 1861, *CCD* 9:238.

[53] Henry Walter Bates (1825–1892), English entomologist, traveled on the Amazon, 1848-59, and described "Batesian" mimicry (Bates 1862).

[54] FM to Hermann Müller, 29 October 1866, *Briefe*:94-8.

[55] See Chapter 11.

[56] Alfred Möller *Briefe*:88 n.

[57] Hermann Müller to FM, 22 August 1871, *Leben*:98.

[58] Darwin to Asa Gray, 16 September 1861, *CCD*, 9:265.

[59] FM to Darwin, 1 December 1866, *Briefe*:99-101, a German translation of the lost original.

[60] Darwin 1875 II:114-5.

[61] FM to Darwin, 1 January 1867. English draft, *Briefe*:104-9. Most of the original of this letter is lost; the concluding paragraphs are in DAR 157a, and drawings of orchid pollinia in DAR 70.

[62] Darwin 1875 II:115.

[63] Müller 1868a.

[64] Müller 1868c, 1869c, 1870a.

[65] Darwin 1877a.

[66] Müller 1869c. FM's "two principal groups" were the lady's slippers (now considered a subfamily, Cypripedioideae), with two functional anthers, and the rest of the true orchids, with one (Heywood 1978).

[67] Müller 1870a.

[68] Freeman 1977.

[69] Darwin to FM, 30 January 1868, BL (Loan 10:20).

[70] Darwin 1875 II:369-70.

[71] FM to Darwin, 3 April 1868, German trans. *Briefe*:137-8.

[72] FM to Darwin, 22 April 1868, DAR 86:85-6. Part of the letter appears in German translation, *Briefe*:140.

[73] FM to Haeckel, 7 December 1868, EHH.

[74] Haeckel 1876.

[75] FM to Haeckel, 20 August 1876, EHH.

[76] Gould 1977:97.

[77] Haeckel, quoted by Gould, 1977:97.

[78] FM to Hermann Müller, 9 August 1876, *Briefe*:344.

[79] FM to Hermann Müller, 14 January 1869, *Briefe*:152-3.

[80] FM to Darwin, 12 January 1869, MS. DAR. 76 B:34-5.

[81] Federoff 1984. Barbara McClintock (1902–1992), American geneticist, awarded Nobel prize in 1983 for the discovery of transposable elements.

[82] FM to Hermann Müller, 14 January 1869, *Briefe*:152-3.

[83] Darwin 1875 II:117.

[84] FM to Darwin, 14 March 1869, Linnean Society of London.

[85] Müller 1868b.

86 Gärtner 1849. Carl Friedrich von Gärtner (1772–1850), German physician and botanist, especially plant hybridization.

87 FM to Hermann Müller, 15-17 September 1868, *Briefe*:147-9.

88 Müller 1873a.

89 Darwin 1871b:235.

90 Müller 1870b.

91 Müller 1870c.

92 FM to Ernst Haeckel, 7 December 1868, EHH. Part in *Briefe*:150. Aleksander Onufrievich Kovalevsky (1840–1901), Russian embryologist who found evidence for relationships of lower chordates.

93 FM to Haeckel, 7 December 1868, EHH. Part in *Briefe*:150, but with wrong date.

94 Müller 1870b.

95 FM to Oscar Schmidt, 8 December 1868, *Briefe*:151-2.

96 FM to Hermann Müller, 8 December 1868, *Briefe*:150-1.

97 See note 96.

# Chapter 9. Termites, Ants, Bees, and Sambaquis, 1871–1876

1 This chapter includes Alfred Möller's narrative and documentation of FM's personal affairs, his visits to the shell mounds and how he became a Traveling Naturalist, from Chapter 13 of *Leben*. The author has added FM's observations on termites, bees, leaf-cutting ants and the Müllerian bodies of *Cecropia* trees. The Brazilian word for shell mounds, "sambaqui," is accented on the last syllable.

2 FM to Hermann Hagen, 30 August 1869, MCZ.

3 Müller 1873b.

4 Müller 1871b.

5 Hagen 1858 & 1860. These are the monographs referred to in Müller's papers on termites in 1873 and 1875.

6 FM to Hermann Müller, 9 October 1871, *Briefe*:200-1.

7 Hagen 1858.

8 Müller 1873b.

9 Pierre Gabriel Charles Lespès (1827–1872), French entomologist.

10 FM to Haeckel, 12 July 1872, EHH, part in *Briefe*:203-4.

11 Robert McLachlan (1837–1904), British entomologist, interested especially in caddis flies.

12 Lespès 1856.

13 McLachlan 1873.

14 Henry Smeathman (1750–1787), British naturalist.

15 Müller 1874a.

16 Müller 1873c.

17 See note 15.

18 See note 16, quoted in English from Darwin, 1875 II:126.

[19] Darwin to FM, 1 January 1874, BL (Loan 10:36), *ML*,II:359-60.

[20] Edouard Ménétriés (1802-61), French naturalist.

[21] See note 16.

[22] FM to Hermann Müller, 30 August 1869, *Briefe*:161-163.

[23] Belt 1874. Thomas Belt (1832–1878), British mining engineer, naturalist, geologist.

[24] See note 16.

[25] FM to Darwin, 20 April 1874, published as Müller 1874b.

[26] Belt 1874.

[27] FM to Darwin, 25 December 1875, published as Müller 1876b.

[28] Müller 1876d.

[29] Rickson 1971.

[30] *Leben*:77-8.

[31] FM to Hermann Müller, 10 June 1872, *Briefe*:202-3.

[32] Hermann Müller to FM, 14 May 1872, *Briefe*: 206. Frederick Smith (1805–1879). British entomologist, a specialist in bees.

[33] Müller 1874a. Original letter lost.

[34] Müller 1874c.

[35] See note 34.

[36] See note 34.

[37] H. Müller 1875.

[38] FM to Hermann Müller, 5-10 October 1873, *Briefe*:234-238.

[39] Hermann Müller to FM, 20 December 1873, *Briefe*:238. René-Antoine Ferchault de Réaumur (1683–1757), French naturalist, physicist, and technologist, best known for his thermometer scale.

[40] Müller 1874a.

[41] Poey 1851. FM to Hermann Müller, 17 June 1874, *Briefe*:297-9.

[42] Müller 1875.

[43] Carpenter 1910.

[44] Hermann von Ihering (1850-1930), Brazilian zoologist and Traveling Naturalist of the National Museum; later Director of the State Museum, São Paulo.

[45] Müller 1876c.

[46] FM to Hermann Müller, 25 September 1875, *Briefe*:319.

[47] FM to Ernst Haeckel, 3 October 1875, EHH.

[48] Attributed by Alfred Möller to a letter from FM to Hermann Müller, 10 June 1872, *Leben*:100.

[49] Attributed by Alfred Möller to a letter from FM to Hermann Müller, 14 March 1873, *Leben*:102.

[50] FM to Hermann Müller, New Year 1874, *Leben*:101.

[51] FM to Haeckel, 6 April 1874, EHH.

[52] FM to Hermann Müller, 2 April 1874, *Leben*:101.

[53] Ladislau de Souza Mello Netto (1837–c1894), Brazilian botanist and Director of the National Museum, Rio de Janeiro, 1875–93; editor of the *Archivos* of the museum, 1876–87.

[54] Müller 1892b.

[55] FM to Hermann Müller, 29 January 1875, *Leben*:103.

[56] FM to Haeckel, 3 October 1875, EHH.

[57] Attributed by Alfred Möller to a letter from FM to Hermann Müller, 29 November 1875, *Leben*:103.

[58] FM to Darwin, 25 December 1875; Müller 1876b.

[59] See note 58.

[60] FM to Hermann Müller, 24 January 1876, *Leben*:104-5.

[61] FM to Hermann Müller, 24 January 1875, *Leben*:105.

[62] FM to Hermann Müller, 23 March 1876, *Leben*:106.

[63] FM to Hermann Müller, 5 February 1877, *Leben*:106.

[64] 1876. *Archivos do Museu Nacional do Rio de Janeiro*, 1.

[65] FM to an unidentified correspondent, 21 June 1877, *Leben*:106.

## Chapter 10. Insects, Honors, and Tragedies, 1876–1881

[1] This chapter includes Alfred Möller's narrative and documentation from Chapter 14 of *Leben*, with additions by the author from FM's publications and letters on versicolor flowers, caddis flies, the fauna of bromeliad pools, crustacean life histories, fig wasps, and other scientific subjects.

[2] Um veterano depõe [Reminiscences of Augusto Sievert]. 1960. *Blumenau em Cadernos*, 3:65.

[3] FM to Rosine Müller, 25 December 1876, *Leben*:107.

[4] *Drimys* is a member of the Winteraceae, a primitive family of flowering plants (Heywood 1978).

[5] Müller 1877a.

[6] FM to Hermann Müller, 27 December 1876, *Leben*:109.

[7] August Müller to Hermann Müller, 26 December 1876, *Leben*:108.

[8] Carlos Guilherme Friedenreich arrived in Blumenau in 1850 as one of the original settlers.

[9] FM to Hermann Müller, 30 March 1877, *Leben*:109-10.

[10] FM to Darwin, 25 March 1877, DAR111:89-90.

[11] Müller 1877c, from which Heuvelmans (1995) quotes extensively (with some errors) in his summary of reports on this fabulous mystery animal.

[12] FM to Ernst Krause, 17 April 1877, *Leben*:111.

[13] Müller 1877d.

[14] FM to Hermann Müller, 23 January 1878, *Leben*:112.

[15] Felix d'Avellar Brotero (1744–1828), Portuguese botanist.

[16] Delpino 1874. Giacomo Giuseppe Frederico Delpino (1833–1905), Italian entomologist.

[17] Müller 1877e.

[18] See note 17.

[19] Jones and Cruzan 1999.

[20] See note 17.

[21] Weiss 1991.

[22] The phrase is from Darwin, 1875 II:340, which Fritz had received the year before.

[23] FM to Hermann Müller, 12 June 1869, *Briefe*:157-8.

[24] Müller 1878d.

[25] FM to Hermann Müller, 13 November 1878, *Leben*:113.

[26] Müller 1878/79, part 3.

[27] See note 26.

[28] See note 26.

[29] Müller 1878/79, part 4.

[30] Müller 1878/79, part 6. Eduard von Hartmann (1842–1906), German philosopher, interested in the role of the unconscious mind.

[31] Müller 1878/79, part 6.

[32] Wallace 1869, in the German translation. Alfred Russel Wallace (1823–1913), English naturalist and traveler; Amazon and Rio Negro, 1848–1852; Malay Archipelago, 1854–1862; co-discoverer, with Darwin, of the importance of natural selection.

[33] Müller 1880/81b.

[34] Carl Robert von der Osten-Sacken (1828–1906), German entomologist.

[35] Müller 1880/81c.

[36] FM to Rosine Müller, 22 July 1879, *Leben*:116.

[37] FM to Hermann Müller, 31 July 1879, *Leben*:116-17.

[38] FM to Hermann Müller, 8 September 1879, *Leben*:117.

[39] Darwin to FM, 4 January 1882. BL (Loan 10:58).

[40] FM to Darwin, 31 March 1882. Only a German translation of FM's draft exists, *Briefe*:424-5.

[41] Müller 1879/80. FM to Hermann Müller, 19 October 1879, *Briefe*:391.

[42] Müller 1879c.

[43] Müller 1892a.

[44] Müller 1880. The quote is unidentified.

[45] FM to Hermann Müller, 22 November 1879, *Briefe*:391-3.

[46] Müller 1881.

[47] FM to Friedrich Ludwig, 26 December 1887, *Leben*:115.

[48] The 'Bruchstücke' paper is Müller, 1871a. The first paper on *Entoniscus* is Müller, 1862b. Alfred-Mathieu Giard (1846–1908), French zoologist and founder of a coastal biological station where his student Jules Bonnier (1859–1908) studied crustaceans and annelids and was later director.

[49] [Krause] 1876, a popular work on evolution.

[50] FM to Hermann Müller, 26 September 1880, *Leben*:117-18.

[51] FM to Ernst Krause, 10 January 10 1881, *Leben*:118.

[52] FM to Hermann Müller, 13 October 1880, *Leben*:118.

[53] FM to Ernst Krause, 10 January 1881, *Leben*:118.

[54] *Blumenauer Zeitung* No. 15. 9 April 1881, quoted in *Leben*:119.

[55] Darwin to Hermann Müller, 27 November 1880. DAR 146.

[56] FM to Darwin, 9 January 1881. *ML* II:363-5.

[57] Darwin to FM, 23 February 1881. *ML* II:365-7.

[58] Caprification is the practice of using inedible caprifigs as a pollen source for edible figs by placing them among the branches of the edible fig trees. Tiny female wasps emerge already mated and dusted with pollen from their place of development in the caprifigs, as Paul Mayer's letter describes. Edible figs generally lack male flowers. Caprifigs have both female and male flowers, the latter predominating during the summer months and being the source of pollen for the pollination of both kinds of figs. Some edible fig varieties, however, can develop without caprification, that is without pollination. (Müller 1882a summarizes Solms-Laubach's work.)

[59] FM to Paul Mayer, 26 October 1880, *Briefe*:400-1.

[60] Hermann Solms-Laubach (1842–1915), German botanist and paleobotanist; Professor of botany at Göttingen and Strasburg.

[61] The publication was Mayer 1882.

[62] Achenes are small, dry one-seeded fruits, the "seeds" of figs.

[63] Sachs 1874.

[64] Avellar Brotero 1788.

[65] FM to Hermann Müller, 28 November 1880, *Briefe*:401-2.

[66] FM to Hermann Müller, 29 December 1880, *Leben*:403-4.

[67] Müller 1882b.

# Chapter 11. Butterfly Scent and Mimicry, 1876–1884

[1] This chapter is by the author.

[2] Müller 1877b. (English translation by Elliott in Longstaff, 1912.) Two pages of the manuscript are in the EHH.

[3] Edward B. Poulton (1856–1943), English entomologist, Professor of Zoology at Oxford, 1893–1933.

[4] Poulton in Longstaff, 1912:602.

[5] FM to Darwin, 20 February 1878, OUMNH.

[6] Müller 1877b.

[7] August Weismann (1834–1914), German zoologist, Professor at Freiburg im Breisgau 1863–1912; best known for his germplasm theory, which rejected Lamarckian inheritance.

[8] See Müller 1877d.

[9] See Müller 1878a.

[10] See Müller 1877b and 1877d.

[11] FM to Weismann, 4 January 1877, *Briefe*:325-9 (incorrectly dated "1876").

[12] FM wrote these as family names, "Satyridae" and "Nymphalidae," evidently a slip on his part because in other publications he treated them as sub-families of the Nymphalidae.

[13] Müller 1878b.

[14] Müller 1878a.

[15] Boppré 1984.

[16] FM to Darwin, 5 April 1878, OUMNH. Papal infallibility may have been on FM's mind because of its recent promulgation by Pius IX in 1870.

[17] Bates 1862.

[18] Müller 1881/82.

[19] FM to Hermann Müller, 29 October 1866, *Briefe*:94-8.

[20] Grant & Grant 1968:81-3; Brown & Kodric-Brown 1979.

[21] FM to Darwin, 29 March 1870, DAR 76(ser. 2): 36.

[22] FM to Hermann Müller, 5 May 1870, *Briefe*:175-7.

[23] FM to Hermann Müller, 14 June 1870, *Briefe*:177-9.

[24] Reference in Darwin to FM, 28 August 1870, BL (Loan 10:33).

[25] Poulton 1890.

[26] Darwin 1871a.

[27] Darwin to FM, 28 August 1870. BL (Loan 10:33).

[28] Codella and Lederhouse (1989) do so explicitly.

[29] Prittwitz 1865.

[30] FM to Hermann Hagen, 4 September 1871, MCZ.

[31] West 1994.

[32] FM to Hermann Müller, 22 December 1878, *Briefe*:388.

[33] Darwin 1871a.

[34] See note 33.

[35] FM to Hermann Müller, 28 May 1871, *Briefe*: 193-5.

[36] Wallace to Darwin, 7 August 1871, DAR 89:85-8.

[37] Darwin to FM, 2 August 1871, *LL* II:329.

[38] Wallace to Darwin, 7 August 1871, DAR 89:85-8.

[39] Meldola to Darwin, 12 March 1872, DAR 171.

[40] Müller 1876a.

[41] Darwin to Meldola, 23 January 1872, OUMNH. In Poulton, 1901.

[42] Darwin to Meldola, 23 January 1872, OUMNH.

[43] Darwin to FM, 2 August 1871, *LL* II:329.

[44] Walter F. H. Blandford, English entomologist, Fellow of the Entomological Society of London 1889–1911.

[45] Blandford 1897.

[46] FM to Darwin, 14 June 1871, DAR 89:91-3.

[47] FM to Darwin, 14 June 1871, DAR 89:91-3. The butterfly wings are in MS. DAR 14:58.

[48] Schmidt 1873:147.

[49] von Hartmann 1872:11.

[50] Müller 1876a.

[51] Mimicry in butterflies explained. . . . 1876.

[52] Müller 1876a.

[53] Bates 1862:507.

[54] Bates 1862:511.

[55] Bates 1862:514.

[56] FM to Hermann Hagen, 4 September 1871, MCZ.

[57] Müller 1878a, a collection of excerpts from FM's letters organized for publication by Meldola. This quotation is in FM to Darwin, 20 February 1878, copy in OUMNH.

[58] Wallace 1889:265.

[59] Gayon 1998:56.

[60] Belt 1874, p. 385 in 2nd ed., 1888.

[61] FM to Darwin, 14 June 1871, DAR 89:91-3.

[62] FM to Weismann, 12 March 1878, *Briefe*:377.

[63] Ackery and Vane-Wright 1984.

[64] Bates 1862:507; Meldola 1882.

[65] FM to Weismann, 25 June 1878, *Briefe*:379-81.

[66] Müller 1879a.

[67] Müller 1878c.

[68] See note 67.

[69] See note 66.

[70] Müller 1879b.

[71] Meldola to Darwin, 4 June 1879, DAR 171.

[72] Comments in Müller, 1879b.

[73] Blandford 1897.

[74] Meldola 1896.

[75] Gayon 1998: 194-5.

[76] Müller 1881/82.

[77] Wallace 1878:254-64.

[78] Wallace 1878:216.

[79] Müller 1876a.

[80] Wallace 1882.

[81] Meldola to Darwin, 18 June 1879, DAR 171.

[82] Wallace 1882.

[83] Meldola 1882.

[84] Müller 1883.

[85] FM to Meldola, 9 April 1883. Passmore Edwards Museum, *Briefe*:441-2.

[86] Müller 1883.

[87] FM to Krause, 23 May 1884, *Briefe*:448-50.

[88] Roland Trimen (1840–1916), English zoologist, lepidopterist; Curator of the South African Museum, Capetown.

[89] Trimen 1898.

[90] Bates 1862.

[91] Wallace 1865.

[92] Trimen 1898.

[93] Blandford 1897.

[94] Punnett 1915. Reginald Crundall Punnett (1875–1967), English zoologist and Mendelian geneticist.

## Chapter 12. Visitors, Losses, and Dismissal, 1881–1891

[1] This chapter is based largely on Alfred Möller's narrative and documentation in Chapter 14 of *Leben*, with additions by the author from FM's correspondence with Darwin on plant movement.

[2] Darwin 1880.

[3] FM to Ernst Krause, 10 January 1881, *Leben*:123.

[4] Müller 1870b.

[5] FM to Darwin, 9 January 1881, *ML*:363-5.

[6] See n. 5.

[7] Darwin 1881.

[8] Darwin to FM, 12 April 1881, *ML* II:367-8.

[9] Darwin to FM, 4 July 1881, BL (Loan 10:52).

[10] H. Müller 1881.

[11] FM to Hermann Müller, 24 June 1882, cited in *Leben*:123. See also *Werke*:928.

[12] Krause 1876.

[13] FM to Hermann Müller, 22 March 1881, *Leben*:123.

[14] FM to Hermann Müller, 8 September 1881, *Leben*:123.

[15] FM to Hermann Müller, 3 July 1882, *Leben*:124.

[16] Probably the human bot fly, *Dermatobia hominis* (Borror, et al. 1976).

[17] Quoted in *Leben*:124.

[18] FM to Ernst Krause, 7 May 1882, *Leben*:120.

[19] FM to Ernst Krause, 27 September 1882, *Leben*:121.

[20] FM to Ernst Krause, 1 January 1883, *Leben*:124.

[21] FM to Hermann Müller, 13 September 1883, *Leben*:124.

[22] Krause 1884.

[23] FM to Friedrich Ludwig, 24 October 1883, *Leben*:125.

[24] FM to Ernst Krause, 1 December 1883, *Leben*:125.

[25] FM to Ernst Krause, 31 March 1884, *Leben*:125.

[26] FM to Ernst Krause, 20 July 1885, *Leben*:126.

[27] Müller 1899.

[28] W. Müller 1886.

[29] Wilhelm Müller to Ernst Krause, 12 June 1884, *Leben*:126.

[30] Ernst Ule (1854–1915), German-Brazilian botanist; commercial scientific collector, 1883–91; Assistant Director of the National Museum, 1891–1900; independent explorer in Brazil, 1900–12.

[31] Brief summary in Müller 1888; the mass of observations appears only in the Museum reports, *Briefe*:574-605.

[32] Andreas Franz Wilhelm Schimper (1856–1901), Pioneer German plant ecologist, and his colleague Heinrich Schenck (1860–1927).

[33] Schimper 1888a & b; Schenck 1892–93.

[34] Steinen 1886.

[35] FM to Ernst Krause, 9 July 1887, *Leben*:130.

[36] August Müller to Hermann Müller, 8 September 1880, *Leben*:132.

[37] August Müller to Hermann Müller, 9 April 1882, *Leben*:133.

[38] Bernardo Scheidemantel (1834–1908), German lithographer in Blumenau, founder of the *Immigrant*, 1883.

[39] Paul Schwarzer (1844–1906), German lawyer in Blumenau.

[40] August Müller to Hermann Müller, 20 April 1878, *Leben*:134. See also Wettstein 1907:229.

[41] FM to von Ihering, 21 June 1884, *Leben*:134-5.

[42] Müller 1892b. Couty is unidentified.

[43] FM to von Ihering, 17 March 1884, *Leben*:135.

[44] FM to von Ihering, 14 November 1889, *Leben*:135.

[45] Dom Pedro (1825–1891) ruled under a regency 1831–40 and as emperor 1840–89. *EB*, 4:459-60.

[46] German translation from the original Portuguese, *Leben*:136. In 1887 there were only five Traveling Naturalists listed in the *Archivos*: other than FM and von Ihering, they were attached to the Museum in Rio. The *Archivos* then lapsed, and at its next appearance in 1892 no Traveling Naturalists were listed.

[47] *Leben*:136, in Portuguese.

[48] Netto to FM, 31 July 1891, German translation from the original Portuguese, *Leben*:136.

[49] FM to von Ihering, 5 June 1891, *Leben*:137.

[50] Müller 1892b.


# 13. Heredity and Variation: Agreements and Arguments with Weismann, 1885–1888

[1] This chapter is by the author.

[2] Weismann 1904:25-56.

[3] Weismann 1882.

[4] Darwin 1875 II:366-70.

[5] Weismann 1889a:191. A lecture given early in 1885 and written in final form in June.

[6] Weismann 1889a:205. Weismann's only exception to the idea that all embryonic cells would for a long time be somatic cells was in the flies that he studied twenty years earlier, in which some very early embryonic cells (pole cells) were set aside as the foundation of the gonads.

[7] Weismann 1889a:205.

[8] Eduard Adolf Strasburger (1844–1912), German botanist and plant cytologist; "clarified cell division and the role of the nucleus and chromosomes in heredity." *DSB*, 13:87-90. His criticism is in Weismann 1889a:209.

[9] Weismann 1889b:279.

[10] FM to Weismann [1885], a lost letter quoted in an appendix to Weismann's lecture (Weismann 1889b:320). Weismann wrote to FM on 5 December 1885 that he was going to communicate the *Abutilon* observations in something that he was then writing, presumably that appendix, Weismann letterbooks, vol. 1,

Universitätsbibliothek, Freiburg im Breigau, nearly illegible. FM's results were first reported in a letter to Hermann Müller, 12 September 1872, *Briefe*:206-8.

[11] Weismann 1889b.

[12] Weismann 1889b:320.

[13] Weismann 1889b:322.

[14] Weismann 1889b:322. My emphasis.

[15] Weismann 1889b. The first 19 pages (251-66 in the translation) are mostly an argument for natural selection as the motive force for adaptation and evolution in general.

[16] The quote is from Weismann 1889b:266-7.

[17] FM to Weismann, 19 February 1886, *Briefe*:466.

[18] See note 17.

[19] FM to Weismann, 5 May 1888, *Briefe*:512.

[20] Weismann 1889b:269.

[21] FM to Weismann, 5 May 1888, *Briefe*:513.

[22] Weismann 1889b:272.

[23] FM to Weismann, 19 February 1886, *Briefe*:467.

[24] Weismann 1889b:275.

[25] Darwin 1875 I:443. The quote is in English.

[26] Müller 1879d.

[27] FM to Weismann, 19 February 1886, *Briefe*:468.

[28] FM to Weismann, 5 May 1888, *Briefe*:513.

[29] FM to Weismann, 21 June 1886, *Briefe*:472-3.

[30] Francis Galton (1822–1911), English statistician and scientific writer, interested in heredity.

[31] Weismann 1889b:279.

[32] FM to Weismann, 21 June 1886, *Briefe*:472-3.

[33] FM to Hermann Müller, 12 September 1872, *Briefe*:206-7.

[34] FM to Hermann Müller, 12 September 1872, *Briefe*:207.

[35] Müller 1886, *Werke*:1106.

[36] Galton 1885.

[37] Müller 1886.

[38] Müller 1886, *Werke*:1106-7.

[39] Müller 1886, *Werke*:1106.

[40] Sturtevant 1965:22. Alfred Henry Sturtevant (1891–1970), American geneticist.

[41] Haeckel 1876.

## 14. Birthday Honors, Civil War, and the Last Years, 1891–1897

[1] This chapter is based on Alfred Möller's narrative and documentation from Chapter 15 of *Leben*, with additions on tropical research stations, the civil war, and FM's last work with plant hybrids.

[2] Oskar Brefeld (1839-1925), German botanist and mycologist, at the Forestry Academy in Eberswalde 1878–1884.

[3] *Leben*:138-9.

[4] Möller 1893.

[5] See Reitz 1983, for illustrations of the bromeliads of Santa Catarina.

[6] *Leben*:140-2.

[7] Krause 1897.

[8] Hermann Blumenau to Heinrich Probst, 1892. Published in 1968 in Portuguese translation from the German original. *Blumenau em Cadernos*, 9:114-7.

[9] Trimen 1898.

[10] *Vossische Zeitung*, No. 445, 24 September 1891.

[11] *Die Natur* No. 43, 24 October 1891, *Leben*:144.

[12] FM to Haeckel, 11 January 1892, *Leben*:145.

[13] Emil August Göldi (1859–1917), German ornithologist, resident in Brazil.

[14] Orville A. Derby (1851–1915), North American geologist active in Brazil. Director, Geological and Mineralogical Service of Brazil, 1907–1915.

[15] FM to Haeckel, 11 January 1892, EHH.

[16] Ferdinand Jakob Heinrich von Mueller (1825–1896). "German-born explorer and botanist who emigrated to Australia in 1847. Director, Botanic Garden, Melbourne, 1857-73." (*CAL*)

[17] Erich V. Haase (1857–1894), German entomologist in southeast Asia; especially butterfly mimicry and defense.

[18] FM to Ernst Ule, 12 May 1895, *Leben*:145.

[19] The full text and list of well-wishers is in *Leben*:146-7.

[20] *Leben*:140.

[21] *Die Natur* No. 20, 19 May 1892, *Leben*:147.

[22] *Leben*:148.

[23] FM to Ernst Krause, 31 May 1892, *Leben*:148.

[24] Müller 1892b.

[25] FM to v. Ihering, 20 February 1893, *Leben*:149.

[26] FM to Ernst Krause, 11 July 1895, *Leben*:151.

[27] *Leben*:150-1.

[28] *Leben*:151-2.

[29] Desterro was later renamed Florianópolis in his honor.

[30] *EB* 4:460-1.

[31] *Leben*:152 note.

[32] FM to Friedrich Ludwig, 23 August 1894, *Leben*:153.

[33] FM to Ernst Krause, 4 November 1894, *Leben*:153.

[34] FM to Alfred Möller, 12 September 1894, *Leben*:152.

[35] *Blumenauer Zeitung* No. 17, 23 April 1892, *Leben*:153.

[36] FM to Alfred Möller, 24 August 1895, *Leben*:153-4.

[37] FM to Alfred Möller, 1 February 1897, *Leben*:154. Quotation from Prutz not identified.

[38] FM to Friedrich Ludwig, 26 March 1893, *Leben*:154. Reitz, 1974, shows such a floral sheath being used as a sled.

[39] FM to Friedrich Ludwig, 26 March 1893, *Leben*:155.

[40] FM to Rosine Müller, 28 August 1895, *Leben*:154.

[41] FM to Alfred Möller, 4 November 1894, *Leben*:156.

[42] Schimper 1888b.

[43] FM to Ernst Krause, 4 November 1894, *Leben*:157-8.

[44] FM to Alfred Möller, 4 November 1894, *Leben*:156.

[45] Strasburger et al. 1895.

[46] Müller 1898.

[47] The statements are in Weismann 1889b:275, 293.

[48] Müller 1897a.

[49] Gärtner 1849.

[50] Joseph Gottlieb Kölreuter (1733–1806), German botanist and pioneer plant hybridizer.

[51] Müller 1897b.

[52] See note 51.

[53] *Leben*:159.

[54] See note 51.

[55] FM to Alfred Möller, 24 August 1895, *Leben*:160.

[56] FM to Ernst Ule, 13 December 1896, *Leben*:161.

[57] FM to Luise Pfeifer, 29 January 1896, *Leben*:161.

[58] Anna Brockes to Alfred Möller, 24 May 1897, *Leben*161-2.

[59] August Müller to Luise Pfeifer, 23 May 1897, *Leben*:162. Werneck de Castro, whose father was acquainted with Fritz's doctor Hugo Gensch, gives the cause of death as a clot followed by blood poisoning (Castro 1992:11, 136). Dr. William T. Hendricks suggested to the author that the infection started as an abscess on the thigh, moved down the leg, became more generalized and brought on fever, and finally blood poisoning.

[60] *Blumenauer Zeitung* No. 22, 29 May 1897, *Leben*:162.

[61] B. Scheidemantel to Alfred Möller, 29 August 1897, *Leben*:162-3.

[62] Haeckel 1897.

[63] Blandford 1897. Blandford had been handed the job of writing Fritz's obituary: "[E. B] Poulton went off and left me a nice legacy in the shape of his article on Fritz Müller which he asked me to write. I have been tearing my hair over it ever since. I can put a plain statement or argument, on a specific subject if necessary, but I am hopelessly destitute of that particular quality of literary skill which is necessary in order to frame a panegyric and I really funk the thing. Moreover M. was a man who wrote on so many and varied subjects that it really wants a lot of time and trouble before one is in a position to speak authoritatively about his output." Blandford to F. A. Dixey, 16 August 1897, OUMNH.

[64] Krause 1897. See Grimm & Grimm 1893, 8:994-5 for this meaning of "*die Ringe.*"

## Locations of Fritz Müller's Correspondence

[1] *Briefe*:IV.

[2] Burkhardt and Smith 1994.

[3] *Briefe*:71n.

[4] "I have translated into German all the letters to Darwin that Mr. Fr. D. sent me." Alfred Möller to Ernst Haeckel, 18 November 1898, EHH.

[5] Letter from Stephen Pocock to the author, 14 July 1987.

[6] Mayer 1999.

[7] *Leben*:144.

[8] According to the note in Möller's hand on the cover folder of the letters, BL (Loan 10).

[9] Henry Fairfield Osborn (1857–1935), American vertebrate paleontologist, who founded the departments of biology at Columbia and vertebrate paleontology at the AMNH, and was president of the Museum for 25 years. (*DSB*)

[10] Osborn 1929, and Correspondence of H. F. Osborn, AMNH.

[11] In *LL*, *ML*, and *CCD*.

[12] Osborn 1929.

[13] Alfred Möller to Ernst Haeckel, 18 November 1898, EHH.

[14] Agassiz 1913.

[15] Alfred Möller to Ernst Haeckel, 18 February 1917, EHH.

[16] Letter from Dr. Erika Krauße to the author, 27 February 1997.

[17] Personal communication from Dr. Joachim-Hans Bergmann, Eberswalde, April 1993.

[18] Letter from Dr. Christian Friedrich to the author, 30 August 2002; Lauterbach 2000.

[19] Lauterbach 2000.

# Bibliography

Ackery, P. R., and R. I. Vane-Wright. 1984. *Milkweed butterflies, their cladistics and biology.* Ithaca: Cornell University Press.

*ADB: Allgemeine deutsche Biographie.* 1875–1912. 56 vols. Reprint 1967-71. Berlin: Duncker & Humblot.

Agassiz, Alexander. 1872–74. Revision of the Echini. *Memoirs of the Museum of Comparative Zoology* 3. Cambridge: [Harvard] University Press.

Agassiz, George R., ed. 1913. *Letters and recollections of Alexander Agassiz with a sketch of his life and work.* Boston: Houghton Mifflin.

Agassiz, Louis, and A. A. Gould. 1856. *Principles of zoology,* rev. ed. Boston: Gould & Lincoln.

Avellar Brotero, Felix de. 1788. *Compêndio de botânica....* I. Paris.

Avise, John C. 1994. *Molecular markers, natural history and evolution.* New York: Chapman & Hall.

Baker, Herbert G. 1956. Pollen dimorphism in the Rubiaceae. *Evolution* 10:23-31.

Barnes, Robert D. 1980. *Invertebrate zoology.* 4th ed. Philadelphia: Saunders.

Bate, Charles Spence. 1865. [Review of *Für Darwin*] in Crustacea:261-70. *The record of Zoological Literature* 1. London: van Voorst.

Bates, Henry Walter. 1862. Contributions to an insect fauna of the Amazon Valley. Lepidoptera: Heliconidae. *Transactions of the Linnean Society, London* 23:495-566.

————. 1863. *The naturalist on the river Amazons.* 2 vols. London: John Murray.

*BE*: see *Brockhaus Enzyklopädie.*

Belt, Thomas. 1874. *The naturalist in Nicaragua.* London: John Murray. 2nd ed., 1888. Reprint 1985. Chicago: University of Chicago Press.

Bigg-Wither, Thomas P. 1878. *Pioneering in South Brazil. Three years of forest and prairie life in the province of Paraná.* London: John Murray. Reprint 1968. New York: Greenwood Press.

B[landford], W. F. H. 1897. Fritz Müller. *Nature* 50:546-8, (7 October).

Blumenau, Hermann. 1850. *Südbrasilien in seinen Beziehungen zu deutscher Auswanderung und Kolonisation.* Rudolstadt: Froebel.

————. 1856. *Deutsche Kolonie Blumenau in der Provinz Santa Catharina in Süd-Brasilien.* Rudolstadt: Froebel.

*Blumenau em Cadernos.* [Historical records of the colony, published monthly 1957–84, 25 volumes.] Blumenau.

Blumenbach, Johann Friedrich. 1825. *Handbuch der Naturgeschichte.* 11th ed. Göttingen: Dietrich.

Boppré, Michael. 1984. Chemically mediated interactions between butterflies. In *The biology of butterflies,* ed. Richard I. Vane-Wright and Phillip R. Ackery, 259-75. London: Academic Press.

Borror, Donald J., Dwight M. DeLong, and Charles A. Triplehorn. 1976. *An introduction to the study of insects.* 4th ed. New York: Holt, Rinehart & Winston.

Bowler, Peter J. 1984. *Evolution, the history of an idea.* Berkeley: University of California Press.

Bravais, Louis F., and Auguste Bravais. 1838. *Mémoires sur la disposition géométriques des feuilles et des inflorescences.* Paris: Paul Renourd.

*Briefe*: see Möller 1921.

*Brockhaus Enzyklopädie.* 1966-74. 17th ed. Wiesbaden: F. A. Brockhaus.

Brown, James H., and A. Kodric-Brown. 1979. Convergence, competition, and mimicry in a temperate community of hummingbird-pollinated flowers. *Ecology* 60:1027-35.

Browne, E. Janet. 1995. *Charles Darwin: voyaging.* Princeton: Princeton University Press.

————. 2002. *Charles Darwin: the power of place.* New York: Knopf.

Burkhardt, Frederick et al., eds. 1985–. *The correspondence of Charles Darwin.* Cambridge: Cambridge University Press.

Burkhardt, Frederick, and Sydney Smith, eds. 1994. *A calendar of the correspondence of Charles Darwin, 1821–1882,* with supplement. 2d ed. Cambridge: Cambridge University Press.

Burmeister, Hermann. 1853. *Reise nach Brasilien.* Berlin: G. Reimer.

————. 1855. *Geologische Bilder zur Geschichte der Erde und ihrer Bewohner.* 2d ed. Vol. II. Leipzig: Wigend.

*CAL*: see Burkhardt and Smith 1994.

Carpenter, G. H. 1910. [Article on Bee.] *Encyclopædia Britannica,* 3:625-8. New York: Encyclopædia Britannica Co.

Castro, Moacir Werneck de. 1992. *O sábio e a floresta. O extraordinária aventura do alemão Fritz Müller no trópico brasiliro.* Rio de Janeiro: Editora Rocco Ltda.

*CCD*: see Burkhardt 1985–.

Chase, Enoch. 1856. *Cleveland's exchange tables*. 3d ed. Boston.

Churchill, Frederick B. 1991. The rise of classical descriptive embryology. In *Developmental biology*, Volume 7. *A conceptual history of modern embryology*, ed. Scott F. Gilbert. New York: Plenum.

Codella, Sylvio G., and Robert C. Lederhouse. 1989. Intersexual comparison of mimetic protection in the black swallowtail, *Papilio polyxenes*: experiments with captive blue jays. *Evolution* 43:410-20.

Craig, Gordon A. 1983. *The Germans*. New York: New American Library.

Craw, Robin. 1992. Margins of cladistics: Identity, difference and place in the emergence of phylogenetic systematics, 1864–1975. In *Trees of life*, ed. Paul Griffiths. *Australasian Studies in History and Philosophy of Science*, 11. Dordrecht: Kluwer.

Crofton, Ursula Brigitte. 1972. Blumenau, a city of German origin in Brazil. San Francisco: Unpubl. M.A. Thesis, San Francisco State College.

Darwin, Charles Robert. 1844a. *Naturwissenschaftliche Reisen*. Translated and edited by E. Dieffenbach. Braunschweig: F. Vierweg & Sohn.

—————. 1844b. Brief descriptions of several terrestrial planariae. . . . *The annals and magazine of natural history* 14:241-51.

—————. 1859. *On the origin of species by means of natural selection*. . . . London: John Murray. Facsimile 1964. Cambridge: Harvard University Press.

—————. 1860. *Charles Darwin über die Entstehung der Arten im Thier- und Pflanzen-Reich durch natürliche Züchtung*. . . . Translated and edited by Heinrich G. Bronn. Stuttgart: Schweizerbart.

—————. 1862. *On the various contrivances by which British and foreign orchids are fertilised by insects, and the good effects of intercrossing*. London: John Murray.

—————. 1864. On the existence of two forms . . . of the genus *Linum*. *Journal of the Proceedings of the Linnean Society of London (Botany)* 7:69-83. (Read February 5, 1863)

—————. 1865. On the sexual relations of the three forms of *Lythrum salicaria*. *Journal of the Linnean Society of London (Botany)* 8:169-96. (Read June 16, 1864)

—————. 1867. On the movements and habits of climbing plants. *Journal of the Linnean Society of London (Botany)* 9:1-118. (Read February 2, 1865)

—————. 1871a. *The descent of man, and selection in relation to sex*. London: John Murray.

—————. 1871b. *On the origin of species*. . . . 5th [American] ed. New York: D. Appleton & Co.

Darwin, Charles Robert. 1875. *The variation of animals and plants under domestication.* 2nd ed. 2 vols. London: John Murray.

—————. 1877a. *On the various contrivances by which British and foreign orchids are fertilised by insects, and the good effects of intercrossing.* 2d ed. London: John Murray.

—————. 1877b. *The different forms of flowers on plants of the same species.* London: John Murray.

—————. 1878. *The effects of cross and self fertilisation in the vegetable kingdom.* 2d ed. London: John Murray.

—————. 1880. *The power of movement in plants.* London: John Murray.

—————. 1881. Movements of plants. *Nature* 23:409. [Quotations and paraphrases from a letter from F. Müller]

—————. 1888. *The different forms of flower on plants of the same species.* 2nd ed. London: John Murray.

Darwin, Francis, ed. 1887. *The life and letters of Charles Darwin, including an autobiographical chapter.* 3 vols. London: John Murray.

Darwin, Francis and A. C. Seward, eds. 1903. *More letters of Charles Darwin: a record of his work in a series of hitherto unpublished letters.* 2 vols. London: John Murray.

Delpino, Federico. 1874. *Ulteriori osservazioni sulla dicogamia nel regno vegetale.* Milano: G. Bernardoni.

*DSB: Dictionary of scientific biography.* 1970-80. Charles Coulston Gillespie, ed. New York: Scribners.

*EB: The Encyclopædia Britannica.* 11th ed. 1910-11. New York: The Encyclopædia Britannica Company.

Falck, Richard. 1927. Nachruf auf Alfred Möller. *Hausschwammforschungen* 9:1-11.

Federoff, Nina. 1984. Transposable genetic elements in maize. *Scientific American* June:84-98.

Ferraz, Paulo Malta. 1949. *Apontamentos para a história da colonização de Blumenau 1850–1860.* São Paulo: Instituto Hans Staden.

Ferreira da Silva, José. 1931. *Fritz Müller. Bio-bibliographia de um grande scientista.* Rio de Janeiro: Ed. Alba.

—————. 1950. História de Blumenau. In *Centenário de Blumenau, 1850-2 de setembro-1950,* 115-51. Blumenau: Edição da Commissão de Festejas.

—————. 1959. Indígenas da bacia do Itajaí. *Blumenau em Cadernos* 2(4):61-6.

Feuerbach, Ludwig. [1841] 1957. *The essence of Christianity.* Translated by George Eliot. New York: Harper & Bros.

Fouquet, Carlos. 1950. Vida e obra de Doutor Blumenau. In *Centenário de Blumenau, 1850-2 de setembro-1950*, 52-115. Blumenau: Edição da Commissão de Festejas.

Freeman, Richard B. 1977. *The works of Charles Darwin. An annotated bibliographical handlist*. Folkestone and Hamden: Dawson and Archon Books.

Friesen, Gerhard K. 1995-6. Ein Brief und ein Tagebuchfragment von Fritz Müller in Blumenau. *Staden-Jahrbuch* 43/44:53-9.

————. 1997-8. Fritz Müllers Fabeln. *Staden-Jahrbuch* 45/46:57-75.

————. 1999-2000. Fritz Müller in seinen Zeitverhältnissen. *Staden-Jahrbuch* 47/48:43-63.

Fröbel, Julius. 1850. *System der socialen Politik*. 2 vols. 2nd ed. of *Neue Politik*, published under the pseudonym 'C. Junius,' 1846. Leipzig: Verlagsbureau.

Galton, Francis. 1885. [Opening address to the Anthropological Section of the British Association: Types and their inheritance.] *Nature* 32:507-10. (24 September 1885)

Gärtner, Karl Friedrich von. 1849. *Versuche und Beobachtungen über die Bastarderzeugung im Pflanzenreich*. Stuttgart: K. F. Hering.

Gayon, J. 1998. *Darwinism's struggle for survival*. Cambridge: Cambridge University Press.

Gerstaecker, K. E. A. 1865. Bericht über die wissenschaftlichen Leistungen im Gebiete der Entomologie während der Jahre 1863-64. 4. Crustaceen. *Archiv für Naturgeschichte* 31 (2):604-7.

Gervinus, Georg Gottfried. 1845. *Die Mission der Deutsch-Katholiken*. Heidelberg: C. F. Winter.

Ghiselin, Michael T. 1996. Charles Darwin, Fritz Müller, Anton Dohrn, and the origin of evolutionary physiological anatomy. In *Systematic Biology as an Historical Science. Memorie della Società Italiana di Scienze Naturali e del Museo Civico di Storia Naturale di Milano* 27:49-58.

Glaßbrenner, Adolf. 1845. *Neuer Reineke Fuchs*. Leipzig: C. B. Lorck.

Gould, Stephen J. 1977. *Ontogeny and phylogeny*. Cambridge: Belknap Press.

Grant, K. A., and V. Grant. 1968. *Hummingbirds and their flowers*. New York & London: Columbia University Press.

Gregory, Frederick. 1977. *Scientific materialism in nineteenth century Germany*. Dordrecht: D. Reidel.

————. 1992. *Nature lost? Natural science and the German theological traditions of the nineteenth century*. Cambridge: Harvard University Press.

Grimm, Jacob, and Wilhelm Grimm. 1893. *Deutsches Wörterbuch*, Vol. 8. Leipzig: S. Hirzel.

Haeckel, Ernst. 1866. *Generelle Morphologie der Organismen*. Berlin: G. Reimer.

————. 1872. *Die Kalkschwämme (Calcispongae). Eine Monographie*. Part I. Berlin: G. Reimer.

————. 1876. *Die Perigenesis der Plastidule, oder die Wellenzeugung der Lebenstheilchen*. Berlin: G. Reimer.

————. 1897. Fritz Müller-Desterro. Ein Nachruf. *Jenaische Zeitschrift für Naturwissenschaft* 1897:156-73.

Hagen, Hermann A. 1858. Specielle Monographie der Termiten. *Linnaea entomologica* 12:4-339.

————. 1860. Monographie der Termiten. *Linnaea entomologica* 14:73-128.

Harris, Horton. 1973. *David Friedrich Strauss and his theology*. Cambridge: Cambridge University Press.

[Hartmann, E. von]. 1872. *Das Unbewusste, vom Standpunkte der Physiologie und Descendenztheorie*. Berlin: C. Duncker.

Hensen, Viktor von. 1863. Studien über das Gehörorgan der Decapoden. *Zeitschrift für wissenschaftliche Zoologie* 13:319-412.

Heuvelmans, Bernard. 1995. *On the track of unknown animals*. 3d ed., translated by R. Garnett. London and New York: Kegan Paul.

Heywood, Vernon H., ed. 1978. *Flowering plants of the world*. Oxford: Oxford University Press.

Jeter, A. F. 1854. *Poisoned wounds. . . .* Quincy: Herald office.

Jones, C. E., and M. B. Cruzan. 1999. Floral morphological changes and reproductive success in deer weed (*Lotus scoparius*, Fabaceae). *American Journal of Botany* 86:273-7.

[Krause, Ernst] Carus Sterne. 1876. *Werden und Vergehen. Eine Entwicklungsgeschichte des Naturganzen in gemeinverständlicher Fassung*. Berlin: Gebrüder Borntraeger.

Krause, Ernst. 1883. Prof. Dr. Hermann Müller von Lippstadt. Ein Gedenkblatt. *Kosmos* 13:393-401.

————. 1884. *Hermann Müller von Lippstadt. Ein Gedenkblatt*. Lippstadt: Kommissionsverlag P. Rempels Buchhandlung.

[Krause, Ernst] Carus Sterne. 1897. Erinnerungen an Fritz Müller. *Vossische Zeitung* (*Königlich privilegirte Berlinische Zeitung*) No. 250, 30 May.

Lang, Arnold. 1891. *Text-book of comparative anatomy*. I. London: Macmillan. [Translation of the original German ed. of 1889]

Langer, William. 1969. *Political and social upheaval, 1832–1852*. New York: Harper & Row.

Lauterbach, Irene R. 2000. *Christian Wilhelm Hermann Trommsdorff (1811–1884). Zu Leben und Werk eines pharmazeutischen Unternehmers.* Stuttgart: Wissenschaftliche Verlagsgesellschaft.

*Leben*: see Möller 1920.

[Leifchild, John]. 1869. Review of *For Darwin [Facts and Arguments for Darwin]. The Athenaeum*, No. 2161, March 27:431.

Lespès, C. 1856. Recherches sur l'organization et les moeurs du Termite lucifuge. Paris, *Comptes rendus* 43:426-8.

[Linnaeus] Linné, Carl von. 1735. *Systema naturae.* 1st ed. [Leiden]: Haak.

*LL*: see Darwin, F., 1887.

Loew, H. 1864. On the Diptera or two-winged insects of the amber-fauna. (Ueber die Diptern-fauna des Bernsteins): a lecture by Director Loew at the meeting of the German Naturalists, Königsberg, 1861. *American Journal of Science and Arts* 2d ser. 37:305-24.

Longstaff, George B. 1912. *Butterfly-hunting in many lands.* London: Longmans, Green.

Lubbock, John. 1869. Review of *Facts and Arguments for Darwin. The Academy* 1 (October 9):14-15.

Ludwig, Friedrich. 1897. Ueber das Leben und die botanische Thätigkeit Dr. Fritz Müller's. *Botanisches Centralblatt* 71:291-302, 347-63, 401-8.

McClelland, Charles E. 1980. *State, society, and university in Germany, 1700–1914.* Cambridge: Cambridge University Press.

McKinney, H. Lewis. 1974. Fritz Müller (Johann Friedrich Theodor) In *DSB*, 9:559-61.

McLachlan, Robert. 1873. [FM on termites]. *The Zoological Record* 10:433-4.

Mädler, J. H. von. 1858. *Der Fixsternhimmel.* Leipzig: F. A. Brockhaus.

Mayer, Anna-K. 1999. Note on the Fritz Müller—Charles Darwin correspondence. *Archives of Natural History* 26:283-95.

Mayer, Paul. 1882. Zur Naturgeschichte der Feigeninsekten. *Mittheilungen aus der zoologischen Station zu Neapel* 3:551 ff.

Mayr, Ernst. 1982. *The growth of biological thought.* Cambridge: Belknap Press.

Meldola, Raphael. 1882. Mimicry between butterflies of protected genera. *The Annals and Magazine of Natural History*, 5th Series, 10:417-25.

———. 1896. The speculative method in entomology. *Proceedings of the Entomological Society of London* 1895:52-68.

Mimicry in butterflies explained by natural selection. 1876. [Summary of Müller, 1876a.] *American Naturalist* 10:534-6.

*ML*: see Darwin, F. and Seward 1903.

Möller, Alfred. 1893. Die Pilzgärten einiger südamerikanischer Ameisen. *Botanische Mitteilungen aus den Tropen* 6. Jena: Gustav Fischer.

—————, ed. 1915. *Fritz Müller. Werke, Briefe und Leben.* Vol. 1, *Gesammelte Schriften.* Jena: Gustav Fischer.

—————, ed. 1920. *Fritz Müller. Werke, Briefe und Leben.* Vol. 3, *Fritz Müllers Leben.* Jena: Gustav Fischer.

—————, ed. 1921. *Fritz Müller. Werke, Briefe und Leben.* Vol. 2. *Briefe und noch nicht veröffentliche Abhandlungen aus dem Nachlaß, 1854–1897.* Jena: Gustav Fischer.

Montgomery, William H. 1974. Germany. In *The comparative reception of Darwin*, ed. Thomas F. Glick. Austin: University of Texas Press.

Müller, Fritz. 1844a. Ueber *Hirudo tessulata* und *marginata* O. F. Müll. *Archiv für Naturgeschichte* I:370-6.

—————. 1844b. *De Hirudinibus circa Berolinum hucusque observatis.* Berolini, typis fratrum Schlesinger.

—————. 1846. [Letter]. *Kirchliche Reform* (Halle), 1846 (Dec.):31-2.

—————. 1851a. Die Heiligkeit Gottes nach den Begriffen der Philosophie und der gewöhnliche Menschenverstand. *Neue Reform* (Halle), 1851: columns 130-5.

—————. 1851b. Die Natur als moralisches Vorbild des Menschen. *Neue Reform* (Halle) 1851: columns 220-5.

—————. 1852. Noch einige Worte über Auswanderung. *Neue Reform* (Halle) 1852: columns 152-60.

—————. 1860. Das Kolonialnervensystem der Moosthiere, nachgewiesen an *Serialaria Coutinhii* n. sp. *Archiv für Naturgeschichte* 26(1):311-18.

—————. 1862a. Die Rhizocephalen, eine neue Gruppe schmarotzender Kruster. *Archiv für Naturgeschichte* 28(1):1-9.

—————. 1862b. *Entoniscus porcellanae*, eine neue Schmarotzerassel. *Archiv für Naturgeschichte* 28(1):10-18.

—————. 1863a. Die Verwandlung der Garneelen. *Archiv für Naturgeschichte* 29(1):8-23.

—————. 1863b. Die zweite Entwicklungsstufe der Würzelkrebse (Rhizocephalen). *Archiv für Naturgeschichte* 29(1):24-33.

—————. 1864. *Für Darwin.* Leipzig: W. Engelmann.

—————. 1865. *V'zaschitu Darvina* [In defense of Darwin]. Translated by Nikolai D. Nozhin. Reprinted as Za Darvina [For Darwin] in Nozhin, N. D. 1940. [Collected works].

—————. 1866. Ueber die Befruchtung der *Martha* (*Posoqueria?*) *fragrans*. *Botanische Zeitung* 24:129-33.

Müller, Fritz. 1867. Notes on some of the climbing-plants near Desterro in South Brazil. *Journal of the Linnean Society of London* (Botany) 9:344-9. (Read 7 Dec. 1865.)

——. 1868a. Notizen über die Geschlectsverhältnisse brasilianscher Pflanzen. [From a letter to Friedrich Hildebrand.] *Botanische Zeitung* 26:113-116.

——. 1868b. Befruchtungsversuche an cipó alho (*Bignonia*). *Botanische Zeitung* 26:625-9.

——. 1868c. Ueber Befruchtungserscheinungen bei Orchideen. *Botanische Zeitung* 26:629-31.

——. 1869a. *Facts and arguments for Darwin*. Translated by William Sweetland Dallas. London: John Murray.

——. 1869b. Excursionsberichte aus Südbrasilien. *Flora* 1869:337-48, 353-64.

——. 1869c. Ueber einige Befruchtungserscheinungen. *Botanische Zeitung* 27:224-6.

——. 1869d. Ueber eine dimorphe *Faramea*. *Botanische Zeitung* 27:606-11.

——. 1870a. Umwandlung von Staubgefässen in Stempel bei *Begonia*. Uebergang von Zwitterblüthigkeit in Getrennblüthigkeit bei *Chamissoa*. Triandrische Varietät eines monandrischen *Epidendrum*. *Botanische Zeitung* 28:149-53.

——. 1870b. Die Bewegung des Blüthestieles von *Alisma*. *Jenaische Zeitschrift für Naturwissenschaft* 5:133-7.

——. 1870c. Bemerkungen über *Cypridina*. *Jenaische Zeitschrift für Naturwissenschaft* 5:255-76.

——. 1871a. Bruchstücke zur Naturgeschichte der Bopyriden. *Jenaische Zeitschrift für Naturwissenschaft* 6:53-72.

——. 1871b. Remarks on some white ants. *Proceedings of the Boston Society of Natural History* 1871:205-6.

——. 1873a. Bestäubungsversuche an *Abutilon*-Arten. *Jenaische Zeitschrift für Naturwissenschaft* 7:22-45, 441-50.

——. 1873b. Beiträge zur Kenntniss der Termiten. II. Die Wohnungen unserer Termiten. *Jenaische Zeitschrift für Naturwissenschaft* 8:341-58.

——. 1873c. Beiträge zur Kenntniss der Termiten. III. Ein Sultan in seinem Harem. *Jenaische Zeitschrift für Naturwissenschaft* 7:451-63.

——. 1874a. Recent researches of termites and honey-bees. (From a letter to Ch. Darwin). *Nature* 9:309.

——. 1874b. The habits of various insects (A letter to Ch. Darwin). *Nature* 10:102-3.

Müller, Fritz. 1874c. Der Haushalt der stachellosen Honigbienen. [Lecture to the Blumenau Cultural Society, in letter to Hermann Müller, 23 March 1874.] *Briefe*:257-67.

―――――――. 1875. Poey's Beobachtungen über die Naturgeschichte der Honigbiene von Cuba. *Melipona fulvipes* Guér. *Zoologisches Garten* 16:291-7.

―――――――. 1876a. Einige Worte über Leptalis. *Jenaische Zeitschrift für Naturwissenschaft* 10:1-12.

―――――――. 1876b. On Brazil kitchen middens, habits of ants etc. [Letter to Mr. Darwin.] *Nature* 13:304-5.

―――――――. 1876c. *Aglea Odebrechtii* n. sp. *Jenaische Zeitschrift für Naturwissenschaft* 10:13-24.

―――――――. 1876d. Ueber das Haarkissen am Blattstiel der Imbauba (Cecropia), das Gemüsebeet der Imbaubaameise. *Jenaische Zeitschrift für Naturwissenschaft* 10:281-6.

―――――――. 1877a. Aus einem Brief von Fritz Müller aus Brasilien. *Flora* 1877:239-40.

―――――――. 1877b. Ueber Haarpinsel, Filzflecke und ähnliche Gebilde auf den Flügeln männlicher Schmetterlinge. *Jenaische Zeitschrift für Naturwissenschaft* 11:99-114. [Translation in Longstaff 1912.]

―――――――. 1877c. Der Minhocão. *Zoologisches Garten* 1877:298-302.

―――――――. 1877d. Beobachtungen an brasilianischen Schmetterlingen. I. *Kosmos* 1:388-95. [Part translation in Longstaff 1912.]

―――――――. 1877e. A correlação das flores versicolores e dos insectos pronubos. *Archivos do Museu Nacional do Rio de Janeiro* 2:19-23. [German translation in *Werke*:1427-31, with errors corrected.]

―――――――. 1878a. Notes on Brazilian entomology. *Transactions of the Entomological Society of London* 1878:211-23.

―――――――. 1878b. On the scent-organs of *Antirrhaea archaea*, Hübn. In Longstaff 1912, 634-8. [Translation of original, 1878, in *Archivos do Museu Nacional do Rio de Janeiro* 3:1-7.]

―――――――. 1878c. Ueber die Vorteile der Mimicry bei Schmetterlingen. *Zoologischer Anzeiger* 1:54-5.

―――――――. 1878d. Sobre as casas construidas pelas larvas de insectos trichopteros da província de Sa. Catharina. *Archivos do Museu Nacional do Rio de Janeiro* 3:99-124. [German trans., *Werke* 694-741].

―――――――. 1878/79. Phryganiden-Studien. *Kosmos* 4:386-96.

―――――――. 1879a. *Ituna* und *Thyridia*. Ein merkwürdiges Beispiel von Mimicry bei Schmetterlingen. *Kosmos* 5:100-8.

Müller, Fritz. 1879b. *Ituna* and *Thyridia*; a remarkable case of mimicry in butterflies. (With members' comments.) *Proceedings of the Entomological Society of London* 1879:xx-xxix.

————. 1879c. Descripção do *Elpidium bromeliarum*. *Archivos do Museu Nacional do Rio de Janeiro* 4:27-34. [German trans., *Werke*:1463-69.]

————. 1879d. Bud-variation in bananas. *Nature* 20:146.

————. 1879/80. Wasserthiere in Baumwipfeln (*Elpidium bromeliarum*). *Kosmos* 6:386-8.

————. 1880. *Palaemon potiuna*. Ein Beispiel abgekürzter Verwandlung. *Zoologischer Anzeiger* 3:152-7.

————. 1880/81a. Haeckel's biogenetisches Grundgesetz bei der Neubildung verlorener Glieder. *Kosmos* 7:388-9.

————. 1880/81b. *Paltostoma torrentium*. Eine Mücke mit zweigestaltigen Weibchen. *Kosmos* 8:37-42.

————. 1880/81c. On female dimorphism of *Paltostoma torrentium*. *The Entomologist's Monthly Magazine* 17:225.

————. 1881. *Atyoida potimirim*: eine schlammfressende Süsswassergarneele. *Kosmos* 9:117-24.

————. 1881/82. Bemerkenswerte Fälle erworbener Aehnlichkeit bei Schmetterlingen. *Kosmos* 10:257-67, n. 3.

————. 1882a. Bericht über Graf zu Solms-Laubach, Die Herkunft, Domestication und Verbreitung des gewöhnlichen Feigenbaums (Ficus Carica L.). *Kosmos* 11:306-15.

————. 1882b. Caprificus und Feigenbaum. *Kosmos* 11:342-46.

————. 1882/83. Pour Darwin. Translated by F. Debray. *Bulletin scientifique du Départment du Nord et des pays voisin* 14:354-382, 418-462; 15:10-47.

————. 1883. Angebissene Flügel von *Acraea thalia*. *Kosmos* 13:197-201.

————. 1885. Die Zwitterbildung im Tierreiche. *Kosmos* 17:321-34.

————. 1886. Ein Züchtungsversuch an Mais. *Kosmos* 19:22-6.

————. 1888. Zweimännige Zingiberaceenblumen. *Berichte der deutschen botanischen Gesellschaft* 6:95-100.

————. 1892a. *Trichodactylus*, siri de agua doce sem metamorphose. *Archivos do Museu Nacional do Rio de Janeiro* 8:125-33. [German trans., *Werke*:1171-85.]

————. 1892b. Aus dem Leben eines deutschen Kolonisators und Naturforschers. *Das Ausland* 65:631-4.

————. 1897a. Ein Fall von Naturauslese bei ungeschlechtlicher Fortpflanzung. *Flora oder Allgemeine botanische Zeitung* 84, supplemental volume (1):96-9.

Müller, Fritz. 1897b. Ein Versuch mit Doppelbestäubung. *Flora* 83:474-86.

————. 1898. Die Mischlinge von *Ruellia formosa* und *silvaccola*. *Jenaische Zeitschrift für Naturwissenschaft* 31:153-5.

————. 1899. Observações sobre a fauna marinha de costa de Santa Catharina. *Revista Museu Paulista* 3:31-40.

Müller, Fritz, and Max Schultze. 1856. Beiträge zur Kenntniss der Landplanarien. *Abhandlungen der Naturforschenden Gesellschaft Halle* 4:19-38.

Müller, Hermann. 1875. Stachellose brasilianische Honigbienen. *Zoologisches Garten* 1875:41-55.

————. 1881. *Alpenblumen, ihre Befruchtung durch Insekten und ihre Anpassung an dieselben*. Leipzig: W. Engelmann.

Müller, Johannes Peter. 1842. *Elements of physiology*, vol 2. London: Taylor & Walton. (Translation of *Handbuch der Physiologie*.)

Müller, Wilhelm. 1886. Südamerikanische Nymphalidenraupen. Versuche eines natürlichen Systems der Nymphaliden. *Zoologische Jahrbücher* 1:417-678.

*NEB: New Encyclopaedia Britannica*. 1992. 15th ed. Chicago: Encyclopaedia Britannica, Inc.

Odebrecht, Emilio. 1875. Erforschung des oberen Itajahy. *Zeitschrift, Gesellschaft für Erdkunde zu Berlin* 10:74-6.

Oesterlen, Friedrich. 1856. *Handbuch der Heilmittellehre*. 6th ed. Tübingen: H. Laupp'schen.

Osborn, Henry Fairfield. 1929. Gift to Down House of the original letters of Charles Darwin to Fritz Müller. *Science* 69:645.

Paulsen, Friedrich. 1895. *The German universities, their character and historical development*. Translated by Edward D. Perry. New York: Macmillan & Co.

Poey y Aloy, F. 1851. *Memorias sobre la historia natural de la isla de Cuba*. Vol. I. Habana: Barcina.

Poulton, Edward B. 1890. *The colours of animals, their meaning and use*. London: Kegan Paul, Trench, Trübner, & Co.

Poulton, Edward B. 1901. *Charles Darwin and the theory of natural selection*. London: Cassell & Co.

Prittwitz, O. von . 1865. Beitrag zur Fauna des Corcovado. *Stettiner entomologische Zeitung* 1865:123-43, 307-25.

Prutz, Robert E. 1843. *Gedichte. Neue Sammlung*. Zurich & Winterthur: Druck und Verlag des literarischen Comptoirs.

————. 1845. *Die politische Wochenstube. Eine Komödie. . . .* Zurich and Winterthur: Literarisches Comptoir.

Punnett, Reginald C. 1915. *Mimicry in butterflies*. Cambridge: Cambridge University Press.

*Reiseführer, Deutsche Demokratische Republik.* 1981. Berlin/Leipzig: VEB Tourist Verlag.

Reitz, Raulino. 1974. Palmeiras. *Flora illustrada catarinense*. Itajaí.

—————. 1983. Bromeliáceas e a malária-bromélia endêmica. *Flora illustrada catarinense*. Itajaí.

Review of *For Darwin*. 1869. *Scientific Opinion* 1:473-4 (April 21).

Rickson, Fred R. 1971. Glycogen plastids in Müllerian body cells of *Cecropia peltata* — a higher green plant. *Science* 173:344-7.

Roquette Pinto, E. 1979. *Glória sem rumor*. 2d ed. Blumenau.

Rosenhainer, O. and H. Trommsdorff, eds. 1913. *Johann Bartolomäus Trommsdorff (1770–1837)*. Jena: Verlag von Bernhard Vopelius.

Sachs, Julius. 1874. *Lehrbuch der Botanik*. 4th ed. Leipzig: W. Engelmann.

Schenck, Heinrich. 1892-93. Beiträge zur Biologie und Anatomie der Lianen in Besonderen der im Brasilien einheimischen Arten. *Botanische Mittheilungen aus den Tropen* 4 and 5. Jena: Gustav Fischer.

Schimper, A. F. W. 1888a. Die Wechselbeziehungen zwischen Pflanzen und Ameisen in tropischen Amerika. *Botanische Mittheilungen aus den Tropen* 1. Jena: Gustav Fischer.

—————. 1888b. Die epiphytische Vegetation Amerikas. *Botanische Mittheilungen aus den Tropen* 2. Jena: Gustav Fischer.

Schmidt, [Eduard] Oscar. 1873. *Descendenzlehre und Darwinismus*. Leipzig: F. A. Brockhaus.

Schultze, Max. 1857. *Lumbricus corethrurus*, Bürstenschwanz. [Note to Müller's paper.] *Werke*:75.

Steenstrup, Johann Iapetus Smith. 1846. *Untersuchungen über das Vorkommen des Hermaphroditismus in der Natur. Ein historischer Versuch.* Translated by Dr. C. F. Hornschuch. Greifswald: Ferd. Otte.

Steinen, Karl von den. 1886. *Durch central-Brasilien*. Leipzig: F. A. Brockhaus.

Strasburger, E., E. Noll, H. Schenck, and A. F. W. Schimper. 1895. *Lehrbuch der Botanik für Hochschulen*, 2d ed. Jena: Gustav Fischer.

Strauss, David Friedrich. [1835-6] 1860. *The life of Jesus critically examined*. Translated by Marion Evans [George Eliot]. New York: Calvin Blanchard. Reprint 1970. St. Clair Shores: Scholarly Press.

—————. 1840-41. *Die christliche Glaubenslehre.* . . . 2 vols. Tübingen: Ossiander.

Sturtevant, Alfred H. 1965. *A history of genetics*. New York: Harper & Row.

Taylor, James L. 1970. *A Portuguese-English dictionary*. Revised ed. Stanford: Stanford University Press.

The Darwinian hypothesis supported by observations on Crustacea. By Fritz Müller, of Desterro. 1865. *The Annals and Magazine of Natural History* 15:410-16. [Translated from *Bibliothèque Universelle et Revue Suisse. Archives des Sciences Physique et Naturelles* 22:154-63. (1865)]

Trimen, Roland. 1898. Mimicry in insects. Presidential Address for 1897. *Proceedings of the Entomological Society of London* 1898:lxxiv-xcvii.

Tschudi, Johann Jakob von. 1868-69. *Reisen durch Südamerika.* 5 vols. Leipzig: F. A. Brockhaus.

Valentin, Veit. 1930-31. *Geschichte der deutschen Revolution von 1848–49.* 2 vols. Berlin: Verlag Ullstein.

Vischer, Friedrich Theodor. 1845. Gervinus und die Deutschcatholiken. *Jahrbücher der Gegenwart* 3:1086-114.

Vogel, Peter. 1892. Ein deutscher Pionier der Wissenschaft in Brasilien. *Die Gartenlaube* 1892:276.

Vogt, Carl. 1851. *Zoologische Briefe.* Frankfurt: G.M. Literarische Anstalt.

Wallace, Alfred Russel. 1865. On the phenomena of variation and geographical distribution as illustrated by the Papilionidae of the Malayan region. *Transactions of the Linnean Society, London* 25:1-71. (Read 17 March 1864).

————. 1869. *The Malay Archipelago.* 2 vols. London: Macmillan & Co.

————. 1878. *Tropical nature.* London: Macmillan & Co.

————. 1882. Dr. Fritz Müller on some difficult cases of mimicry. *Nature* 26:86-7. (25 May 1882)

————. 1889. *Darwinism.* London: Macmillan & Co.

Walther, Lena. 1882. *Tante Jettchen.* Gotha: Perthes.

————. 1901. *Aus meiner Jugendzeit.* Gotha: Schlössmann.

Wappäus, Johann Eduard. 1846. *Deutsche Auswanderung und Colonisation.* Leipzig: J. C. Hinrichs.

Weismann, August. 1882. Studies in the theory of descent. Translated and edited by R. Meldola. London: Sampson Low, Marston, Searle, & Rivington.

————. 1889a. The continuity of the germ-plasm as the foundation of a theory of heredity, 1885. In *Essays upon heredity and kindred biological problems.* Translated and edited by E. B. Poulton, S. Schönland, and A. E. Shipley, 161-249. Oxford: Clarendon Press.

————. 1889b. The significance of sexual reproduction in the theory of natural selection, 1886. In *Essays upon heredity and kindred biological problems.* Translated and edited by E. B. Poulton, S. Schönland, and A. E. Shipley, 251-332. Oxford: Clarendon Press.

Weismann, August. 1904. *The evolution theory*. Translated by J. Arthur Thomson and Margaret R. Thomson. London: Edward Arnold.

Weiss, Martha R. 1991. Floral colour changes as cues for pollinators. *Nature* 354:227-9.

*Werke*: see Möller 1915.

West, David A. 1994. Unimodal Batesian polymorphism in the Neotropical swallowtail butterfly *Eurytides lysithous* (Hbn.). *Biological Journal of the Linnean Society* 52:197-224.

Wettstein, Karl A. 1907. *Brasilien und die deutsch-brasilianische Kolonie Blumenau*. Leipzig: W. Engelmann.

Wislicenus, Gustav Adolf. 1846. Vorwort. *Kirchliche Reform* (Halle) 1846:1-3.

# Acknowledgments

I gratefully acknowledge the permissions granted by the following to use materials in their possession. The British Library; the Syndics of Cambridge University Library; HarperCollins Publishers, London; the Ernst-Haeckel-Haus, Friedrich-Schiller Universität, Jena; the Ernst Mayr Library of the Museum of Comparative Zoology, Harvard University; the Houghton Library, Harvard University; the Librarian, Oxford University Museum of Natural History; the Senckenbergische Bibliothek, Johann Wolfgang Goethe-Universität, Frankfurt-am-Main; and Prof. Dr. Christoph Friedrich, Institut für Geschichte der Pharmazie, Philipps-Universität, Marburg.

The following responded generously to my visits or enquiries.

In Germany: Dr. Wolfgang Götz, Ahaus; Dr. Hannelore Landsberg, Musem für Naturkunde der Humboldt-Universität, Berlin; Dr. Jutta Weber, Staatsbibliothek zu Berlin – Preußicher Kulturbesitzt; Dr. Alden Dittman and Dr. Renate Löschner, Ibero-Amerikanisches Institut Preußischer Kulturbesitz, Berlin; Dr. Monika Minninger, Stadtarchiv und Landesgeschichtliche Bibliothek, Bielefeld; Sabine Happ, Archiv der Rheinischen Friedrich-Wilhelms-Universität, Bonn; Dr. Albrecht Milnik, Forstliche Forschungsanstalt Eberswalde; Dr. Winifried Hagenmaier, Universitätsbibliothek, Freiburg im Breisgau; Dr. Bernd Bader, Justus-Liebig-Universität, Giessen; Dr. H.-J. Subklew, Greifswald; Hagen Rüster, Thüringisches Staatsarchiv, Greiz; Prof. Dr. Walther Liese, Universität Hamburg; Prof. Dr. Erika Krauße and Frau Nöthlich, Ernst-Haeckel-Haus, Friedrich-Schiller Universität, Jena; Herr Luttmer, Niedersächsisches Staatsarchiv, Wolfenbüttel.

In Italy: Dr. Christiane Groeben, Stazione Zoologica 'Anton Dohrn', Naples.

In Britain: Members of the Darwin Letters Project, especially Janet Browne, Joy Harvey, Thomas Junker, Anna-K. Mayer, Stephen Pocock, Duncan Porter, Marsha Richmond, and Jonathan Topham, who have answered queries on many subjects over the years; the staff of the Manuscripts Room at the Cambridge University Library, especially Godfrey Waller; Grenville Lucas, Keeper of the Herbarium and Library, and Sylvia FitzGerald and Cheryl Piggott, Library of the Royal Botanic Gardens, Kew; the late John Thackray, Natural History Museum Library, London; Virginia Murray, John Murray (publishers) Ltd., London; Gina Douglas, Librarian of the Linnean Society of London; Sue Holland, *Athenaeum* Indexing Project, The City University, London; Valerie Bott, Curator, Passmore Edwards Museum, London; Stephen J. Simpson, Curator, and Stella Newton, Librarian, Oxford University Museum of Natural History.

In the United States: Mary Brockenbrough and Dana Fisher, Ernst Mayr Library, MCZ, Harvard; Joel Sweimler and R. David Wells, Special Collections, American Museum of Natural History, New York; Rachel Barreto Edensword, Oliveira Lima Library, Catholic University, and Bill Cox, Smithsonian Institute Archives, Washington D.C.; Arthur Donovan of the United States Merchant Marine Academy, Kings Point; Wendy Schnur of the Mystic Seaport Museum Library; Allen C. West, Cambridge, Massachusetts.

I thank William Darwin for permission to quote from unpublished letters of Charles Darwin.

I am grateful to Janis Antonovics, Wade N. Hazel, and Duncan Porter for their encouragement after reading an early draft of the manuscript, to Ernst Mayr for suggestions on a later draft, and especially to Janet Browne, whose valuable suggestions drove me to many useful revisions.

I thank colleagues at the Virginia Polytechnic Institute and State University for their help: the staff of the Carol Newman Library, Andrew Becker and the late Thomas O. MacAdoo for translations from Latin, and Arnold Schuetz for German information. I am most grateful to the Department of Biology and its Heads, Ernest Stout and Joe Cowles, for their support, and to Mrs Jacqueline Hamblin, who read my handwriting and managed the early drafts of the manuscript.

Much of the work was done while my wife and I were visiting scholars in the Cambridge Wellcome Unit for the History of Medicine, Department of the History and Philosophy of Science, and I thank the late Roger French (Director, 1993), Andrew Cunningham (Acting Director, 1997), and particularly Harmke Kamminga, for making available the incomparable research facilities of the University.

We had the great pleasure of meeting Fritz Händel, a resident of Fritz Müller's birthplace Windischholzhausen, and a Müller enthusiast, who with his wife introduced us in 1993 to the scenes of Fritz's youth in Thuringia.

Our search for the "lost treasures"of Alfred Möller's archive took us to the Fortstliche Forschungsanstalt Eberswalde, where the Director, Prof. Dr. Dieter Heinsdorf and his colleagues welcomed us warmly, and Dr. J.-H. Bergmann gave us local information and led us through the forest to the site of Alfred Möller's research building and his grave.

It has been a pleasure to work with Mary Holliman and Bruce Wallace of Pocahontas Press. And I thank Jim Glanville and Deena Flinchum for their friendship and for underwriting the publication of this book.

I especially thank Lindsay Butte West for her support, for her help in many a library and archive, and for her sharp editorial eye.

# Index

Page numbers in italics refer to words in figure captions.